Realignment and
Party Revival

Realignment and Party Revival

Understanding American Electoral Politics at the Turn of the Twenty-First Century

Arthur Paulson

PRAEGER

Westport, Connecticut
London

Library of Congress Cataloging-in-Publication Data

Paulson, Arthur C.
  Realignment and party revival : understanding American electoral politics
at the turn of the twenty-first century / Arthur Paulson.
    p. cm.
  Includes bibliographical references and index.
  ISBN 0-275-96865-0 (alk. paper)
    1. Presidents—United States—Election. 2. Political parties—United States.
  I. Title.

JK528.P38 2000
324'.0973—dc21   99-054877

British Library Cataloguing in Publication Data is available.

Library of Congress Catalog Card Number: 99-054877
ISBN: 0-275-96865-0

First published in 2000

Praeger Publishers, 88 Post Road West, Westport, CT 06881
An imprint of Greenwood Publishing Group, Inc.
www.praeger.com

Printed in the United States of America

10 9 8 7 6 5 4 3 2

To
the memory of my father,
Carl Paulson,
with thanks

Contents

Preface

The impeachment of President William Jefferson Clinton in 1999 was certainly a rare event in American history; so rare, in fact, that no living American had ever witnessed a previous impeachment of a President of the United States. Indeed, impeachment was meant to be a rare constitutional and political event, reserved for the most extreme of offenses by a President against the constitutional order.

According to polling data during the impeachment process, however, most Americans did not consider the offenses by President Clinton to be that grave. The affair with Monica Lewinsky, most Americans seemed to think, was more a personal than a public matter. The Republicans in the House of Representatives who pursued impeachment were themselves perceived widely as extremists who were making their personal contempt for President Clinton a public issue, thereby seriously misusing the impeachment tool. As the process proceeded, observers were increasingly incredulous about the impeachment strategy and how far it was proceeding.

I remember seeing more than one television interview during the Clinton impeachment process with Howard Baker, the Tennessee Republican who served on the Senate Select Committee investigating Watergate, the scandal that led to the resignation of President Richard Nixon in 1974. Mr. Baker commented that the impeachment process was both a political and a constitutional one. If it now descended into a purely political fight, he warned, it would become very much like a vote of no confidence against a prime minister in a parliamentary democracy. This would be unhealthy, Baker cautioned, because parliamentary democracy is based on party government and a fusion of powers, both of which are contrary to the constitutional separation of powers. Moreover, he said, the very notion of a parliamentary vote of no confidence in the executive is outside the "American political personality."

The Watergate investigation in which Senator Baker took a leading role was often offered by journalists and the media as a case that stood in contrast to the investigation of President Clinton. Although many Americans may not remember the political infighting involved in the Watergate process, it is certainly true that Watergate involved much more clearly public issues and Presidential behavior presenting a much more serious threat to the constitutional order than did "Monicagate." In addition, despite the political infighting, Watergate did not take on overtones of a parliamentary vote of no confidence. Many southern Democrats supported Nixon until almost the end of the process, and some Republicans, including Baker, Senator Barry Goldwater of Arizona, and Senator Lowell Weicker of Connecticut, were harshly critical of the President early in the process. As late as July 1974, when the House Judiciary Committee began its hearings into Watergate, it was unclear that the votes for impeachment would be found. The Democrats were in the majority in Congress and on the committee, but the White House was counting on a number of southern Democrats to vote against impeachment, while the advocates of impeachment were hopeful of finding support from moderate-to-liberal Republicans. In the end, the Democrats on the committee voted unanimously for bills of impeachment, joined by a number of Republicans. Only the resignation of President Nixon, encouraged at an Oval Office meeting by Senator Goldwater, Senate Minority Leader Hugh Scott, and House Minority Leader John Rhodes, all Republicans, prevented the bills from going to the floor of the House of Representatives. The Watergate case was a very rare phenomenon that Americans hoped would not soon be replicated.

Indeed, I would argue, it hasn't been. The investigation of President Clinton was conducted not only on very different issues but also in a very different political environment. Whereas Watergate was visibly an exercise in the separation of powers, the Clinton impeachment seemed much more like a parliamentary motion for no confidence. Had it been literally that, of course, the President would have been removed from office on an almost entirely party-line vote. The fact that, constitutionally, this remained impeachment conducted in a bicameral legislature, rather than a vote of confidence by the lower house of the legislature, prevented Clinton's removal from office. Bill Clinton was saved by the constitutional fact that he was the President, and not a prime minister.

But what explains an impeachment process that went so much further than anyone expected it would? Why would House Republicans push the process despite its apparent unpopularity? Why is it that, except for the outcome itself, the Clinton impeachment so resembled a parliamentary motion of no confidence, even in defiance of what Howard Baker called the "American political personality"?

This book suggests that the politics of the Clinton impeachment is understood much better than it has been if we understand change in the political environment, particularly the change in the American political parties and party system that has come about since a period of critical electoral change that can be dated to just before the Watergate affair.

At that time, between 1964 and 1972, the resolution of factional struggles within both major parties resulted in the most profound electoral realignment in American history; so profound, in fact, that it violated most of the paradigms of electoral analysis, and most political scientists missed it. The most compelling ingredient of the electoral change was the disintegration of the solid south and the movement of most of its white voters from the Democrats to the Republicans in Presidential elections. As the south continued to vote Democratic in congressional elections for almost thirty years, the American electorate produced divided government most of the time for the remainder of the twentieth century. So it was that realignment was not observed, and political analysts called it "dealignment." However, the change in party coalitions that reached critical proportions in the 1964–1972 period reversed electoral patterns that had been in place since the earliest foundations of the party system almost two centuries ago.

Which brings us to the second point of this book. Not only has electoral behavior changed, as it does periodically, the parties have changed to the point that the party system has been altered very fundamentally. Most political scientists have seen this as party decay, observing correctly that the parties founded in the nineteenth century are growing institutionally weaker. But this book presents evidence that our system is not going through simple party decay. Rather, American political parties are being revived in new form. The decisive factional struggles of 1964 to 1972 have yielded two parties that are ideologically polarized to a degree that would seem foreign to the historic "American political personality." Unlike the party system that persisted from the early nineteenth century into the 1960s, the party system that has emerged since then features a liberal party (the Democrats) and a conservative party (the Republicans). Stimulated by the civil rights issue in the 1960s, deepened by Vietnam and the abortion debate, the American political system now features an ongoing debate about an agenda of cultural issues in which conservative (and Republican) confronts liberal (and Democrat) over a divide that is more and more polarized. This is not an accident of who happens to run for or occupy public office. It has been institutionalized in our new party system.

The impeachment of President Clinton probably would not have taken place at all in the old party system. The fact that it did take place in the new party system reflects not only the personalities involved but, even more, a new political environment that will define issues and alignments well into the twenty-first century. To Republicans who impeached President Clinton, he represents the ascendancy of a permissive counterculture, which they detest, to power in America. To the Democrats who defended him (regardless of their view of his personal conduct), the pro-impeachment Republicans present a threat of using government to pass judgment on personal moral choices, a threat that, if it were to come to pass, would endanger the very foundations of a free society. These are what Walter Dean Burnham calls "either-or" issues that defy the accommodations that are necessary to a pluralist democracy.

Add to the above issues the fact that we live in a rapidly changing economy, in which growth and insecurity seem to develop simultaneously, and we have a society in which the ability to debate such "either-or" issues intelligently and amicably will be essential to democratic life in the twenty-first century. The philosophical hope that we can develop that ability underlies the research that this book presents.

Acknowledgments

When I think of all of those who have played a role in the development of this book, I am inspired by the level of generosity offered by so many.

I want to thank my colleagues at Southern Connecticut State University who granted me the sabbatical leave that gave me the time to focus on this project and to write the first draft of the manuscript.

I want to thank my colleagues in the Department of Political Science, all of whom are worthy of naming for the support and advice they have offered, and for the pleasure I have in working with them: Harriet Applewhite, Paul Best, John Critzer, Robert Gelbach, John Iatrides, Kul Rai, David Walsh, and Clyde Weed. A special thank you to Professor Applewhite, who read early drafts of several chapters and offered commentary that greatly improved the final product.

I am particularly grateful to Jean Polka, our department secretary, who aided in a big way on so many tasks in putting this book together. Jean's professionalism and skill help us get our job done, and her personality and spirit contribute in subtle but important ways to the very pleasant atmosphere of our workplace.

I am indebted, again, to Edward S. Greenberg of the University of Colorado, who reviewed early drafts of the theoretical chapters and commented wisely on them. Professor Greenberg, who was my Ph.D. advisor, seems to influence my career periodically, always to my great benefit.

Thank you to many others who commented on conference papers that contributed to the development of this work, including Gerald Pomper of Rutgers University and John K. White of the Catholic University of America.

Thanks to the many people involved in the production of this book. The efforts of Jim Sabin at Greenwood Publishing and George Ernsberger at Publishing Synthesis are representative of the labors of many more. The copy editing of Henry Lazarek, for example, saved me from myself at numerous points in the text.

Thanks to my students, who have motivated this work and shown interest in it. Thanks particularly to Mario Martins, Chris Fitzgerald, Richard Haskell, Jodi Hoss, and John Mulcahy for their invaluable assistance with data input and other details of this project.

Thanks to Alan and Betty Jepson, known in my home town as "Mr. and Mrs. Milford," for their constant interest in my work. Betty has continually asked, "Where's the book?" Here it is, Betty.

Finally, thank you with love to my wife, Lynn Greer, who has lived with the ups and downs of this project as much as I have. She has shared in this as she has shared a life with me, for which I am eternally grateful.

Introduction: Realignment and the Revival of Political Parties

Observers of electoral change in American politics over the last half of the twentieth century have noted persuasive evidence of dealignment and party decay. As if "waiting for Godot," political scientists and journalists who have taken up the language have been frustrated in the search for the sort of partisan realignment that has periodically restructured the electoral environment and the party system.[1] Not so long ago, the concept of realignment, introduced in the classic work of V. O. Key, was central to studies of American elections. Now, it is almost as paradigmatic for scholars, impatient for evidence of a new realignment, to conclude that dealignment and party decay have rendered the concept useless.

This book enters into a two-pronged debate, first on the usefulness of the concept of realignment in understanding electoral change, and second, on the prospects for party decay versus party renewal in American politics. My central thesis is that the dealignment of recent decades should not be equated with the decline of political parties, *per se*. Rather, dealignment should be understood as realignment by other means, and party decay should be understood as a transition to a new party system, ideologically polarized according to standards of the American experience. Certainly, the American parties born in the nineteenth century have decayed, as have their coalitions of electoral support, but they have not been replaced by electoral vacuum. The emerging parties, conceived in a realignment in the 1960s, represent an almost unAmerican potential to develop a "responsible" party system. Such a party system would present American democracy with both very serious challenges and very important opportunities in the twenty-first century.

REALIGNMENT AND DEALIGNMENT IN AMERICAN POLITICS

Introduced in the classic work of V. O. Key, the concept of realignment brings historical perspective to electoral analysis, locating patterns of stability and change and distinguishing long-term from short-term trends.[2] A rich body of literature has developed around the concept, generated especially by the early work of Walter Dean Burnham, James L. Sundquist, Everett Carll Ladd, and Gerald Pomper.[3] The literature presents a broad consensus about the characteristics of realignment. First, critical realignment involves significant and relatively persistent shifts in the makeup of the coalitions supporting the two major parties. Whereas secular realignment evolves incrementally over extended periods of time, critical realignment appears suddenly, over no more than two or three Presidential elections.[4]

Second, critical realignment is usually accompanied by relatively high issue salience among voters and ideological polarization within and between the parties. Realignment often seems to begin as an internal factional struggle is resolved within one or both major parties.

Third, the shift of "decisively large minorities" of voters from one party coalition toward the other results in new majorities in Presidential and Congressional elections, spreading among the national, state, and local levels.[5] Fourth, this new "normal" majority enables party leaders to establish a relatively stable governing coalition. This new governing coalition, in turn, shapes an agenda that sets new directions in public policy and redefines the salient issues of American politics for an extended period of time.

Finally, critical realignment occurs with remarkable periodicity. A broad consensus in the literature places previous realignments in the 1830s, the 1860s, the 1890s, and the 1930s. The periodicity of realignments may reflect waves of economic modernization and political development, with new issues and interests accompanying the decline of old partisan alignments and the rise of new ones.[6] Emerging electoral coalitions reflect varying combinations of vote switching, voter mobilization, and generational change.[7]

Presidential elections have been classified according to the change or continuity in partisan coalitions, and the success or failure of the normal majority party.[8] Most elections are *maintaining elections*: The majority party wins with a stable electoral coalition, the governing coalition remains intact, and the policy agenda reflects the status quo. Once or twice in every realignment cycle, short-term forces produce a *deviating election*. The minority party wins the Presidency, perhaps with the benefit of an unusually popular candidate, a split in the majority party, a recession, or a particularly salient, if transient issue operating against the majority party. Democrat Woodrow Wilson was elected in 1912 because the majority Republicans were so badly split that former President Theodore Roosevelt was running as a third-party candidate. Republican Dwight D. Eisenhower was so popular that he twice overcame the majority Democrats. Although the minority party wins a deviating election, the electoral coalitions are relatively stable, and the result does not represent a significant disturbance of the electoral order.

Occasionally, however, such a disturbance is found in a *converting election*. The majority party wins, but with an altered electoral coalition. The 1928 Presidential election, for example, served as the basis of Key's early presentation of the concept of realignment. Democrat Alfred E. Smith was soundly defeated by Republican Herbert C. Hoover, a landslide victory for the majority party. But Smith drew Catholic, urban, and working-class voters to the polls and to the Democratic coalition, while losing usually solid Democratic ground in the south to Hoover. Similarly, Republican Barry Goldwater lost in a record landslide to President Lyndon Johnson in 1964, but he gained support for the Republicans in the South, while losing much of the historic GOP base in the northeast. If majority party leaders celebrated these victories, perhaps they should not have, for these converting elections signaled an approaching realignment.

By definition, *critical elections* that consummate critical realignments are most rare. The majority party, its electoral coalition cracked, is defeated and displaced for an extended time by a new majority party, as occurred in 1932 with the election of Democrat Franklin D. Roosevelt to the Presidency. The New Deal coalition would enable the Democrats to win five consecutive presidential elections and assemble an almost permanent majority in Congress.

Dealignment and Party Decay

For elections over the last half of the twentieth century, the realignment model has been at least as confusing as it has been enlightening.

Realignment was widely anticipated in the 1960s, and there is strong evidence of significant electoral change at that time. Three decades had passed since the New Deal realignment. Increased issue voting in the electorate and ideological polarization within and between the major political parties seemed to indicate an approaching realignment.[9] But observers who were waiting for realignment were apparently disappointed. For most analysts, electoral change in the 1960s and early 1970s, though important, was insufficiently partisan and perhaps even insufficiently persistent to qualify as realignment.[10] As David Broder put it in 1978, "We are now in the fifth decade since the last realignment—two or three elections past the point at which the cycle should have produced a new mandate, and a clear governing coalition."[11]

The consensus that has emerged in electoral analysis since then amounts to variations on a theme of dealignment. Dealignment theorists recognize the significant coalitional shift and ideological polarization of the 1960s. With the nominations of Republican Barry Goldwater in 1964 and Democrat George McGovern in 1972, both parties fell under the influence of their more ideological factions. Civil rights, the Vietnam War, and the "social issue" all contributed to ideological polarization within and between the parties and to a shift in patterns of support in Presidential elections. The shift was cross-cutting: Democrats gained slightly among middle-class voters and solidified their support in cities and among blacks. Republicans gained in the once Democratic solid south and benefited from a backlash on the race issue among working-class whites. Clearly, the New Deal alignment, which produced normal Democratic majorities, was no longer dominant in Presidential elections. Scammon and Wattenburg said elections would be won by candidates who were centrists on the "social issue."[12] Ladd found an "inversion of the New Deal order."[13] Burnham drew on David Apter to foresee partisan alignments based on a technologically based class system, forming a top-bottom coalition against the middle: the technologically competent and the technologically superfluous against the technologically obsolete.[14]

Evidence of the passing of the New Deal party system in the 1960s and 1970s was strong, but dealignment theorists pointed out that there were no new normal partisan majority, no new and stable governing coalition, and no emergence of a new policy agenda.

In his analysis of the 1988 election, Burnham stated what realignment has historically involved and what has been missing in the current electoral age:

> Traditional realignments . . . uniformly entailed capture of control by a single party of all branches of the federal government and (usually) a

preponderant majority of state legislative seats and control of state governments, too. As well, all of them were marked either by very high turnout rates or by sharply increased levels of participation. . . . Both were features of a system of action in which critical realignment deeply engaged the public-at-large, and in which elites, policy consequences, and new majority coalitions were solidly anchored in the electorate itself.[15]

Although the Republicans won the Presidency in five out of six elections starting in 1968, that did not constitute realignment, according to dealignment theorists. First, instead of control of all branches of government by a single party, a "two-tier" party system had emerged,[16] marked by increased split-ticket voting,[17] divided government, increasingly autonomous trends in elections for national and state office, and candidate-centered elections with a structural electoral bias in favor of incumbents of both parties, particularly in the United States House of Representatives.[18]

Second, instead of the increased voter turnout or "sharply increased levels of participation" found in past realignments, there has been a sizeable and consistent decline in voter turnout since 1960, a mark of the declining capacity of political parties to mobilize the general electorate. To the degree that the function of political mobilization is being performed in the American system, it is increasingly done by interest groups more than by political parties. Interest groups have been for some time playing the increasingly important role in nominations, elections, and policy formulation, to the detriment of the role of parties. Issue activists have come to manipulate nominations in both parties, using the parties to articulate interests. The result is a decreased capacity of party leaders to aggregate interests, either for making broad appeals to the electorate, or for the purpose of governing.[19]

Finally, over the last half of the twentieth century, there has been decreasing evidence that political parties or governing coalitions are "solidly anchored in the electorate" as Burnham would expect in a realigning period. The series of Republican Presidential victories did not translate into majorities of American voters identifying themselves as Republicans. Indeed, Americans are increasingly disassociated from political parties and likely to identify themselves as independents.[20]

Everett Carll Ladd has expressed the emerging consensus among political scientists and journalists:

It is wholly evident that the dealignment interpretation of American politics is the correct one. Ideological and partisan preferences apart, there is an impressive body of theory and data that supports the argument that the present era of American electoral politics is one of dealignment and party decay.[21]

Alas, there is no realignment cycle, no striking rhythm, no necessity that the old majority party will be replaced by a new majority, no reason even to be particularly attentive to the prospects of the latter development.[22]

What emerges from the dealignment thesis is a picture of electoral disaggregation and party decomposition. In his classic work on critical elections nearly thirty years ago, Burnham posed the question of whether realignment is even possible under such conditions:

Since at least the mid-1960's, increasing evidence has been accumulating that a nationwide critical realignment may be in the making. Yet electoral disaggregation has very obviously undergone immense, almost geometric expansion in the same period. Since these two processes are inversely related to each other—electoral disaggregation carried beyond a certain point would, after all, make critical realignment in the classic sense impossible—an analytical dilemma arises when one considers the two sets of phenomena together.[23]

Burnham's dilemma is logically central to the analysis of realignment and dealignment. A general consensus seems to have emerged in political science that realignment is, indeed, impossible; that, as Burnham argued, realignment requires strong parties, and party decay by definition means dealignment of the electorate.

Drawing on Burnham's work, Silbey traces dealignment and party decay back to 1893 and considers the last half century as a period of "postalignment." Burnham's dilemma informs Silbey's logic: "The cyclical pattern of realignment does not extend to non-party, anti-party or post-party periods." Silbey thus concludes that "realignments are not the normal dynamic of the American political order."[24]

RECONSIDERING REALIGNMENT AND THE PARTY SYSTEM

If the relationship between realignment and electoral disaggregation is as inverse as Burnham says it is, and if political parties are in decay as the consensus in the literature suggests, the concept of realignment would, indeed, seem to be moribund. Certainly, under conditions of party decay, realignment "in the classic sense" would appear unlikely. But, ironically, to expect realignment to occur necessarily "in the classic sense" renders ahistorical a concept was developed precisely for the purpose of lending historical perspective to electoral analysis. Given the structural change reported by advocates of the dealignment thesis, however, realignment should be expected to appear in altered form.

Burnham himself, running against the tide in political science, observes a new realignment in the 1990s.[25]

I do not take issue with empirical observations of dealignment and electoral disaggregation; these trends have been demonstrated conclusively. Rather, the argument presented here emphasizes theoretical context and conceptual definition: Realignment on the one hand and party decay and electoral disaggregation on the other should not be considered, by definition, mutually exclusive. Nor should electoral disaggregation and party decay be considered to be irreversible, linear processes. Viewed instead as part of a dialectical process, the dealignment of the last half of the twentieth century may yet serve as the stimulus to realignment and the renewal of parties in the twenty-first. However altered the form of its appearance, realignment remains a useful analytical tool. Regardless of terminology, very significant electoral change in the 1960s and another wave of change that seems to be developing at the turn of the century would indicate that periodic sea change in aggregate voting behavior remains characteristic of the American political system.

Burnham's dilemma aside, the questions of realignment versus dealignment and party renewal versus party decay are analytically distinct and autonomous in reality. Nevertheless, dealignment theorists tell a story that presents a picture of linear and uniform dealignment and party decay. Dealignment is the decay of party-in-the-electorate, demonstrated by decreasing voter turnout and party identification among voters and by increasing split-ticket voting and candidate-centered elections. The decay of party-as-organization is linked to waves of electoral and party reform, particularly in the progressive era, and again in the 1960s. Reform opened the party-as-organization to previously exogenous forces, issue activists, and ideologues whose first loyalty was not to the party, and it weakened institutional mechanisms for making collective decisions.[26] Finally, the decay of party-in-government is, by definition, divided government, the split control of the executive and legislative branches by the major parties, which has been the case more frequently than not for almost a half century.[27]

My analysis, by contrast, recognizes the autonomy of processes of party and electoral change. The result is a story of dealignment as realignment by other means and party decay leading to party renewal.

Realignment has been a characteristic of the American electoral system in the past at least partly because of the nature of American political parties. First, the American party system is a two-party system. Spatial theories of electoral behavior would indicate that to win, both parties must appeal to voters neither can count on, voters typically in the center of the ideological spectrum.[28]

Second, American political culture is a Lockean liberal culture, with strong mainstream consensus on the value of individual liberty and private property.[29] Both political parties, thus, strongly support both capitalism and limited republican government. Any party that does not is relegated to minor party status on the fringes of the system, often does not survive for long, and certainly will not win elections.

Third, strong social consensus belies the diversity of American society. Across all electoral eras going back to the 1830s, both major parties have been "umbrella" parties. That is, each party has been a coalition of diverse interests. Most of the time, these coalitions have been relatively stable. Periodically, however, these coalitions have destabilized, resulting in electoral realignment.

To win two-sided elections, the major parties must be umbrella parties, making broad appeals to the variety of interests in the electorate. For example, American political culture is known for its very limited degree of class consciousness.[30] Rather than thinking of themselves as members of social classes, most Americans, at most times in our history, have thought of themselves as individuals, relatively free of social structural limitations on their life choices. Neither major party can assemble stable majorities by making narrow, doctrinaire appeals to a limited class base.

Expressed in functional terms, parties in the American political system historically have performed interest aggregation far more than they have interest articulation. When interests are articulated, it is often in cultural terms, on issues of tradition versus modernization, race and civil rights, or abortion and women's rights. The most successful economic appeals have been made in relation to the business cycle rather than the polarization of class interests; economic growth is a valence issue in American politics rather than a position issue, and when the economy is salient, voting tends to be a retrospective evaluation of incumbents.[31] Thus, the Great Depression was essential to the emergence of a stable Democratic majority, with the working class at its base, during the New Deal realignment. In 1992, it was "the economy, stupid," because of recession, not a narrow appeal to class interests.

Fourth, American political parties are historically decentralized. Operating in a federal system, parties have drawn their power from electoral bases at the state and local levels. The Daley machine in Chicago, Tammany Hall in New York, the Democratic Farmer Labor Party founded by Hubert Humphrey and his allies in Minnesota, the Frank Hague machine in Jersey City, the Pendergast machine in Kansas City, the Connecticut Democratic Party under John M. Bailey, the Democratic Party assembled by Edmund Muskie in Maine, the Pennsylvania Republican Party (including its Philadelphia machine) in the first half of the twentieth century, and the Long Island Republican machine that

still survives, are all examples of strong state and local party organizations that have never been replicated at the national level.[32] National
party committees exist structurally but have been for the most part
functionally powerless.[33] Parties and candidates, then, focus on winning elections in their states and localities and appeal primarily to state
and local electorates. For this reason, regional and ideological factions
have emerged historically within political parties more than between
parties.

Fifth, American political parties historically are patronage-oriented
rather than issue-oriented. Winning elections and control of government is the main goal of American parties. Issues have been important
to the extent that they serve the purpose of winning elections and
governing.[34] Dating back at least to the birth of the Democratic Party
and the spoils system under Andrew Jackson, most particularly in the
cases of urban machines, party organizations have been patron-client
organizations, designed to win elections, maintain control of government, and provide positions and services for supporters.[35]

Finally, along with the division of powers, the constitutional separation of powers reinforces the lack of ideological or policy cohesion
found historically within American political parties. Although parties
and candidates seek to win elections and organize government, they do
so in the context of executive leadership separated from legislative
leadership, both chosen in temporally staggered elections. The United
States, since 1789, has never had the sort of national general election
that the United Kingdom holds at least every five years. Although
divided government has been the exception rather than the rule until
recently, it has been the rule in at least one previous electoral period
(immediately previous to the realignment of 1896) and is a predictable
outgrowth of the American constitutional system. As a result, American
politics has not featured "responsible" parties, or party government,
usually found in parliamentary democracies.[36]

Parties and Factions

The two-party system, by its generally successful aggregation of
interests, has served to camouflage a multifactional electoral system
that is even more persistent in American politics. As umbrella parties,
American political parties are best understood not as responsible parties, or even rational-acting organizations, but as factional systems—the
Democrats a multifaction system, and the Republicans a two-faction
system. The Democratic umbrella historically has covered the Solid
South, the party regulars of the big-city machines of the north and their
working-class constituencies, and the more middle-class reform elements of the party. The Democratic Party generally has been the party

through which new demographic sectors of the population have been mobilized into the electorate. The Republican umbrella, on the other hand, has covered a more uniformly middle-class electorate, with its Wall Street and Main Street factions battling for power.

Except during critical realignments, ideological polarization in American politics has occurred more often within than between the parties. Over the first half of the twentieth century, and through two realignments, change in the ideological centers of gravity within the two major parties was incremental in pace and minor in degree, although somewhat more visible among the Democrats than among the Republicans. Then, in the 1964–1972 period, ideological change within and between the parties was abrupt and pronounced, as factional struggles within the parties reached critical stages. The result was not only a major electoral realignment, but very fundamental change in the American party system.

AN ALTERNATIVE THEORY OF REALIGNMENT AND PARTY DEVELOPMENT

The party-decay thesis enjoys reasonably broad support in political science but has not achieved unanimity among scholars, nor even the near consensus that the dealignment thesis enjoys. The debate poses the question "Are American political parties in decline, or are they reviving?" But that question presents another set of alternatives as if they were mutually exclusive, when perhaps they are not. The hypothesis behind this research is that both questions can be answered in the affirmative. That is, the American political parties born in the nineteenth century are in decline; the American political parties of the twenty-first century, conceived in the realignment of the 1960s, are emerging.

The analysis I present is based on the following six propositions:

1. *The most compelling electoral realignment in American history occurred in the 1960s.* The realignment of the 1960s was actually something of an inversion of all previous alignments, particularly when state-level data in Presidential elections is examined. The south, historically solidly Democratic since the end of Reconstruction, shifted toward the Republicans in Presidential elections and now is the most Republican section of the country. The northeast, once the most Republican region of the country, is now the most Democratic. This resulted, at the very least, in the decline of the New Deal party system, and, as one author put it, "the collapse of the Democratic Presidential majority."[37]

2. *The realignment of the 1960s occurred because of the resolution of factional struggles within both major parties in favor of the more ideological factions.* As interest groups and issue activists gained control of Presidential nominations, as noted by the party-decay theorists, conservative Republicans and liberal Democrats came to dominate their national parties. This ideological polarization was reflected, almost immediately, in the national Presidential coalitions of both parties.

3. *Increased split-ticket voting and divided government, which has become the norm in American politics, has been structured by ideological polarization as well as by incumbency advantages at the polls.* No effort is made in this analysis to deny that the electoral change of the 1960s was one of dealignment. But dealignment should be understood as realignment by other means, or as James Q. Wilson put it, "realignment at the top, and dealignment at the bottom."[38] The result was a "two-tier" party system, as Ladd observed, usually featuring a Republican President and always featuring a Democratic Congress. The swing vote in the electorate was not an independent centrist vote. Rather, the swing voters were disproportionately conservative Democrats, from the south, voting Republican for President and Democratic for Congress. Republican Presidents and Democratic incumbents in Congress were both the beneficiaries at the polls.

4. *There was, starting in the 1970s, a new policy agenda, displacing the New Deal and the Great Society.* It was a conservative agenda, reflecting the conservative governing coalition of Republicans and conservative Democrats that had emerged. This coalition reached the peak of its powers during the Reagan Presidency, but its electoral roots are found in the 1960s and its policy roots are found in the Nixon administration.

5. *The "realignment at the top" of the 1960s has spread to the bottom in the 1990s.* The conservative Republicans and liberal Democrats who gained control of Presidential nominations in the 1964–1972 period have since consolidated their power over nominations at the state level and in Congressional elections, leading to a decline in the ideological content of split-ticket voting. The Republicans won both houses of Congress in 1994 for the first time in over four decades. That victory was not so important for realignment analysis as the fact that the Republican presidential coalitions had spread to congressional elections. For the first time ever, in 1994, the Republicans won a majority of House seats in the South, and the national Republican vote for Congress very much resembled the Republican vote for president over the previous thirty years. This outcome does not necessarily mean that we are headed for a persistent national Repub-

xxvi   Introduction

lican majority, although that may yet be the case. What it does mean
is that we now have presidential and congressional election coalitions that are quite similar. The result is likely to be a decrease in the
frequency of divided government.

6. *We now have two major political parties that are, by standards of the
American experience, ideologically polarized:* a Republican Party that is
conservative and a Democratic Party that is liberal. The umbrellas
of both parties seem to be less inclusive, and American parties,
though still not ideologically distinct to the degree of European
parliamentary parties, may come to resemble the responsible party
model more than they ever have. This would have important implications for American democracy in the twenty-first century.

The chapters that follow present evidence and test these propositions.
Chapter 1 examines realignment in the twentieth century, focusing on
a comparison of the "systems of '96." The realignment surrounding
William Jennings Bryan, which began the process of party decay according to Burnham and Silbey, is compared with alignments since: the New
Deal system and the dealignment system. The data from these realignments is used to critique the concept of realignment and how it has been
operationalized.

The political parties themselves is the subject of Chapters 2 through
6. The changing power of the factions within the major political
parties, particularly their influence over presidential nominations, is
examined to draw some conclusions about the relationship between
ideological polarization and electoral realignment. Chapters 2 and 3
discuss the Democratic and Republican parties as the umbrella parties
that were formed in the nineteenth century. Chapter 4 examines the
decisive factional struggles of the 1964–1972 realignment. Chapter 5
discusses the party decay from that period until 1980, and Chapter
6 portrays party revival since 1980. Because factions are not as formal
or identifiable as organizations as parties are, extensive description
of the history of factions in American politics accompanies the
presentation of data.

Chapter 7 discusses the electoral foundations of divided government,
particularly the impact of incumbency and ideology on split-ticket
voting between presidential and congressional elections.

The shifting roles of race and class, widely considered to be central
to electoral change since the 1960s, is the subject of Chapter 8.

Chapters 9 and 10 offer a two-part conclusion. Chapter 9 discusses
the usefulness of the realignment theory to the analysis of American
elections. In Chapter 10, I evaluate the prospects for a responsible party
system in the United States and the implications of that question for
American democracy.

NOTES

1. Expression taken from Everett Carll Ladd, "Like Waiting for Godot: The Uselessness of 'Realignment' for Understanding Change in Contemporary American Politics," in Byron E. Shafer, ed., *The End of Realignment? Interpreting American Electoral Eras* (Madison: University of Wisconsin Press, 1991), pp. 24–36.

2. V. O. Key, "A Theory of Critical Elections," *Journal of Politics* 17 (1955): 3–18.

3. See, for example, Walter Dean Burnham, *Critical Elections and the Mainprings of American Politics* (New York: Norton, 1970); Everett Carll Ladd, "The Shifting Party Coalitions—1932–1976," in Seymour Martin Lipset, ed., *Emerging Coaliions in American Politics* (San Francisco: Institute for Contemporary Studies, 1978); Ladd with Charles D. Hadley, *Transformations of the American Party System: Political Coalitions from the New Deal to the 1970s* (New York: Norton, 1978); David G. Lawrence, *The Collapse of the Democratic Presidential Majority: Realignment, Dealignment and Electoral Change from Franklin Roosevelt to Bill Clinton* (Boulder: Westview Press, 1997); Gerald Pomper, "From Confusion to Clarity: Issues and American Voters, 1956–1968," *The American Political Science Review* 66 (1972): 415–428; Pomper with Susan Lederman, *Elections in America: Control and Influnce in Democratic Politics* (New York: Longman, 1980); Byron E. Shafer, ed., *The End of Realignment? Interpreting American Electoral Eras* (Madison: University of Wisconsin Press, 1991); James L. Sundquist, *The Dynamics of the American Party System: Alignment and Realignment of Political Parties in the United States* (Washington, D.C.: Brookings Institution, 1983).

4. V. O. Key, "Secular Realignment and the Party System," *Journal of Politics* 23 (1959): 198–210.

5. Burnham, *Critical Elections*, p. 67.

6. See particularly Burnham, *Critical Elections*; Ladd with Hadley, *Transformations of the American Party System*; and Sundquist, *Dynamics.*

7. See Kristi Andersen, "Generation, Partisan Shift, and Realignment: A Glance Back to the New Deal," in Norman H. Nie, Sidney Verba, and John R. Petrocik, *The Changing American Voter* (Cambridge, Mass.: Harvard University Press, 1976), and *The Creation of a Democratic Majority: 1928–1936* (Chicago: University of Chicago Press, 1979).

8. See Angus Campbell, "A Classification of Presidential Elections," in Angus Campbell, Philip E. Converse, Warren E. Miller, and Donald E. Stokes, *Elections and the Political Order* (New York: John Wiley and Sons, 1960). See also Pomper with Lederman, 82–105.

9. See, for example, Burnham, *Critical Elections*; Pomper, "From Confusion to Clarity;" Kevin Phillips, *The Emerging Republican Majority* (New Rochelle, N.Y.: Arlington House, 1969); and Richard Scammon and Ben Wattenburg, *The Real Majority* (New York: Coward-McCann, 1970).

10. See, for example, Walter Burnham, "American Politics in the 1970s: Beyond Party?" in Jeff Fishel, ed., *Parties and Elections in an Anti-Party Age* (Bloomington: Indiana University Press, 1978); Walter Burnham, "American Politics in the 1980s," in Burnham, *The Hidden Crisis in American Politics* (New York: Oxford University Press, 1982); Walter Burnham, "Into the 1980s with Ronald Reagan," in Burnham, *The Hidden Crisis in American Politics*; Walter Burnham, "The Reagan Heritage," in Gerald Pomper, et al., *The Election of 1988: Reports and Interpretations* (Chatham, N.J.:

Chatham House, 1989); Everett Carll Ladd, "The Shifting Party Coalitions—1932–1976"; Everett Carll Ladd, "The Brittle Mandate: Electoral Dealignment and the 1980 Presidential Election," *Political Science Quarterly* 96 (1981): 1–25; Ladd with Charles D. Hadley; Ladd, "Like Waiting for Godot."

11. David Broder, "Introduction," in Seymour Martin Lipset, ed., *Emerging Coalitions in American Politics* (San Franciso: Institute for Contemporary Studies, 1978), p. 5.

12. Scammon and Wattenburg.

13. See particularly Everett Carll Ladd, "Liberalism Upside Down: The Inversion of the New Deal Order," in William Crotty, ed., *The Party Symbol: Readings on Political Parties* (San Francisco: W. H. Freeman and Company, 1980).

14. Burnham, "American Politics in the 1970s." See also David Apter, "Ideology and Discontent," in David Apter, ed., *Ideology and Discontent* (New York: The Free Press, 1964).

15. Burnham, "The Reagan Heritage," p. 16.

16. Ladd with Hadley, p. 266; Ladd, "Like Waiting for Godot," p. 31.

17. See especially Walter DeVries and V. Lance Terrance, *The Ticket Splitter: A New Force in American Politics* (Grand Rapids, Mich.: William B. Eerdmans, 1972).

18. See Walter Burnham, "Insulation and Responsiveness in Congressional Elections," *Political Science Quarterly* 90 (1975): 411–435; Barbara Hinckley, *Congressional Elections* (Washington, D.C.: Congressional Quarterly Press, 1981); Gary C. Jacobson, *The Electoral Origins of Divided Government: Competition in U.S. House Elections, 1946–1988* (Boulder: Westview Press, 1990); Thomas E. Mann and Raymond E. Wolfinger, "Candidates and Parties in Congressional Elections," *The American Political Science Review* 74 (1980): 617–632; and David R. Mayhew, "Congressional Elections: The Case of the Vanishing Marginals," *Polity* 6 (1974): 295–317.

19. See William Crotty, *American Parties in Decline*, 2nd ed. (Glenview, Ill.: Scott, Foresman, 1984), especially pp. 142–196.

20. See especially Martin P. Wattenberg, *The Decline of American Political Parties* (Cambridge: Harvard University Press, 1990).

21. Ladd, "The Brittle Mandate," p. 3.

22. Ladd with Hadley, p. 333.

23. Burnham, *Critical Elections*, pp. 91–92.

24. Joel H. Silbey, "Beyond Realignment and Realignment Theory," in Byron E. Shafer, ed., *The End of Realignment? Interpreting American Electoral Eras* (Madison: University of Wisconsin Press, 1991), pp. 15–18.

25. Walter Burnham, "Realignment Lives: The 1994 Earthquake and Its Implications," in Colin Campbell and Bert A. Rockman, eds., *The Clinton Presidency: First Appraisals* (Chatham, N.J.: Chatham House, 1996), pp. 363–395.

26. Whereas Burnham and Silbey trace party decay to reforms associated with the realignment of 1896, Nelson Polsby and Austin Ranney emphasize the 1960s. See Polsby, *The Consequences of Party Reform* (Oxford: Oxford University Press, 1983) and Ranney, *Curing the Mischiefs of Faction: Party Reform in America* (Los Angeles: University of California Press, 1975).

27. See Paul Allen Beck and Frank Sorauf, *Party Politics in America*, 7th ed. (New York: HarperCollins, 1992), for the classic presentation of the categories of party-in-the-electorate, party-as-organization, and party-in-government.

28. The classic spatial theory of electoral democracy, of course, was presented by Anthony Downs. See *An Economic Theory of Democracy* (New York: Harper and Row, 1957).

29. See especially Louis Hartz, *The Liberal Tradition in America* (New York: Harcourt, Brace and World, 1955).

30. For discussions of class consciousness, or lack of it, in American political culture, see Stanley Aronowitz, *False Promises: The Shaping of American Working Class Consciousness* (New York: McGraw-Hill, 1973); Daniel Bell, *The End of Ideology: On the Exhaustion of Political Ideas in the Fifties* (New York: The Free Press, 1960); Richard Centers, *The Psychology of Social Classes* (Princeton, N.J.: Princeton University Press, 1949); Alexis De Tocqueville, *Democracy in America* (New York: Doubleday, 1969); Hartz; Robert E. Lane, *Political Ideology: Why the American Common Man Believes What He Does* (New York: The Free Press, 1962); Arthur Paulson, *Political Attitudes of the Unemployed: Interviews with Fifteen Men* (Unpublished Ph.D. dissertation, University of Colorado, 1985); Kay Lehman Schlozman and Sidney Verba, *Injury to Insult: Unemployment, Class, and Political Response* (Cambridge, Mass.: Harvard University Press, 1979); Frederick Jackson Turner, *The Frontier in American History* (New York: Holt, 1947).

31. For the classic discussion of the difference between position and valence issues, see Donald E. Stokes, "Spatial Models of Party Competition," in Angus Campbell, Philip E. Converse, Warren E. Miller, and Donald E. Stokes, *Elections and the Political Order* (New York: John Wiley and Sons, 1966), pp. 161–179. For the classic work on retrospective voting, see Morris P. Fiorina, *Retrospective Voting in American National Elections* (New Haven: Yale University Press, 1981).

32. Beck and Sorauf.

33. Cornelius P. Cotter and Bernard C. Hennessy, *Politics without Power* (New York: Atherton, 1964).

34. John H. Aldrich, *Why Parties? The Origin and Transformation of Party Politics in America* (Chicago: University of Chicago Press, 1995).

35. See Beck and Sorauf, pp. 78–82; L. Sandy Maisel, *Parties and Elections in America: The Electoral Process* (New York: McGraw-Hill, 1993), pp. 55–73; and David R. Mayhew, *Placing Parties in American Politics* (Princeton, N.J.: Princeton University Press, 1986).

36. Aldrich, *Why Parties*, pp. 3–27; Beck and Sorauf, pp. 426–456; Austin Ranney. Classic works in the comparative analysis of party systems include Robert A. Dahl, *Political Oppositions in Western Democracies* (New Haven: Yale University Press, 1966); Leon Epstein, *Political Parties in Western Democracies* (New York: Praeger, 1967); Seymour Martin Lipset and Stein Rokkan, eds., *Party Systems and Voter Alignments* (New York: Cambridge University Press, 1976).

37. Lawrence.

38. See James Q. Wilson, "Realignment at the Top, Dealignment at the Bottom," in Austin Ranney, ed., *The American Elections of 1984* (Durham, N.C.: AEI/Duke University Press, 1985).

A Century of Presidential Elections: From "System of '96" to System of '96

Looking ahead to the Presidential election of 1996, Rhodes Cook of *Congressional Quarterly* wrote that to win, Republican Robert Dole would have to reassemble the normally Republican coalition of states in the south and west, what Cook called the "Republican L."[1] Mr. Dole did, indeed, carry most of those states, but not enough of them. President Bill Clinton, the incumbent Democrat, cracked both the south and the west, and nearly swept the northeast quadrant of the country. The result was that President Clinton was the first Democratic President to win re-election since 1944, more than half a century before, when Franklin D. Roosevelt was re-elected to a fourth term.

The Presidential election of 1996 provided further evidence of two realities of electoral change. First, the Democratic Party is no longer the nation's majority party, as it had been in 1944, and it has not been for some time. Before Bill Clinton was elected President in 1992, the Republicans had won five of the previous six Presidential elections. Moreover, during the Clinton Presidency, the Republicans have won control of Congress and have retained it even in the face of his re-election.

Second, the election provided further evidence that there has been a partisan reversal in the political geography of American Presidential elections. The "Republican L" of 1996 would have been the "Democratic L" in 1896. In that realigning election, which gave birth to what Walter Dean Burnham has called the "system of '96," Democrat William Jennings Bryan carried all of the south and most of the west in a losing cause.[2] Republican William McKinley swept the northeast quadrant and was elected President with a coalition of states very similar to the coalition that would be assembled by Democrat Bill Clinton a century later. The coalitions of states in the Presidential elections of 1896 and 1996 are compared in Table* 1.1.[3] Only nine of the forty-five states participating in the two elections voted for the same party in both: two Republican states and seven Democratic states. The other thirty-six all switched. States switching from the Democrats to the Republicans between 1896 and 1996 are found predominantly in the south and west; those switching from the Republicans to the Democrats are found mostly in the northeast quadrant.

If the comparison of the electoral maps of 1896 and 1996 amounted to a mirror-image coincidence, it would be a curiosity of only passing interest. But, the reversal across a century represents a persistent pattern of state electoral behavior. This chapter reconsiders the concept of realignment by examining that pattern.

REALIGNMENT AND STATES IN PRESIDENTIAL ELECTIONS: A METHODOLOGY

The remainder of this chapter illustrates stability and change in Presidential elections by examining the electoral behavior of the states between 1896 and 1996. The data demonstrate a realignment of states in Presidential elections reaching critical proportions in the 1964–1972 period.

States are the central unit of analysis for the following reasons. First, states are the constitutional and political building blocks of Presidential elections. The contest for victory in the Electoral College has always made states the focus of campaign strategy; the winning coalition is a coalition of states.

Second, previous studies have demonstrated a political geography in which states and regions are observed to have relatively autonomous political subcultures. Results at the state level in Presidential elections reflect not only partisan loyalties in voting behavior but also a persistent relative ideological position of the states, particularly on cultural issues.[4] But related issues of traditional versus modern values have lingered across previous alignments in American politics, uniting coali-

*Tables will be found at the ends of chapter texts.

tions that have been consistent in their support of one side or the other.[5] These coalitions have also had a consistent geographic base. Generally speaking, traditional values have drawn most of their support from the south and interior west and rural areas, whereas modern values find their support in the northeast quadrant and urban areas. The traditional-versus-modern debate has shaped coalitions on numerous issues that are not necessarily linked by definition. Race has historically been the most persistently divisive of the traditional versus modern issues, but the debate has extended from the ratification of the Constitution, to state versus national authority, to foreign policy, to economics. Social class interests and economic issues, however, have often cut across these cultural coalitions. The cultural coalitions have also cut across party lines, periodically with realigning consequences. Table 1.2 illustrates general ideological positions on issues involving traditional versus modern values. Although Table 1.2, of necessity, generalizes broadly, it reflects a consensus of political historians, including the literature cited here thus far.

What is important to electoral analysis is the observation in studies cited here that states retain approximately the same relative ideological position in the cultural coalitions over time. The tendency is, for example, that a culturally conservative state in 1896 will remain culturally conservative in 1996.

In this chapter, I use two measures to study electoral change and stability across alignment eras. First, states are classified according to their partisan loyalties within each era. Democratic states in any era are those that voted Democratic and more Democratic than the nation in most of the Presidential elections of the period. Likewise, Republican states are those that voted Republican and more Republican than the nation in most Presidential elections. All other states are classified for the era as "competitive." The importance of considering the vote of a state relative to the national vote makes intuitive sense and is well developed in the work of Louis H. Bean, who observed that not only for residents of Maine, but for everyone, "As your state goes, so goes the nation."[6] His point is that whereas parties gain and lose votes, states tend to vote with amazing consistency, relative to the national vote in Presidential elections, over extended periods of time.

Second, Pearson's r will be used to correlate the state level vote in Presidential elections. The central focus will be on the beginning and end of the twentieth century, comparing state-level coalitions in each election with those of 1896 and 1996. Shorter-term evaluations of electoral stability and change are also made to highlight periods of critical realignment.

These two measures, taken together, consider both the winning party at the state level in Presidential elections and the relative strength of the parties in the various states. Put in the language of realignment theory, these measures incorporate what Clubb, Flanigan, and Zingale offered as the two distinct dimensions of electoral change: across-the-board or surge change, in which the electorate moves rather uniformly toward one party or the other, often producing new majorities without significant change in party coalitions; and differential or interactive change, in which there is a cross-cutting change in the coalitions of the two parties, whether new majorities result or not.[7]

The model for this study is based on the hypothesis that partisan electoral change between 1896 and 1996 is strongly related to cultural coalitions based on state political ideology. For purposes of testing and illustrating this hypothesis, states are sorted according to their ideological position in Presidential elections during the period of ideological polarization and critical electoral change between 1964 and 1972. The nomination of the ideological "extremists," conservative Republican Barry Goldwater in 1964 and liberal Democrat George McGovern in 1972, and the third-party candidacy of George Wallace in 1968, have had an enduring impact on the party system, which I argue should be understood as a critical realignment during that period.

Those states that voted more Republican than the country in both 1964 and 1972, cast a higher total vote for Nixon and Wallace than the country in 1968, and voted less Democratic than the country in all three elections are classified as the most conservative. States that voted more Democratic than the country in all three elections, less Republican than the country in 1964 and 1972, and cast a lower total vote for Nixon and Wallace than the country in 1968 are classified as the most liberal. All other states are classified as "moderate." If ideology has much to do with electoral realignment, a strong relationship between these classifications and electoral alignments before and since would be expected. This chapter concludes with an illustration of the relationship between ideological polarization and electoral realignment. The relationship between ideological polarization and change within the parties is the subject of the five chapters that follow.

A CENTURY OF PRESIDENTIAL ELECTIONS

The following analysis is based on three striking observations of state behavior in Presidential elections.

First, *partisan continuity has been the general rule*. The relationship between the south and the northeast in Presidential elections actually extends all the way back to the 1830s, when Presidential elections came to be based on the popular vote. The south was the most Democratic region of the country, even before the solid south emerged after Reconstruction, and continued to be until the 1960s. The northeast was consistently the strongest region for the Federalists, the Whigs, and the Republicans over the same period of time. The west, as states are admitted to the union, varies more over time but is generally less Democratic than the south and less Republican than the northeast. The west did, however, vote for William Jennings Bryan in 1896 and for all three Democratic winners of the next half century: Woodrow Wilson, Franklin D. Roosevelt, and Harry S. Truman. To win, the Democrats needed the "Democratic L."

Second, *there was a disruption in the partisan alignment of states starting in 1948. The result is a mirror-image reversal of the historic partisan pattern by the 1960s.* The 1944 Presidential election, the most recent re-election of a Democratic President until 1996, was also the last election in which the continuity in the coalition of states remained undisturbed. Thereafter, the south was loosened from the Democratic coalition in the Dixiecrat rebellion of 1948, and Republicans Dwight D. Eisenhower and Richard M. Nixon cracked the south between 1952 and 1960. The south nevertheless remained the most Democratic region of the country until it became the least Democratic region in the Democratic landslide of 1964. Since then, the south and interior west have generally voted Republican, and the northeast quadrant of the country has consistently been the most Democratic region of the country.

The correlations in Table 1.3 illustrate the long-term continuity between 1896 and 1944, the mid-century disruption, and the fact that since the 1964–1972 period, state-level returns are positively and strongly correlated with the coalition of 1996. Table 1.4 compares the partisan alignment of states in Presidential elections between 1896 and 1944 with the alignment that emerged starting in 1964. Put again in the language of Clubb, Flanigan, and Zingale, Table 1.4 shows compelling differential change in the coalition of states between the first half of the twentieth century and the latter third of the century.

Third, *the partisan disruption was thus not a disruption in the coalition of states. The same states have continued to vote generally together*—the south and interior west, once relatively Democratic, now relatively Republican; and the northeast, once relatively Republican, now relatively Democratic. The historic coalition of states is *reversed almost intact.* The electoral change in the partisan alignment of states, then, has not been chaotic or without direction. Rather, it seems that although the partisan coalitions have reversed, there has been a persistence of ideological coalitions among the states. Prior to the New Deal, the Democratic Party tended to be the party of traditional values, most popular in the south and interior west. The Republican Party, founded as the anti-slavery party, represented the commercial interests of a modernizing elite based in the more industrial and urban northeast. After the New Deal, the

Democrats came to be associated with modern values such as internationalism and the welfare state and picked up the standard of civil
rights in the 1960s. The Republicans have become the party of traditional values. Thus, if the partisan continuity of the states in Presidential elections has been a general rule, the *ideological continuity of states
has been much closer to an absolute rule.*

THE SYSTEM OF 1896

Even in the realignment of 1896, William Jennings Bryan was inher-
iting as much as creating a Democratic coalition that was rural, southern, and—to a lesser degree—western. Bryan was the Presidential
nominee of a party that had its roots in the Anti-Federalist movement,
the small government, states' rights philosophy of Thomas Jefferson,
the anti–National Bank, pro-frontier philosophy of Andrew Jackson, the
declining aristocracy of the ante-Bellum south, and the post-Reconstruction solid south. Now he was offering himself and his party as the
vehicle of rural America.

The salient issue of the 1896 campaign was silver. President Grover
Cleveland, the Democratic incumbent who was retiring from office,
favored the gold standard. So did the Republicans and the business
interests who supported their nominee, William McKinley. Bryan and
the Democrats who supported him favored the free coinage of silver, to
create easier credit for small, independent farmers. Bryan's support of
free silver was certainly a self-consciously economic agenda. But his
eloquent expression of it, for example in the "Cross of Gold" speech at
the Democratic convention, was delivered largely in cultural terms. He
was a cultural conservative, seeking to maintain a way of life against
the tide of capitalist modernization. Bryan's populism was a combination of economic progressivism and traditional values based on "the
Social Gospel."[8]

As opposed to Bryan, the Republican mainstream of 1896 was conservative on economic issues, representing established corporate and financial interests. But it was in these interests to promote the
industrialization that rural populists saw as so threatening to their way
of life. These issues were cross-cutting ideologically in that the populists were thus progressive on economic issues and at the same time
conservative on social issues. This apparent irony is actually more the
rule than the exception in American political life.

Although the Presidential election of 1896 is properly recognized as
a realigning election, and although Bryan and the populists represented
a very new leadership for the Democratic Party, the electoral continui-
ties between 1896 and previous elections should not be overlooked. The

regional patterns of 1896 carried all the way back to the Presidential election of 1824, which was the first in which a popular vote for Presidential electors was recorded in most states, and gave birth to the second party system. The 1824 election was thrown into the House of Representatives when Andrew Jackson won a plurality of both the popular and Electoral Vote but could not muster a majority of the latter. Without exception, where John Quincy Adams won in 1824, mostly in the northeast, William McKinley would win in 1896. In 1896, Bryan carried all of the southern states won by Jackson or William H. Crawford in 1824. In 1896, McKinley and Bryan battled closely for the three states won by Henry Clay in 1824. Ultimately, the 1824 election had been settled in the House in favor of Adams. The result gave fuel to the popular movement behind Jackson, leading to his election in 1828, and to the birth of the Democratic Party. Although the south was not immediately solid, it voted generally for Democrats starting with Jackson. Before voting for John Quincy Adams, the northeast was the strongest section for the Federalists, as it would later be for the Whigs and the Republicans. (See Table 1.5.)

Similarly, the regional patterns of 1896 were even closer to those of the hotly contested pre–Civil War election of 1860, the year of Bryan's birth. The election of Abraham Lincoln establishes 1860 as a realigning election, and rightly so. It is only the second Presidential election the Republicans contested, and the first they won. But the splintering of the parties in a four-way race in 1860 exaggerates the realigning appearance of that election. A combination of the northern and southern Democratic votes reveals regional patterns very similar to the ones that existed both before and after 1860.

In 1896 William McKinley carried all the northern states that had been won by Lincoln. Bryan carried all the southern states that had been won by Vice President John Breckinridge, the southern Democrat, in 1860. McKinley and Bryan battled closely for the states that had been carried by Senator Stephen A. Douglas of Illinois, the northern Democrat, and by Constitutional Unionist John C. Bell. (See Table 1.6.)

Although the Presidential election of 1896 reveals the persistence of historic coalitions in American politics, it is still classified as a realigning election, and properly so, for two reasons. First, the 1896 election established a normal Republican national majority with control of the Presidency and Congress. Second, the 1896 election solidified the Republican base in the east and strengthened the Democrats in the west. Prior to 1896, there was no clear majority party. Although the Republicans won six consecutive Presidential elections starting in 1860, their dominance ended with the end of Reconstruction and the readmission of the south to the union. Thereafter, elections were very closely contested, and control of national government shifted back and forth, until

1896. The Republicans won three out of five Presidential elections between 1876 and 1892, including the stolen election of 1876, in which Governor Samuel J. Tilden of New York, the Democratic nominee, was denied the Presidency. The Democrats won the popular vote for President in four out of the same five elections, including all three in which Grover Cleveland was their nominee. Cleveland won in 1884 and 1892, losing in 1888. He is the twenty-second and twenty-fourth President because in 1888 he won the popular vote and lost the electoral college in an election as close as his victory four years before. He remains not only the only President to regain the office but also the only candidate to win the popular vote and lose the Presidency in the electoral college after an election in which the result was undisputed and decided at the polls.[9] His experience reflects how close the elections of the time were: Between 1876 and 1892, the popular vote margin was never more than three percentage points; in the 1880s, never so much as a percentage point.

At the same time, control of Congress fluctuated. In the twenty years before 1896, divided government was the rule rather than the exception, just as it has been since the 1960s.

Then in 1896 a persistent Republican majority emerged, with its base in the east. Bryan, who effectively outlined an agenda for the progressive era, swept the south and carried most of the interior west, whose states had entered the union in the previous two decades. Bryan thus inherited the frontier coalition of Andrew Jackson and extended it westward into the area of the old Louisiana Purchase. In elections after 1896, the west wavered, and they supported Republicans for President more often than not. But the west was essential to Democratic national victories when they occurred, which was only twice until the Depression.

In a sense, the 1896 election is the model for realignment, even more than 1932 would later become. The 1896 election offers not only a new partisan majority but much more evidence than 1932 would provide (although much less than 1964) of differential electoral change. Thus, 1896 fits what we would expect to find in a realigning election according to correlation analysis popularized by Gerald Pomper and Susan Lederman.[10] The post-Reconstruction elections correlate very positively and significantly with each other. The Presidential election of 1892 is converting, the Republicans losing much of the west to James B. Weaver, the Populist candidate. Then, 1896 realigns and subsequent elections correlate highly with it. (See Table 1.7.)

After Reconstruction, and until 1896, the Republicans generally carried the northeast and the west, the Democrats the solid south. When the Democrats won in 1884 and 1892, it was because they were able to crack the northeast quadrant. Indeed, in 1884 the result turned only on

New York. Grover Cleveland of New York carried the state for the Democrats by only 1,000 votes out of more than 1,100,000 cast (48.2 percent for each major candidate), and then only because of the support of the reform Republican "mugwumps" and because of the counterproductive "rum, Romanism, and rebellion" remark by a supporter of Republican James G. Blaine. Had New York voted for Blaine, the Republican would have been elected.[11]

After 1896 the Democrats became reliant on the west and could only crack the east if they did not need it. William Jennings Bryan was the Democratic nominee for President twice more, always running a competitve race, sweeping the south, carrying at least some of the west, and losing everywhere in the east. Despite the realignment, the coalition of states after 1896 is not radically altered. But electoral change is sufficient to establish a Republican majority, by solidifying the east in the GOP camp. As Table 1.8 illustrates, almost all the states of the northeast quadrant voted reliably Republican in Presidential elections between 1896 and 1908. Most notably, New York, a closely competitive state before 1896, and New Jersey, a Democratic state, voted Republican in the four Presidential elections starting in 1896. Meanwhile, only the eleven states of the old Confederacy plus Kentucky remained reliably Democratic in the same period.

Between 1896 and 1932, the only Democrat elected President was Woodrow Wilson in 1912 and 1916. Wilson won in 1912 only because of the Bull Moose split from the Republicans, to be discussed in Chapter 2. Wilson won with less than 42 percent of the total popular vote, almost exactly the same proportion and geographic distribution of the vote received by Bryan three times. In 1916, President Wilson, even with the power of incumbency, was re-elected so narrowly that Republican Charles Evans Hughes and most of the country went to bed on election night thinking that Hughes had won. Hughes carried almost all of the northeast quadrant, while Wilson reassembled what was then a "Democratic L" of the south and west. Thereafter, the Republicans were reinstated in 1920 and remained in control of the White House and the Hill until dislodged by the Great Depression and the New Deal. The Republican coalition that elected Harding, Coolidge, and Hoover in the 1920s was still rooted in the northeast quadrant, essentially unchanged from the coalition that elected McKinley, Roosevelt, and Taft two decades before. The Democrats remain cornered, in the south. (See Table 1.9.)

THE NEW DEAL SYSTEM

The realigning election of 1932 saw the emergence of the Democratic majority, which persisted for most of the next three decades. The 1928–

1936 period has often been cited as the prototype of realignment, particularly in the classic seminal work of V. O. Key.[12] It offers not only the new Democratic majority but also a stable governing coalition and a dramatic new policy agenda. As an across-the-board surge toward the Democrats, the New Deal realignment is the most compelling in American history. Indeed, contrary to the impression left by most of the realignment literature, the realignment of the 1930s is the only one in which a normal partisan majority for one party is replaced by a new normal partisan majority for the other party.

However, even this realignment fails to fit the model perfectly, featuring very little change in the coalitions of the two major parties. Indeed, the differential change associated with the New Deal realignment has been overplayed, possibly because Key's exploratory work on realignment focused on the disproportionately Catholic, northern, urban, working-class, and labor union vote for Democrat Al Smith in 1928. Kristi Andersen, building an argument for mobilization more than vote change to explain realignment, focused on the same demographics of the vote for Smith in Chicago.[13] These observations are accurate and important. A working-class base that would be central to the Democratic coalition of the New Deal period did emerge in 1928, as Key points out. And, as Andersen argued, record numbers of voters were mobilized, for both major parties. The 21,000,000 votes for Republican Herbert Hoover was a record, and the 15,000,000 votes for Smith was a record for a losing Presidential nominee.

The Presidential election of 1928 is usually classified as a converting election, and considering the evidence cited here, properly so. But considering the electoral behavior of the states, the conversion is overestimated. Though Governor Smith lost five historically Democratic states of the rim south and carried historically Republican Massachusetts and Rhode Island, those results represented more of a deviation than a conversion. Thereafter, patterns of relative support of the parties that had predated 1928 were restored. Even after the New Deal realignment, the Democrats still swept the solid south and won in the west; the Republicans did best in the northeast quadrant, consistently running better there than across the country.

When Franklin D. Roosevelt was elected President in 1932, he carried all but six states: Delaware and five of the six New England states. Four years later, when FDR was re-elected in a record landslide, he lost only Maine and Vermont, and his performance in the northeast generally was not up to his showing across the country. In 1940 and 1944, FDR again swept the south and won most of the west. His Republican opponents, Wendell L. Willkie and Governor Thomas E. Dewey of New York, each carried a bloc of plains states and ran better in the northeast quadrant than they did nationally. Willkie and

Dewey both carried Maine, Vermont, and Indiana; Willkie carried Michigan, and Dewey carried Ohio. Thus, in the four Roosevelt elections, the Democrats won big where they had always run strongest; the Republicans ran best in historically Republican territory. Table 1.10 shows the generally stable correlations of the state-level vote in Presidential elections before and after the New Deal realignment. Table 1.11 illustrates the unidirectional movement of states toward the Democrats in the New Deal realignment. There is no evidence of a cross-cutting realignment among the states in Presidential elections, which was found to some degree in the 1890s and which would be even more evident in the 1960s.

All this should not undercut the status of the 1928–1936 period as one of critical realignment. But the economic and class basis of the New Deal realignment would explain the continuity in the relative strength of the political parties in the states. The Great Depression had a much more national impact rather than the disparate regional impacts found in other realignments, and the social class polarization of the New Deal realignment was a national phenomenon. But the 1928–1936 period certainly differs from either the 1890s or the 1960s. The salient issues of the 1890s and the 1960s were expressed in more cultural terms, with disparate regional results, and were thus much more disturbing on the historic coalition of states.

The Secular Realignment to Dealignment

The first four elections of the New Deal period show remarkable stability in electoral coalitions. Franklin D. Roosevelt was elected President four times, and the Democrats retained control of Congress throughout his Presidency. According to Table 1.10, the Democratic vote at the state level correlates from one election to the next at .93 or higher, stability even greater than the glory days of political parties before 1896. The state-level correlation of the Democratic vote between 1940 and 1944 is an unprecedented and unmatched .99. But the re-election of President Roosevelt in 1944 ran out the string to a degree not appreciated at the time. Polling 54 percent of the popular vote, sweeping the solid south, and winning an overwhelming victory of 432 to 99 in the Electoral College, FDR became not only the first but also the last Democrat to be elected fundamentally on the strength of the New Deal coalition.

The second half of the New Deal alignment cycle might best be understood as a secular realignment from the pre-exisiting historic pattern of partisan coalitions to the system of dealignment that emerged by the 1960s.[14] The Dixiecrat rebellion in 1948 and Republican gains in the rim south over the next decade would set the stage. In the 1960s, the embrace of civil rights by the national Democrats and the seizure of the Republican Party by its conservatives would push the realignment to critical proportions.

The Dixiecrat rebellion draws special attention to the Presidential election of 1948. As a result of the candidacy of Governor J. Strom Thurmond of South Carolina, the States' Rights Democratic nominee, the state-level correlations of the national Democratic vote with other elections foreshadow the correlations that would emerge more regularly, starting in 1964. Thurmond carried South Carolina, Mississippi, Louisiana, and Alabama. President Harry S Truman carried the rest of the south, although with reduced percentages.

President Truman, of course, was widely expected to lose in 1948. The universal indication of a Republican victory in opinion polls was supported by the fact that the Democrats were split not two, but three ways. Thurmond was threatening Truman in the south, while former Vice President Henry A. Wallace, the Progressive nominee opposed to administration Cold War policy, was threatening to draw ultraliberal Democrats from the ticket. Just as the Dixiecrats foreshadowed electoral change in the south, so Henry Wallace foreshadowed the antiwar Democrats at the 1968 and 1972 conventions.[15]

Nevertheless, outside the south, the New Deal coalition remained intact, both demographically and geographically. President Truman retained the disproportionately Catholic, urban working-class, and labor union vote that had always delivered for FDR. Generally speaking, outside the south, Truman won in 1948 where Wilson had won in 1916, while Governor Thomas Dewey, the Republican, won in 1948 where Hughes had won in 1916. The national margin was similar: Wilson defeated Hughes by 49 percent to 46 percent, Truman defeated Dewey by 50 to 45. The erosion of Democratic support in the south was overlooked, partly because Thurmond was a third-party candidate supported by many southern leaders in the Democratic Party and partly because President Truman had scored a stunning upset victory. And, after all, from the perspective of 1948, could you expect the south to actually vote Republican? Where else would the south go but back to the Democratic fold?

The next three Presidential elections gave indications of growing Republican support in the south. Dwight D. Eisenhower reassembled the Republican base in the northeast quadrant and at the same time cracked the south twice in his two landslide victories. In 1960 Vice President Richard M. Nixon carried Virginia, Tennessee, and Florida. Although the Republican national vote declined by eight percentage points in 1960, Nixon lost no ground in the south and only barely lost the total vote of the eleven states of the old Confederacy.

The Democrats may have carried the south in 1960 only because Senator John F. Kennedy of Massachusetts, the Democratic nominee for President, found it wise to protect his southern flank by inviting Senate Majority Leader Lyndon B. Johnson to join him on the ticket. Prior to 1948, the idea of a Democrat having to worry about the south in a national election would have seemed farfetched. But Kennedy, as a Catholic, was concerned about losing southern states as Al Smith had in 1928. More important, the political environment had changed. It was now clear that no Democrat could take the south for granted.

Thus, between 1948 and 1960, the south was no longer solid for the Democrats in Presidential elections and not yet Republican. Less noticed, but related to the shift of the south, the interior west and the northeast quadrant also shifted in the same period, the former region toward the Republicans, the latter toward the Democrats. Dwight D. Eisenhower swept both the northeast and the west in his 1952 and 1956 landslides. His sweep of the northeast was no surprise. But his percentages in the west also outstripped his national performance.

In the 1960 Presidential election, decided by only one-tenth of 1 percent, all three regions were competitive. Nixon won the interior west, carrying all the plains states and six of the eight mountain states. Kennedy won the south but failed to sweep it. What was suddenly new in 1960 was that the Democrats won most of the northeast quadrant. Kennedy carried his home state of Massachusetts, plus New York, New Jersey, Pennsylvania, Michigan, and Illinois; to do so in such a closely contested election, he had to run better in these states than across the country, thus reversing the historic pattern. Not only had Republicans McKinley and Lincoln won these states, so had every Republican winner and some of the losers over the previous century. Charles Evans Hughes had won them all in his narrow loss to Wilson, and the Republicans who lost to Roosevelt and Truman had won some of these states and had run better here than nationally. Because both Wilson in 1916 and Kennedy in 1960 polled between 49 and 50 percent of the national popular vote, the two elections are excellent for comparison. Table 1.12 shows the state-by-state distribution of net change in the Democratic vote between 1916 and 1960, Kennedy gaining in the northeast quadrant while losing ground in the south and interior west.

For a nearly a century, a solid south for the Democrats was the most reliable rule of the American electoral environment. Second only to that, perhaps, was the fact that the northeast would be a base of any Republican victory coalition. But in 1960, outside the south, Kennedy won most of the states where Lincoln and McKinley had won; Nixon carried most of the states Bryan had carried. What was unraveling was not only the New Deal coalition but a coalition of states a century old.

THE DEALIGNMENT REALIGNMENT

In 1964 President Johnson defeated Barry Goldwater by almost exactly the same margin by which President Roosevelt disposed of Alf Landon in 1936. Both Presidents polled 61 percent of the popular vote. Both could lay claim to a record landslide that stands to this day: FDR won by the largest Electoral Vote in American history (523 to 8), and LBJ won by the largest share of the popular vote (61.1 percent). Each carried overwhelming Democratic majorities into Congress, and each could interpret his victory as a mandate.

There the similarities between the two Democratic landslides end. In fact, the two elections are radically different from each other, and, in terms of electoral analysis, the differences are far more instructive than the similarities. In 1936 the "Democratic L" was intact. FDR swept a solid south that still had, for all practical purposes, a one-party system. FDR swept the west as well. Governor Landon carried only Maine and Vermont and ran better in the northeast quadrant than anywhere else in the country. In 1964, LBJ, a Texan, ran weakest in the south, splitting the popular vote about evenly with Goldwater and losing the five deep south states. Johnson also won all of the west except Goldwater's Arizona but did not do so well there as across the country. LBJ ran best in the northeast quadrant, carrying, for example, Rhode Island by better than 4–1, Massachusetts by better than 3–1, and Maine, Vermont, Connecticut, New York, and Pennsylvania by 2–1 or better. (See Tables 1.13 and 1.14.)

A map of the United States, constructed on the basis of where each party ran better than its national percentage, reveals the emergence of the "Republican L" for the first time. The "Republican L" has remained standard in every Presidential election since, except 1976, when Democrat Jimmy Carter was elected President.

The Presidential election of 1964 is a genuine converting election. What was then the normal majority party won, but with its electoral coalition altered. But 1964 goes beyond previous conversions, as illustrated by comparing Table 1.15 with Tables 1.7 and 1.10. Whereas 1928, for example, represented a disruption that was followed by a new Democratic majority based on restored coalitions, 1964 represents a sharp and relatively sudden break with the past and guide to the future. This clarifies the longer-range findings from Table 1.2. Both the Republican and Democratic vote at the state level in all Presidential elections through 1940 are positively correlated with the Presidential election of 1896 and negatively correlated with 1996, and 1944 is much more closely correlated to 1896 than 1996. Then, there is the secular realignment of 1948 through 1960. The election of 1964 suddenly correlates positively with 1996, and negatively with 1896, for both parties. With one exception, this new pattern has been undisturbed ever since. The correlations in Table 1.2 might be taken to be explained as normal in the passage of time. But in fact the change is not temporal, it is abrupt. The historic coalition of states, dating back to before the Civil War and central to the system of 1896, is still in place in 1944, apparently as strong as ever. Over two decades it is disturbed. By 1964 it is gone.

The "Emerging Republican Majority"

If the 1964 Presidential election provided the Democrats with a sense of security, it was illusory. The Johnson landslide muted the reality that the most important political outcome of 1964 was the takeover of the Republican Party by its conservatives. As the Presidential nominee of the party of Lincoln, Senator Goldwater opposed the Civil Rights Act of 1964 and pursued an aggressively southern electoral strategy. If Alfred E. Smith laid the groundwork for the New Deal realignment, then even more, Barry Goldwater ushered in the alignments of the post–New Deal party system.[16]

Starting in 1968, the Republicans won five out of the six Presidential elections, combining a new coalition with a new Presidential majority to a degree unmatched either after 1896 or after 1932. Ever since then, the "Republican L" has been a consistent ingredient in Republican Presidential victories.

When Republican Richard M. Nixon was elected President in a three-way race in 1968, he carried the south by a small plurality, swept the interior west, and cracked the northeast quadrant. The third-party candidacy of George C. Wallace of Alabama served as a way station for conservative Democrats no longer willing to vote the party line, not yet willing to vote Republican.

The Democratic nominee, Vice President Hubert H. Humphrey, was locked in as the most liberal alternative in the race. Although consistent with the personal commitments of a long and honorable career in public life, this was ironic, as Humphrey represented an administration unpopular for the war in Vietnam, particularly among the liberal Democrats Humphrey most needed to attract. He did in fact attract them, particularly after indicating that he would change direction in Vietnam, and he came very close to defeating Mr. Nixon. But the national distribution of his vote revealed the same coalition that liberal Democrats would show in defeat over the next two decades. Humphrey was literally cornered into the northeast and nearly shutout everywhere else. Though Nixon was only narrowly elected, Humphrey was buried in a conservative landslide.

The electoral patterns set in 1968 persisted into the 1990s. The Republicans as a rule won the Presidency while the Democrats generally retained both houses of Congress. Wallace voters and their demographic heirs, almost all white and disporportionately southern, were historically conservative Democrats who held the swing vote in both Presidential and Congressional elections. They also held the swing vote in Congress, and thus, the balance of power in the resulting divided government.[17]

That pattern should have been clear in the results of the 1972 Presidential election. President Nixon was re-elected by a landslide, but the Democrats retained Congress. Senator George McGovern of South Dakota, the Democrat, carried only Massachusetts and the District of Columbia, running better in the northeast than anywhere else in the country. Nixon ran best in the south and west. The conservative Democrats who voted for Wallace in 1968 now generally voted Republican for President and Democratic for Congress.

The 1964–1972 elections, taken together, seem to play the same role for the post–New Deal era as the 1928–1936 elections did for the New Deal period: a converting election in 1964 won by the Democrats, but with a noticeably altered national coalition; a realigning election in 1968, with a Republican plurality and a conservative electoral majority; and a Republican landslide in 1972.

The realignment of 1964–1972 might have been more recognized in its own time had its electoral patterns continued without interruption. Kevin Phillips predicted an "emerging Republican majority" even before Nixon was elected, and Richard Scammon and Ben Wattenburg explained Nixon's election in terms of new alignments on "the social issue."[18]

However, Watergate intervened, and for a time, the elections between 1964 and 1972 were widely interpreted as electoral accidents.[19] Yet even the self-destruction of a Republican Presidency, plus the nomination of the most conservative Democrat possible, could result only in a very narrow victory for Jimmy Carter of Georgia in 1976. The election of 1976 deviates from the post–New Deal mold, not only because a Democrat was elected President, but also because he carried ten of the eleven states of the south. But even when Carter carried the south, it was only because of the black vote, most of which had materialized in the previous decade, since the passage of the Voting Rights Act. Even Carter lost the white south, once so solidly Democratic.

The Watergate affair stalled the emergence of a Republican Presidential majority but did not abort it. The next three Presidential elections resulted in Republican victories, and in 1984 and 1988, the coalitions of the 1964–1972 period were largely restored. (See Tables 1.16 and 1.17.) In 1980 Ronald Reagan carried all of the south but Carter's Georgia, and in 1984 he carried forty-nine states, all but Minnesota and the District of Columbia. The "Republican L" was particularly visible on the electoral map of 1988. Vice President George Bush swept the south and interior west. Governor Michael Dukakis of Massachusetts, his Democratic opponent, ran best in the northeast quadrant, carrying Massachusetts, Rhode Island, New York, West Virginia, Wisconsin, Minnesota, and Iowa, all Republican states in the system of 1896.

The "Republican L" has survived while the Democrats regained the Presidency. Even Democratic tickets of Bill Clinton of Arkansas and Albert Gore of Tennessee could not carry more than four southern states in either of their two national victories, and in both the Democratic base remained the northeast quadrant. The 1996 Presidential election illustrates both the difficulty with which the Democrats have won the Presidency since 1968 and the mirror image between the normal coalition of states now and the coalition of a century ago. In 1996, President Clinton, even as a reasonably popular incumbent benefiting from a strong economy, could only poll about 50 percent of the total popular vote. Democrats have won with about 50 percent of the popular vote in five Presidential elections over the past century: Woodrow Wilson in 1916, Harry S Truman in 1948, John F. Kennedy in 1960, and Jimmy Carter in 1976, then Clinton in 1996. Table 1.18 shows the changing distribution by states of the Democratic Presidential vote in those elections. The Democratic vote has grown consistently in the northeast quadrant, while declining in the south and the west. The fact that Clinton in 1996 could not come close to matching the 1976 Carter vote in the south illustrates the persistence of that pattern.

Ideological Polarization and the Dealignment Realignment

The thesis of the preceding analysis is that there was a critical realignment in Presidential elections between 1964 and 1972 that was related to ideological polarization between the major political parties. This thesis is illustrated in Table 1.19, which compares the electoral change in the coalition of states in Presidential elections between the 1896–1944 period and the 1964–1996 period and the ideological polarization of 1964–1972. Elections between 1948 and 1960, when the New Deal alignment was in decline but not yet displaced by the critical change of 1964–1972, are excluded from this analysis. The partisan realignment of states between 1896–1944 and 1964–1996 is shown in Table 1.4. As introduced in the methodology section of this chapter, states that voted more Republican than the country in both 1964 and 1972, cast a higher combined percentage of the vote for Nixon and Wallace than the country in 1968, and voted less Democratic than the country in all three elections are classified as "conservative." States that voted more Democratic than the country in all three elections, voted less Republican than the country in 1964 and 1972, and cast a lower combined percentage of the vote for Nixon and Wallace than the country in 1968 are classified as "liberal." All other states are classified as "moderate." These classifications are valid because the Republican Presidential nominees in all three elections, Goldwater and Nixon, are clearly more conservative than the Democrats Johnson, Humphrey, and McGovern. The Wallace candidacy of 1968 represents a nonpartisan but decidedly conservative vote. Finally, all three elections represent cases in which the electorate was polarized over the salient issues, particularly civil rights and the Vietnam War.

Table 1.19 illustrates the political geography of both the electoral change and the ideological polarization. Eight of the ten most liberal states are found in the northeast quadrant, with the other two on the west coast. All ten have shifted dramatically toward the Democrats in Presidential elections. Almost all of the most conservative states are found in the south and west and have shifted toward the Republicans in Presidential elections. These conservative states make up the "L" on the electoral map so central to the Democratic coalitions of a century ago and the Republican coalitions of today. Finally, the states in the ideological center show the greatest degree of electoral stability.

The next five chapters develop this theme by addressing the ideological alignment of states in factions within the political parties.

CONCLUSION

As the turn of the twenty-first century approaches, Presidential elections continue to be shaped by a realignment that reached critical proportions between 1964 and 1972. In terms of the change in the coalition of states, the 1964–1972 period represents the most profound realignment in American history. The question remains: Why was it not recognized as such?

The central methodological problem is that dealignment theorists who have been "waiting for Godot" have been waiting for something that even realignment theory, properly understood, would not predict. They have been waiting for a realignment that would fit a rigid ahistorical model and appear just like 1932, or perhaps 1896. But our review demonstrates what many dealignment theorists forget, that previous realignments have not looked much like each other, either.

For example, critical realignment is expected to displace the normal majority party and produce a new national majority party. This did in fact take place in 1932, to a degree that the New Deal realignment fits the model on that score perfectly. But the realignment of 1896 fits the model only imperfectly, and, of course, the dealignment period since the 1960s does not satisfy that prediction at all. Prior to 1896 there was no clear majority party to displace. Presidential elections were very closely contested, and divided government was a frequent result. After 1896 the Republicans became dominant nationally, but they did not displace the Democrats. This imperfect fit should not disqualify 1896 as a realignment; nor should divided government disqualify the 1860–1896 period as a realignment cycle. The two periods represent qualitatively different electoral environments with differing alignments.

Critical realignment is also expected to produce a major shift in the issue cleavages and electoral coalitions between the two major parties. Here 1896 fits reasonably well, with its shift of the interior west toward the Democrats. As we have seen, the New Deal realignment gives some evidence of this, with the movement of an urban working class into the Democratic coalition starting in 1928. But after 1932 the aggregate change in coalitions between the two parties was in fact very small. In fact, there is significant electoral stability across all realignments previous to 1964. In terms of differential electoral change featuring a shift in the relative composition of party coalitions, only the post-1964 realignment is both compelling and persistent.

Critical realignment is expected to produce unified control of the elected branches of the national government for one party. This was certainly the case starting in 1896 and 1932. But it was no more true after the 1860s than it has been since the 1960s. Yet neither of the latter periods should be dismissed as a realignment cycle. Each period had its own persistent electoral environment and governing coalition.

Finally, critical realignment is expected to be accompanied by increased voter turnout, as was the case with the New Deal realignment. But this standard in the model is as violated by the 1896 realignment as it has been by the declining voter turnout since the 1960s. Yet 1896 should not be disqualified for that reason as a realignment.

Dealignment theorists place great weight in their analysis on party decay, not only in the past half century but since the 1890s. Joel Silbey has referred to electoral politics since 1893 as a "post-party" system. Ironically, Walter Dean Burnham, who continues to consider periodic realignment as a central characteristic of the electoral system would agree that party decay is traced back that far. But even if American political parties, as they were constructed in the nineteenth century, have declined through the twentieth, that did not prevent persistent partisan majorities from emerging in the 1890s and the 1930s.

The periodic markings of sea change in the party system should not be analyzed by requiring any period to pass inspection according to a checklist that must be satisfied. Rather, realignment, if it is to add grounding in history to electoral analysis, should be understood contextually in terms of the system change it represents.

First, realignment involves a persistent systemic change in the electoral environment, producing a new pattern of outcomes. There will be new cleavages and coalitions, or a new and normal majority, or both. Second, the result of these electoral outcomes will be a new and persistent governing coalition, which will produce a new policy agenda.

Starting in 1964, there was a new electoral environment. New cleavages and coalitions reflected an ideological polarization between the parties, unprecedented since the early republic. The normal majority Democrats lost their control of the elected branches of government and were replaced by a new governing coalition. This governing coalition featured divided government, usually a Republican President and a Democratic Congress. A new policy direction developed, certainly more conservative than was the case during the New Deal period. And, all this happened in a period that might have been predicted, about three decades after the previous realignment.

Periodic realignment, even in altered form—indeed, especially in altered form—remains central to understanding the linkage between parties and government, and between elections and policy, in the American political system. The current period is not a simple story of party decay. Rather, like previous realignments, and perhaps even more so, it is the story of the decline of one party system and the birth of another.

TABLES

Table 1.1

Comparing the Systems of '96: Coalitions of States in Presidential Elections, 1896 and 1996

1896	1996 Republican	1996 Democratic
Republican	Indiana	California
	North Dakota	Connecticut
		Delaware
		Illinois
		Iowa
		Kentucky
		Maine
		Maryland
		Massachusetts
		Michigan
		Minnesota
		New Hampshire
		New Jersey
		New York
		Ohio
		Oregon
		Pennsylvania
		Rhode Island
		Vermont
		West Virginia
		Wisconsin
Democratic	Alabama	Arkansas
	Colorado	Florida
	Georgia	Louisiana
	Idaho	Missouri
	Kansas	Nevada
	Mississippi	Tennessee
	Montana	Washington
	Nebraska	
	North Carolina	
	South Carolina	
	South Dakota	
	Texas	
	Utah	
	Virginia	
	Wyoming	

$G = -.91$

Derived from data in *Presidential Elections, 1789–1996* (Washington, D.C.: Congressional Quarterly, 1997), pp. 102–127.

Table 1.2
Modern and Traditional Values in American Politics: Ideological Positions on Issues across Electoral Eras

Issue/Alignment	Modern Values	Traditional Values
Geographic Base	Northeast	South, West
	Urban	Rural
Constitutional Ratification	Federalist	Anti-Federalist
Constitutional Interpretation	Loose Construction	Strict Construction
Centralization/ Decentralization	National Authority	States' Rights
National Banks	For	Against
Slavery	Limit/Oppose	Extend/Favor
Industrialization	For	Against
Free Silver	Against	For
League of Nations	For	Against
Foreign Policy	Internationalism	Isolationism
Civil Rights	For	Against
Vietnam War	Against	For
Welfare State	For	Against
Abortion	Pro-Choice	Pro-Life
Clinton Impeachment	Against	For

The above generalizations are made on polarizing issues, according to a consensus of the literature cited in the text.

Table 1.3
Comparing the "Systems of '96": Correlations of Partisan Vote in Presidential Elections 1896–1996, with 1896 and 1996 Presidential Elections

Election	Democratic 1896	1996	Republicans 1896	1996
1896	1.00	−.56	1.00	−.62
1900	.82	−.26	.78	−.44
1904	.52	.01	.43	−.27
1908	.66	−.20	.74	−.45
1912	.53	−.10	.46	−.31
1916	.72	−.24	.78	−.51
1920	.58	−.16	.66	−.41
1924	.47	−.05	.72	−.49
1928	.47	.08	.49	−.12
1932	.68	−.24	.70	−.45
1936	.76	−.24	.75	−.41
1940	.60	−.04	.64	−.29
1944	.57	.01	.61	−.25
1948	−.22	.09	.65	−.29
1952	.29	.24	.33	−.02
1956	.41	−.01	.56	−.29
1960	−.18	.51	.27	.24
1964	−.60	.49	−.69	.68
1968	−.66	.72	.19	.35
1972	−.66	.76	−.56	.76
1976	−.06	.71	−.01	.57
1980	−.15	.73	−.44	.80
1984	−.57	.88	−.50	.83
1988	−.53	.82	−.53	.83
1992	−.35	.92	−.44	.83
1996	−.56	1.00	−.62	1.00

Correlations are Pearson's *r* at the state level.
Derived from *Presidential Elections, 1789–1996*, pp. 102–127.

Table 1.4
Comparing Coalitions of States in Presidential Elections: 1896–1944 and 1964–1996

	1964–1996		
	Republican	*Cyclical/ Competitive*	*Democratic*
1896-1944			
Republican	Kansas	Connecticut	Massachusetts
	New Jersey	Illinois	Minnesota
	North Dakota	Iowa	Pennsylvania
	South Dakota	Maine	Rhode Island
		Michigan	
		Oregon	
		Vermont	
		Wisconsin	
Cyclical/ Competitive	Colorado	California	Maryland
	Idaho	Delaware	New York
	Indiana	Missouri	Washington
	Nebraska	Ohio	West Virginia
	New Hampshire		
	Utah		
	Wyoming		
Democratic	Alabama	Arkansas	
	Arizona	Kentucky	
	Florida	Tennessee	
	Georgia		
	Louisiana		
	Mississippi		
	Montana		
	Nevada		
	New Mexico		
	North Carolina		
	Oklahoma		
	South Carolina		
	Texas		
	Virginia		

G = −.73

States classified in party coalitions voted for the indicated party, with percentages larger than the national vote for the party, in most elections in the period. All states not fitting in either party coalition are classified as cyclical/competitive.
Derived from *Presidential Elections, 1789–1996*, pp. 102–127.

Table 1.5
Coalitions of States Compared: Presidential Elections of 1824 and 1896

	COALITION OF STATES 1896	
	McKinley (R)	*Bryan (D-P)*
1824		
Adams	Connecticut	
	Illinois	
	Maine	
	Maryland	
	Massachusetts	
	New Hampshire	
	Rhode Island	
Clay	Kentucky	Missouri
	Ohio	
Jackson	Indiana	Alabama
	New Jersey	Mississippi
	Pennsylvania	North Carolina
		Tennessee
Crawford		South Carolina

G = .90

	MEAN POPULAR VOTE 1896	
	McKinley (R)	*Bryan (D-P)*
1824		
In states carried by:		
Adams	**65**	33
Clay	49	**50**
Jackson	44	**55**
Crawford	14	**86**

Derived from *Presidential Elections, 1789–1996*, pp. 32 and 87.

Table 1.6
Coalition of States Compared: Presidential Elections of 1860 and 1896

	COALITION OF STATES 1896	
	McKinley (R)	Bryan (D-P)
1860		
Lincoln	California	
(R)	Connecticut	
	Illinois	
	Indiana	
	Iowa	
	Maine	
	Massachusetts	
	Michigan	
	Minnesota	
	New Hampshire	
	New York	
	Ohio	
	Oregon	
	Pennsylvania	
	Rhode Island	
	Vermont	
	Wisconsin	
Bell	Kentucky	Tennessee
(CU)		Virginia
Douglas	New Jersey	Missouri
(ND)		
Breckinridge	Delaware	Alabama
(SD)	Maryland	Arkansas
		Florida
		Georgia
		Louisiana
		Mississippi
		North Carolina
		Texas

G = .92

(continued)

Table 1.6 (continued)

	MEAN POPULAR VOTE 1896	
1824	*McKinley (R)*	*Bryan (D-P)*
In states carried by:		
Lincoln	**61**	38
Bell	48	**52**
Douglas	**53**	45
Breckinridge	34	**65**

Derived from *Presidential Elections, 1789–1996*, p. 93.

Table 1.7
State-Level Correlations: Democratic Vote for President, 1884–1908

Election	1888	1892	1896	1900	1904	1908
1884	.92	.66	.57	.79	.84	.82
1888		.77	.60	.85	.92	.88
1892			.08	.50	.72	.57
1896				.82	.63	.76
1900					.85	.95
1904						.94

Correlations are Pearson's *r*.
Derived from *Presidential Elections, 1789–1996*, pp. 100–105.

Table 1.8
Comparing Coalitions of States in Presidential Elections: 1880–1892 and 1896–1908

1880-1892	1896-1908		
	Republican	*Cyclical/ Competitive*	*Democratic*
1880-1892			
Republican	California Illinois Iowa Maine Massachusetts Michigan Minnesota New Hampshire Ohio Oregon Pennsylvania Rhode Island South Dakota Vermont Wisconsin Wyoming	Colorado Kansas Nebraska	
Cyclical/ Competitive	New York Washington	Indiana Montana	Nevada
Democratic	Connecticut New Jersey West Virginia	Delaware Maryland Missouri	Alabama Arkansas Florida Georgia Kentucky Louisiana Mississippi North Carolina South Carolina Tennessee Texas Virginia
Populist	North Dakota	Idaho	

G = .70

For each period, states voting for one party with percentages higher than the national percentage in three out of four elections are classified in that party coalition. States that fit in neither coalition are classified as cyclical or competitive. North Dakota and Idaho participated only in the 1892 election.
Derived from *Presidential Elections, 1789–1996*, pp. 98–105.

Table 1.9
Comparing Coalitions of States in Presidential Elections: 1896–1908 and 1920–1928

	1920-1928		
	Republican	Cyclical/ Competitive	Democratic
1896-1908			
Republican	California Connecticut Illinois Iowa Maine Massachusetts Michigan New Hampshire New Jersey New York Ohio Oregon Pennsylvania Rhode Island South Dakota Vermont Washington Wyoming	Minnesota North Dakota West Virginia Wisconsin	
Cyclical/ Competitive	Colorado Delaware Idaho Indiana Kansas Montana Nebraska	Maryland Missouri Utah	
Democratic		Kentucky Nevada Oklahoma Tennessee	Alabama Arkansas Florida Georgia Louisiana Mississippi North Carolina South Carolina Texas Virginia

G = .87
See Table 1.8 for partisan classification of states.
Derived from *Presidential Elections, 1789–1996*, pp. 102–110.

Table 1.10
State-level Correlations: Democratic Vote for President 1916–1944

Election	1920	1924	1928	1932	1936	1940	1944
1916	.91	.86	.80	.88	.90	.91	.89
1920		.97	.75	.79	.82	.91	.88
1924			.76	.79	.77	.88	.86
1928				.77	.76	.80	.82
1932					.93	.86	.84
1936						.93	.91
1940							.99

Correlations are Pearson's *r* at the state level between indicated presidential elections.
Derived from *Presidential Elections, 1789–1996*, pp. 108–114.

Table 1.11
Comparing Coalitions of States in Presidential Elections: 1920–1928 and 1932–1944

		1932-1944	
	Republican	Cyclical/ Competitive	Democratic
1920–1928			
Republican	Maine	Colorado	California
	Vermont	Connecticut	Montana
		Delaware	Washington
		Idaho	
		Illinois	
		Indiana	
		Iowa	
		Kansas	
		Massachusetts	
		Michigan	
		Nebraska	
		New Hampshire	
		New Jersey	
		New York	
		Ohio	
		Oregon	
		Pennsylvania	
		Rhode Island	
		South Dakota	
		Wyoming	

Table 1.11 (continued)

	Republican	Cyclical/ Competitive	Democratic
1932-1944			
Cyclical/ Competitive		Minnesota	Arizona
		Missouri	Kentucky
		North Dakota	Maryland
		West Virginia	Nevada
		Wisconsin	New Mexico
			Oklahoma
			Tennessee
			Utah
Democratic			Alabama
			Arkansas
			Florida
			Georgia
			Louisiana
			Mississippi
			North Carolina
			South Carolina
			Texas
			Virginia

G = .97
See Table 1.8 for partisan classification of states.
Derived from *Presidential Elections, 1789–1996*, pp. 108–114.

Table 1.12
Comparing Coalitions of States in Presidential Elections: 1916 and 1960

	1960		
	Republican	Cyclical/ Competitive	Democratic
1916			
Republican	Indiana		Connecticut
	Iowa		Delaware
	Maine		Illinois
	Oregon		Masachusetts
	South Dakota		Michigan
	Vermont		Minnesota
	Wisconsin		New Jersey
			New York
			Pennsylvania
			Rhode Island
			West Virginia
Cyclical/ Competitive	California		
	New Hampshire		
	North Dakota		
	Washington		
Democratic	Arizona	Mississippi	Alabama
	Colorado		Arkansas
	Florida		Georgia
	Idaho		Louisiana
	Kansas		Maryland
	Kentucky		Missouri
	Montana		Nevada
	Nebraska		New Mexico
	Ohio		North Carolina
	Oklahoma		South Carolina
	Tennessee		Texas
	Utah		
	Virginia		
	Wyoming		

G= −.23
See Table 1.8 for partisan classification of states.
Derived from *Presidential Elections, 1789–1996*, pp. 107 and 118.

Table 1.13

Comparing Coalitions of States in Presidential Elections: 1936 and 1964

	1964		
	Republican	*Cyclical/ Competitive*	*Democratic*
1936			
Republican			Maine
			Vermont
Cyclical/		Delaware	Connecticut
Competitive		Illinois	Iowa
		Indiana	Kentucky
		Kansas	Massachusetts
		Nebraska	Michigan
		North Dakota	New Hampshire
		South Dakota	New Jersey
		Wyoming	New York
			Ohio
			Pennsylvania
			Rhode Island
			West Virginia
Democratic	Alabama	Arkansas	Colorado
	Arizona	California	Maryland
	Georgia	Florida	Minnesota
	Louisiana	Idaho	Missouri
	Mississippi	Montana	Oregon
	South Carolina	Nevada	Texas
		New Mexico	Washington
		North Carolina	Wisconsin
		Oklahoma	
		Tennessee	
		Utah	
		Virginia	

G = −.64
See Table 1.8 for partisan classification of states.
Derived from *Presidential Elections, 1789–1996*, pp. 112 and 119.

Table 1.14
Democratic Presidential Vote by State, 1936 and 1964

State	1936	1964	Net Change
South Carolina	99	41	−58
Mississippi	97	13	−84
Louisiana	89	43	−46
Texas	87	63	−24
Georgia	87	46	−41
Alabama	86		−86
Arkansas	82	56	−26
Florida	76	51	−25
North Carolina	73	56	−17
Nevada	73	59	−14
Virginia	70	54	−16
Arizona	70	50	−20
Montana	69	59	−10
Utah	69	55	−14
Tennessee	69	56	−13
California	67	59	−8
Oklahoma	67	56	−11
Washington	66	62	−4
Oregon	64	64	0
Wisconsin	64	62	−2
Idaho	63	51	−12
New Mexico	62	59	−3
Maryland	62	66	+4
Minnesota	62	64	+2
Missouri	61	64	+3
Wyoming	61	57	−4
West Virginia	61	68	+7
Colorado	60	61	+1
North Dakota	60	58	−2
New Jersey	60	66	+6
New York	59	69	+10
Kentucky	59	64	+5
Ohio	58	63	+5
Illinois	58	60	+2
Nebraska	57	53	−4
Pennsylvania	57	65	+8
Indiana	57	56	−1
Michigan	56	67	+11

(continued)

Table 1.14   (continued)

State	1936	1964	Net Change
Connecticut	55	68	+13
Delaware	55	61	+6
Iowa	54	62	+8
South Dakota	54	56	+2
Kansas	54	54	0
Rhode Island	53	81	+28
Massachusetts	51	76	+25
New Hampshire	50	64	+14
Vermont	43	66	+23
Maine	42	69	+27
U.S.	61	61	0

Derived from *Presidential Elections, 1789–1996,* pp. 112 and 119.

Table 1.15
State-Level Correlations: Democratic Vote for President, 1940–1972

Election	1944	1948	1952	1956	1960	1964	1968	1972
1940	.99	−.36	.77	.65	.26	−.65	−.59	−.59
1944		−.39	.79	.64	.27	−.66	−.55	−.55
1948			−.17	−.10	.19	.73	.39	.29
1952				.83	.56	−.44	−.32	−.32
1956					.36	−.50	−.43	−.31
1960						.23	.32	.33
1964							.82	.68
1968								.89

Correlations are Pearson's *r*.
Derived from *Presidential Elections, 1789–1996,* pp. 113–121.

Table 1.16
State-Level Correlations: Democratic Vote for President, 1964–1996

Election	1968	1972	1976	1980	1984	1988	1992	1996
1964	.82	.68	.10	.08	.42	.55	.36	.49
1968		.89	.28	.31	.69	.80	.56	.72
1972			.43	.40	.81	.88	.69	.76
1976				.91	.76	.60	.82	.71
1980					.80	.62	.84	.73
1984						.92	.91	.88
1988							.83	.82
1992								.92

Correlations are Pearson's *r* at the state level.
Derived from *Presidential Elections, 1789–1996*, pp. 119–127.

Table 1.17
Coalition of States in Presidential Elections: 1964–1972 and 1980–1996

	1980–1996		
	Republican	Cyclical/ Competitive	Democratic
1964–1972			
Republican	Alabama	Kentucky	
	Alaska	Louisiana	
	Arizona	Missouri	
	Colorado	Nevada	
	Georgia	New Jersey	
	Idaho	New Mexico	
	Indiana	Vermont	
	Kansas		
	Mississippi		
	Nebraska		
	New Hampshire		
	North Dakota		
	Oklahoma		
	South Carolina		
	Utah		
	Virginia		
	Wyoming		
Cyclical/ Competitive	Florida	Arkansas	Iowa
	North Carolina	California	
	South Dakota	Delaware	
	Texas	Illinois	
		Montana	
		Ohio	
		Oregon	
		Tennessee	
		Wisconsin	
Democratic		Connecticut	D.C.
		Maine	Hawaii
		Maryland	Massachusetts
		Michigan	Minnesota
		Pennsylvania	New York
			Rhode Island
			Washington
			West Virginia

G = .89
See Table 1.8 for partisan classification of states.
Derived from *Presidential Elections, 1789–1996*, pp. 123–127.

Table 1.18
Democratic Presidential Vote, by State, at 50 Percent Democratic in the National Vote, 1916–1996

State	1916	1948	1960	1976	1996	Net Change
South Carolina	97	24	51	56	44	−53
Mississippi	93	10	36	50	45	−48
Louisiana	86	33	50	52	53	−33
Georgia	80	61	63	67	46	−34
Texas	77	66	51	51	44	−33
Alabama	76		57	56	44	−32
Florida	69	49	49	52	48	−21
Virginia	67	48	47	48	46	−21
Arkansas	66	62	50	65	55	−11
Colorado	61	52	45	43	46	−15
Utah	59	54	45	34	34	−25
North Carolina	58	58	52	55	44	−14
Arizona	57	54	44	40	47	−10
Montana	57	53	49	45	42	−15
Tennessee	56	49	46	56	48	−8
Nebraska	55	46	38	39	35	−20
Wyoming	55	52	45	40	37	−18
Nevada	53	50	51	46	46	−7
Maryland	53	48	54	53	55	+2
Idaho	52	50	46	37	34	−18
Ohio	52	50	47	49	48	−4
Kentucky	52	57	46	53	46	−6
Oklahoma	51	63	41	49	41	−10
Missouri	51	58	50	51	48	−3
New Mexico	50	56	50	48	51	+1
Kansas	50	45	39	45	37	−13
New Hampshire	49	47	47	44	50	+1
West Virginia	49	57	53	58	52	+3
Washington	48	53	48	46	52	+4
North Dakota	48	43	45	46	40	−8
Delaware	48	49	51	52	52	+4
Maine	47	42	43	48	54	+7
Connecticut	47	48	54	47	54	+7
California	47	48	50	48	53	+6
Massachusetts	47	55	60	56	62	+15
Indiana	47	49	45	46	42	−5
Minnesota	46	57	51	55	52	+6
Rhode Island	46	58	64	55	61	+15

(continued)

Table 1.18   (continued)

State	1916	1948	1960	1976	1996	Net Change
Oregon	46	46	47	48	50	+4
South Dakota	46	47	42	49	43	−3
New York	45	45	53	52	61	+16
Michigan	44	48	51	46	52	+8
Illinois	43	50	50	48	55	+12
Wisconsin	43	51	48	49	50	+7
Iowa	43	50	43	49	51	+8
New Jersey	43	46	50	48	55	+12
Pennsylvania	40	47	51	50	50	+10
Vermont	35	37	41	43	55	+20
U.S.	49	50	50	50	50	+1

Data drawn from *Presidential Elections, 1789–1996*, pp. 107–127.

Table 1.19
Ideological Realignment and Partisan Realignment, 1964–1972

Ideological Alignment of States, 1964–1972		
liberal	*moderate*	*conservative*

Electoral Change

	liberal	moderate	conservative
Toward Democrats	Connecticut Massachusetts Michigan Minnesota New York Oregon Pennsylvania Rhode Island Washington Wisconsin	Illinois Iowa Maine Maryland Vermont West Virginia	
Electoral Stability		California Delaware Missouri New Jersey Ohio South Dakota	Kansas North Dakota
Toward Republicans		Colorado Kentucky Montana New Hampshire Texas	Alabama Arizona Arkansas Florida Georgia Idaho Indiana Louisiana Mississippi Nebraska Nevada New Mexico North Carolina Oklahoma South Carolina Tennessee Utah Virginia Wyoming

G = .96

"Electoral Change" represents the realignment of states in Presidential elections between the 1896–1944 and 1964–1996 eras. See Table 1.4 for that realignment expressed in partisan terms. See the text for an explanation of the ideological classification of states according to the 1964–1972 Presidential elections.
Derived from *Presidential Elections, 1789–1996*, pp. 102–127.

NOTES

1. Rhodes Cook, "Dole's Job: To Convince His Own Party," *Congressional Quarterly Guide to the 1996 Republican National Convention*, August 3, 1996, pp. 7–11.

2. See Walter Dean Burnham, *Critical Elections and the Mainsprings of American Politics* (New York: Norton, 1970).

3. Most of the data on Presidential elections is drawn from *Presidential Elections, 1789–1996* (Washington, D.C.: Congressional Quarterly, 1997).

4. J. Clark Archer, Fred M. Shelly, Peter J. Taylor, and Ellen R. White, "The Geography of U.S. Presidential Elections," *Scientific American* 259 (1988): 44–51; Burnham, *Critical Elections*; Daniel J. Elazar, *American Federalism: A View from the States* (New York: Harper and Row, 1984); Richard Jensen, "Party Coalitions and the Search for Modern Values," in Seymour Martin Lipset, ed., *Emerging Coalitions in American Politics* (San Francisco: Institute for Contemporary Studies, 1978); Everett Carll Ladd with Charles D. Hadley, *Transformations of the American Party System* (New York: Norton, 1975), particularly pp. 129–177; George Rabinowitz and Stuart Elaine MacDonald, "The Power of the States in U.S. Presidential Elections," *The American Political Science Review* 80 (1986): 65–87; Harvey L. Schantz, "Sectionalism in Presidential Elections," in Schantz, ed., *American Presidential Elections: Process, Policy, and Political Change* (Albany: State University of New York Press, 1996), pp. 9–50. William Schneider, "Democrats and Republicans, Liberals and Conservatives," in Seymour Martin Lipset, ed., *Emerging Coalitions in American Politics* (San Franciso: Institute for Contemporary Studies, 1978); James L. Sundquist, *The Dynamics of the American Party System: Alignment and Realignment of Political Parties in the United States* (Washington, D.C.: Brookings Institution, 1983).

5. See particularly Burnham, *Critical Elections* and "Into the 1980s with Ronald Reagan"; Jensen; Schneider; and Sundquist, *Dynamics*. Obviously, the distinction between economic and cultural issues is somewhat arbitrary and artificial. Most, if not all issues, have both economic and cultural dimensions. The distinction has more to do with how issues are presented and debated by political elites, opinion leaders, activists, and candidates; how the agenda is set; and the electoral coalitions that emerge.

6. Louis H. Bean, *How to Predict Elections* (New York: Knopf, 1948). In this work, actually prepared about a year before the Presidential election, Bean stands almost alone in predicting that President Truman would be elected in 1948. As his data is drawn from Presidential elections between 1896 and 1944, the relative position of the states in Presidential election coalitions is undisturbed by the 1964–1972 realignment. His data, in fact, is drawn entirely from the relatively stable partisan alignment of states that persisted until a secular realignment began around 1948, as discussed in the introduction of the current work.

7. Jerome M. Clubb, William H. Flanigan, and Nancy H. Zingale, *Partisan Realignment: Voters, Parties and Government in American History* (Boulder, Colo.: Westview, 1990), pp. 77–118.

8. See Robert W. Cherry, *A Righteous Cause: The Life of William Jennings Bryan* (Boston: Little, Brown, 1985), pp. 113–188. A more detailed discussion of Bryan as the leader of the Democratic Party appears in Chapter 2.

9. Interesting, and usually overlooked, is the fact that Grover Cleveland is also the only candidate other than Franklin D. Roosevelt to win the popular vote in more than two Presidential elections.

10. See Gerald Pomper with Susan Lederman, *Elections in America: Control and Influence in Democratic Politics* (New York: Longman, 1980). See also Pomper, "Alive! The Political Parties after the 1980–1992 Presidential Elections," in Harvey L. Schantz, *American Presidential Elections: Process, Policy, and Political Change* (Albany: State University of New York Press, 1996), pp. 135–156.

11. *Presidential Elections*, pp. 47 and 124. See also Roger Butterfield, *The American Past* (New York: Simon and Schuster, 1957), pp. 236–241; Stefan Lorant, *The Glorious Burden: The History of the Presidency and Presidential Elections from George Washington to James Earl Carter, Jr.* (Lenox, Mass.: Authors Edition, 1977), pp. 388–391; and Rexford G. Tugwell, *Grover Cleveland* (New York: Macmillan, 1968), pp. 94–98.

12. See V. O. Key, "A Theory of Critical Elections," *Journal of Politics* 17 (1955): 3–18; Kristi Andersen, "Generation, Partisan Shift, and Realignment: A Glance Back to the New Deal," in Norman H. Nie, Sidney Verba, and John R. Petrocik, *The Changing American Voter* (Cambridge: Harvard University Press, 1976) and *The Creation of a Democratic Majority: 1928–1936* (Chicago: University of Chicago Press, 1979).

13. Andersen, *The Creation of a Democratic Majority*.

14. David G. Lawrence has referred to 1948 and the 1960s together as two mini-realignments. See Lawrence, *The Collapse of the Democratic Presidential Majority* (Boulder: Westview Press, 1997).

15. Clubb, Flanigan, and Zingale, p. 122.

16. Chapters 2, 3, and 4 focus on the factional struggles within the parties that combine to produce this analogy.

17. Split-ticket voting and divided government in the post–New Deal party system are discussed in detail in Chapter 7.

18. Kevin Phillips, *The Emerging Republican Majority* (New Rochelle: Arlington House, 1969); Richard Scammon and Ben Wattenburg, *The Real Majority* (New York: Coward-McCann, 1970).

19. Ladd with Hadley, pp. 280–290.

2

The Democratic Party as a Multifactional System, 1896–1964

The Democratic Party, the oldest political party in the world, has been throughout its history a multifactional system. Its urban-rural and north-south divides, taken alone, would oversimplify the reality. Southern Democrats, disproportionately conservative, pro-slavery before the Civil War and pro–white supremacy after Reconstruction, were often found in rural alliance with western populists at the turn of the twentieth century. Northern Democrats were divided between the party regulars of the urban machines, supported by a largely working-class electoral base, and reform factions with a more middle-class electoral base. Though a liberal-versus-conservative framework for analyzing Democratic Party politics, then, would also be an oversimplification, conservative Democrats had decidedly more power within their party early in the twentieth century than they do now.

The purpose of this chapter is to examine the Democratic Party as a multifactional system prior to the electoral realignment of 1964–1972. The ideological alignment of states originally presented in Chapter 1 is used to illustrate the shift in power at Democratic National Conventions from the more conservative states of the south and west in the system of 1896 to the more liberal states of the east by the middle of the twentieth century.

THE SOLID SOUTH AND THE DEMOCRATIC PARTY

The Solid South was as central to the definition of the Democratic Party from the end of Reconstruction to the middle of the twentieth century as it was to the partisan structure of national electoral coalitions. The fact that the critical realignment of 1896 and the United States Supreme Court decision in *Plessy v. Ferguson* were virtually simultaneous events was not coincidence. Although the Jim Crow laws emerged slowly after the Union occupation of the old Confederacy ended, *Plessy* gave federal legitimacy to the legal structure of white supremacy in the south. Emboldened by the action of the court, southern states took action to effectively deny the right to vote to African Americans.[1] In the decade after 1896, the total vote cast across the south in Presidential elections was reduced by more than half, reflecting the disappearance of southern blacks from the electorate. The decline was sharpest in the deep south, where the African American population was highest.[2] At the same time the Democratic Party in the south improved its position, from being dominant in most states even before 1896 to being practically unopposed in any state after the turn of the century.

The political reforms of the progressive era only enhanced the one-party system in the south. The advance of primary elections was particularly convenient in the south, where elections for public office at all levels, from local to the national Congress, came to be decided in the Democratic primary. In many states, even though African Americans had a *de jure* right to vote, they had no such *de facto* right because the Democratic Party was defined as a private club and allowed to limit its membership by race. In those states, African Americans could vote in meaningless general elections, but only after being excluded from the decisive Democratic primary.[3]

The existence of a one-party south should not be taken to mean that electoral politics was without conflict; the alignments were factional rather than partisan. In some states, there was issue-conflict between conservative Democrats and populists. The reforms supported by populists were often considered dangerous, because they might benefit and empower blacks as well as poor whites. Thus, conservatives were not bothered by the fact that such tactics as literacy tests and poll taxes might disenfranchise poor whites as well as African Americans; the result would only strengthen conservative Democrats in primaries. More often, southern factionalism was as much or more personal than issue-oriented: Voters were for or against, for example, Huey Long in Louisiana, or Herman Talmadge in Georgia, or Harry F. Byrd in Virginia.

In any case, in national politics, populist and conservative Democrats in the south often maintained an uneasy alliance against the urban north and the federal government. While populists were opposed to the financial elite of the north, conservatives prioritized the maintenance of white supremacy. But in national party affairs, both southern factions were usually united in support of states' rights. It was thus worthy of notice when southern unity would occasionally crack at Democratic national conventions over southern candidates like Oscar Underwood and Estes Kefauver, who challenged the status quo of southern isolation and white supremacy.

The south maintained a general isolation from the incursions of national policy, particularly on matters of race, until the mid-twentieth century. The economic underdevelopment of the south was part of what made the region different. But two political institutions served the purposes of the southern elite in protecting the south's status quo and system of white supremacy. First, because of the one-party system in the south, the institutionalization of the seniority system in Congress served to advance the power of incumbent Democrats from the south. The role of southern conservative Democrats in Congressional coalitions is discussed in Chapter 7.

The second political institution protecting the south in national politics was found strictly within the Democratic Party: The two-thirds rule at Democratic national conventions gave the south a veto power over the national Democratic ticket and served as an invaluable bargaining chip on matters of national policy.

With the seniority system in Congress and the two-thirds rule at Democratic conventions, it was in the interest of southern Democrats to promote national Democratic candidates. Democratic control of Congress would put southerners in committee chairs; Democratic Presidents would owe their nominations (and renominations) to southern support, or at least, acquiescence. Thus, for the south, even progressive Democrats were preferable on the national level to Republicans, whose party was, after all, the party of Abraham Lincoln, and whose party had no institutional interest in protecting southern white supremacy.[4]

Because of its position in the party system, the south held a general veto power over the Democratic Presidential nomination and probably over policy in a government in which the Democrats had control of the Presidency or Congress, or both. On the other hand, although the south was guaranteed an acceptable Democratic nominee for President, the region would never be able to put over the nomination of a preferred candidate of its own. The south was so solidly Democratic that the national Democratic Party did not need to make any special appeal to win the states of the old Confederacy. The south would thus remain isolated, able to prevent national policy but not to promote it.

The south's special status in the Democratic Party would be severely weakened in the twentieth century by demographic, economic, and political change. Urbanization would increase the power of labor and northern big-city organizations in the Democratic Party, and the migration of large numbers of blacks from the south to northern cities in states with large blocs of electoral votes would give national Democrats an electoral interest in supporting the growing civil rights movement. In 1936, the Democratic National Convention would repeal the two-thirds rule, removing the south's veto over Presidential nominations, and in 1948 the Democratic Party would, for the first time, endorse civil rights reform. Table 2.1 illustrates the declining power of the south in the national nominating coalitions at Democratic national conventions between the realignment of 1896 and the emergence of the post–New Deal Democratic Party by 1972, using the ideological classification of states introduced in Chapter 1. The south, with its veto power, always cast a majority of its vote on decisive ballots for Presidential nominees until 1928, when most of its delegates opposed Al Smith. The south formed the base of the nominating coalition for Franklin D. Roosevelt in 1932, but its power in the Democratic Party thereafter would be short-lived. After the New Deal, the south increasingly found itself on the outside looking in at the centers of power in the national Democratic Party, a majority of its delegates opposing the nominations of Harry Truman, Adlai E. Stevenson, John F. Kennedy, and George McGovern. Only the south's support of the Johnson administration on the Vietnam War and Hubert Humphrey for President in 1968 interrupted the pattern. The decline of the south in the Democratic Party would fundamentally reorder the American party system and realign the electorate.

THE DEMOCRATS IN THE SYSTEM OF 1896: THE PARTY OF WILLIAM JENNINGS BRYAN

The factional system of the Democratic Party of the early twentieth century, and its relation to the south, is illustrated by the position in that system held by William Jennings Bryan, certainly the central character of the realignment of 1896.[5] Using the language of his day, and in some ways of any day, Bryan was a progressive Democrat. His support of free silver reflected a commitment on his part to economic populism and, to a large degree, egalitarianism. "The Great Commoner" saw himself as the candidate of the common man, whom he envisioned as a rural individual whose life, community, and values were threatened by modernization promoted by distant economic elites in the east. His political base was western, but he represented the interests of rural America, generally. Just as much, he opposed the interests of the center of an industrializing America: the financial interests of the east and the values of an urban culture that seemed foreign. In some of his economic views, he anticipated the programs of a later Democratic Party, the party of the New Deal and Great Society.

In foreign affairs, Bryan also subscribed to views that later liberal Democrats might have shared. He opposed an American war in the jungles of the Far East, for example. He argued against the use of military force in putting down the Philippine Insurrection, predicting that America would have to choose between the values of empire and democracy. As Secretary of State under President Woodrow Wilson a decade and a half later, Bryan would resign in protest over the drift toward entry into World War I.

But on cultural issues, Bryan, like many western and southern Democrats of his day, stood for traditional values. Some of these cultural views were then called "progressive," particularly support for prohibition, and Bryan saw them as progressive: He was a defender of traditional values against the invasion of modern values representing the interests of monopoly capital. For nearly two decades after his first nomination for the Presidency in 1896, Bryan remained the undisputed leader of the rural progressive faction of the Democratic Party. But William Jennings Bryan was also a Christian fundamentalist who tolerated the Ku Klux Klan and who would come to represent the state in the Scopes Monkey Trial of 1925. Bryan's opposition to Darwinism came not only from his religious faith but also from his progressive economic philosophy: He considered "Social Darwinism" to be a rationalization of class exploitation in modern society.[6] In any case, Bryan lived long enough to be called conservative, even reactionary, as he lost his influence in the Democratic Party during his final years.

For a quarter century after his first nomination for the Presidency, support for or opposition to William Jennings Bryan seemed to define the factional alliances within the Democratic Party. The rural populist faction, based in the west, made up the base of Bryan's support. The urban faction, based in the east, opposed him whenever there was a viable alternative. Southern Democrats supported Bryan whenever he ran and accomodated themselves to others when he did not. In four of the five national conventions starting with 1896, Bryan exercised decisive influence. He was nominated for the Presidency three times—in 1896, 1900, and 1908—and his decision to shift his vote from Champ

Clark to Woodrow Wilson was the turning point at the 1912 convention. Only in 1904, when Bryan declined to seek renomination for President or to endorse any other candidate, was a Bryan opponent nominated for the Presidency: Alton B. Parker of New York. Bryan's neutrality in the 1904 preconvention campaign probably represented his effort to retain leadership of the rural faction while not being a candidate himself.[7]

The "Cross of Gold"

The issue of free silver was the vehicle that carried Bryan to the Democratic Presidential nomination in 1896. It was an issue on which Bryan could preach his brand of economic progressivism combined with a cultural conservatism that appealed to rural America. After the recession of the 1890s, populist Democrats advocating free coinage of silver took control of the party at local caucuses and state conventions. Supporters of President Grover Cleveland from the eastern, urban, "gold" faction of the party lacked the delegates to the Democratic National Convention in 1896 and did not seriously contest the nomination for the Presidency. When Bryan gave his "cross of gold" speech, advocating the free coinage of silver, he was preaching to the converted, who were in firm control of the proceedings. His eloquence allowed him to win the Democratic Presidential nomination on the fifth ballot, after an intrafactional contest among pro-silver candidates. More than the "cross of gold" or "crown of thorns" metaphors, Bryan expressed his national vision and his role as a factional and party leader when he said, "The great cities rest upon our broad and fertile prairies. Burn down your cities and leave our farms, and your cities will spring up again, as if by magic; but destroy our farms, and the grass will grow in the streets of every city in the country."[8]

The power of the states of the south and west at the 1896 Democratic National Convention is illustrated in Table 2.2, which sorts states according to their majority vote on free silver at that convention, and by ideological classification in the 1964–1972 alignment, as explained in Chapter 1.[9] Chapter 1 also discusses the body of literature that shows the persistence of the ideological coalitions in American politics. The high value of the gamma indicates the similar polarization between those states, mostly from the east, that would become the most liberal in the 1964–1972 alignment, and those states, mostly from the south and west, that would become the most conservative. The negative value of the gamma indicates the victory for the latter faction. In addition to carrying the day on free silver, the rural faction of the south and west would provide the base of support for Bryan both at the convention and in the Presidential election that November.

Bryan and Wilson

Over a dozen years, Bryan would wage three spirited, if losing, campaigns for the Presidency. After his third defeat in 1908, Bryan remained the titular leader of the Democratic Party, and his continuing real influence was demonstrated at the Democratic National Convention of 1912, to which he had been elected as a delegate in the Nebraska primary. The 1912 convention also illustrates how Bryan and subsequent leaders of the rural and southern elements of the Democratic Party used a divide-and-conquer strategy against northern Democrats, who were split between the party regulars and the reformers.

The front-runner for the Democratic Presidential nomination was House Speaker Champ Clark, a Missouri Democrat whose base of support was in the western and rural faction of the party. His leading opponent was Governor Woodrow Wilson of New Jersey, a progressive reformer. The south was not united on any candidate; a plurality of its delegates were held by Representative Oscar Underwood of Alabama. Tammany Hall had no candidate of its own but settled on favorite son Governor L. Judson Harmon of Ohio, whose prospects at the convention were not promising. Tammany's support would ultimately decide the nomination counterproductively, due to Bryan's intervention.

Clark led on the first ballot and gradually gained ground thereafter. His support came primarily from the west and increasingly from the south. Wilson found his base in the east and gained ground as the vote for Harmon declined.

On the tenth ballot, Clark achieved a majority, thanks to his gaining all ninety votes of the New York delegation, with the support of Tammany Hall. With Harmon effectively out of the race, Tammany had to choose between Clark, the candidate of the rural faction, and Wilson, the urban reformer. Given that dilemma, Tammany chose Clark.

But owing to the two-thirds rule, the nomination was not yet Clark's. Nor would it be. During the fourteenth ballot, Bryan requested, and was granted, permission to address the convention to explain his vote. He was switching from Clark to Wilson, he said, because he could not support any candidate backed by Tammany.[10]

Support for Clark slowly deflated, while Wilson continued to gain. By the thirtieth ballot, Wilson assumed the lead; he won the Democratic Presidential nomination on the forty-sixth ballot.

Table 2.3 illustrates the changing geographic and ideological distribution of the convention vote during the balloting, using the 1964–1972 alignment. In the early balloting, Clark found his base in the west, Wilson found his in the east. Though Wilson did not lose votes in the east, his gains after the fourteenth ballot came in the south and west, mostly at the expense of Clark. The geographic differences in the vote for the two leading candidates had disappeared. Wilson adhered to the old formula for an eastern, urban Democrat to be nominated for the Presidency: obtain the support of the south. And Bryan, with his appeal in the south and west, had effectively delivered the nomination.

Bryan had no such power at the 1920 Democratic convention, for at least two reasons. First, the urban population of the country was growing rapidly. In 1920 the United States census listed a majority of the population as "urban" for the first time.[11] Big-city Democratic organizations were gaining strength, and three of the four leading candidates for the Democratic Presidential nomination were from large northern states: Governor James M. Cox of Ohio; A. Mitchell Palmer of Pennsylvania, who, as Attorney General in the Wilson administration had been initiating the "Red Scare"; and Governor Alfred E. Smith of New York, the candidate of Tammany Hall. Bryan, for his part, remained a leader to many rural Democrats of the south and west, but while he opposed Cox and Smith at the 1920 convention, his focus was now on issues more than candidates. Indeed, Bryan's religious fundamentalism now led him to emphasize the cultural conservatism in his agenda, particularly his support for prohibition.

Second, Woodrow Wilson had served as President for eight years, and Bryan had lost whatever influence he had in the Wilson administration by resigning as Secretary of State in 1915 over the drift toward American entry into World War I. President Wilson figured decisively, if passively, in the Democratic nominating politics of that year. Wilson privately hoped for a third term, although his poor health and declining popularity foreclosed any real possibility of that. Nevertheless, the President declined to close the door on his own renomination or to endorse another candidate. Thus, although the three leading candidates, Cox, Palmer, and former Treasury Secretary William Gibbs McAdoo, were products or allies of the Wilson administration, none could command the support of two-thirds of the convention delegates. To confuse matters more, McAdoo, the early front-runner and son-in-law of the President, hesitated too long. Not wanting to appear to oppose Wilson if the President ran again, and hoping for his endorsement and a convention draft if he did not, McAdoo withdrew from the race days before the convention opened.[12]

The result was a long and open convention that took forty-four ballots to nominate Cox for President. With the two-thirds rule, no candidate could win without at least measurable backing from the south, and no faction, acting alone, could deliver the nomination. But the growing power of the east in party affairs was demonstrated by the fact that the convention produced a ticket of two internationalist liberal Democrats who supported President Wilson and the League of Nations: Cox and

Assistant Navy Secretary Franklin D. Roosevelt, a New Yorker and supporter of Al Smith.

William Jennings Bryan was particularly discouraged by the outcome of the convention, not only by its nomination of Cox but also by the fact that his one direct effort to influence the proceedings, a platform minority report endorsing prohibition, was defeated decisively, by a vote of 929.5 to 155.5. "This is not my kind of convention," he said. "Four years from now it will be my kind of convention."[13]

The Fight at the Garden

Bryan was wrong. The 1924 Democratic National Convention was, perhaps, nobody's kind of convention, lasting through 103 ballots over two weeks at Madison Square Garden in New York. It was the ultimate showdown between the urban and rural factions of the Democratic Party, and no one was left standing. The bitterness peaked well before the long Presidential balloting, when a platform committee minority report condemning the Ku Klux Klan was defeated, 543.35 to 543.15, the closest roll call in the history of American political conventions.

The vote on the Klan minority report demonstrates the enduring ideological coalitions in American politics that defined the factional struggle at the 1924 convention. The vote for the report and against the Klan was based in the northeast quadrant, among the states that would be the most liberal in the ideological alignment of 1964–1972. The support for the Klan came from states, mostly in the south and west, that would be among the most conservative states in the 1964–1972 alignment. The high value of gamma in Table 2.4 indicates the polarization in the vote on the Klan, and the negative gamma indicates the victory of the more conservative rural faction of the party. The composition of the winning coalition on the Klan vote of 1924 was highly similar to the composition of the winning coalition on Free Silver in 1896, illustrated in Table 2.2.

The result of the Klan vote was a victory for rural and conservative Democrats, but its closeness demonstrated that no one was likely to approach the two-thirds vote necessary to achieve a Presidential nomination in the early balloting. William G. McAdoo was again the front-runner on the first ballot and throughout most of the ballots that followed. The base of his support was in the south and west and among supporters of the Klan. Governor Smith, backed by Tammany Hall and a bloc of anti-Klan and liberal Democrats, was his leading opponent.

No end was yet in sight when William Jennings Bryan, now a Florida delegate, asked permission to address the convention during the thirty-eighth ballot, hoping for a replay of his decisive role in 1912. He sought to explain his opposition to Smith, whom he saw as a creature of

Tammany, the east, and Wall Street. He was hooted off the rostrum, and having spoken to no effect, returned to his hotel room to listen to the convention by radio.

Ultimately, having no hope to obtaining two-thirds of the delegates, both McAdoo and Smith withdrew. Most of the Smith vote went to Senator Oscar Underwood of Alabama, a southern progressive who had supported the anti-Klan minority report. Because of his position against the Klan, however, Underwood could not gain much support from the south, even as a regional favorite son. Most of the anti-Smith delegates voted for John W. Davis of West Virginia, a moderate-to-conservative Democrat, who was also opposed by Bryan because he was a Wall Street lawyer. Davis was nominated on the 103rd ballot. (See Table 2.5.)

The 1924 experience exhausted Democrats, who over the next four years seemed to seek party unity for its own sake. McAdoo decided not to run for President again, fearing a repeat of the 1924 convention. Without McAdoo, rural and conservative Democrats found themselves without a candidate who could compete against Al Smith. Governor Smith defeated his leading opponents in the primaries and had the Democratic Presidential nomination clinched before the 1928 convention met. Even the south acquiesced in the nomination of Al Smith, and was rewarded with the nomination of Senator Joseph T. Robinson of Arkansas for Vice President.

The nomination of Alfred E. Smith for the Presidency was a decisive victory for the eastern, urban, liberal faction of the party, and led to the converting election of 1928, discussed in Chapter 1, which played such a role in building what would become the New Deal coalition.

THE NEW DEAL DEMOCRATS

Holding their national convention in the midst of the Great Depression, the Democrats were hopeful of regaining the Presidency in 1932. Thus, the Democratic Presidential nomination was a prize worth having, and all the factions of the party had candidates in the running. Alfred E. Smith was seeking renomination for President, with support from Tammany Hall. House Speaker John Nance Garner, a Texan, sought to unify the south and win the support of conservative Democrats.

But Garner was hampered by an obsession across the south with stopping Al Smith. The beneficiary of that obsession was Governor Franklin D. Roosevelt of New York. A longtime friend of Al Smith, Roosevelt had been narrowly elected governor in 1928, while Smith was losing the Presidential election to Republican Herbert Hoover. Re-elected by a landslide in 1930, Governor Roosevelt had fallen out of favor with Tammany Hall over the state's investigation of scandals surrounding Mayor James J. Walker of New York. Now the Presidential candidate of reform liberal Democrats, Roosevelt found himself as the south's anti-Smith vehicle. When Roosevelt emerged as the front-runner in the primaries, southern delegates were all the more willing to jump on the bandwagon.

As the convention opened, Roosevelt enjoyed the support of a majority of the delegates. Only twice in the history of the Democratic Party had a candidate achieved a majority without being nominated: Martin Van Buren in 1844 and Champ Clark in 1912. Roosevelt's opponents hoped to make it happen again. But when Roosevelt led on the first ballot with 666.25 delegate votes to 201.75 for Smith and 90.25 for Garner, and gained on the next two ballots, Garner was readily persuaded to throw in his support. With the California and Texas delegations joining the drive, Roosevelt was nominated on the fourth ballot with 945 votes to 190.5 for Smith. Garner then was nominated for Vice President.[14] In an arrangement among strange bedfellows, Roosevelt, a liberal Democrat, found his strongest support coming from conservatives opposed to his old friend, Al.

Table 2.6 illustrates the vote of state delegations for President at the 1932 Democratic convention. The relatively low value of the gamma indicates a fair degree of consensus, although its negative direction indicates the importance of conservative Democrats to the nomination of Governor Roosevelt. Even when the battle narrowed to two New Yorkers, the south was decisive. Based on interests similar to those expressed by William Jennings Bryan in explaining his switch to Wilson at the 1912 convention, when presented with a choice between a candidate from Tammany Hall (and a Catholic at that) and a relatively anti-Tammany reformer, the south went with the reformer.

Such was Roosevelt's need for southern support at the convention that his operatives decided against their early inclination to push for an end to the two-thirds rule in 1932. As President, needing the support of southern Democrats in Congress for the New Deal, he made no effort to advance the power of the federal government to dismantle white supremacy in the south.

But Roosevelt did attempt, with some success, to reduce the power of the south and gain power for liberal Democrats in party affairs. In 1936, with the renomination of the President uopposed, the Democratic National Convention eliminated the two-thirds rule by voice vote. The south was thus deprived of its veto power over the Democratic Presidential nomination, a fact that was not immediately relevant to any major contest but that would promote the power of liberal Democrats within the party in the long run.

Encouraged by his record landslide re-election, FDR moved after 1936 to more vigorously exercise his role not only as President and leader of his party, but as the leader of the liberal faction of his party. When he tried to pack the Supreme Court, he failed, and engaged the opposition of conservative Democrats particularly, even Vice President Garner. But he lost the battle and won the war, as the court effectively reversed itself on the constitutionality of the economic regulatory power created by the New Deal.[15]

In 1938 the President defied accepted political form by campaigning in several primaries against conservative Democrats, with little success. He endorsed Senator Alben W. Barkley of Kentucky, who won renomination over A. B. Chandler, but he failed in efforts to unseat Senator Guy Gillette of Iowa and Senator Walter F. George of Georgia. When FDR ran for third and fourth terms in 1940 and 1944, what little opposition he encountered within his own party came from conservative Democrats. Even as an unannounced candidate in 1940, FDR eliminated Vice President Garner in the primaries. In 1944 he won renomination by a vote of 1,086 to 89 over Senator Harry F. Byrd of Virginia. Still, most southern delegates voted for FDR at the 1940 and 1944 conventions, and the south remained solidly Democratic for FDR through four elections.[16]

The fact that liberal Democrats still could not unilaterally deliver majorities at Democratic conventions was dramatized in 1944, when Vice President Henry A. Wallace was denied renomination and his place on the ticket was handed to Senator Harry S Truman of Missouri on the second ballot. As the convention approached, President Roosevelt indicated his support for his Vice President but also indicated that he would not split the party over the issue of his running mate. Truman was something of a compromise between liberal Democrats backing Wallace and conservative Democrats who preferred Supreme Court Justice James F. Byrnes. Truman, in fact, had been ready to place Byrnes in nomination at the convention. But the President, persuaded by Democratic National Chairman Walter Henneman that a compromise choice was necessary for party unity, called Senator Truman privately and urged him to run for Vice President. Henneman, a Missourian, proceeded to lobby for Truman, who was thus Vice President when Franklin D. Roosevelt died in office on April 12, 1945.[17]

Table 2.7 shows the distribution of state delegations on the second ballot for the Democratic Vice Presidential nomination at the 1944 convention and illustrates the compromise status of the Truman candidacy. Though the vote was very close with Wallace finding his base among liberal Democrats, the balloting was not highly polarized. Truman drew his support from party regulars in the north, including Tammany Hall in New York, as well as from the south, to take the lead.

Immediately thereafter, the opposition to Truman collapsed, and he was nominated.

The Democrats and Civil Rights

It is an example of the irony of politics that Harry Truman, after being used by conservative Democrats as a vehicle for stopping Henry Wallace, would be used by 1948 as a reluctant vehicle by liberal Democrats in making the party's first national commitment to civil rights reform. The national convention of 1948 marked the beginning of the decisive transition period for the national Democratic Party in the position it would take on civil rights, a transition that climaxed with the passage of the Civil Rights Act of 1964. Over the same period, there would be a secular realignment of the "L" of the south and west from the Democrats toward the Republicans in Presidential elections, while the urban states of the northeast quadrant moved from the Republicans toward the Democrats, a process discussed in detail in Chapter 1.

Well before the 1948 convention, the Truman administration had become an advocate of civil rights reform, initiating desegregation of the military and advocating an anti-lynching bill in Congress. Southern Democrats feared that the accommodation they had long enjoyed with the national Democratic Party was in jeapordy. As the convention met, most southern delegates opposed the nomination of President Truman, while northern liberal Democrats were praising the President even as they lobbied for a faster pace of change.

The President and his closest allies tried to prevent a showdown, but southern segregationists and northern liberals could agree only that the showdown had to occur. The southerners understood that the national Democrats could not promote national action that would end white supremacy in the south and retain the region's support. However, northern liberals were moved not only by a moral atmosphere that accompanied defeating Hitler in the recent world war but also by the demographic reality of black migration into the urban areas of the north; an increasing portion of electoral support for northern liberal Democrats was African American.

The showdown finally came in the debate over civil rights on the platform. The platform committee, still hoping to maintain party unity, had fashioned a moderate plank on civil rights that was supported by President Truman. However, the Texas delegation proposed a minority report for states' rights. Supported across the south and opposed by nearly everyone else, the states' rights plank was defeated, 924 to 310.

The liberal Democrats presented a minority report for a more vigorous civil rights plank:

Civil Rights. We highly commend President Harry S Truman for his courageous stand on the issue of civil rights.

We call upon the Congress to support our President in guaranteeing these basic and fundamental American Principles:

(1) the right of full and equal political participation; (2) the right of equal opportunity of employment; (3) the right of security of person; (4) and the right of equal treatment in the service and defense of our nation.[18]

Put in terms of the issues of the day and the next decade and a half, the platform effectively endorsed what would become the Voting Rights Act of 1965, the equal employment opportunity sections of the Civil Rights Act of 1964, an anti-lynching law, and desegregation of the armed services.

Mayor Hubert H. Humphrey of Minneapolis provided the dramatic expression of the liberal minority plank: "It is time for the Democratic Party to get out of the shadows of States' Rights, and walk forthrightly into the bright sunshine of human rights."[19]

The pro–civil rights plank passed, 651.5 to 582.5. The south voted solidly against it; the larger delegations of the northeast quadrant voted for it; the rest of the delegates divided closely.

The civil rights plank passed over the opposition of the President, who preferred party unity to commendation. His Missouri delegation voted nay, unanimously.

Table 2.8 illustrates the vote of state delegations on the two civil rights planks taken together. States are sorted into three groups: Those that voted for the states' rights plank presented by the south, those that voted for the civil rights plank presented by the liberals, those that voted against both. The polarization on civil rights, and the long-term ideological coalition of states, is exhibited on these votes. States from the northeast quadrant that are classified as "liberal" in the 1964–1972 alignment voted for the civil rights plank. The south voted uniformly for states' rights. Most other delegations voted against both planks. The large blocs of votes from California, Illinois, Michigan, New Jersey, New York, Pennsylvania, and Ohio were decisive for the civil rights plank.

Table 2.9 compares the Ku Klux Klan vote at the 1924 Democratic Convention with the civil rights votes of 1948. The similarity of state voting behavior on those two ballots and the fact that both roll calls fit rather neatly into the 1964–1972 alignment amount to further evidence of the persistent ideological coalition of states, at least on the issue of race. In addition to the relative stability of coalitions of states, Table 2.9 illustrates the shift in power within the Democratic Party from conservatives to liberals on the issue of race.

President Truman won the Democratic nomination by a vote of 926 to 266 over Senator Richard B. Russell of Georgia. Numerous southern delegates bolted the convention, as threatened, and convened as the States' Rights Democratic Party to nominate Governor J. Strom Thurmond of South Carolina for President.

What followed, of course, was the classic election upset. Behind in public opinion polls, his party split three ways, President Truman was elected. As discussed the Chapter 1, the divisions in the Democratic Party led to a pattern of election returns that foreshadowed the realignment of the 1964–1972 period.

The experience of 1948 demonstrated the difficulty the Democrats now faced in extending their umbrella over the diverse elements of their coalition. So long as the economic priorities of the New Deal or winning the war defined the most-salient issues and so long as there was no effort to disturb white supremacy in the south, African Americans, southern whites, and the northern urban working class could coexist under the Democratic umbrella. But black migration to northern cities changed the electoral equation for northern Democrats. And even the first halting steps by northern Democrats to dismantle southern white supremacy threatened the party's national coalition. The closeness of the 1948 Presidential election thus indicated the Democrats' vulnerability: They needed all the parts of their coalition to keep the sum of their victory. In 1948, labor was still solidly in the Democratic column. Even in the face of the Dixiecrat challenge, President Truman had carried seven of the eleven states of the old Confederacy. And, at the same time, the urban black vote was crucial to narrow victories in Ohio, Illinois, and California. With any of those pieces of the puzzle removed, Truman would have lost.

From 1948 on, liberal Democrats could claim voting majorities at the party's national conventions. This was now enough to control nominations, because the south no longer had the veto power drawn from the two-thirds rule. But liberal Democrats also knew that they had to be careful of what they did with their majority. They needed both blacks in the north and whites in the south to win national elections, and the 1948 election had demonstrated how dangerous a split in the party could be. The result, over the next three Presidential elections, was the nomination of Democratic national tickets with a moderate liberal from the north as the nominee for President and a southerner as his running mate, offering a cautious approach to civil rights reform. Briefly, that formula extended the umbrella enough to keep the increasingly tenuous New Deal coalition from collapsing.

The uneasy compromise is illustrated vividly by the nominating politics of the 1952 convention. The two leading candidates going to the convention were southerners: Senator Estes Kefauver of Tennessee, who favored civil rights, and Senator Russell, a segregationist. Senator Kefauver had emerged as the front-runner by upsetting President Truman in the New Hampshire primary, and he went on to win primaries in Nebraska, Ohio, Oregon, and California. He lost only the Florida primary, to Senator Russell.

Neither candidate was acceptable at the White House. Kefauver was not a team player, holding televised hearings in the Senate that embarrassed the administration and entering the race for the Presidency before Truman had announced his plans. Russell, as a segregationist, had opposed the administration on civil rights and had challenged the President at the 1948 convention.

The President, for his part, never declared his candidacy and did not campaign; he ultimately announced that he would not run for a third term a few weeks after the New Hampshire primary. But he would have a hand in deciding the Democratic Presidential nomination.

That hand would have to be played by uniting moderate and liberal Democrats on an alternative to Kefauver. The leading candidates for supporters of the Truman administration were W. Averill Harriman of New York, the candidate of Tammany Hall; Governor Adlai E. Stevenson of Illinois, a reform liberal Democrat who proclaimed that he was not running for President; and Vice President Alben W. Barkley. The 74-year old Barkley, beloved across factions of the party, was nevertheless rejected by labor as too old and too conservative, leaving Harriman and Stevenson as possibilities.[20]

Although it was almost identical to the 1948 platform, the civil rights plank did not encounter major controversy at the 1952 convention. Rather, the civil rights fight was over the relationship between party loyalty and delegate credentials. A resolution requiring credentialed delegates to take a loyalty oath to the national Democratic ticket, proposed by Representative Blair Moody of Michigan, passed by voice vote. When the Virginia delegation inquired about its own credentials because its members would not take such an oath, a floor fight developed. A motion to seat the Virginia delegation led to a roll-call vote.

On the roll call, delegates for Russell were solid for seating Virginia; delegates for Kefauver and Harriman were against. The decisive delegates were the supporters of Governor Stevenson, who voted for the motion to seat the Virginia delegates. The motion passed, 650.5 to 518. The Missouri delegation, including the alternate serving in place of President Truman, voted to seat Virginia, as did most moderates.

The result was that Stevenson became the most broadly acceptable candidate, in spite of his claim that he was not a candidate at all. Kefauver was unacceptable to the administration; Harriman was too liberal; Russell was too conservative. Kefauver led on the first ballot with 340 votes out of 1230, well short of the 616 needed to win. Stevenson had 273 votes, Russell 268, and Harriman 123.5. All gained on the second ballot, except for Harriman. During a recess after the second ballot, Harriman and other favorite sons withdrew in favor of Stevenson, who was nominated on the third ballot. Table 2.10 illustrates the relationship between the Virginia credentials vote and the delegate vote for President.

After losing the 1952 election to Republican Dwight D. Eisenhower, Stevenson won renomination in 1956, holding off a challenge from Kefauver in the primaries and defeating Averill Harriman on the first ballot at the convention. Stevenson presented himself as a moderate liberal, acceptable to the south, and won a majority of delegates from every section of the country and every faction of the party.

In 1960, unlike 1956, the south had a candidate of its own again for the Democratic Presidential nomination. But the decline in the south's power to protect white supremacy was illustrated by the fact that their candidate, Senate Majority Leader Lyndon B. Johnson, a Texas Democrat, had made himself a national candidate by supporting the Civil Rights Bills of 1957 and 1960 and guiding them to passage. Johnson hoped to move beyond his base in the south by reconstructing the convention coalition that had nominated William Jennings Bryan three times between 1896 and 1908: the "L" of the south and the west.[21]

But when Senator John F. Kennedy of Massachusetts emerged as the front-runner by sweeping the primaries, most western delegates jumped on the Kennedy bandwagon. Kennedy was nominated on the first ballot by a vote of 806 to 409 for Johnson. The only western delegation for Johnson was New Mexico; otherwise Johnson assembled majorities only in southern and border state delegations. Although Kennedy was not considered the most liberal of the candidates for the nomination, his first ballot victory provided evidence of the emerging liberal nominating coalition in the Democratic Party, based in the northeast. (See Table 2.11.)

Kennedy did, of course, make an appeal to the south by adding Johnson to the ticket. Even then, the Democratic ticket only narrowly carried the south in an even more narrow national victory. During the 1960 campaign, however, Senator Kennedy made a strategic choice of historic importance when he interceded with Georgia Democrats to have Martin Luther King released from jail after a civil rights demonstration in Atlanta.[22] Kennedy showed his awareness of the importance of the black vote in northern cities, and it proved essential to his carrying New York, New Jersey, Pennsylvania, Michigan, and Illinois. Had he lost New York, or any two of the others, he would not have been elected.

This reality, plus the pressure of the Civil Rights movement, including the march on Washington on August 28, 1963, plus violence practiced against civil rights demonstrators by extreme segregationists across the south, led the Kennedy administration to introduce the Civil

Rights bill. After the assassination of President Kennedy, President Johnson pushed vigorously for passage of the bill. The politics of passing the bill in Congress is discussed in Chapter 7. But starting in 1964, the Democrats came to be associated with civil rights nationally and in the south. The resulting electoral change would lead to the historic realignment discussed in Chapter 2. But even as late as 1964, the factional struggle within the Democratic Party was yet to be resolved decisively. That resolution would not have taken the form it did, nor would the realignment have taken place, without profound and sudden change within the Republican Party.

TABLES

Table 2.1
Decline of the South at Democratic National Conventions, 1896–1972

IYear/Contest	Non-South	South	liberal	moderate	conservative	National
1896: Bryan (5th ballot)	**60**	**100**	23	**80**	**99**	**70**
1904: Parker (1st)	**56**	**98**	69	54	77	**66**
1912: Wilson (43rd)	**55**	**51**	**52**	55	**54**	**55**
1920: Cox (44th)	**67**	51	**72**	66	**52**	**64**
1924: Davis (103rd)	**46**	72	32	**55**	68	**52**
1928: Smith (1st)	**79**	19	**98**	67	31	**66**
1932: Roosevelt (1st)	**53**	73	**54**	40	**82**	58
1948: Truman (1st)	**99**	4	**100**	88	41	**77**
1952: Stevenson (3rd)	**63**	10	**77**	43	33	**50**
1956: Stevenson (1st)	**71**	48	**65**	66	**64**	**66**
1960: Kennedy (1st)	**68**	3	**81**	51	29	**53**
1968: Humphrey (1st)	**63**	83	**55**	67	**79**	**67**
1972: McGovern (1st)	**66**	24	**66**	66	32	**57**

These figures represent the percentage of the delegate vote for the winning candidates in contested nominations at Democratic National Conventions. The south includes all eleven states of the Confederacy. The remainder of the continental forty-eight states are "non-south." States are sorted by ideology according to the 1964–1972 classification introduced in Chapter 1 and presented in Table 1.19. Figures in bold indicate plurality or majority on roll call.

Derived from *National Party Conventions* (Washington, D.C.: Congressional Quarterly, 1997), pp. 215–247.

Table 2.2
**Delegate Vote on Free Silver, 1896 Democratic National Convention,
by 1964–1972 Ideological Alignment of States**

	Ideological Alignment of States, 1964–1972		
	liberal	*moderate*	*conservative*
1896 Convention Free Silver Vote			
Nay	Michigan	California	Alabama
(For	Oregon	Colorado	Arizona
Free Silver)	Washington	Illinois	Arkansas
		Iowa	Florida
		Kentucky	Georgia
		Missouri	Idaho
		Montana	Indiana
		Ohio	Kansas
		Texas	Louisiana
		West Virginia	Mississippi
			Nebraska
			Nevada
			New Mexico
			North Carolina
			North Dakota
			Oklahoma
			South Carolina
			Tennessee
			Utah
			Virginia
			Wyoming
Yea	Connecticut	Delaware	
(Against	Massachusetts	Maine	
Free Silver)	Minnesota	Maryland	
	New York	New Hampshire	
	Pennsylvania	New Jersey	
	Rhode Island	South Dakota	
	Wisconsin	Vermont	

G = −.89

States sorted by majority vote on Free Silver Minority Report. The ideological
classification of states is based on the three Presidential elections between 1964
and 1972, as explained in Chapter 1 and presented in Table 1.19.
Derived from *National Party Conventions*, p. 215.

Table 2.3
Delegate Vote for Democratic Presidential Nomination, 1912

	By 1964-1972 ideological classification of states					
	liberal	*moderate*	*conservative*	*Non-South*	*South*	*National*
1st Ballot						
Clark	24	**57**	**32**	**47**	14	**40**
Wilson	**45**	24	24	28	31	30
Harmon	31	8	3	17	3	14
Underwood		1	32		**35**	11
10th Ballot						
Clark	**55**	**58**	**34**	**60**	16	**51**
Wilson	41	27	26	28	23	32
Underwood	3		26	1	**24**	11
30th Ballot						
Clark	**45**	**50**	24	**47**	16	**42**
Wilson	45	35	**46**	41	**42**	42
Underwood	1	3	30	2	41	11
43rd Ballot						
Clark	37	31	19	34	13	30
Wilson	**52**	**55**	**54**	**55**	**51**	**55**

Figures are percentages of delegate vote, by delegation, according to ideological classification of states. Ideological classification of states is based on voting in the 1964–1972 Presidential elections and is explained in detail in the Introduction and Chapter 1 and presented in Table 1.19. States that voted more Democratic than the country in all three Presidential elections 1964–1972, voted less Republican than the country in 1964 and 1972, and cast a lower percentage of their vote for Nixon and Wallace than the country in 1968 are listed as "liberal." States that voted less Democratic than the country in all three elections, less Republican than the country in 1964 and 1972, and cast a higher percentage of the vote for Nixon and Wallace than the country in 1968 are listed as "conservative." All other states are listed as "moderate." Ideological and geographic data are counted separately.
Derived from *National Party Conventions*, p. 221.

Table 2.4
Delegate Vote on Ku Klux Klan Minority Report at 1924 Democratic National Convention, by 1964–1972 Ideological Alignment of States

	Ideological Alignment of States, 1964–1972		
	liberal	*moderate*	*conservative*
Nay	Michigan	California	Arizona
(For Klan)	Oregon	Kentucky	Arkansas
	Washington	Missouri	Florida
		Montana	Georgia
		New Hampshire	Idaho
		Texas	Indiana
		West Virginia	Kansas
			Louisiana
			Mississippi
			Nebraska
			Nevada
			New Mexico
			North Carolina
			Oklahoma
			South Carolina
			Tennessee
			Virginia
			Wyoming
Even Split		Colorado	Utah
Yea	Connecticut	Delaware	Alabama
(Against Klan)	Massachusetts	Illinois	North Dakota
	Minnesota	Iowa	
	New York	Maine	
	Pennsylvania	Maryland	
	Rhode Island	New Jersey	
	Wisconsin	Ohio	
		South Dakota	
		Vermont	

G = –.66

States sorted by majority vote on Minority Report on Ku Klux Klan. The ideological classification of states is explained in Chapter 1 and presented in Table 1.19. Colorado and Utah split evenly on the Minority Report.
Derived from *National Party Conventions*, p. 228.

Table 2.5
Delegate Vote on Ku Klux Klan and for President, 1924 Democratic National Convention

KU KLUX KLAN MINORITY REPORT

	By 1964–1972 ideological classification of states					
	liberal	*moderate*	*conservative*	*Non-South*	*South*	*National*
Yea	**80**	**54**	18	**61**	14	50
Nay	20	46	**80**	39	**83**	**50**

	By delegation support for candidate (1st Ballot)			
	Smith	*Other*	*McAdoo*	*National*
Yea	**99**	**53**	23	50
Nay	1	47	**75**	**50**

DEMOCRATIC PRESIDENTIAL NOMINATION

1st Ballot	By 1964–1972 ideological classification of states					
	liberal	*moderate*	*conservative*	*Non-South*	*South*	*National*
McAdoo	18	**48**	**49**	**33**	58	**39**
Smith	**63**	7	1	30		22

	By vote on Ku Klux Klan Minority Report		
	Yea	*Nay*	*National*
McAdoo	20	**59**	**39**
Smith	**44**	1	22

102nd Ballot	By 1964–1972 ideological classification of states					
	liberal	*moderate*	*conservative*	*Non-South*	*South*	*National*
Davis	15	**42**	**55**	29	**67**	**38**
Underwood	**56**	17	13	**33**	10	29
Walsh	10	15	9	15	2	11

	By vote on Ku Klux Klan Minority Report		
	Yea	*Nay*	*National*
Davis	17	**61**	**38**
Underwood	**48**	6	29
Walsh	7	16	11

103rd Ballot (before shift)	By 1964–1972 ideological classification of states					
	liberal	*moderate*	*conservative*	*Non-South*	*South*	*National*
Davis	32	**55**	**68**	**46**	72	**52**
Underwood	**41**	17	11	26	12	23

Figures of percentages of delegate vote. See Table 1.19 for ideological classification of states.
Derived from *National Party Conventions*, pp. 228–229.

Table 2.6
Delegate Vote for President, 1st Ballot, 1932 Democratic National Convention, by 1964–1972 Ideological Alignment of States

	Ideological Alignment of States, 1964–1972		
	liberal	*moderate*	*conservative*
Roosevelt	Michigan	Colorado	Alabama
	Minnesota	Delaware	Arizona
	Oregon	Iowa	Arkansas
	Pennsylvania	Kentucky	Florida
	Washington	Maine	Georgia
	Wisconsin	Montana	Idaho
		New Hampshire	Indiana
		New Mexico	Kansas
		South Dakota	Louisiana
		Vermont	Mississippi
		West Virginia	Nebraska
			Nevada
			North Carolina
			North Dakota
			South Carolina
			Tennessee
			Utah
			Wyoming
Smith	Connecticut	New Jersey	
	Massachusetts		
	New York		
	Rhode Island		
Garner		California	
		Texas	
Favorite Sons		Illinois	Oklahoma
and		Maryland	Virginia
Other		Missouri	
		Ohio	

G = –.36
States sorted by plurality vote of delegation in 1932 and ideological alignment for 1964–1972 Presidential elections, explained in Chapter 1 and illustrated in Table 1.19.
Derived from *National Party Conventions*, p. 231.

Table 2.7
Delegate Vote for Vice President, 2nd Ballot, 1944 Democratic National Convention, by 1964–1972 Ideological Alignment of States

	Ideological Alignment of States, 1964–1972		
	liberal	*moderate*	*conservative*
Truman	Massachusetts	Delaware	Arizona
	New York	Maine	Arkansas
	Rhode Island	Maryland	Louisiana
		Missouri	Mississippi
		Montana	New Mexico
		New Hampshire	Oklahoma
		New Jersey	South Carolina
		Vermont	Virginia
Wallace	Connecticut	California	Florida
	Michigan	Colorado	Georgia
	Minnesota	Iowa	Kansas
	Oregon	Ohio	North Dakota
	Pennsylvania	South Dakota	Utah
	Washington	Texas	
	Wisconsin	West Virginia	
Favorite Sons		Illinois	Alabama
and		Kentucky	Idaho
Other			Indiana
			Nebraska
			Nevada
			North Carolina
			Tennessee
			Wyoming

$G = .20$

States sorted according to majority or plurality vote of delegation at 1944 convention and the ideological alignment for 1964–1972 Presidential elections explained in Chapter 1 and presented in Table 1.19.

Derived from Richard C. Bain and Judith H. Parris, *Convention Decisions and Voting Records* (Washington, D.C.: Brookings Institution, 1973), Appendix.

Table 2.8

Delegate Vote on Civil Rights, 1948 Democratic National Convention, by 1964–1972 Ideological Alignment of States

	Ideological Alignment of States, 1964–1972		
	liberal	*moderate*	*conservative*
For *Civil Rights*	Connecticut Massachusetts Michigan Minnesota New York Pennsylvania Washington Wisconsin	California Colorado Illinois Iowa New Jersey Ohio South Dakota Vermont	Indiana Kansas Wyoming
Against *Both* *Planks*	Oregon Rhode Island	Delaware Kentucky Maryland Maine Missouri Montana New Hampshire West Virginia	Arizona Idaho Nebraska Nevada New Mexico North Dakota Oklahoma Utah
For *States' Rights*		Texas	Alabama Arkansas Florida Georgia Louisiana Mississippi North Carolina South Carolina Tennessee Virginia

$G = .79$

Delegations "for civil rights" voted for the Civil Rights plank to the Democratic Platform and against the States' Rights plank; delegations "for states' rights" voted for the States' Rights plank and against the Civil Rights plank; delegations "against both" voted against both planks. States sorted by ideological alignment of states in 1964–1972 Presidential elections (see Table 1.19).

Derived from *National Party Conventions*, p. 236.

Table 2.9
Democratic Convention Votes on Race Issues, 1924–1948

	1948		
	For Civil Rights	*Against Both*	*For States' Rights*
1924			
Against	California	Arizona	Arkansas
Anti-Klan	Indiana	Idaho	Florida
Minority Report	Kansas	Kentucky	Georgia
	Michigan	Missouri	Louisiana
	Washington	Montana	Mississippi
	Wyoming	Nebraska	North Carolina
		Nevada	South Carolina
		New Hampshire	Tennessee
		New Mexico	Texas
		Oklahoma	Virginia
		Oregon	
		West Virginia	
For	Connecticut	Delaware	Alabama
Anti-Klan	Illinois	Maine	
Minority Report	Iowa	Maryland	
	Massachusetts	North Dakota	
	Minnesota	Rhode Island	
	New Jersey		
	New York		
	Ohio		
	Pennsylvania		
	South Dakota		
	Vermont		
	Wisconsin		

G = −.63
States classified according to majority vote on platform planks.
Derived from *National Party Conventions*, pp. 228 and 236.

Table 2.10
1952 Democratic National Convention Delegate Vote on Virginia Credentials and for President, by 1964–1972 Ideological Alignment of States

SEATING VIRGINIA DELEGATION

	By 1964–1972 ideological classification of states					
	liberal	moderate	conservative	Non-South	South	National
Yea	30	**58**	**70**	47	**75**	**53**
Nay	**70**	40	17	**52**	10	42

	By delegation support for President					
	Harriman	Kefauver	Stevenson	Russell	Other	National
Yea	9	26	**62**	**79**	**68**	**53**
Nay	**91**	**71**	37	4	30	42

DEMOCRATIC PRESIDENTIAL NOMINATION

	By 1964–1972 ideological classification of states					
	liberal	moderate	conservative	Non-South	South	National
1st Ballot						
Kefauver	**33**	**35**	14	**32**	14	**28**
Stevenson	20	30	15	29	2	22
Russell	0	17	**48**	4	**76**	22
Harriman	25	3	4	13		10
2nd Ballot						
Kefauver	**39**	**36**	14	**34**	14	**29**
Stevenson	24	34	19	33	14	26
Russell	0	18	**46**	4	**76**	24
Harriman	25	3	3	13		10
3rd Ballot						
Kefauver	20	33	12	25	14	22
Stevenson	**77**	**43**	33	**63**	10	**50**
Russell	0	15	**49**	4	**76**	21

Figures are percentages of delegate vote, by delegation, according to ideological classification of states in 1964–1972 Presidential elections, as explained in Chapter 1 and presented in Table 1.19.
Derived from *National Party Conventions,* p. 238.

Table 2.11
**Delegate Vote for President, 1st Ballot, 1960 Democratic Convention,
by 1964–1972 Ideological Alignment of States**

	Ideological Alignment of States, 1964–1972		
	liberal	*moderate*	*conservative*
Kennedy	Connecticut	Alaska	Arizona
	Massachusetts	California	Idaho
	Michigan	Colorado	Indiana
	New York	Illinois	Kansas
	Oregon	Iowa	Nebraska
	Pennsylvania	Maine	North Dakota
	Rhode Island	Maryland	Utah
	Washington	Montana	Wyoming
	Wisconsin	New Hampshire	
		Ohio	
		South Dakota	
		Vermont	
		West Virginia	
Johnson		Delaware	Alabama
		Kentucky	Arkansas
		Texas	Georgia
			Louisiana
			Nevada
			New Mexico
			North Carolina
			Oklahoma
			South Carolina
			Tennessee
			Virginia
Favorite Sons	Minnesota	Hawaii	Florida
and		Missouri	Mississippi
Other		New Jersey	

G = .50
States sorted according to plurality vote for Democratic Presidential nomination
in 1960 and ideological alignment of states in Presidential elections of 1964–1972,
as explained in Chapter 1 and illustrated in Table 1.19.
Derived from *National Party Conventions*, p. 241.

NOTES

1. See *Plessy v. Ferguson* 163 U.S. 537 (1896). Among state actions taken to keep African Americans from voting, I refer particularly to the literacy test in states where it had been illegal to teach African Americans to read, the poll tax, and the grandfather clause.

2. See Walter Dean Burnham, *Critical Elections and the Mainsprings of American Politics* (New York: Norton, 1970), pp. 77–79.

3. This particular tactic was ruled unconstitutional by the Supreme Court in *Smith v. Allwright* 321 U.S. 649 (1944).

4. The classic study of southern politics in the period of the solid south remains V. O. Key, Jr., *Southern Politics in State and Nation* (New York: Knopf, 1949). Key's study is all the more instructive because it was published the year after the climactic Democratic Convention of 1948, which passed the civil rights platform plank sponsored by Americans for Democratic Action (ADA), leading to the bolt of the Dixiecrats. Thus, Key reports about a solid south just about to come apart.

5. On the life of William Jennings Bryan, see Paolo E. Coletta, *William Jennings Bryan*, Volume I: *Political Evangelist 1860–1908* (Lincoln: University of Nebraska Press, 1964); Volume II: *Progressive Politician and Moral Statesman 1909–1915*; and Volume III: *Political Puritan 1915–1925*. See also Louis W. Koenig, *Bryan* (New York: G.P. Putnam's Sons, 1971); Lawrence W. Levine, *Defender of the Faith, William Jennings Bryan: The Last Decade 1915–1925* (New York: Oxford University Press, 1965); David J. Nordloh, *William Jennings Bryan* (Bloomington: Indiana University Press, 1981); and Donald K. Springen, *William Jennings Bryan: Orator of Small-Town America* (Westport, Conn.: Greenwood Press, 1991).

6. See Louis W. Koenig, *Bryan: A Political Biography of William Jennings Bryan* (New York: G.P. Putnam's Sons, 1971), pp. 605–609.

7. Coletta, Volume I, pp. 319–344.

8. Ibid., p. 140.

9. Unless otherwise noted, data on convention voting is drawn or derived from *National Party Conventions, 1831–1996* (Washington, D.C.: Congressional Quarterly, 1997). Data on Presidential primaries is drawn from *Presidential Elections, 1789–1996* (Washington, D.C.: Congressional Quarterly, 1997). Data is also drawn from Richard C. Bain and Judith H. Parris, *Convention Decisions and Voting Records* (Washington, D.C.: The Brookings Institution, 1973).

10. *National Party Conventions*, p. 72. See also Robert W. Cherry, *A Righteous Cause: The Life of William Jennings Bryan* (Boston: Little, Brown, 1985), pp. 125–127, and Koenig, *Bryan*, pp. 491–496.

11. Robert K. Murray, *The 103rd Ballot* (New York: Harper and Row, 1976), p. 23. Much of the following discussion on the 1920 Democratic National Convention draws on Murray's account, pp. 3–92.

12. Ibid., p. 40.

13. Ibid., p. 83.

14. Whether an explicit deal was made promising the Democratic Vice Presidential nomination to Garner is unclear. An agreement can be attributed to a number of communications between the Roosevelt and Garner camps, including conversations between Joseph P. Kennedy and William Randolph Hearst, a Garner delegate from California; and between James A. Farley and Representative Sam Rayburn of

Texas. In any case, it would appear that surrender in the name of party unity was as much Garner's idea as anyone's. One wonders whether he would have made a deal in which he gave up the Speakership of the House to take an office he considered to be worth no more than "a bucket of warm spit." For an excellent discussion of the Roosevelt campaign and the Democratic National Convention of 1932, see Kenneth S. Davis, *FDR: The New York Years, 1928–1933* (New York: Random House, 1994), pp. 195–250.

15. See particularly the "switch in time that saved nine," from *Schecter Poultry Corporation v. U.S.* 295 U.S. 495 (1935) to *West Coast Hotel Co. v. Parrish* 300 U.S. 379 (1937), *NLRB v. Jones and Laughlin Steel Corporation* 301 U.S. 1 (1937) and *U.S. v. Darby* 312 U.S. 100 (1941). Chief Justice Charles Evans Hughes, the Republican nominee for President in 1916, wrote the opinions in both *Schecter* and *NLRB v. Jones and Laughlin* and couched the latter in legal terms that would allow the court to uphold strict precedent even while reversing *Schecter* in effect. See Bernard Schwartz, *A History of the Supreme Court* (New York: Oxford University Press, 1993), pp. 236–245.

16. FDR might have been opposed for renomination in 1936 by Senator Huey P. Long of Louisiana, had Long not been assassinated by Dr. Carl Weiss in 1935.

17. See *National Party Conventions, 1831–1996*, pp. 91–92.

18. Ibid., p. 95.

19. Hubert H. Humphrey, *The Education of a Public Man* (New York: Doubleday, 1976), p. 459.

20. See Harry S Truman, *Memoirs by Harry S Truman*, Vol. II: *Years of Trial and Hope* (New York: Doubleday, 1956), pp. 495–497. See also Porter McKeever, *Adlai Stevenson: His Life and Legacy* (New York: William Morrow and Co., 1989), pp. 196–197, and Bert Cochran, *Adlai Stevenson: Patrician among Politicians* (New York: Funk and Wagnalls, 1969), pp. 203–204.

21. Theodore H. White, *The Making of the President 1960* (New York: Atheneum, 1961), pp. 134–135.

22. Ibid., pp. 321–323.

3

The Republican Party as a Bifactional System, 1896–1964

The factional struggle within the Democratic Party that contributed to electoral realignment in the 1960s was a long process in which, over a period of about forty years, the south gradually lost power within the party. The factional struggle within the Republican Party was as long and severe, but its resolution in 1964 much more sudden, reversing historic patterns of Republican politics. This chapter examines the factional politics of the Republican Party prior to 1964.

The Republican Party has always had a simpler factional structure than the Democratic Party, even if the ideological divisions have been as intense. Whereas the Democratic Party is a multifactional system, the Republican Party is fundamentally a two-faction system. This fact can be attributed to three observations comparing the Republicans to the Democrats.

First, until the mid-twentieth century when the Democratic solid south began to break up, the south never represented an autonomous faction within the Republican Party, as it did by its defense of white supremacy within the Democratic Party. Republicans had little or no electoral base in the south. Except for isolated regions, like the Appalachians of eastern Tennessee and western North Carolina, the route to public office for a southern Republican politician was by Presidential appointment rather than election. Therefore, motivated by patronage interests, southern Republicans joined alliances with the supporters of Republican Presidents, or Republicans who appeared poised to win national elections. The south's support was essential to the renomination of President William Howard Taft in 1912, for example, but most southern states were closely contested forty years later between his son Senator Robert A. Taft of Ohio and General Dwight D. Eisenhower. Not until civil rights achieved salience as a national issue did the south come to be consistently allied with conservative Republicans in party affairs.

Second, Republican national conventions were governed by majority rule. With no two-thirds rule, no minority faction could veto the majority, as the south could at Democratic national conventions. Therefore, winning coalitions were assembled earlier, before, or during Republican national conventions, encouraging the development of fewer factions than within the Republican Party.

Finally, the Democratic Party's umbrella always covered more-diverse interests than the Republican umbrella. The Republican Party has always been, and remains, disproportionately white, Anglo-Saxon, Protestant, and middle class. Both of its factions have always been electorally based in the middle class, and its elites have represented the interests of competing sectors of capital.

THE REPUBLICAN FACTIONS: WALL STREET VERSUS MAIN STREET

The two persistent factions in Republican politics have been labeled "Wall Street" versus "Main Street."[1] The tags certainly amount to an oversimplification, but perhaps the most instructive one available. The names certainly indicate accurately the interests represented by each faction. The Wall Street faction has represented the interests of big business: monopoly and international capital. The Main Street faction has represented small, competitive capital, with its local roots and (sometimes) national markets.

No ideological generalization for either faction would cover the 1896–1964 period accurately. During the system of 1896, the Wall Street faction was the old guard of the Republican Party, economic conservatives who supported the gold standard and high tariffs, and generally opposed government regulation of the economy. This faction produced five of the six Republican Presidents of the period, William McKinley, William Howard Taft, Warren G. Harding, Calvin Coolidge, and Herbert C. Hoover, the first three of whom were products of the Ohio Republican establishment. This was the faction particularly despised by and fearful of their Democratic opponent, William Jennings Bryan.

The Main Street faction was the more progressive wing of the Republican Party during the system of 1896, sharing some common ground with the populists who supported Bryan in the Democratic Party. More flexible on financial issues and supportive of government regulation of the economy, this faction produced one President, Theodore Roosevelt, and the period's leading Republican insurgents, including Robert M. LaFollette, Hiram Johnson, George W. Norris, and William E. Borah. As President, Theodore Roosevelt was so active in both foreign and domestic affairs as to practically invent the modern Presidency.[2]

During the New Deal alignment, Wall Street and Main Street reversed positions on a left-right ideological continuum in Republican politics. As the New Deal became an accomplished reality, and with the approach of World War II, the Wall Street faction, representing the interests of large corporations and banks, became more internationalist, more tolerant of government intervention in the economy, and thus, the more liberal of the two Republican factions. The Main Street faction, still representing small and local business, retained its more parochial vision and emerged as the more isolationist and conservative Republican faction. To this day, the Main Street faction remains the more conservative of the two and is now the electoral home of traditional values in American politics.

The electoral map within the Republican Party is similar to both the factional pattern within the Democratic Party and the historic geography of Presidential elections, with the important qualifications regarding the south. The Wall Street faction of the Republican Party has found the base of its support in the northeast quadrant, particularly the New England and Mid-Atlantic states. The Main Street faction draws its greatest support historically from the interior west. The north central states have generally been a battle ground between Wall Street and Main Street. The south, as discussed earlier, generally sided with incumbents and apparent winners, until the emergence of civil rights as a salient electoral issue. The result was that until the New Deal realignment, the south was often found in alliance with the Wall Street faction supporting Republican Presidents. After the New Deal realignment, with the Republicans out of the White House and the Wall Street faction more liberal, the south gave relatively strong support to Robert Taft who was the Main Street candidate for the Republican Presidential nomination three times. By 1964, of course, the south would be the engine of the conservative revolt that seized control of the Republican Party from the Wall Street faction.

Until 1964 the Wall Street faction was always the Presidential and executive wing of the Republican Party, able to deliver Presidential nominations at national conventions, regardless of its ideological position in the party. The Wall Street faction was the base of the nominating coalition that produced McKinley, Taft, Harding, Coolidge, and Hoover, as well as the more moderate-to-liberal Republicans of the New Deal period: Alf Landon, Wendell Willkie, Thomas Dewey, and Dwight D. Eisenhower.[3]

During the New Deal period, the Main Street faction emerged as generally the Congressional and legislative wing of the party, particularly as Main Street became more conservative in Republican politics. Thus, while Main Street Republicans would control the party caucuses in both houses of Congress, the Wall Street Republicans would mobilize to decide Presidential nominations at the party's national convention. This repeating pattern is explained by electoral dynamics. To win national elections prior to 1964, Republicans had to appeal to the large, closely contested states, with large blocs of Electoral votes, located mostly in the northeast quadrant of the country. The south was solidly Democratic. The Republicans were generally strongest in the northeast and could win in the west. They could win without the west, as they did in 1896; but they could not win without the Electoral votes in the northeast quadrant. In every Republican victory in a Presidential election between 1896 and 1956, the northeast quadrant was solid, or nearly solid, for the Republican. New York, New Jersey, Pennsylvania, Ohio, Michigan, and Illinois all voted Republican in every Republican Presidential victory throughout that sixty-year period.

Between 1896 and 1928, the incumbent President was usually a Republican, and usually an old-guard Republican. The nominating coalition was usually based in the east, with support from southern Republicans hoping for Presidential largesse. There were progressive challenges by the Main Streeters, but even if they enjoyed some success in the primaries, all of them were turned aside at the convention, all but one of them easily.

After the New Deal realignment, as the Wall Streeters emerged as the internationalist, liberal wing of the Republican Party, electoral considerations discussed earlier applied, perhaps even more so. Wall Street candidates were better able to appeal to swing voters, who were perceived as more liberal than most Republicans, even if less liberal than most Democrats. Moreover, Electoral votes remained heavily weighted toward the northeast quadrant.

The Wall Street faction would retain its control of Republican Presidential nominations so long as the Republican electoral base was in the northeast and the south remained solidly Democratic. The salience of civil rights would decisively change the electoral environment in the mid-twentieth century and, by 1964, the nominating politics of the Republican Party.

THE REPUBLICAN PARTY IN THE SYSTEM OF 1896

During the system of 1896, when the Republicans were the majority party, only three Republican Presidential nominations were contested seriously at the national convention. Two of them involved factional confrontations between the old guard of Wall Street and the progressives of Main Street, both won by the former with the support of the south.

The Old Guard and the Bull Moose

The first, in 1912, resulted in the great divide that led to the election of the only Democratic President between 1896 and the New Deal, Woodrow Wilson. In that case, former President Theodore Roosevelt challenged President William Howard Taft in the primaries and won nearly all of them, including Illinois, Pennsylvania, California, and New Jersey. Roosevelt even won Taft's own Ohio, by an impressive 55 percent to 40 percent. Taft won only the Massachusetts primary, and even that by only 3,000 votes.[4] But the Republican National Committee, and the convention machinery, were controlled by the Taft forces, who steamrollered the renomination of the President.

At the convention, Taft and his allies first won the contest to select the temporary chair of the convention when the post went to Senator Elihu Root of New York, by a vote of 558 to 501. Next, the Roosevelt forces challenged seventy-two Taft delegates, all of whom had been seated by the credentials committee. Supporters of Roosevelt moved to prevent challenged delegates from voting, a strategically important move because a majority of the unchallenged delegates were for Roosevelt. But the Taft forces moved to table the motion, and with their challenged delegates still voting, the motion carried, 567 to 507. All the credentials were then decided in favor of Taft. With most Roosevelt delegates now abstaining in protest over what they regarded as a stolen convention, President Taft won renomination on the first ballot. Roosevelt delegates bolted the Republican convention, formed the Progressive Party, and nominated Roosevelt for the Presidency. The election of Democrat Woodrow Wilson followed, with Roosevelt running second and Taft third.

Tables 3.1 and 3.2 illustrate patterns of support in the roll call votes at the 1912 Republican convention, using the 1964–1972 ideological alignment of states. The tables demonstrate the alliance of that time between the Wall Street faction and the south in Republican politics. Most of the northeastern base of the Wall Street faction, states that would be the most liberal in the 1964–1972 alignment, and ten of the eleven states of the old Confederacy, which would be the most conservative, supported President Taft. Roosevelt found most of his support elsewhere in the country, to the west, although his broad strength in the primaries crossed regional and factional lines.

In 1916 there was again a contest for the Republican Presidential nomination at the convention, but it did not break down along factional lines. The exhausted Republicans, not unlike the Democrats after their seventeen-day convention of 1924, convened in 1916 with party unity as their top priority. A joint committee of Republicans and leaders of the still surviving Progressive Party even negotiated the basis for a unity ticket, although with difficulty. When Theodore Roosevelt declined renomination by the Progressives, they returned to their Republican home. With Roosevelt's endorsement, the Republicans nominated Supreme Court Justice Charles Evans Hughes. Hughes was a progressive Republican acceptable to the old guard and, as a Supreme Court Justice, had not been involved in the blood-letting of 1912.[5] With the Republicans once again united and Roosevelt campaigning for the ticket, perhaps harder than the candidate himself, Hughes only narrowly lost the election to President Wilson.

After the respite, the factional struggle between Wall Street and Main Street was rejoined in 1920. As in 1912, the progressive Republicans of Main Street, this time divided between Senator Hiram Johnson of California and General Leonard Wood, dominated the primaries. Once again as well the Wall Street old guard controlled the convention.

Wood was the early front-runner at the convention, but neither he nor Johnson had a real hope of gaining the support of party leaders. Governor Frank Lowden of Illinois, who had lost several primaries, winning only in his home state, was the strongest old-guard candidate, but not nearly strong enough to be nominated. The old guard, then, held large blocs of delegates in reserve behind favorite sons from large states in the northeast quadrant, like Senator Warren G. Harding of Ohio and Governor Calvin Coolidge of Massachusetts. They held on long enough to bypass Wood and Johnson until, on the ninth ballot, Harding emerged as the front-runner, with a majority of delegates from the south in addition to a plurality from the northeast quadrant. After the famous meeting in the "smoke-filled room," the old guard settled on Harding, who was nominated on the tenth ballot. Once again, the Wall Street faction delivered the nomination with the support of the south (see Table 3.3). Although a dark horse when nominated, Harding was elected by a landslide that November, in the first of three consecutive Republican Presidential victories.

THE REPUBLICAN PARTY IN THE NEW DEAL AGE

The Wall Street faction of the Republican Party retained its control of GOP national conventions for another four decades, well beyond the New Deal realignment, which relegated the Republicans to minority-party status.

The Willkie Crusade

A turning point in national Republican politics was reached in 1940, when Wendell L. Willkie was nominated for the Presidency. Willkie and his crusade, even more after the election of 1940 than during that campaign, were the stimulus through which the Republican Party polarized internally: The Wall Street faction became decidedly more liberal, and the Main Street faction more conservative.

By 1940 the Republicans had been out of the White House for eight years, having lost the Presidency to Franklin D. Roosevelt in the midst of the Great Depression. FDR had been re-elected by a record landslide in 1936, and many Republicans on both Wall Street and Main Street saw their party as being in crisis. With the New Deal largely an accomplished reality by 1940, the fall of France to Hitler's troops just before the Republican National Convention only increased the pressure for new party leadership.

The early front-runner was Senator Arthur Vandenburg of Michigan. Although an old-guard Republican, Vandenburg recognized that the New Deal, if imperfect, needed to be salvaged rather than dismantled.[6] But the Senator still harbored the isolationist views he would later reject, when he would take a leadership role in building the bipartisan foreign policy after the war.

Senator Vandenburg was effectively eliminated in the primaries by District Attorney Thomas E. Dewey of New York. Dewey, who swept the primaries, went to the convention as the front-runner for the Republican Presidential nomination, but his candidacy had some fatal flaws. He had been very narrowly defeated in his bid to unseat Governor Herbert Lehman two years before. Although that race, and his well-publicized experience as a prosecutor, had brought him name recognition, the defeat had put a heavy burden of proof on his claims, which even his victories in the primaries did not overcome. At thirty-eight years of age, he was widely regarded as too young and inexperienced, particularly in view of the war in Europe. Finally, he was moderately liberal on domestic issues and popular with the Wall Street faction, but many of them regarded Dewey as too isolationist on foreign policy. His isolationist views might have appealed to Main Street Republicans, but they regarded him as too liberal.

On Main Street, the candidate of choice was Senator Robert A. Taft of Ohio, the son of William Howard Taft, who had lived in the White House as a young man and dearly wanted to do so again. Taft was an isolationist, conservative Republican whose supporters admired him. Although Dewey had more delegates, Taft had delegates who were more committed. But Taft's isolationism made it nearly impossible for him to win delegates outside the Main Street faction of the party, and he was feared to be too conservative to be elected.

The man of the hour as the convention approached was Wendell Willkie, an Indiana-born New Yorker, who was President of a utility company, Commonwealth and Southern.[7] Willkie, a renegade Democrat turned liberal Republican, had never held public office, although he had been a New York delegate to the Democratic National Convention in 1924, pledged to Al Smith, and a member of the Democratic County Committee in Manhattan just before switching parties in 1939. Drawn to anti–New Deal politics by his opposition to government regulation of public utilities in general and the Tennessee Valley Authority in particular, Willkie was nevertheless a liberal who supported the social welfare aspects of the New Deal and an internationalist who supported aid to the Allies in Europe. He was particularly attractive to the more liberal elements of the Wall Street faction because he was the only Republican running for President who took both of those positions.

Willkie, the candidate, was to a large degree the creation of the idea brokers and image makers of Manhattan who in 1940 had much more control of national print and electronic media than they do now. His appearance on a radio quiz show that had intellectual appeal, *Information Please*, increased his name recognition and public support, as did his article for *Fortune* magazine, "We the People." He was promoted by Henry Luce and Russell Davenport at *Time-Life*, Dorothy Thompson at the New York *Herald Tribune*, and by Arthur Krock at the *New York Times*. Unknown by most Americans early in 1940, Willkie drew the support of 1 percent of self-identified Republicans in the Gallup Poll in April, 10 percent by the end of May, and 17 percent just before the convention opened in June. In a Gallup Poll taken during the convention, Willkie was the front-runner, with 44 percent. During the same period, Dewey fell from 67 percent to 29 percent; Taft support was steady, at 12 percent in April and 13 percent at convention time.[8]

The Republican National Convention of 1940 has become a piece of American political folklore, with its nomination of Wendell Willkie for the Presidency. As the convention met, Dewey was a front-runner whose campaign was deflating, and many delegates expected to nominate Taft. For liberal Republicans, Willkie was a compelling alternative, and they slowly united around him. Dewey led on the first ballot, with

360 votes, to 189 for Taft, 105 for Willkie, and 346 scattering among other candidates. Dewey began to lose support immediately thereafter, while Taft and Willkie gained. Willkie took the lead on the fourth ballot, with 306 votes, to 254 for Taft and 250 for Dewey. On the fifth ballot, the contest narrowed to Willkie and Taft. The New York delegation switched to Willkie, who led 429 to 377. On the sixth ballot, with the galleries chanting "We Want Willkie" and the Michigan and Pennsylvania delegations leading the shift to his candidacy, Willkie was nominated, with 655 votes to 318 for Taft. The factional structure of the party was revealed by the voting on the fifth and sixth ballots. Taft won in the south on both ballots, and Willkie won in the more liberal states of the northeast. The nomination is decided elsewhere around the country. (See Table 3.4.)

Willkie ran a vigorous campaign, losing to FDR by 55 to 45 percent and carrying ten states, an impressive recovery for the Republicans from the landslide defeat of 1936. But neither his miracle nomination at the Philadelphia convention nor his campaign against "the champ" was the source of his real contribution to the development of the Republican Party or to public policy in the years after his candidacy. That came in his crusade for internationalism within the Republican Party, and his failed bid for renomination in 1944. Indeed, the crusade of 1944, more than his nomination in 1940, makes Wendell Willkie almost as important to the history of the Republican Party as William Jennings Bryan is to the Democrats.

In the four years after the 1940 campaign, Willkie did little to ingratiate himself with Republican leaders and much to aggravate them. Indeed he seemed to do more to cooperate with the Democratic President than to express his own party loyalty. Willkie stood almost alone among Republican leaders in his advocacy of active aid to the Allies prior to the Japanese attack on Pearl Harbor in 1941. He endorsed the administration's Lend-Lease program and was able to deliver enough Republican votes in Congress to guarantee its passage. He took a world tour as the personal representative of President Roosevelt and came home to publish his pamphlet *One World*, in which he expressed his views that the United States should join an international organization for world peace after the war, and that the principles for which the war was being fought required both an end to racial discrimination in the United States and an end to European colonialism in Africa and Asia.[9] Even Harold E. Stassen, a liberal Republican and old Willkie supporter, argued that *One World* took too much notice of the danger of British colonialism and not enough of the danger of communism. To make himself even more the ideological misfit, Willkie argued a civil liberties appeal on behalf of a communist before the Supreme Court of the United States and won the case.[10]

Willkie was particularly sensitive to the relationship between the war effort and social justice at home. In an address to a meeting of the National Association for the Advancement of Colored People (NAACP) Willkie said:

> It is becoming apparent to thoughtful Americans that we cannot fight the forces of imperialism abroad and maintain a form of imperialism at home. . . . Our very proclamations of what we are fighting for have rendered our own inequities self-evident. When we talk of freedom and opportunity for all nations, the increasing paradoxes in our own society become so clear that they cannot be ignored.[11]

Willkie directed his criticism on the race issue at both political parties:

> One party cannot go on fooling itself that it has no further obligation to the Negro citizen because Lincoln freed the slave, and the other is not entitled to power if it sanctions and practices one set of principles in Atlanta and another in Harlem.[12]

So frustrated was Willkie with the leadership of both parties that he considered seriously running for President as an independent in 1944. He found the laws for qualifying for state ballots so difficult, however, that he decided that he must enter the Republican primaries.[13]

Willkie's attitude toward the mainstream of his own party is demonstrated by his statement at a luncheon in St. Louis late in 1943: "I don't know whether you're going to support me, or not, and I don't give a damn. You're a bunch of political liabilities who don't know what's going on."[14]

The feeling was mutual. In 1943, when Republican National Chairman Harrison E. Spangler called a conference of party leaders on the postwar world at Mackinac Island, Wendell Willkie was not invited. But he was having an effect. At Mackinac, only Senator Taft among the conferees attempted to maintain isolationism. While Senator Vandenburg was looking for a middle ground, Thomas E. Dewey, now Governor of New York, took a decidedly internationalist position. When the conference passed a resolution calling for "participation by the United States in a postwar cooperative organization," Willkie called it "a step forward. . . . When one measures against what we could have gotten a few years ago, it seems amazing."[15]

But if Willkie had a hand in moving his party on the issues, he did so at a cost to his personal support. With the near consensus achieved at Mackinac in favor of internationalism, isolationists and conservative Republicans moved to support Dewey for President in 1944, if only to stop Willkie.

The stop-Willkie combine came together in the Wisconsin primary, where he was making his stand. Wisconsin had a reputation, from its LaFollette tradition, of being both isolationist and progressive. If he could make a strong showing there, Willkie thought, he would be on his way to renomination. It was an all-or-nothing gamble that did not work. Fred R. Zimmerman, an America First isolationist and former governor, filed a slate of delegates in the primary pledged to Dewey, who was not an announced candidate. When Dewey won a majority of the delegates and Willkie won none, Willkie withdrew. Governor Dewey went on to win the Republican Presidential nomination on the first ballot with all but one vote.

Willkie never endorsed Dewey. Supporters of both Dewey and President Roosevelt were still lobbying for Willkie's endorsement when he died, on October 8, 1944, at the age of 52, after a series of heart attacks. Although decisively defeated in his last campaign, Willkie had taken the lead in preparing his party to participate in a bipartisan foreign policy in the postwar world. After the war, Governor Dewey emerged as an internationalist liberal Republican who was generally recognized as the leader of the Wall Street faction of the party, and Senator Vandenburg became the main architect of the bipartisan foreign policy in the Senate. Both had presented themselves as isolationists in the 1940 race against Willkie, but the world had changed.[16]

Dewey, Taft, and Ike

For two decades after World War II, the Main Street faction shaped Republican behavior on domestic issues in Congress, while the Wall Street faction continued to control the quadrennial Republican national conventions. Twice more, Robert Taft, "Mr. Republican," the candidate of Main Street, would be frustrated in his dream for the Presidency at Republican conventions. Both times, Thomas E. Dewey would have a decisive hand in his frustration.

Governor Dewey won renomination for President in 1948, although he had to overcome a serious challenge in the primaries by the insurgent liberal Republican, former Governor Harold E. Stassen of Minnesota. After Stassen scored upset victories in the Wisconsin and Nebraska primaries, Dewey effectively eliminated him by narrowly winning the Oregon primary.

The manner of Dewey's renomination at the 1948 convention illustrates the degree to which the Wall Street faction remained at the ideological center of the Republican Party. Dewey went to the convention as the front-runner, with Senator Taft his leading opponent. Stassen had the third largest bloc of delegates. Two favorite sons, Senator Vandenburg and Governor Earl Warren of California, had serious hopes for the nomination, in the event of a convention deadlock. Vandenburg especially was expected to benefit from a deadlock, because he had one foot on Wall Street and one foot on Main Street: He was an internationalist, Chair of the Senate Foreign Relations Committee, and a leader of his party's Congressional wing. But Dewey, as it turned out, was similarly positioned: The distribution of his delegate support indicates that he was acceptable across all factions of the party (see Table 3.5).

Dewey led on the first ballot, followed by Taft. Both gained on the second ballot. Dewey was within thirty-three votes of the nomination after the second ballot and confidently allowed the convention to recess.

During the recess, the stop-Dewey forces attempted to find an acceptable alternative candidate but failed. There had been speculation that Dewey could be stopped by a Taft-Stassen unity ticket; but Taft and Stassen each preferred Dewey to the other. There was also speculation that Taft and Stassen could each settle on Vandenburg; but even combined, the three candidates did not have the votes to stop Dewey after the second ballot. Finally, Taft was too conservative; given the choice between Dewey and Taft, Stassen, Vandenburg, and Warren, all preferred Dewey. Dewey, it appeared, was the optimum choice, less conservative than Taft or Vandenburg, more conservative than Stassen or Warren. Thus Taft, Stassen, Vandenburg, and Warren all withdrew and endorsed Dewey, who was nominated unanimously on the third ballot.[17]

Dewey's defeat at the hands of President Truman in 1948 ended his Presidential ambitions. When Senator Taft was re-elected by a landslide in Ohio in 1950, he was widely regarded as the front-runner for the Republican Presidential nomination in 1952, particularly because the Wall Street faction of the party was without a candidate. But Taft and his conservative Republican supporters on Main Street would be turned away again.

By the end of 1951, Governor Dewey, Senator Henry Cabot Lodge of Massachusetts, and Representative Hugh Scott of Pennsylvania had built an organization of internationalists and liberal Republicans to draft General Dwight D. Eisenhower for the Presidency. Ike hesitated, but he was persuaded by Lodge to allow his name and delegate slates to be entered in the New Hampshire primary. After Eisenhower defeated Taft in New Hampshire and polled 108,692 write-in votes in the Minnesota primary (narrowly won by Stassen as a favorite son) two weeks later, the General announced that he would resign as NATO Commander and seek the nomination actively.

Eisenhower went on to win primaries in New Jersey, Pennsylvania, Massachusetts, and Oregon. Taft recovered to win primaries in Wisconsin, Nebraska, Illinois, Ohio, West Virginia, and South Dakota. As the

Republican convention opened, Taft had a narrow lead in delegates over Eisenhower. Warren of California and Stassen, both liberal Republicans, held blocs of delegates as favorite sons.

The 1952 convention was almost a replay of 1912. Once again, conservative Republicans supporting a Taft for President controlled the Republican National Committee and the Rules and Credential committees of the convention. But this time, they did not have support from the Wall Street faction of the party, and more important, their candidate was not the incumbent President.

The strategy of the Eisenhower forces in 1952 was very similar to the strategy of the Roosevelt forces in 1912: Being a little short of delegates, they challenged the credentials of Taft delegates. Their focus was in the south, where conflicting delegations had been sent by Texas, Louisiana, and Georgia. In all three cases, the Credentials Committee had decided for Taft.

Once again, as in 1912, the Eisenhower forces proposed a "Fair Play" Amendment to the rules, requiring that challenged delegates whose credentials had not been approved by two-thirds of the Republican National Committee not be allowed to vote on roll calls until they had been approved on the floor. This amendment, if passed, would deprive Taft of the votes he needed in the credentials floor fights. The decisive test of strength took place when the Taft forces proposed a substitute, exempting seven Louisiana delegates from the rule. The Taft substitute was defeated, 658 to 548, and the Fair Play Amendment passed by a voice vote. The rules vote, which determined control of the convention, was decided when the delegates pledged to Warren of California and Stassen of Minnesota voted with the Eisenhower forces. The Eisenhower forces then won all the credentials contests. Prior to the rules and credentials floor fights, Taft had the lead in delegates and an overwhelming majority in the south; thereafter, Eisenhower had a slim majority in the south and was very close to a majority of all delegates.

Eisenhower almost won the Republican Presidential nomination on the first ballot, with 595 votes, just nine short of victory, to 500 for Taft. The Minnesota delegation switched its support to Eisenhower, putting him over the top. He was ultimately nominated with 845 votes.

The contest for the Republican Presidential nomination in 1952 revealed another approaching turning point in the politics of the GOP. The Wall Street faction had delivered yet another nomination, but this time only narrowly after a particularly bitter struggle. The fact that this victory was such a near thing, even with a candidate as strong as Dwight D. Eisenhower, indicated the vulnerability of the liberal wing of the party and the growing power of the conservatives. Moreover, the 1952 primaries and convention balloting established that the factional divisions within the Republican Party had reached a point of extreme ideological polarization. Ike swept the northeast, while Taft won eight of the eleven delegations from the south and most of the interior west. Indeed, had it not been for the rules and credentials floor fights, Taft would have swept the south. The bitterness and polarization of the 1952 struggle would linger, and set the stage for the conservative revolt against the party establishment in 1964. Tables 3.6 and 3.7 show the factional distribution of support for the candidates at the 1952 convention. The very high gamma on Table 3.7 illustrates the degree of polarization in the delegate vote.

The Eisenhower Administration

Elected twice, by landslides each time, Dwight D. Eisenhower was the only Republican President of the New Deal era. He was preferred by liberal Republicans because he was an internationalist, he could defeat Robert Taft, and he could be elected. But he had few strong commitments on domestic issues and was surprised to find, by his own assessment, that Taft was less conservative than he was.[18] At heart, Ike was a moderate. He did little either to reverse or advance the legacy of the New Deal. He did play a significant role in the growth of the federal government in the economy, with the passage of the Federal Highway Act in 1956. He appointed Earl Warren as Chief Justice of the United States, partly as a result of Warren's help on rules and credentials at the 1952 convention, and was not happy with the court's decisions in *Brown v. Board of Education* (1954 and 1955). But President Eisenhower believed in the rule of law, and he enforced *Brown* and *Cooper v. Aaron* (1958) by using federal troops to desegregate Little Rock High School.[19] He was aware of the role of his party as the party of Lincoln and was proud of his administration's support of the Civil Rights Acts of 1957 and 1960, moderate as they may have been.

Not an ideologue, President Eisenhower had a practical view of government. "The legitimate object of government," he said, quoting Abraham Lincoln, "is to do for a community of people whatever they need to have done, but cannot do at all, or cannot so well do, for themselves, in their separate and individual capacities."[20] The President called his philosophy "modern Republicanism," and liberal Republicans were perfectly comfortable with it.[21]

Yet President Eisenhower disappointed liberal Republicans by not taking a very active role in party affairs. Aside from deciding to run again after his heart attack at least partly because he could not find a suitable Republican candidate to take his place, Ike did little to advance the interests of "modern Republicans" within the party.

For example, Eisenhower did little to confront Senator Joseph R. McCarthy (R-Wisconsin), who was already engaged in his anti-Communist witch-hunt during the 1952 campaign. Although originally inclined not to, Eisenhower agreed to appear with McCarthy in Wisconsin during the 1952 campaign. It is not as if there was no Republican opposition to McCarthy for Ike to lead. Early on, Senator Margaret Chase Smith of Maine had circulated an anti-McCarthy petition, "Declaration of Conscience," among her liberal Republican colleagues in the Senate, several of whom signed it. But even as President, Eisenhower believed that public confrontation with McCarthy would enflame the situation. He therefore would not go beyond covert support for McCarthy opponents.[22]

The heir apparent to President Eisenhower was Vice President Richard M. Nixon, who had some appeal across the ideological spectrum of the Republican Party. For conservative Republicans, there was his rabid anti-Communism and fiscal conservatism; for liberal Republicans, there was his internationalism and support of the Civil Rights bills of 1957 and 1960, in addition to his early support for Eisenhower. Governor Nelson Rockefeller of New York, a liberal Republican, briefly explored running for President in 1960, but found party leaders united behind the Vice President, and announced that he would not seek the nomination.[23]

Nixon therefore had the Republican Presidential nomination clinched well before the 1960 convention, but the remaining factionalism was demonstrated by the protests he encountered both from liberals and from conservatives within the GOP. Governor Rockefeller was dissatisfied with the party platform and beckoned Nixon to meet with him. Nixon complied, and during the convention, flew in secret from Chicago to New York to meet with Rockefeller at his apartment on Fifth Avenue. The two agreed on platform planks for stronger national defense and vigorous federal policy in support of civil rights. Nixon then executed his agreement by imposing it on the platform committee at the convention, much to the chagrin of some conservative Republicans.[24]

In response to the "Compact of Fifth Avenue" between Nixon and Rockefeller, there was a brief movement among conservatives at the convention to nominate Senator Barry Goldwater of Arizona for the Presidency. When his name was placed in nomination, although without hope of beating Nixon, Goldwater promptly withdrew, admonishing his supporters: "Let's grow up conservatives! If we want to take this party back, and I think we can, some day, let's get to work!"[25]

It was a rallying cry that the conservative Republicans of Main Street would take to heart.

TABLES

Table 3.1
Roll Call Votes at 1912 Republican National Convention

TEMPORARY CHAIR OF THE CONVENTION

| | By 1964–1972 ideological classification of states | | | | | |
	liberal	moderate	conservative	Non-South	South	National
Root	**50**	41	**64**	43	**79**	**52**
McGovern	49	**58**	35	**56**	21	46

| | By delegation support for President | | |
	Roosevelt	Taft	National
Root	26	**84**	**52**
McGovern	**73**	16	46

TABLE RULES MINORITY REPORT

| | By 1964–1972 ideological classification of states | | | | | |
	liberal	moderate	conservative	Non-South	South	National
Yea	**51**	41	**65**	44	**78**	**53**
Nay	49	**59**	34	**56**	21	47

| | By delegation support for President | | |
	Roosevelt	Taft	National
Yea	25	**84**	**53**
Nay	**75**	15	47

REPUBLICAN PRESIDENTIAL NOMINATION

| | By 1964–1972 ideological classification of states | | | | | |
	liberal	moderate	conservative	Non-South	South	National
1st Ballot						
Taft	**48**	**36**	**61**	**39**	**83**	**52**
Roosevelt	8	21	4	15	1	10

Figures are percentages of delegate vote, by delegation, according to ideological alignment of states. The 1964–1972 ideological alignment of states, and the methodology, is explained in Chapter 1. The ideological alignment is initially used in Table 1.19.

Derived from *National Party Conventions, 1831–1996* (Washington, D.C.: Congressional Quarterly, 1997), p. 222.

Table 3.2
Balloting for President, 1912 Republican National Convention, by 1964–1972 Ideological Alignment of States

	Ideological Alignment of States, 1964–1972		
	liberal	*moderate*	*conservative*
Taft	Connecticut	Colorado	Alabama
	Massachusetts	Delaware	Arizona
	Michigan	Iowa	Arkansas
	New York	Kentucky	Florida
	Rhode Island	Montana	Georgia
	Washington	New Hampshire	Indiana
		Texas	Louisiana
		Vermont	Mississippi
			Nevada
			New Mexico
			South Carolina
			Tennessee
			Utah
			Virginia
			Wyoming
Roosevelt	Minnesota	California	Kansas
	Oregon	Illinois	Nebraska
	Pennsylvania	Maine	North Carolina
		Maryland	Oklahoma
		Missouri	
		New Jersey	
		Ohio	
		South Dakota	
		West Virginia	
LaFollette	Wisconsin		North Dakota
			Idaho

G = –.19

States sorted according to plurality vote on roll call for President. States with a plurality of delegates recorded as "present, not voting" are counted for Roosevelt. The 1964–1972 ideological alignment of states, and the methodology, is explained in Chapter 1. The ideological alignment is initially used in Table 1.19. Derived from *National Party Conventions*, p. 222.

Table 3.3
Delegate Vote for Republican Presidential Nomination,
1920 Convention

	By 1964–1972 ideological classification of states					
	liberal	moderate	conservative	Non-South	South	National
1st Ballot						
Wood	**15**	**31**	**43**	**27**	**37**	**29**
Lowden	6	31	28	19	32	21
Johnson	13	15	14	15	5	14
9th Ballot						
Wood	19	25	32	26	22	25
Lowden	5	19	13	12	16	12
Harding	**25**	**38**	**52**	**33**	**61**	**38**
10th Ballot						
Wood	20	18	17	20	10	18
Harding	**62**	**61**	**75**	**61**	**89**	**66**

	By First Ballot Vote for President				
	Johnson	Wood	Lowden	Other	National
10th Ballot					
Harding	**40**	44	**79**	**76**	**66**
Wood	10	**48**	4	12	18

Figures are percentages of delegate vote, by delegation, according to 1964–1972
ideological alignment of states. The 1964–1972 ideological alignment of states,
and the methodology, is explained in Chapter 1. The ideological alignment is
initially used in Table 1.19.
Derived from *National Party Conventions*, p. 226.

Table 3.4
Delegate Vote for Republican Presidential Nomination, 1940 Convention

	By 1964–1972 ideological classification of states					
	liberal	moderate	conservative	Non-South	South	National
1st Ballot						
Dewey	**31**	**35**	**43**	**36**	35	**36**
Taft	3	29	23	13	**44**	19
Willkie	11	11	10	11	7	11
5th Ballot						
Taft	33	**51**	**48**	33	**61**	38
Willkie	**46**	37	48	**45**	34	**43**
6th Ballot						
Taft	12	**50**	37	28	**58**	32
Willkie	**85**	48	**61**	**69**	40	**66**

Figures are percentages of delegate vote, by delegation, according to 1964–1972 ideological alignment of states. The 1964–1972 ideological alignment of states, and the methodology, is explained in Chapter 1. The ideological alignment is initially used in Table 1.19.
Derived from *National Party Conventions*, p. 234.

Table 3.5
Delegate Vote for Republican Presidential Nomination, 1948 Convention

	By 1964–1972 ideological classification of states					
	liberal	moderate	conservative	Non-South	South	National
1st Ballot						
Dewey	**51**	20	**53**	**40**	37	**40**
Taft	9	**28**	23	15	**44**	20
Stassen	13	15	15	16	6	14
2nd Ballot						
Dewey	**52**	33	**58**	**48**	41	**47**
Taft	11	**37**	26	20	**49**	25
Stassen	13	14	14	15	7	14

Figures are percentages of delegate vote, by delegation, according to 1964–1972 ideological alignment of states. The 1964–1972 ideological alignment of states, and the methodology, is explained in Chapter 1. The ideological alignment is initially used in Table 1.19.
Derived from *National Party Conventions*, p. 237.

Table 3.6
Roll Call Votes, 1952 Republican National Convention

TAFT SUBSTITUTE TO FAIR PLAY AMENDMENT TO THE RULES

	By 1964–1972 ideological classification of states					
	liberal	moderate	conservative	Non-South	South	National
Yea	14	48	75	39	75	45
Nay	86	52	25	61	25	55
	By delegation support for President			
	Eisenhower	Other	Taft	National
Yea	12	37	85	45
Nay	88	63	15	55

REPUBLICAN PRESIDENTIAL NOMINATION

	By 1964–1972 ideological classification of states					
	liberal	moderate	conservative	Non-South	South	National
Eisenhower	76	39	36	50	51	49
Taft	17	47	61	40	48	41

Figures are percentages of delegate vote, by delegation, according to 1964–1972
ideological alignment of states. The 1964–1972 ideological alignment of states,
and the methodology, is explained in Chapter 1. The ideological alignment is
initially used in Table 1.19.
Derived from *National Party Conventions*, p. 239.

Table 3.7

Balloting for President, 1952 Republican National Convention, by 1964–1972 Ideological Alignment of States

	Ideological Alignment of States, 1952		
	liberal	*moderate*	*conservative*
Eisenhower	Connecticut	Colorado	Georgia
	Massachusetts	Delaware	Kansas
	Michigan	Iowa	Louisiana
	New York	Maine	
	Oregon	Maryland	
	Pennsylvania	Missouri	
	Rhode Island	New Hampshire	
	Washington	New Jersey	
		Texas	
		Vermont	
Taft	Wisconsin	Illinois	Alabama
		Kentucky	Arizona
		Montana	Arkansas
		Ohio	Florida
		South Dakota	Idaho
		West Virginia	Indiana
			Mississippi
			Nebraska
			Nevada
			New Mexico
			North Carolina
			North Dakota
			Oklahoma
			South Carolina
			Tennessee
			Utah
			Virginia
			Wyoming
Favorite Sons	Minnesota	California	

G = .83

States sorted according to vote of plurality of delegates for President. The 1964–1972 ideological alignment of states, and the methodology, is explained in Chapter 1. The ideological alignment is initially used in Table 1.19.
Derived from *National Party Conventions*, p. 239.

NOTES

1. See Nelson Polsby, "Coalition and Faction in American Politics: An Institutional View," in Seymour Martin Lipset, ed., *Emerging Coalitions in American Politics* (San Francisco: Institute for Contemporary Studies, 1978), pp. 103–123.

2. See Stephen Skowronek, *The Politics Presidents Make: Leadership from John Adams to Bill Clinton* (Cambridge: Harvard University Press, 1997), pp. 227–259. See also H. W. Brands, *T.R.: The Last Romantic* (New York: Basic Books, 1997), pp. 417–637; and Samuel and Dorothy Rosenman, *Presidential Style: Some Giants and a Pygmy in the White House* (New York: Harper and Row, 1976), pp. 1–123.

3. For the classic discussion of the executive and legislative wings of the Democratic and Republican parties, see James MacGregor Burns, *The Deadlock of Democracy: Four Party Politics in America* (Englewood Cliffs, N.J.: Prentice Hall, 1967).

4. Unless otherwise noted, all data on Presidential primaries is drawn from *Presidential Elections, 1789–1996* (Washington, D.C.: Congressional Quarterly, 1997). Convention data is drawn or derived from *National Party Conventions, 1831–1996* (Washington, D.C.: Congressional Quarterly, 1997). Discussion of conventions is drawn from *National Party Conventions* and from Richard C. Bain and Judith H. Parris, *Convention Decisions and Voting Records* (Washington, D.C.: Brookings Institution, 1973).

5. For an interesting account of the concurrent 1916 Republican and Progressive conventions, see William Draper Lewis, *The Life of Theodore Roosevelt* (United Publishers, 1919). Lewis's book is a generally admiring biography of the late President, published just after Roosevelt's death, but its account is consistent with the record of the conventions. See also *National Party Conventions*, pp. 72–73.

6. Steve Neal, *Dark Horse: A Biography of Wendell Willkie* (Lawrence, Kans.: University Press of Kansas, 1989), p. 58.

7. Most of the discussion of the Willkie campaign is drawn from Neal, pp. 45–180, and from Ellsworth Barnard, *Wendell Willkie: Fighter for Freedom* (Marquette, Mich.: Northern Michigan University Press, 1966), pp. 142–268. See also Herbert S. Parmet and Marie B. Hecht, *Never Again: A President Runs for a Third Term* (New York: Macmillan, 1968).

8. Neal, pp. 78 and 108.

9. See Wendell L. Willkie, *One World* (New York: Simon and Schuster, 1943) and Willkie, *An American Program* (New York: Simon and Schuster, 1944).

10. Neal, *Dark Horse*, pp. 267–270. The case was *Schneiderman v. U.S.* 320 U.S. 118 (1943).

11. Ibid., p. 273.

12. Ibid., p. 275.

13. Ibid., p. 291.

14. Ibid., p. 290.

15. Ibid., p. 284. See also Barnard, pp. 406–421.

16. See Neal, pp. 308–324, and Barnard, pp. 470–503.

17. William R. Keech and Donald R. Matthews, *The Party's Choice* (Washington, D.C.: Brookings Institution, 1977), pp. 172–177.

18. See Dwight D. Eisenhower, *Mandate for Change* (New York: Doubleday, 1965), pp. 218–222.

19. See *Brown v. Board of Education* 347 U.S. 483 (1954); *Brown v. Board of Education II* 349 U.S. 294; and *Cooper v. Aaron* 357 U.S. 566 (1958). See also Dwight D.

Eisenhower, *Waging Peace* (New York: Doubleday, 1965), pp. 148–176, for a discussion of President Eisenhower's attitudes toward civil rights and school desegregation.

20. Robert J. Donovan, *Eisenhower: The Inside Story* (New York: Harper Brothers, 1956), pp. 207–208.

21. Eisenhower, *Waging Peace*, p. 375.

22. For an excellent account on Eisenhower and McCarthy, see Stephen E. Ambrose, *Eisenhower the President* (New York: Simon and Schuster, 1984) pp. 58–66. See also Fred I. Greenstein, *The Hidden Hand Presidency: Eisenhower as Leader* (New York: Basic Books, 1982), pp. 155–227. On Margaret Chase Smith and the "Declaration of Conscience," see William S. White, "Seven GOP Senators Decry 'Smear' Tactics of McCarthy," *New York Times*, June 2, 1950. See also Margaret Chase Smith, *Declaration of Conscience*, William C. Lewis, ed. (New York: Doubleday, 1972), and Patricia Ward Wallace, *The Politics of Conscience* (Westport, Conn.: Praeger, 1995).

23. Keech and Matthews, pp. 48–49.

24. For the best reporting on the "Compact of Fifth Avenue," see Theodore H. White, *The Making of the President 1960* (New York: Atheneum, 1961), pp. 180–212.

25. *National Party Conventions*, p. 105.

Ideological Polarization and Party Change: Realignment of the Factional Systems, 1964–1972

4

The umbrellas of both major parties have historically covered the ideological spectrum, providing shelter for both the multifactional system of the Democratic Party and the two-faction system of the Republican Party. The result, until the 1960s, was two parties that were ideologically almost indistinguishable. The Democrats, with a working-class appeal, were somewhat more progressive on economic issues; but given the electoral strength and veto power of the Solid South, the Democrats were also somewhat more conservative on cultural issues, particularly race. The post-Reconstruction system of white supremacy in the south was authored by southern Democrats, but it was maintained by Democrats everywhere in the interest of preserving their tenuous national coalition. The Republicans, on the other hand, had a greater upper-class and middle-class bias, and were more conservative on economic issues. At the same time, as the party of Lincoln without the presence of an autonomous southern faction, the Republicans were generally more liberal on cultural issues, particularly race, again until the 1960s.

Multifactionalism is at least as important a cornerstone to American electoral politics as is the two-party system. Moreover, partisan realignment seems to be as much the result of what happens among factions within political parties as it is electoral change in coalitions between the parties. The internal dynamics of the minority party is particularly important.[1] The presence of incumbents generally discourages or marginalizes factional conflict in the majority party, and party elites in the majority party seek to maintain an electoral environment that has delivered victory at the polls.[2] But party and factional elites in the minority party, once they understand that they are the minority, seek to build new electoral coalitions that might produce victory. Factional conflict, then, develops in the minority party over clashing interests, ideology, and differences over electoral strategy.

The resolutions of factional conflicts in the Democratic Party, leading to the nomination of William Jennings Bryan for the Presidency in 1896, and the nomination of Alfred E. Smith in 1928 followed by the election of Franklin D. Roosevelt in 1932, both contributed to critical realignments. In much the same manner, so did the nominations of Republican Barry Goldwater in 1964 and Democrat George McGovern in 1972. Indeed, in the 1964–1972 period, the nearly simultaneous resolution of factional struggles in both parties produced the most profound electoral realignment in American history and fundamentally altered the two-party system.

IDEOLOGICAL POLARIZATION AND THE BIRTH OF THE SIXTH AMERICAN PARTY SYSTEM

The current electoral era emerged in the 1964–1972 period, defined by ideological polarization between the parties unprecedented since mass political parties developed in the United States in the 1830s. The two-party system remains, with both major parties still as anchored as ever in the Lockean liberalism of American political culture.

In that sense, American political parties still do not offer the range of ideological choice that might be found in parliamentary democracies. But the decentralized, patronage-oriented, umbrella parties born in the nineteenth century have declined, as has been so widely noted by political scientists, journalists, and other observers of American politics. This decline, however, has not been a matter of linear decay; rather it has been a matter of institutional change that may yet come to be understood as revival. The new parties being born toward the end of the twentieth century are more nationalized and issue-oriented than the parties that were born in the nineteenth century. They remain umbrella parties that aggregate interests; but the umbrellas of the two parties no longer overlap ideologically as they did until the 1960s. Each party umbrella covers interests that, taken together, are more homogeneous ideologically.

Thus, the new parties are very different parties, both structurally and functionally, than the old parties. First, the new parties articulate interests as much as they aggregate interests, perhaps even more so. Party decay theorists were quite right to point out the growing power of special interest groups in American politics, but increasingly they operate within one of the major political parties rather than in both parties or outside the parties. Certainly, the interests of large corporations operate within both parties, as would seem inevitable in a Lockean liberal political culture and a democratic capitalist political economy. But most other interests operate, at least for election campaigns, within one party or the other. Interests considered to be "liberal," such as labor, civil rights, abortion rights, and environmentalism, fit more comfortably under the Democratic umbrella; interests considered to be "conservative," such as the gun lobby, opponents of affirmative action, and the Christian right, are associated with the Republicans. There are exceptions to the rule. There is still a small pro-choice Republican presence, for example, but an equally small pro-life presence in the Democratic Party. But the generalization holds true, particularly for single-issue special interests.[3]

Issue activists have gained power over nominations in both parties. The Goldwater movement was populated not only, or even primarily, by the conservative Republicans who had supported Robert Taft but by self-identified ideologues and issue activists of the right.[4] Democratic Party reforms then opened up first the Democratic Party, and more slowly through legislation, the Republican Party to the power of issue activists in determining nominations. To a large extent, these issue activists not only supplemented but replaced party leaders in the nominating process. Where patronage-oriented party leaders were often motivated by a Downsian rationality to move to the center to win elections, nomination activists in both parties often placed their salient issues ahead of winning elections. The strategy for issue activists was first to take over the party, as Goldwater and his supporters did, then build a winning strategy, in that order.

In the issue-oriented party, nomination activists and convention delegates are much more ideologically extreme than the general electorate, and even more extreme than party identifiers of their own party.[5]

The nationalization of communications media, the nationalization of a policy agenda, and ideological polarization have combined to nationalize the parties. As national interest groups and activists became stronger, state and local party leaders and their organizations became weaker. Party reforms promoted national fundraising for candidates, whose sources of support increasingly became the single-issue interest groups rather than the party. As conservative Republicans and liberal Democrats each gained power over nominations nationally, that power filtered to the state and local levels. Whereas there were once liberals and conservatives in both parties, with similar regional coalitions within both parties, Democrats now tend to be more liberal than Republicans everywhere in the country, while Republicans generally are everywhere more conservative.

It is because of this nationalization combined with ideological polarization that in 1994, the Republicans could run a national campaign based on a national and ideologically conservative agenda, the "Contract with America." Furthermore, party loyalty votes are now much more common in Congress than prior to 1964, and the conservative coalition emerges on Congressional roll calls much less frequently.[6]

Of course, the emergence of nationalized, issue-oriented parties did not occur overnight, even after the initial ideological polarization of Presidential nominations in 1964 and 1972. Thus, "realignment at the top, dealignment at the bottom" contributed to a radical increase in split-ticket voting and divided government.[7] Chapter 7 addresses split-ticket voting, divided government, and the Presidential and Congressional parties since 1964.

The balance of this chapter addresses the Presidential nominations of the 1964–1972 period as they contributed to realignment and the new party system.

IDEOLOGICAL POLARIZATION: THE REPUBLICANS

The very narrowness of his defeat for the Presidency in 1960 exposed Richard M. Nixon to second-guessers from every corner of the Republican party, instead of gaining him credit for a close race well run. According to liberal Republicans, Nixon could have carried Illinois, Pennsylvania, New Jersey, and Michigan, more than enough to win the election, if only he had more vigorously endorsed civil rights. But conservative Republicans answered that by endorsing states' rights and a reversal of the growth of the welfare state, Nixon could have carried the south and won the election. The debate within the Republican Party was more than a discussion of strategy of course; it was a conflict over ideology that would split the party in 1964 and alter its direction thereafter.[8]

The outcome of lasting importance from the 1964 Presidential election is not that President Johnson was elected, or that Senator Barry Goldwater of Arizona was defeated by a landslide, but that the Goldwater movement took over the Republican Party from the ground up.

From the time F. Clifton White assembled a dozen friends in Chicago in 1961 to plot a coup for 1964, to the party's national convention three years later, conservative Republicans gave an exhibition of an ideologically based citizen activism that would become the norm in the internal politics of both parties in years to come. Over the next two years, White and his coconspirators recruited allies down to the state and local levels who put together an organization from the grass roots up. By the end of 1963, they could cite two accomplishments, one of which was pure luck, the other of which was the result of hard work. First, as the election year 1964 began, Senator Goldwater had emerged as the front-runner for the Republican Presidential nomination, largely because his leading potential opponents had nearly self-destructed. Nixon had been defeated in a bid to unseat Governor Edmund G. Brown of California in 1962, apparently ending his political career with his "last press conference." And Governor Nelson Rockefeller of New York, who had emerged as the front-runner with the demise of Nixon, had divorced and remarried, and then watched his support among Republican voters deflate. But more important was the fact that the Goldwater movement was on the ground, ready to, in Goldwater's words, "take this party back."

And that is what they did.[9] Their organization at the grass roots was such an effective guerilla operation that no one, not even the leaders of the Republican Party, knew what was going on until it was too late to stop it. At least until after the California primary, most moderate-to-liberal Republicans remained confident that Goldwater was too conservative to be nominated, not to mention elected, and that he would be stopped at the convention. Their confidence was encouraged when Henry Cabot Lodge won the New Hampshire primary on a write-in vote. Goldwater won primaries in Illinois, Indiana, and Nebraska, with unimpressive showings against token opposition. Then, in a surprise, Governor Rockefeller won the Oregon primary, with Goldwater finishing a poor third, behind Lodge.

But moderate-to-liberal Republicans realized only too late that Goldwater already had the delegates to be nominated.[10] The Goldwater activists were not playing what was, before 1964, the normal preconvention game, in which supporters of a candidate would lobby party leaders for endorsements and then allow the leaders to deliver the delegates. Instead, while Goldwater was only holding his own in the primaries, his supporters were taking over the party in the states selecting delegates by convention. Having won in the precinct caucuses, the Goldwater activists then won most or all of the delegates at county conventions and Republican state conventions. Party leaders who would not support Goldwater were simply removed in the process. In many cases, it was not until state conventions met that party leaders recognized that they had lost control of the state party apparatus and the delegation to the national convention.

After the Oregon primary, Goldwater could only be stopped if Rockefeller beat him in California, and perhaps not even then. When Goldwater won the California primary, he clinched the nomination. Rockefeller withdrew and backed an eleventh hour stop-Goldwater drive led by Governor William W. Scranton of Pennsylvania. But Scranton never had a chance. The Republican National Convention of 1964 was actually a coronation of Barry Goldwater as the party's nominee for President, much as party conventions would generally become in later years.

Nevertheless, the Republican National Convention was a battle ground, even if the nomination was predetermined, and the factional divisions of that convention illustrate what became a persistent shift in control of the Republican Party to its conservatives. As with the Democrats at the 1948 convention, the key issue at the turning point was not only the Presidential nomination itself but the battle over the civil rights issue in the party platform.

The platform plank on civil rights, presented by a platform committee controlled by Goldwater supporters, promised "full implementation and faithful execution" of the Civil Rights Act of 1964, but liberal Republicans proposed an amendment that went further. Presented by Senator Hugh Scott of Pennsylvania, the amendment promised increased personnel for the Justice Department Civil Rights Division, strict requirements for school desegregation, equal protection for voting rights in state as well as federal elections, and elimination of racial discrimination in hiring.[11]

The stop-Goldwater forces were hoping to use the civil rights issue to generate national sympathy for their cause, which would pressure delegates to vote not only for a strong civil rights plank but also for Scranton for President, in the hope of a Republican victory in the general election. What they did not understand was that the Goldwater delegates were conservatives first and Republicans second; they would not desert Goldwater even if they were persuaded that he would lose the election. The convention voted against the minority report on civil rights by 897 to 409.[12] Support for the minority report was concentrated in the northeast and among delegates pledged to Scranton or Rockefeller. Goldwater delegates voted uniformly against the minority proposal.[13] The convention also defeated a platform minority report, presented by stop-Goldwater forces, to condemn extremist groups like the Ku Klux Klan and the John Birch Society. The debate and vote were reminiscent of the unsuccessful effort to condemn the Klan at the long 1924 Democratic National Convention.

The voting for President on the first ballot, a foregone conclusion, reflected the outcome of the platform floor fights: 883 for Goldwater, 214 for Scranton, 114 for Rockefeller, and 97 scattering. Every state that cast a majority of its vote for Goldwater voted against the minority report for civil rights, except for Delaware. Without exception, every state that voted against Goldwater voted for the minority report. Table 4.1 shows the strong relationship between the balloting on civil rights and the Presidential ballot. Table 4.2 illustrates the ideological divide within the Republican Party at the 1964 convention, using the alignment of states between parties in the 1964–1972 Presidential elections. Every state classified as "conservative" according to its vote for the Republicans or George Wallace in the 1964–1972 Presidential elections was for Goldwater at the Republican convention. All eleven states of the old Confederacy voted for Goldwater. Eight of the ten most liberal states according to the same electoral classification voted against Goldwater at the convention.

The southern strategy did not win Goldwater the election, of course, but the five states he carried, other than his home state of Arizona, were all in the deep south. For conservative Republicans, the southern strategy remained a potentially viable route to the Presidency. They had completed the task of taking their party back; now they had to nominate a candidate who could be elected.

The New Nixon

That candidate turned out to be Richard M. Nixon. Nixon had originally run for President in 1960 as a moderate Republican, the heir apparent to President Eisenhower. But he understood after 1964 that there had been a realignment within the party and that the nominating coalition would be a conservative one in 1968.[14]

Understanding that conservative Republicans had taken over the party, Nixon appealed to them as the candidate who could retain control of the party for them and, at the same time, win the next election. Though some southern party leaders, like Republican State Chairman Clarke Reed of Mississippi, wished to remain uncommitted until the convention, others, such as Senator J. Strom Thurmond of South Carolina, endorsed Nixon early. Thurmond was particularly important, because he was the Democrat who had led the Dixiecrat revolt of 1948, before coming over to the Republican Party to support Goldwater in 1964. Even more important for Nixon, Goldwater endorsed his nomination well in advance of the 1968 election year.[15]

Nixon swept the contested Republican primaries against what turned out to be token opposition and went to the convention as the front-runner. Governor Rockefeller, entering the race late, was the candidate of liberal Republicans at the convention. Governor Ronald Reagan of California did not announce his candidacy until the convention. Rockefeller had more delegates, but Reagan, as the most conservative Republican, presented the greater danger to Nixon. While Rockefeller and Reagan agreed to work together in an effort to stop Nixon, the front-runner visited southern delegations, where Reagan was an ideological favorite, and promised a conservative administration, particularly with the appointment of "strict constructionists" to the Federal courts. Senator Thurmond was a particularly useful ally at the convention, cajoling southern Republicans to back Nixon as the candidate who could be elected. Southern delegates could hardly question the credibility of Strom Thurmond, the leader of the 1948 Dixiecrat revolt, as a supporter of states' rights against civil rights.[16]

It was enough—barely. Nixon was nominated on the first ballot with 692 delegate votes, to 277 for Rockefeller, 182 for Reagan, and 182 scattering. Table 4.3 illustrates the nominating coalition of states at the 1968 Republican convention. The negative gamma indicates that the coalition for Nixon was a conservative one, although its lower value indicates accurately that Nixon was stronger among moderate Republicans than Goldwater had been. Six delegations voted against Goldwater in 1964 but for Nixon in 1968: Alaska, D.C., Maryland, New Hampshire, Oregon, and Vermont. But the differences in the nominating coalitions between 1964 and 1968 are more apparent than real, as the presence of both Nixon and Reagan divided the votes of conservative Republicans in 1968. The factional divisions in the party were nevertheless almost exactly the same in 1968 as they had been in 1964. The vote for Nixon and Reagan combined was virtually the same in size and distribution as the vote for Goldwater in 1964. Nixon won about 63 percent in the states that had supported Goldwater at the 1964 convention, compared with his 52 percent of the national total, and Reagan won all of his delegates in those states. (See Table 4.4.) In all, twenty-seven of the thirty-three states that cast at least a plurality of their votes for Goldwater at the 1964 convention voted for Nixon at the 1968 convention, and two of those states voted for Reagan. All the delegations that voted for Rockefeller in 1968 were from states that had voted for Scranton or Rockefeller in 1964. Historic coalitions of states also remained intact. The states that voted for Goldwater in 1964 and Nixon or Reagan in 1968 were disproportionately from the south and interior west. The states that voted for Scranton or Rockefeller in 1964 and for Rockefeller in 1968 were all located in the northeast.

The Republican convention of 1964, then, had been no accident. Nominating a mainstream candidate in 1968, conservative Republicans nevertheless retained control of the party and elected a President.

IDEOLOGICAL POLARIZATION: THE DEMOCRATS

The Democratic Party was taken over by its liberals during the New Deal period, with the crucial turning point coming when a progressive civil rights program was endorsed at the 1948 convention. For Democrats outside the south, the successful fight to pass the Civil Rights Act of 1964 made civil rights a matter of consensus rather than conflict. What remained, between 1964 and 1972, was a showdown between the party's liberal factions: the party regulars versus the reformers. The regulars were party loyalists first, products of party organizations in large cities, with a labor and working-class electoral base. The reformers, ideologues when compared with the regulars, were issue activists who generally placed policy ahead of party. Their electoral base was younger, more highly educated, and more middle class. Whereas the liberal Democrats of both factions could be united on economic issues and civil rights, the party regulars and reformers had long been divided over political reform and power within the party. That divide was magnified when the Vietnam War split the Democratic Party as it did the country.

The war in Vietnam led, in 1968, to the most serious challenge to the renomination of a sitting President since 1912. When Senator Eugene McCarthy of Minnesota announced that he would enter several primaries against President Johnson, few took his quixotic campaign seriously. Anti-war liberal Democrats hoped, instead, that Senator Robert F. Kennedy of New York would carry their banner against the President. But Kennedy was persuaded that such a challenge would split the party beyond repair, and that the result would be the election of Richard Nixon to the Presidency. He announced repeatedly that he would not be a candidate.[17]

But 1968 would not be an orderly or predictable election year. The Tet Offensive in Vietnam, the decision of President Johnson not to run again, and the assassinations of Martin Luther King and Robert Kennedy made 1968 a year in which traumatic events exposed underlying social crises. These events not only reshaped the electoral environment of 1968, they contributed to building the electoral environment that persists to this day.

Even after the Tet Offensive, the McCarthy challenge was not taken seriously until the results of the New Hampshire primary were known. President Johnson, not on the ballot, won the Presidential Preference primary with 50 percent of the vote, but McCarthy polled an impressive 42 percent, and won twenty out of twenty-four elected delegates.

The result pulled Robert F. Kennedy into the race for the Democratic Presidential nomination and may have had a hand in pushing President Johnson out. Thereafter, the Democratic primaries of 1968 were contests almost entirely between anti-war candidates, McCarthy and Kennedy. Vice President Hubert H. Humphrey, the candidate of the Johnson administration, announced his candidacy too late to enter the primaries.

Kennedy and McCarthy, then, battled through the remaining primaries almost head-on. When Kennedy won the California primary, hope that he could win the nomination lasted literally a few minutes, until he was shot and fatally wounded by an assassin after proclaiming his victory in Los Angeles.

Taken together, the factional structure of the Democratic Party and the delegate selection process of the time explain why Robert F. Kennedy might have won the nomination, whereas McCarthy had no chance at the convention. Both of the anti-war candidates did respectably in the primaries. McCarthy won in Wisconsin, Pennsylvania, Massachusetts, Oregon, and, after Kennedy's death, in New York; Kennedy won in the District of Columbia, Indiana, Nebraska, South Dakota, and California. But in 1968, only fifteen states and D.C. held Presidential primaries, about the same number of states as had been holding primaries for decades before that time. And there was a contest for delegates between national candidates in only eight states. In the other seven states, delegates sponsored by state parties running uncommitted or pledged to favorite sons won most of the convention seats. Even in Pennsylvania, where McCarthy polled 72 percent of the Presidential Preference vote, the Democratic State Committee, which had already endorsed President Johnson, sponsored officially uncommitted delegates, who won a majority of the seats, and would vote for Humphrey at the convention.

In 1968, then, a candidate could not yet secure the nomination, even by winning all of the primaries, much as Estes Kefauver had discovered in 1952. It was still a matter of winning primaries to persuade party leaders to nominate the candidate at the convention, as John F. Kennedy had done in 1960. This, McCarthy had no chance of doing, and Robert Kennedy might have done in 1968.

Eugene McCarthy was a reform liberal of intellectual style and middle-class appeal. Outside Minnesota, where McCarthy had long been a political ally of Hubert Humphrey in the Democratic-Farmer Labor Party (DFL), he had no strong party connections; his was a single-issue-movement candidacy.

Robert F. Kennedy, however, was a liberal Democrat with leadership credentials in both the regular and reform factions of the party. He appealed to working-class voters and union members, as well as reform activists; to racial minorities as well as whites. He was an anti-war candidate well connected to the party machinery. Indeed, his younger, more ideological supporters referred to Kennedy the anti-war activist and Kennedy the party leader as the "good Bobby" and the "bad Bobby" respectively. Because he represented a bridge between the liberal factions of the party, however, Kennedy's supporters had reason to believe that he could be nominated at the convention.[18]

Even so, it is hardly likely that Robert F. Kennedy would have been the Democratic nominee in 1968. The Johnson administration was solid behind Vice President Humphrey, who thus had the support of party leaders in most states. And in 1968 it was still party leaders who delivered delegates. Even before Kennedy died, and even projecting a Kennedy victory in California, Humphrey was the front-runner, although he had entered no primaries. Put in terms of party factionalism, Humphrey had the support of the party regulars and the south, while the anti-war opposition was found almost entirely within the party's reform faction. It was the south in particular that President Johnson could hold over his Vice President's head to get Humphrey to restrain himself from making concessions he may even have wanted to make to the anti-war delegates.

If Kennedy were to have been nominated, he would have had to win over most of the party regulars. Specifically, he would have had to persuade Mayor Richard J. Daley of Chicago to abandon the Johnson-Humphrey administration at the convention by endorsing him. In such an event, delegates who were officially uncommitted or pledged to favorite sons, but otherwise headed for voting for Humphrey, might have instead jumped on a Kennedy bandwagon. These delegates, mostly party regulars and moderate liberals, would have to be found, if at all, predominantly in the large urban states of the north, such as New Jersey, Pennsylvania, Ohio, Michigan, and Illinois. It was a long shot, at best.

After Robert Kennedy died, this was the scenario that lay behind the "Ted" offensive for Senator Edward M. Kennedy of Massachusetts, which incubated briefly at the convention, apparently with covert and tentative support from Daley. The "Ted" offensive even achieved an offer of support from McCarthy, but it wasn't enough. Uncertainty over whether Ted Kennedy would run, and even more doubt about the possibility of winning control of the convention from Johnson and Humphrey, led Daley to second guess the idea and stay with Humphrey.[19]

In any case, Vice President Humphrey was nominated on the first ballot. Despite the deep divisions apparent within the party, and the confrontations inside and outside the convention hall in Chicago, Humphrey won a majority of delegates from across the ideological spectrum of the party, including a majority from the most-liberal delegations. The factional divisions in the party are much better illustrated by the roll call votes on credentials and on the minority report opposed to the Johnson administration on the Vietnam War than by the vote on the

Democratic Presidential nomination itself. All four roll calls are structured by ideology, and much more, split according to candidate support. On all of the platform and credentials roll calls, the McCarthy delegates voted overwhelmingly for the minority reports and challengers, and the Humphrey delegates overwhelmingly for the committee report and regular delegates.

The most lasting accomplishment by the reformers at the 1968 convention, in terms of Democratic nominating politics, was the abolition of the unit rule, a long-standing rule that allowed state delegations to mandate a unanimous vote in favor of the majority position. On the unit-rule issue, the party was more united than on the other issues, and liberal Democrats carried the day, because Humphrey released his delegates to vote their conscience. A substantial number of Humphrey delegates joined the McCarthy delegates in voting for the motion. See Table 4.5 for a breakdown of the 1968 convention roll calls.

Reform and the New Democratic Party

The abolition of the unit rule set the stage for the establishment of the McGovern-Fraser Reform Commission, authorized by the 1968 convention to set rules for delegate selection to future Democratic national conventions. The appointment of its leadership and membership demonstrated the power of reform liberal Democrats in setting the new rules. Humphrey, as the titular leader of the Democratic Party, appointed Senator Fred Harris of Oklahoma, a self-proclaimed liberal ideologue, as the Democratic National Chairman in 1969. Harris, with Humphrey's approval, appointed Senator George McGovern of South Dakota, an anti-war liberal Democrat and long-time Humphrey friend, to chair the commission. When McGovern resigned from the commission to run for President, he was replaced by Representative Donald M. Fraser of Minnesota, a Humphrey protégé and a decidedly liberal Democrat who was one of the rising stars of the DFL. It was as if Humphrey was attempting to retrieve his liberal soul by approving reformers to lead the party and its reform process.[20]

The McGovern-Fraser Commission would produce rules that would directly shape the nominating politics of 1972 and beyond, and along with subsequent reform commissions, shape the modern national Democratic Party as it stands at the turn of the twenty-first century. Indeed, once they were used as models for state legislation on delegate selection influencing both parties, the McGovern-Fraser reforms would play a central role displacing the party-centered nomination process with a candidate-centered nomination process.[21]

The central principles of the McGovern-Fraser reforms were openness and proportional representation. The delegate selection process would have to be open and public; no longer could a governor or a party committee appoint delegates well in advance of the election year. Instead, the selection process must be based on public participation in a timely manner, during the election year. Candidates would be awarded delegates in proportion to their share of support from Democratic voters, so long as they qualified by meeting a threshold of at least 15 percent of the vote. Finally, there would also be proportional representation for demographic groups by race, sex, and age—an affirmative action program for delegates.[22]

The immediate result of the reforms was the beginning of the proliferation of primaries. State parties and legislatures would find it easiest to comply with participation rules by passing primary laws. In 1972, twenty-two Democratic Presidential primaries would be conducted, compared to sixteen in 1968; 65 percent of the delegates would be selected in primaries, up from 40 percent in 1968.[23] Thus, a strategy for winning nominations without running in primaries, as Hubert Humphrey did in 1968, was no longer very viable.

More important, for the time being, would be the delegate selection processes of non–primary states. Previously, party leaders controlled delegate selection tightly in most non–primary states. Starting in 1972, local caucuses in convention states would be public, participatory, and candidate-centered.

The leading beneficiary of the reforms was George McGovern, not only because they opened the process to issue activists where they were previously limited or excluded, but also because of the usefulness of his knowledge of the rules in plotting a campaign strategy. McGovern understood better than his rivals the necessity of organizing early and from the grass roots up, and in a system of proportional representation, of competing for delegates everywhere.[24]

Organized early from the ground up by issue activists, the McGovern campaign became the vehicle by which liberal ideologues would take over the Democratic Party. The McGovern campaign was to the Democratic Party in 1972 what the Goldwater campaign had been to the Republican Party in 1964.

The candidates of the Democratic Party establishment in 1972, Senator Humphrey and Senator Edmund S. Muskie of Maine, found themselves in much the same position as Rockefeller and Scranton in the Republican campaign of 1964. Both were organized from the top down, counting on historically reliable avenues of party support for the nomination.

Muskie understood the importance of running everywhere, but because he had little grass-roots organization, he spread his resources too thin. He counted on an impressive array of endorsements from moderate-to-liberal Democrats across the country to deliver delegates. Specifically, he counted on and received endorsements from Senator Harold E. Hughes of Iowa to win the precinct caucuses there; and from Senator Adlai Stevenson of Illinois, Governor John Gilligan of Ohio, and Governor Milton Shapp of Pennsylvania to win primaries in those states. It was a strategy that could work as long as the Muskie bandwagon appeared to be the safe place to be. And so it appeared as the election year opened. The Gallup Poll listed Muskie as the front-runner, with the support of 32 percent of Democrats nationally, to 27 percent for noncandidate Ted Kennedy, 17 percent for Humphrey, and 3 percent for McGovern.[25]

But with McGovern organized at the grass roots and Humphrey waiting to pick up the pieces, Muskie could not afford to stumble—which, of course, he did. In the New Hampshire primary, where Muskie was expected to win big, he won with only 46 percent of the vote, to 37 percent for McGovern. In Florida, where Governor George C. Wallace of Alabama won with 42 percent of the vote, Humphrey placed second with 18 percent. Muskie, with only 9 percent, placed fourth (behind Senator Henry M. Jackson of Washington) and was mortally wounded. Subsequent defeats in Wisconsin, Pennsylvania, and Massachusetts finished him.

It was McGovern who understood from the outset that the campaign would be first an elimination contest within the ideological factions of the Democratic Party and later a showdown among the winners within each faction.[26] McGovern would have to eliminate Mayor John V. Lindsay of New York to secure the united support of liberal issue activists. This McGovern did by entering the Florida primary, where he had no chance of winning, only to limit the vote for Lindsay to 7 percent; then by winning the Wisconsin primary and finishing Lindsay, who again polled only 7 percent. Meanwhile, Humphrey eliminated Muskie and Jackson, first by finishing a disappointing third, but well ahead of both, in Wisconsin, then by winning the Pennsylvania primary on April 25, while McGovern was winning Massachusetts the same day.

By then, McGovern was established as the candidate of reform liberal Democrats; Humphrey was the candidate of the party regulars; and Governor Wallace had conservative Democrats to himself. The outcome of the Democratic primaries generally reflects that historic division of factional support (see Table 4.6).

George Wallace was eliminated by bullets rather than by ballots. He could not have been nominated in any case, with his support limited to the party's conservatives, any more than Richard Russell could have been in 1948 or 1952, or even Lyndon Johnson could have been in 1956 or 1960. But on top of victories in the Florida, Tennessee, and North Carolina primaries, Wallace won the Maryland and Michigan primaries

and demonstrated the presence of conservative Democrats in the elec-
torate, even outside the south, who were ready to be taken by the
Republicans in a Presidential election and who proved central to the
realignment of 1964–1972 (see Table 4.7). Indeed, the re-election of
President Nixon in 1972 was guaranteed by two factors: the decision of
George Wallace to enter the Democratic primaries rather than run for
President again as a third-party candidate, and the nomination by the
Democrats of their most liberal alternative.[27]

The assassination attempt on George Wallace, who up to that point
had won a plurality of votes in the Democratic primaries, left only
McGovern and Humphrey to seriously contest the Democratic nomination. Winning the Rhode Island and Oregon primaries, McGovern
emerged as the clear front-runner. Going into the California primary,
the situation for the Democrats in 1972 was much the same as it had
been for the Republicans in 1964: McGovern had won a strong base of
delegates in precinct caucuses and state conventions, as had Goldwater
in 1964; he had held his own in the primaries. If he won California, it
appeared, the nomination was his. Humphrey, unlike Rockefeller in
1964, might actually win the nomination at the convention, if he could
first win California; or he might stop McGovern, only to have the
convention deadlock and nominate a liberal Democrat who had not
been an active candidate, such as Senator Edward M. Kennedy of
Massachusetts.

In any event, McGovern defeated Humphrey in a hard-fought California primary, by 44 percent to 39 percent. But Humphrey was not
ready to concede the nomination. He decided to use the McGovern-Fraser rules against McGovern, leading to a convention showdown that
left many Americans with the impression, correct or otherwise, that the
Democrats were a disorderly bunch influenced by liberal ideologues
who were out of touch with the American people.[28]

California state law in 1972 still provided for a Presidential primary
in which delegate candidates ran on at-large slates, making the state-
wide result winner-take-all. Thus, when McGovern won the California
primary, although by only five percentage points, he won all 271 delegates. If the party rule for proportional representation were applied
strictly, McGovern would be left with only 120 California delegates and
short of the nomination. Thus, the Humphrey forces challenged the
credentials of 151 California delegates pledged to McGovern.

Meanwhile, the McGovern forces filed a cross-challenge to the seating of the Illinois delegation led by Mayor Daley. Although the Daley
delegates won their seats in the Illinois primary, the McGovern forces
argued that the delegation had been endorsed behind closed doors by
the Daley machine and did not reflect the demographic distribution of
Illinois Democrats. The McGovern forces proposed a delegation

cochaired by Alderman William Singer of Chicago and the Reverend Jesse Jackson.[29]

The Credentials Committee stood by the new party rules and supported both challenges, unseating 151 McGovern delegates from California, 72–66, and unseating Mayor Daley and fifty-eight of his delegates, 71–61. Now both losing sides would challenge the seated delegates on the convention floor, the McGovern forces challenging the 151 Anybody-But-McGovern (ABM) coalition delegates from California, the ABM forces challenging the reform delegates from Illinois.

While the Credentials Committee had applied the reform rules consistently, rules gave way to candidate interest on the convention floor. In a session marked by fascinating, even humorous parliamentary maneuvering and closely fought roll calls in which delegates were highly disciplined to cast votes for the interests of their candidates, the McGovern forces won both of the credentials contests. On California, the McGovern minority report carried, 1,618.28 to 1,238.22; on Illinois, the ABM minority report was defeated, 1,486.04 to 1,371.56.

With credentials settled in McGovern's favor, so was the nomination. After Humphrey withdrew from the race, McGovern was nominated on the first ballot with 1,728.35 delegate votes out of 3,016. See Table 4.8 for an analysis of the credentials and Presidential votes at the 1972 Democratic National Convention.

McGovern's defeat the following November was even more devastating than Goldwater's in 1964, but his nomination at the convention was as important for liberal Democrats as Goldwater's nomination had been for conservative Republicans eight years before, and it had as lasting an effect on the party system.

SUMMARY

This chapter and the previous ones, taken together, demonstrate that each era associated with realignments in the twentieth century featured not only its own electoral coalitions between the major parties but also nominating coalitions within the parties that had much to do with the rise and fall of an electoral order. The nominating coalitions central to the 1964–1972 realignment, however, were unique for the lasting ideological polarization between the parties that they generated.

The shifting position of the south—and its impact on American politics—is illustrated as much by the changing nominating coalitions within the parties as by the decisive realignment of the south between the parties, which reached critical proportions in the 1960s. In the system of 1896, the south was a central ingredient to the nominating coalitions of both parties, for different if related reasons.

In the Democratic Party, the still solid south had a veto power on Presidential nominations because of the two-thirds rule at national conventions. Thus, the recurrent battles between the rural and urban factions of the Democratic Party were settled with candidates the south could at least tolerate, which is to say, candidates who would either support or tolerate white supremacy in the south. Meanwhile, Republicans in the south found themselves in the solidly Democratic region in an era of national Republican victories at the polls. Southern Republicans, then, reliant for political life on patronage appointments, cast their lot with incumbent Republican Presidents.

During the New Deal period, the balance of power in both parties moved north. After the Democrats revoked the two-thirds rule in 1936 with the support of President Roosevelt, liberal Democrats from the north gained power over Presidential nominations. Meanwhile, the relatively liberal Wall Street faction of the Republican Party was able to deliver GOP Presidential nominations from 1940 until 1964. The south in particular and conservatives generally were out in the cold at the national conventions of both parties.

Thus, in both of these periods, the nominating coalitions in both parties had a similar geographic base, and there was little ideological difference between the parties. But the Presidential nominations of the 1964–1972 period broke that pattern. Nominating power gravitated south and west in the Republican Party and moved north in the Democratic Party. Ideologues in both parties, a conservative Republican in 1964 and a liberal Democrat in 1972, secured Presidential nominations.

There had been decisive factional victories in one party or the other before in American politics. Indeed, there had been cases in which ideologues had gained control of their national party apparatus, however briefly. For example, the Republicans of the pre–Civil War period were an abolitionist party, and William Jennings Bryan led the populists to power in the Democratic Party in the realignment of 1896. But factional victories for ideologues in party affairs have been the exception to the rule and of brief duration. The followers of Daniel Webster, for example, never became a majority in the Whig Party, just as at the same time, the followers of John C. Calhoun were a minority in the Democratic Party. Both parties avoided decisive action on slavery rather than break up their factional alliances. Similarly, a century later, Franklin D. Roosevelt and the Democrats constructed an umbrella that covered both southern white supremacists and northern liberals and became the New Deal coalition.

But the factional victories of 1964 and 1972 were very different. For the first time, differing ideologues, conservative Republicans and liberal Democrats, gained power in the two major parties almost simultaneously. In addition, the winning factions would consolidate power within their party.

Whereas the short-term result was the decline of the nineteenth-century party system, the longer-term outcome may be the birth of a new American party system for the twenty-first century.

TABLES

Table 4.1
Roll Call Votes at 1964 Republican National Convention

CIVIL RIGHTS MINORITY REPORT

	By 1964–1972 ideological alignment of states					
	liberal	*moderate*	*conservative*	*Non-South*	*South*	*National*
Yea	**72**	23	1	38		31
Nay	28	**77**	**99**	**62**	**100**	**69**

	By delegation support for president				
	Rockefeller	*Scranton*	*Other*	*Goldwater*	*National*
Yea	**84**	88	**74**	3	31
Nay	16	12	25	**97**	**69**

REPUBLICAN PRESIDENTIAL NOMINATION

	By 1964–1972 ideological alignment of states					
	liberal	*moderate*	*conservative*	*Non-South*	*South*	*National*
Goldwater	24	**80**	**96**	**61**	**97**	**68**
Scranton	**30**	15	2	19	3	16
Rockefeller	29	1		11		9

	By delegation vote on civil rights minority report		
	Yea	*Nay*	*National*
Goldwater	18	**93**	**68**
Scranton	**40**	3	16
Rockefeller	26	1	9

Figures represent percentage of total delegates. Ideological alignment of states based on 1964–1972 Presidential elections as described in Chapter 1 and used in Table 1.19.

Derived from *National Party Conventions, 1831–1996* (Washington, D.C.: Congressional Quarterly, 1997), p. 242.

Table 4.2
Delegation Vote for President, 1964 Republican National Convention,
by 1964–1972 Ideological Alignment of States

	Ideological Alignment of States, 1964–1972		
	liberal	*moderate*	*conservative*
Goldwater	Washington	California	Alabama
	Wisconsin	Colorado	Arizona
		Delaware	Arkansas
		Illinois	Florida
		Iowa	Georgia
		Kentucky	Idaho
		Missouri	Indiana
		Montana	Kansas
		Ohio	Louisiana
		South Dakota	Mississippi
		Texas	Nebraska
		Vermont	Nevada
		West Virginia	New Mexico
			North Carolina
			North Dakota
			Oklahoma
			South Carolina
			Tennessee
			Utah
			Virginia
			Wyoming
Scranton	D.C.	Alaska	
	Connecticut	Maryland	
	Massachusetts	New Hampshire	
	Pennsylvania	New Jersey	
	Rhode Island		
Rockefeller	New York		
	Oregon		
Favorite Sons	Michigan	Hawaii	
	Minnesota	Maine	

G= −.88
See Chapter 1 and Table 1.19 for explanation of ideological alignment of states.
Delegations sorted according to plurality vote for President.
Derived from *National Party Conventions*, p. 242.

Table 4.3

Delegation Vote for President, 1968 Republican National Convention, by 1964–1972 Ideological Alignment of States

	Ideological Alignment of States, 1964–1972		
	liberal	*moderate*	*conservative*
Nixon	D.C.	Alaska	Alabama
	Oregon	Colorado	Arizona
	Washington	Delaware	Florida
	Wisconsin	Illinois	Georgia
		Iowa	Idaho
		Kentucky	Indiana
		Maryland	Louisiana
		Missouri	Mississippi
		Montana	Nebraska
		New Hampshire	Nevada
		South Dakota	New Mexico
		Texas	North Dakota
		Vermont	Oklahoma
		West Virginia	South Carolina
			Tennessee
			Virginia
			Wyoming
Nixon/ Rockefeller		Maine	
Rockefeller	Connecticut		
	Massachusetts		
	Minnesota		
	New York		
	Pennsylvania		
	Rhode Island		
Reagan		California	North Carolina
Favorite Sons & Other	Michigan	Hawaii	Arkansas
		New Jersey	Kansas
		Ohio	Utah

$G = -.36$

See Chapter 1 and Table 1.19 for explanation of ideological alignment of states. Delegations sorted according to plurality vote for President at 1964 convention. Derived from *National Party Conventions*, p. 244.

Table 4.4
1968 Republican Presidential Nomination

	By 1964–1972 ideological alignment of states					
	liberal	*moderate*	*conservative*	*Non-South*	*South*	*National*
Nixon	29	52	72	45	74	52
Rockefeller	57	9	3	27	2	21
Reagan	2	23	14	13	19	14

	By delegation support for President at 1964 Convention				
	Rockefeller	*Scranton*	*Other*	*Goldwater*	*National*
Nixon	20	35	29	63	52
Rockefeller	80	54	25	5	21
Reagan				21	14

Figures represent percentage of total delegates. Ideological alignment of states based on 1964–1972 Presidential elections as described in Chapter 1 and used in Table 1.19.

Derived from *National Party Conventions*, p. 244.

Table 4.5
Roll Call Votes at 1968 Democratic National Convention

BAN UNIT RULE

	By 1964–1972 ideological alignment of states					
	liberal	*moderate*	*conservative*	*Non-South*	*South*	*National*
Yea	60	56	36	60	19	52
Nay	36	44	60	38	79	46

	By delegation support for President:				
	McCarthy	*McGovern*	*Divided*	*Humphrey*	*National*
Yea	88	100	95	39	52
Nay	10		3	58	46

CREDENTIALS: TEXAS, GEORGIA, AND ALABAMA

	By 1964–1972 ideological alignment of states					
	liberal	*moderate*	*conservative*	*Non-South*	*South*	*National*
Regulars	33	50	67	43	76	48
Challengers	36	34	13	34	7	27

	By delegation support for President				
	McCarthy	*McGovern*	*Divided*	*Humphrey*	*National*
Regulars	6		32	61	48
Challengers	81	92	46	16	27

(continued)

Table 4.5 (continued)

VIETNAM MINORITY REPORT

	By 1964–1972 ideological alignment of states					
	liberal	*moderate*	*conservative*	*Non-South*	*South*	*National*
Yea	**56**	41	22	47	14	40
Nay	43	**58**	**78**	**53**	**85**	**60**

	By delegation support for President				
	McCarthy	*McGovern*	*Divided*	*Humphrey*	*National*
Yea	**89**	**100**	66	27	40
Nay	10		33	**72**	**60**

DEMOCRATIC PRESIDENTIAL NOMINATION

	By 1964–1972 ideological alignment of states					
	liberal	*moderate*	*conservative*	*Non-South*	*South*	*National*
Humphrey	55	**67**	**79**	**63**	**83**	**67**
McCarthy	40	21	12	28	7	23
McGovern	2	10	3	7	1	6

	By delegation vote on motion to ban Unit Rule		
	Yea	*Nay*	*National*
Humphrey	**45**	84	**67**
McCarthy	40	10	23
McGovern	10	2	6

	By delegation vote on Credentials			
	Challengers	*Split*	*Regulars*	*National*
Humphrey	17	**57**	84	**67**
McCarthy	**54**	36	11	23
McGovern	23	4	2	6

	By delegation vote on Vietnam Minority Report		
	Yea	*Nay*	*National*
Humphrey	32	**84**	**67**
McCarthy	**49**	11	23
McGovern	14	1	6

Figures represent percentage of total delegates. Ideological alignment of states based on 1964–1972 Presidential elections as described in Chapter 1 and used in Table 1.19. Delegations are sorted according to majority vote on the Presidency or issues. Many delegations were split at the 1968 Democratic convention and did not produce majorities for President; these delegations are classified as "divided" for President. On credentials, delegations that voted for the regular party delegation on all roll calls are sorted for the "regulars." Delegations that voted for the challengers on all roll calls are sorted for the "challengers." Other delegations "split" their support.
Derived from *National Party Conventions*, p. 243.

Table 4.6
1972 Democratic Presidential Primaries

WINNER OF PRESIDENTIAL PRIMARIES

	By 1964–1972 ideological alignment of states		
Winners	*liberal*	*moderate*	*conservative*
McGovern	Massachusetts New York Oregon Rhode Island Wisconsin	California New Jersey South Dakota	Nebraska New Mexico
Wallace	Michigan	Maryland	Florida North Carolina Tennessee
Humphrey	Pennsylvania	Ohio West Virginia	Indiana
Muskie		Illinois New Hampshire	

G = .03

MEAN VOTE IN PRESIDENTIAL PREFERENCE PRIMARIES

	By 1964–1972 ideological alignment of states					
	liberal	*moderate*	*conservative*	*Non-South*	*South*	*National*
McGovern	**37**	**35**	15	**34**	4	**30**
Wallace	23	11	**40**	19	**53**	24
Humphrey	19	25	24	25	8	23
Muskie	13	18	6	14	5	12

Figures represent mean percentage of the vote in Presidential primaries. Ideological alignment of states based on 1964–1972 Presidential elections as described in Chapter 1 and used in Table 1.19.

Derived from *Presidential Elections, 1789–1996* (Washington, D.C.: Congressional Quarterly, 1997), pp. 182–185.

Table 4.7
Wallace Vote, 1968, and Increase in Nixon Vote, 1960–1972

State	Nixon (R) 1960	Wallace 1968	Wallace 1972	Nixon (R) 1972	Nixon Net Change 1960–1972
Mississippi	25	64		78	+53
Georgia	37	43		75	+38
Louisiana	29	65		65	+36
Alabama	42	66		72	+30
Arkansas	43	39		69	+26
South Carolina	49	32		71	+22
North Carolina	48	31		70	+22
Florida	52	29	42	72	+20
Texas	49	19		66	+17
West Virginia	47	10		64	+17
Rhode Island	36	4	15	53	+17
Virginia	52	24		68	+16
Tennessee	53	34	68	68	+15
Oklahoma	59	20		74	+15
Maryland	46	15	39	61	+15
Nevada	49	13		64	+15
Wyoming	55	9		69	+14
New Jersey	49	9		62	+13
Utah	55	6		68	+13
Connecticut	46	6		59	+13
Hawaii	50	2		63	+13
Missouri	50	11		62	+12
New York	47	5		59	+12
Delaware	49	13		60	+11
Indiana	55	11	41	66	+11
New Mexico	50	8		61	+11
New Hampshire	53	4		64	+11
Idaho	54	13		64	+10
Pennsylvania	49	8	21	59	+10
Kentucky	54	18		63	+9
Arizona	56	10		65	+9
Illinois	50	9		59	+9
Nebraska	62	8	12	71	+9
Kansas	60	10		68	+8
Colorado	55	8		63	+8
Alaska	51	12		58	+7

(continued)

Table 4.7 (continued)

State	Nixon(R) 1960	Wallace 1968	Wallace 1972	Nixon (R) 1972	Nixon Net Change 1960–1972
Ohio	53	12		60	+7
Michigan	49	10	51	56	+7
Montana	51	7		58	+7
North Dakota	55	6		62	+7
Washington	51	7		57	+6
California	50	7		55	+5
Massachusetts	40	4	7	45	+5
Maine	57	2		62	+5
Vermont	59	3		63	+4
Minnesota	49	4		52	+3
Wisconsin	52	8	22	53	+1
Iowa	57	6		58	+1
Oregon	53	6	20	52	−1
South Dakota	58	5		54	−4

Wallace 1968: Nixon net change/ $r = .86$
Wallace vote for 1972 in the Democratic primaries he entered.
Derived from *Presidential Elections*, pp. 118–121 and 182–185.

Table 4.8
Roll Calls at 1972 Democratic National Convention

ILLINOIS CREDENTIALS (PRO-DALEY)

	By 1964–1972 ideological alignment of states					
	liberal	moderate	conservative	Non-South	South	National
Yea	37	**46**	**55**	42	**61**	45
Nay	**61**	43	44	**52**	38	**49**

	By support for or opposition to McGovern		
	McGovern	ABM Coalition	National
Yea	29	**65**	45
Nay	**63**	33	**49**

CALIFORNIA CREDENTIALS (PRO-MCGOVERN)

	By 1964–1972 ideological alignment of states					
	liberal	moderate	conservative	Non-South	South	National
Yea	**66**	**51**	41	**58**	33	**54**
Nay	33	37	**59**	35	**67**	41

	By support for or opposition to McGovern		
	McGovern	ABM Coalition	National
Yea	**70**	33	**54**
Nay	21	**66**	41

DEMOCRATIC PRESIDENTIAL NOMINATION

	By 1964–1972 ideological alignment of states					
	liberal	moderate	conservative	Non-South	South	National
McGovern	**66**	**66**	32	**66**	24	**57**
Jackson	18	17	14	18	11	17
Wallace	7	7	31	6	**42**	13
Chisholm	3	4	8	3	9	5

Figures represent percentage of total delegates. Ideological alignment of states based on 1964–1972 Presidential elections as described in Chapter 1 and used in Table 1.19.

Derived from *National Party Conventions*, pp. 246–247.

NOTES

1. For an excellent development of this argument, see Clyde P. Weed, *The Nemesis of Reform: The Republican Party during the New Deal* (New York: Columbia University Press, 1994).

2. Edward G. Carmines and James A. Stimson, *Issue Evolution: Race and the Transformation of American Politics* (Princeton: Princeton University Press, 1989).

3. See, for example, Byron E. Shafer, *Bifurcated Politics: Evolution and Reform in the National Party Convention* (Cambridge, Mass.: Harvard University Press, 1988), pp. 108–147. See also John H. Aldrich, *Why Parties? The Origin and Transformation of Party Politics in America* (Chicago: University of Chicago Press, 1995), pp. 163–193.

4. See Robert Novak, *The Agony of the G.O.P. 1964* (New York: Macmillan, 1965), particularly pp. 118–139, 176–201, 331–354, and 439–469. See also Theodore H. White, *The Making of the President 1964* (New York: Atheneum, 1965), pp. 200–231 and 331–364.

5. See Shafer, *Bifurcated Politics*, pp. 77–147.

6. See Harold W. Stanley and Richard G. Niemi, *Vital Statistics on American Politics* (Washington, D.C.: Congressional Quarterly, 1994), pp. 213–216. Chapter 7 focuses on divided government and split-ticket voting, and the emergence in recent years of ideological polarization between the parties in Congress.

7. James Q. Wilson, "Realignment at the Top, Dealignment at the Bottom," in Austin Ranney, ed., *The American Elections of 1984* (Durham, N.C.: American Enterprise Institute/Duke University Press, 1985), pp. 277–310.

8. Novak, pp. 7–24. See also White, *The Making of the President 1964*, pp. 64–65.

9. Much of the discussion of the Republican nominating politics of 1964 is taken from Novak, pp. 118–139, and White, *The Making of the President 1964*, pp. 94–101.

10. See Novak, pp. 331–354.

11. *National Party Conventions 1831–1996* (Washington, D.C.: Congressional Quarterly, 1997), pp. 107–108.

12. Unless otherwise noted, data from national conventions in text and tables are drawn or derived from *National Party Conventions 1831–1996*, pp. 242–247. Data for Presidential primaries are drawn from *Presidential Elections, 1789–1996* (Washington, D.C.: Congressional Quarterly, 1997).

13. See Novak, pp. 451–456.

14. See Theodore H. White, *The Making of the President 1968* (New York: Atheneum, 1969), pp. 52–53.

15. Lee Edwards, *Goldwater: The Man Who Made a Revolution* (Washington, D.C.: Regnery Publishing, 1995), pp. 372–375. See also Lewis Chester, Godfrey Hodgson, and Bruce Page, *An American Melodrama: The Presidential Campaign of 1968* (New York: The Viking Press, 1969), pp. 433–450, and White, *The Making of the President 1968*, pp. 160–161.

16. See White, *The Making of the President 1968*, pp. 261–299; Chester, Hodgson, and Page, pp. 447–475; and Richard M. Nixon, *RN: The Memoirs of Richard Nixon* (New York: Grossett and Dunlap, 1978), pp. 304–305.

17. Chester, Hodgson, and Page, pp. 51–67.

18. Ibid., pp. 105–126.

19. Ibid., pp. 564–576.

20. See Theodore H. White, *The Making of the President 1972* (New York: Atheneum, 1973), pp. 17–47.

21. Shafer, *Bifurcated Politics*, pp. 77–107.

22. Perhaps the classic on the party reforms after 1968 is Nelson W. Polsby, *The Consequences of Party Reform* (Oxford: Oxford University Press, 1983). See also William Crotty, *Party Reform* (New York: Longman, 1983), and Crotty, *American Parties in Decline*, 2nd ed. (Glenview, Ill.: Scott Foresman, 1984), and White, *The Making of the President 1972*, pp. 17–33. For a concise presentation of reforms in historical context, see *Presidential Elections, 1789–1996* (Washington, D.C.: Congressional Quarterly, 1997), pp. 139–146 and 229–244.

23. Data is drawn and derived from *Presidential Elections, 1789–1996*, pp. 141 and 182–185.

24. See White, *The Making of the President 1972*, pp. 40–45.

25. See White, *The Making of the President 1972*, pp. 73–99, for a discussion of the field of Democratic candidates at the outset of the 1972 campaign, particularly p. 78 for the early Gallup Poll report.

26. Ibid., pp. 40–45.

27. See Dan T. Carter, *The Politics of Rage: George Wallace, the Origins of the New Conservatism, and the Transformation of American Politics* (Baton Rouge: Louisiana State University Press, 1995), pp. 324–450.

28. See Shafer, *Bifurcated Politics*, pp. 169–172 and 232–237. See also White, *The Making of the President 1972*, pp. 167–229.

29. An excellent account of the credentials battles at the 1972 Democratic National Convention is given by White in *The Making of the President 1972*, pp. 167–202. See also *National Party Conventions, 1831–1984*, pp. 119–122 and pp. 211–212, which supplies the data for the convention roll calls.

Party Decay and the New Nominating Politics, 1972–1980

The Presidential elections of 1964 through 1972 were seen widely as electoral accidents not only because they presented unconventional results in the general election (two landslides for different parties sandwiching an election with an important third-party candidate), but also because they involved unconventional and unpredictable nomination campaigns. Neither the nomination of Goldwater nor the nomination of McGovern was commonly expected; both nominations violated what was considered rational behavior by a political party according to spatial theories of the electorate. And certainly neither the challenge to President Johnson in the Democratic primaries of 1968 nor the strength it gathered was expected. But just as realignment between parties yields unexpected election results during the critical period, realignment between or among factions within parties will yield unexpected nominations during the critical period. What was occurring between 1964 and 1972 was not an accident but a critical realignment both within and between parties.

The seizure of power by issue activists within both major parties at that time was not coincidence but a reflection of the rapid social change in society at-large during that period. The Civil Rights revolution, the Vietnam War, and increasing conflict between cultural traditionalists and a counterculture all created the political environment of ideological polarization that inspired durable change in the party system.

REFORM AND THE NEW PARTY SYSTEM

Historically, realignment has meant not only sea change in electoral coalitions but also lasting institutional change in the structure and processes of American political parties. The realignment of the 1830s produced the birth of the Democratic Party and the Whig Party and the introduction of quadrennial national conventions.[1] The realignment of 1860 was built around the birth of the Republican Party. The realignment of 1896 was associated with the reforms of the progressive era, which weakened nineteenth-century parties by advancing civil service reform, weakening patronage systems, and opening nomination processes to greater popular participation, the latter particularly through the introduction of primaries.[2] Yet, the nineteenth-century party system persisted, however unevenly, beyond the New Deal realignment of the 1930s.

Electoral and party reform growing out of the realignment of the 1960s delivered a body blow to the nineteenth-century party system. It came in three waves: the voting rights reforms resulting from the Civil Rights movement, the delegate selection reforms in the wake of the 1968 Democratic National Convention, and campaign finance reform in the shadows of Watergate.

Voting Rights

The 24th Amendment to the Constitution and the Voting Rights Act of 1965 would combine to greatly expand the registration and participation of African Americans in the south.[3] The result would be the further ideological polarization of the national parties. First, white supremacists such as George Wallace would lose Democratic primaries to more-progressive candidates like Jimmy Carter and Bill Clinton. Second, white supremacists and their electoral heirs would move even more decisively into the Republican Party. Finally, numerous African American Democrats would be elected to Congress from districts across the south with large African American populations. Thus the Democratic Party in the south, though generally less liberal than Democrats elsewhere, would become decidedly more liberal than the growing southern Republican Party.

Party Reform

Party reform would grow out of the Democratic convention of 1968, violently divided over the Vietnam War. The reforms of the McGovern-Fraser Commission had a lasting impact beyond facilitating the nomination of George McGovern for the Presidency in 1972.[4] They introduced participatory candidate-centered Presidential nomination systems in both parties, first by requiring reform within the Democratic Party, then by stimulating reforms by the state legislatures with Democratic majorities, which in turn spread reform to the Republican Party. The result was to consolidate the power of issue activists in both parties, further promoting ideological polarization between the parties. The McGovern-Fraser reforms first directly led to a proliferation of Presidential primaries beyond 1972, to over thirty by 1976, with a slower increase continuing thereafter. Second, the McGovern-Fraser reforms required proportional representation according to candidate support, opening the door to a proliferation not only of primaries but of candidates. Third, the new primary laws tended to follow the Oregon model, which required the listing of all candidates on the ballot. No longer could candidates be selective in where they entered primaries. Now most candidates would run everywhere, and primaries would become more decisive in delivering the nomination. The nomination campaign would no longer be a combination of state and local contests. Rather, it was a national contest, requiring candidates to recruit national support. Favorite sons representing state party organizations, or regional candidates who would enter selected primaries, would no longer be viable.

Campaign Finance Reform

The Watergate scandal, itself a product of a President who saw himself as surrounded by political enemies from a liberal counterculture, in turn produced campaign finance reform. The new Federal Election Commission and its matching funds provision would require Presidential aspirants to found national campaign organizations, which functioned like corporations to raise money. The expense of seeking Presidential nominations would be increased by the necessity of national campaigns through numerous primaries, but finance reform would increase the cost even more. Those who could raise the most money would have their funding matched, so long as donations came from twenty states or more in increments of $250.00 or less. This required a large, complex, national organizational structure outside the party and well connected to issue activists and interests that could raise large amounts of money from numerous supporters.[5]

Taken together, these three waves of change in electoral and nominating politics would further weaken the nineteenth-century political parties and consolidate the power of issue activists in party affairs. Candidate-centered nominations would replace party-centered nominations and elections. But the reforms would also plant the seeds of a new ideologically polarized and more nationalized party system. The balance of this chapter discusses the new nominating politics as an agent of party decay in the years immediately following reform. Chapter 6 examines Presidential nominations as an instrument of longer-term party revival.

PARTY DECAY AND THE NEW NOMINATING POLITICS

The long and crowded campaign for the Democratic Presidential nomination in 1972 worked largely as the McGovern-Fraser reformers envisioned it. The process was thoroughly participatory and democratized, and left the national party open to manipulation of its processes and outcomes by issue activists. At the convention, the openness he authored would not be without its costs for Senator McGovern. Even with the nomination clinched, McGovern's convention managers could not control the agenda to give their candidate the best exposure. Instead, the long debates and ballots on rules and credentials had given the convention and the Democratic Party the appearance of chaos to a national audience; and on the night of his acceptance speech, the debate that led to the formation of the McGovern-Fraser Commission and the ballot on the Vice Presidency combined to keep McGovern off the rostrum, and national television, until almost 3 AM.[6] It was a dramatization of the decline of the Democratic Party of Andrew Jackson, William Jennings Bryan, and Franklin D. Roosevelt.

The next two elections, 1976 and 1980, also produced unexpected nomination campaigns that provided further evidence of party decay. The two challenges to incumbent Presidents in the primaries, and the initial nomination of Jimmy Carter were all uncommon events, resulting from rapid change in the party system. None of these events should have been particularly surprising, however. Viewed in the context of ideological polarization, in each challenge to a President, the majority faction of the party in the White House was rebelling against a President who was a product of the "opposition" faction. And although both Presidents survived the primaries and convention, neither won the election, and in both cases the majority faction consolidated its position in party affairs. Meanwhile, the Carter nomination in 1976 represented the seizure of the party apparatus in advance of the convention by a candidate-centered campaign using reform against party leaders, much as McGovern had in 1972.

Ford vs. Reagan

The challenge to President Gerald Ford in the 1976 Republican primaries was the result of a unique political accident: scandal leading to the resignation of Vice President Spiro T. Agnew, and Watergate, leading to the resignation of President Nixon. With the resignation of President Nixon in 1974, Gerald Ford took office as 38th President of the United States. Ford, who before being appointed Vice President in 1973, had been House Minority Leader for eight years, had a solid conservative record in the House but had always allied himself with moderate Republicans in intraparty conflicts. He called himself a conservative on economic issues, a social moderate, and an liberal on foreign policy.[7] He had supported Vandenburg, Eisenhower, and Governor George Romney of Michigan for the Presidency. He was considered a rising star in the Republican Party during the Eisenhower administration and was a leader of a successful coup against the Republican House leadership in 1959, which displaced Joseph W. Martin of Massachusetts and installed Charles Halleck of Indiana as Republican Floor Leader. He led a similar coup himself six years later to seize the leadership from Halleck. He had been a supporter of civil rights in the House and in recent years had come to back Nelson Rockefeller in the latter's anticipated bid for the Republican Presidential nomination in 1976.[8]

Thus, conservative Republicans already did not consider Gerald Ford to be one of their own when he took office as President. Doubt began to turn to opposition when he appointed Rockefeller as the new Vice President and hardened when he set up a system to pardon Vietnam era draft resisters. Finally, as the abortion issue grew in salience, President Ford was pro-choice and did nothing to restrain his wife in her libertarian attitudes toward private personal conduct. It was not long before a movement to challenge President Ford developed among conservative Republicans behind former Governor Ronald Reagan of California.

For a time, it did not appear inevitable that Reagan would challenge an incumbent Republican President. Reagan, as governor of California, had issued the "eleventh commandment"—"Thou shalt not speak ill of any fellow Republican."[9] But conservative opposition to the Ford administration could not be ignored. Briefly, in 1974 and 1975, Howard Phillips and Richard Viguerie had even attempted to assemble a third party behind a ticket of Reagan and George Wallace; but that alternative never went very far.[10]

Any serious candidacy for Reagan was within the Republican Party. President Ford did not enjoy all the normal advantages of incumbency: He had never won the nomination of his party for the Presidency nor built the national organization that such a nomination requires; he was unelected; and he was not a conservative Republican. His ascension to the Presidency, from the point of view of Reagan supporters, was illegitimate. As the ruling faction in their party, conservative Republicans had never accepted Ford. Therefore, challenging him was, in their view, neither an act of disloyalty to the party nor a violation of Reagan's eleventh commandment.

In June of 1975, three conservative Republican Senators, James L. Buckley of New York, James McClure of Idaho, and Jesse Helms of North Carolina, released a joint statement that in effect urged Reagan to run for President:

> as neither the President nor the Vice President was elected to office, it would be in the best interest of the Republican Party and of the country for the 1976 presidential and vice-presidential nominations to be sought and won in an open convention. . . . The merits of the current administration must be judged in 1976 by delegates pledged only to support the principles of their party.[11]

Using such logic, Ronald Reagan announced for the Republican Presidential nomination in 1976, and the party was in for a nominating contest that would rival the contests of 1952 and 1964 for bitterness and intensity.

However, the primary campaign began much as those who expected a President to win the nomination of his party easily would have anticipated, and for a few weeks it looked like Ford would put Reagan away early. Ford narrowly won the New Hampshire primary, then added victories in Florida and Illinois. The Ford and Reagan camps were, at this point, actually negotiating terms for Reagan's withdrawal.[12]

But Reagan rebounded and survived to win North Carolina, thanks to the help of Senator Helms. North Carolina was unlike previous primary states where President Ford had the support of the party, and Reagan was supported by insurgent conservative activists. In North Carolina, it was a battle between two factions of the party leadership, between supporters of Helms and supporters of Governor James Holshouser, a moderate Republican. It was a classic showdown for the new Republican Party of the south, between the ultraconservatives, many of whom had been Dixiecrats, supporting Helms and Reagan, and the country club Republicans supporting Holshouser and Ford. The growing power of the Dixiecrats and ultraconservatives in the new Republican Party of the south was demonstrated by the Reagan victory.

After North Carolina, Ford and Reagan raced stride-for-stride to the convention. Ford won the Wisconsin primary; Reagan won every delegate in the Texas primary, making the national delegate race close. Reagan added victories in Indiana, Georgia, Alabama, Nebraska, South Dakota, and California, while Ford won primaries in Maryland, Michigan, and Ohio.

The results confirmed a classic convention showdown between the Wall Street faction of the Republican Party, supporting President Ford, and the more conservative Main Street faction supporting Reagan. President Ford had won mostly in the northeast quadrant, while Reagan had won most of the "L" of the south and west. See Table 5.1, which demonstrates that the coalition of states for Ford and Reagan replicated the historic ideological pattern.[13]

After the primaries, President Ford had a very narrow lead in the delegate count, although he was short of a majority. The President probably would have won the Republican nomination in any case, but it was virtually guaranteed by Reagan's preconvention blunder: the selection of Senator Richard Schweiker of Pennsylvania, a liberal Republican, to run for Vice President on the Reagan ticket. The design of the Schweiker selection was to win over officially uncommitted delegates in the northeast, particularly Pennsylvania, New York, and New Jersey, a number of whom were considered winnable by the Reagan campaign.

They were not. Mostly moderate-to-liberal Republicans, the delegates of Pennsylvania, New York, and New Jersey were uncommitted in name only and loyal to the President. Ford had won the Pennsylvania and New Jersey Presidential Preference primaries unopposed; in the New York primary, Vice President Rockefeller had won the overwhelming majority of delegates as a stand-in favorite son for the President. Even in Pennsylvania, the addition of Senator Schweiker to the Reagan ticket could do no more than steal a handful of delegates.

The real uncommitted delegates upon whom the convention's decision turned were from the south and west, conservative Republicans torn between their ideology on one side of the equation and their President on the other. The Schweiker candidacy only neutralized the consideration of ideology and drove most of these delegates into the Ford camp. The most public and dramatic case concerned the Mississippi delegation, chaired by Republican State Chairman Clarke Reed. Reed was a conservative, to be sure, and a party man who had to feel some pressure to support the President. The delegates were uninstructed by the Republican State Convention—thirty votes, all conservative Republicans, up for grabs. If Reagan were to overtake Ford for the nomination, these were exactly the delegates he had to have. When he selected Schweiker for Vice President, these were exactly the votes he lost. At the national convention, Mississippi voted 16 for Ford, 14 for Reagan.[14]

The nomination of the President was almost certain, but at the convention, the Reagan forces made a serious effort to motivate conservative Republicans to come over to their side. First, conservative Republicans urged Senator James L. Buckley of New York to seek the nomination, in an effort to deny President Ford a first-ballot victory. On the second ballot, according to this strategy, many conservatives previously pledged to Ford would be free to vote for Reagan.[15] Buckley, who needed the support of Vice President Rockefeller in New York for his own nomination and re-election, declined to run. Second, Reagan supporters attempted to require President Ford to select his running mate publicly, in advance of the Presidential balloting, in the hope that his selection of a moderate Republican would drive conservatives to Reagan. Their proposal, rule 16-C, was defeated in the Rules Committee; their minority report failed on the floor—1,180 to 1,069—delegates voting almost uniformly with their candidates. Finally, Reagan forces proposed a minority report on the platform critical of Ford administration foreign policy. The Reagan strategists hoped that the platform fight would motivate conservative Republicans to vote their ideology on the Presidential ballot. The Ford camp cut short that dream by simply refusing to fight and allowing the minority report to pass by voice vote.[16]

President Ford won the Republican nomination on the first ballot, very narrowly, with 1,187 votes to 1,070 for Reagan. The distribution of the vote reflected ideological patterns very similar to the Presidential ballots at the 1952, 1964, and 1968 conventions (see Table 5.2).

The important outcome of the 1976 Republican Presidential primaries was not the victory of the President, but the fact that Ronald Reagan had come so close. Even in defeat, challenging an incumbent President, conservative Republicans had secured their electoral base and consolidated their power in the GOP.

Jimmy Who?

Watergate, plus the serious split in the Republican Party in 1976, led to the only Democratic victory in a Presidential election between 1964 and 1992. Even so, the Democrats probably would not have won the Presidency had they not nominated a moderate, former Governor Jimmy Carter of Georgia.

The nomination of Jimmy Carter, like the Presidency of Gerald Ford, was the result of a political accident. Unlike the rise of Ford, however, the nomination of Carter was the result of an accident that was purely electoral and hardly unique. Like 1972, the race for the Democratic Presidential nomination in 1976 was at first an elimination contest within ideological factions. In 1976, unlike 1972, liberal Democrats, now the majority faction in their party, failed to unite behind any candidate for the nomination. Carter, on the other hand, would win early primaries with a plurality against divided opposition, emerge as the front-runner, build momentum, unite moderate and conservative Democrats, and clinch the nomination before the convention.[17]

The 1976 Democratic Presidential primaries demonstrated again what the participatory, candidate-centered nominating campaign would be like: a crowded field, with an elimination contest within factions, followed by a decisive showdown between surviving candidates, and the emergence of a presumptive nominee before the convention.

All of this was not entirely clear at the outset of the 1976 primary campaign, when a deadlocked convention was widely expected, for three reasons. First, the system of proportional representation in awarding delegates among candidates made the achievement of a majority appear less likely. Second, at least partly because of proportional representation, the field of active candidates was a crowded one. Finally, none of the natural leaders of either of the liberal factions, the reformers or the regulars, was actively seeking the nomination.

A number of liberal Democrats were seeking to lay claim to the reform faction of the party: Representative Morris K. Udall of Arizona, Senator Birch E. Bayh of Indiana, former Senator Fred Harris of Oklahoma, and Sargent Shriver of Maryland. Each was hoping to eliminate the others by placing first or second in the New Hampshire primary, then winning in Massachusetts, widely considered the most liberal state in the nation because it alone had voted for George McGovern in 1972. None of the liberal Democrats who might have been able to call on a personal base of support within the party was running in the primaries. McGovern and Muskie both harbored some hope for the nomination, and Kennedy may have, too. But Muskie and Kennedy were up for re-election to the Senate, and in any case, any of the three might be well positioned to be nominated at an old-fashioned deadlocked convention: The majority of the delegates would certainly be liberals; even if not united around a particular candidate, they could unite and nominate at the convention.

Senator Henry M. Jackson of Washington was the active candidate of the party regulars. He was hoping to assemble the New Deal coalition in the primaries, with the support of labor. His focus in the early contests would be in the large industrial states of the northeast: Massachusetts, New York, and Pennsylvania. Victories in those states would set him up to clinch the nomination later, by winning primaries in Michigan, New Jersey, and Ohio.

The candidate that party regulars and labor preferred, Hubert Humphrey, was, like McGovern, Muskie, and Kennedy, not making the race. He certainly still wanted to be President, but he, too, was up for re-election to the Senate. And he would be a very strong candidate for the nomination at a deadlocked convention, because he would be broadly acceptable to a coalition of moderate-to-liberal Democrats. Therefore, Humphrey had no apparent motive to enter the primaries, even if he were running for President.

The only factional leader who was running actively was the conservative Democrat, Governor George Wallace of Alabama. Although probably too conservative to be nominated, his solid base of support, his name recognition, and the fact that he was the only conservative Democrat running against a collection of moderates and liberals, made him the early front-runner among the active candidates. With victories in the primaries like those he scored in 1972, Wallace could go to the convention still the front-runner, which would make deadlock all the more likely.

Into this mix Jimmy Carter entered. He did not fit neatly into any faction of the Democratic Party. A southerner like Wallace, a moderate like Henry Jackson, Carter's opening was to build a coalition of moderates and conservatives without making himself unacceptable to liberal Democrats. His strategy did not depend on party leaders and recognized that the nomination would be won before the convention. According to the plan, Carter would emerge as a serious contender by running well in New Hampshire; he would eliminate Wallace in Florida, an achievement that would make him acceptable to liberals even as it united moderates and conservatives behind his candidacy; he would then hold off any liberal candidates in the later primaries and secure the nomination.

That is almost exactly what happened. Carter, running against a collection of liberal Democrats, won the New Hampshire primary with only 29 percent of the vote, to 24 percent for Udall. It was enough to make Carter the front-runner. Jackson won the Massachusetts primary, where Udall ran second, again failing to win because liberals were still scattering their votes. Carter meanwhile, turned south and eliminated Wallace in Florida and North Carolina. Then, Carter edged Udall in the Wisconsin primary by only 7,000 votes; the same day, Jackson won the New York primary, where Udall again ran second. Udall certainly lost Wisconsin because of scattered votes for other liberals, and possibly New York, too; and he might have won either New York or Wisconsin by concentrating his campaign resources there, but he tried to win both and won neither.

Finally, still in the lead with momentum working for him, Carter defeated Jackson and Udall in the Pennsylvania primary, almost clinching the nomination. Jackson, out of money, withdrew.

Now, liberal Democrats hoped that Humphrey would enter the race and challenge Carter in the New Jersey primary, and thus create the deadlocked convention. He considered it briefly, but on the morning of the filing deadline for the New Jersey primary, only some thirty-six hours after the Pennsylvania results were in, Humphrey held a press conference in the Senate Caucus room and announced once more that he would not run.

Two liberals did enter the race late, however: Senator Frank Church of Idaho and Governor Jerry Brown of California. Carter did, indeed, have to hold them off in the later primaries. Church beat Carter in Nebraska and Oregon. Brown beat Carter in Maryland and California. But, with Jackson and Humphrey out of the race, Carter now had the upper hand among party regulars against his reform liberal opposition in most states. He kept winning his share of primaries, in Indiana, Georgia, Michigan, and South Dakota.

When Carter won the Ohio primary in early June, the opposition caved in. Well before the convention met, Carter had the Democratic nomination in hand. He was endorsed by party leaders across factional lines, including Mayor Daley, Senator Jackson, Governor Wallace, and Senator Church. His nomination on the first ballot was decisive, with 2,238.5 delegate votes, to 329.5 for Udall and 300.5 for Brown. Every delegation cast a majority of its votes for Carter, except for two that voted for favorite sons: Arizona for Udall and California for Brown.

The distribution of victories in the 1976 Democratic Presidential primaries is illustrated in Table 5.3, which sorts states according to the 1964–1972 ideological alignment. As the low gamma indicates, Carter assembled a centrist coalition that included broad support across the ideological spectrum.

Nevertheless, the nomination of Jimmy Carter did not represent a reversal of the process of ideological polarization between the parties; nor had liberal Democrats lost their electoral base in the primaries. The most important lasting impact of the Carter victory on the Democratic Party was the defeat of George Wallace and the final elimination of the white supremacist faction of the Democratic Party in the south. The ingredients of Carter's success over Wallace in the Florida, North Carolina, Georgia, Tennessee, and Arkansas primaries had long since been planted. First, the ideological polarization between the parties had already pushed some conservative Democrats into the Republican Party, as early as 1964. Second, the 24th Amendment to the Constitution and the Voting Rights Act had greatly increased the black vote in the south, and particularly in Democratic primaries, pushing even more southern whites toward the Republican camp. Starting in 1970, a number of southern progressives emerged along with Carter in the Democratic Party, including Albert Gore, Jr. of Tennessee, Reuben Askew of Florida, Dale Bumpers of Arkansas, and of course not least, Bill Clinton of Arkansas. Candidates like George Wallace, and the voters who supported him, became dinosaurs in the Democratic Party, and began to appear more often in the Republican Party. This process probably did even more to polarize the national parties ideologically than the nomination of liberal Democrats.

Second, liberals remained the potentially governing faction in the Democratic Party. Despite the margin of his victory and the consensus he enjoyed at the convention, Jimmy Carter may not have been nominated had liberal Democrats united on a single candidate against him early in the primaries. Table 5.4 sorts the 1976 primaries according to the outcome that would have obtained had the cumulative vote for Udall, Brown, Church, Jackson, Bayh, Harris, Shriver, Humphrey, and Kennedy been cast for one candidate against Carter. Table 5.5 shows the mean percentage of the vote for candidates in the primaries by the ideological alignment of states, and the mean percentage for labor and liberal Democrats had their vote been combined. Although no conclusion can be drawn from these tables as to what the outcome might actually have been, both demonstrate the continuing factional divisions in the party, electoral potential of liberal Democrats in the primaries in 1976, and the trouble Carter would have had winning against a united front on his left flank.

If there was a flaw in the Carter blueprint for the 1976 primaries, it was its assumption that a showdown with Ted Kennedy would come in 1976, not 1980. Hamilton Jordan, the author of the original Carter plan, expected Kennedy to run in 1976. Carter would eliminate Wallace, unite moderates and conservatives, then beat Kennedy, who would be burdened by Chappaquiddick.[18] Ironically, had the assumption that Kennedy would run been accurate, Carter probably would not have been nominated, and President Ford, sweeping the south against Kennedy, probably would have been elected. But as it is, Kennedy did not run, liberal Democrats did not unite on anyone, not even in the later primaries, and they had no viable candidate at the convention. Jimmy Carter, the centrist, was nominated and elected.

Carter vs. Kennedy

Thus, the showdown that Carter expected with Kennedy finally took place in 1980. Once again, it seemed surprising that an incumbent President should be challenged within his own party. But as with the Reagan challenge against Ford in 1976, the majority faction of the party in the White House did not control the Presidency. When the Carter administration pursued policies, particularly on the economy, that liberal Democrats considered to be too austere, and when the second wave of oil shocks and the recession struck in 1979, the President was particularly vulnerable to a Kennedy challenge. Indeed, prior to the Iran hostage situation, public opinion polls indicated that Kennedy led President Carter among Democrats.[19]

But the Iran hostage crisis brought the advantages of incumbency into play. Carter in 1980 could put incumbency advantages of the Presidency to use more than Ford could against Reagan in 1976 because, in contrast to Ford, Carter had won his party's nomination for the Presidency, had a national organization within the party loyal to him, and had been elected in his own right. Well before the primaries in 1980, President Carter had reclaimed status as the front-runner.

Nevertheless, liberal Democrats had become as dominant in the nominating politics of their party as conservative Republicans were in the nominating politics of theirs. Even in 1976, with Carter as the nominee, delegates to the Democratic National Convention were distinctly more liberal than Democratic voters and the general electorate, just as the Republican convention delegates were more conservative than Republican voters or the general electorate.[20] And just as the uncommitted delegates in the 1976 Republican contest were conservatives torn between their ideology and their President, the swing vote in the 1980 Democratic primaries would be liberals torn between their ideology and their President. Even as the front-runner with incumbency advantages, President Carter had a viable challenge on his hands.

The primary campaign between Carter and Kennedy in 1980 had many of the same patterns as the 1976 contest between Ford and Reagan. Carter almost eliminated Kennedy early with victories in the New Hampshire and Illinois primaries; then Kennedy salvaged his campaign by winning where he had to, in New York. From then on they battled to the convention, each winning where ideological electoral patterns would lead one to expect: Carter winning almost everywhere in the "L" states of the south and interior west, Kennedy scoring most of his victories in the northeast quadrant. On the final day of primaries in June, Kennedy survived by winning New Jersey and California. President Carter, as had President Ford four years before, secured his front-runner status by winning the Ohio primary. (See Table 5.6.)

The renomination of the President was virtually guaranteed. Kennedy, like Reagan four years before, was left to a convention fight over the rules and the platform. Once again, like four years before, the incumbent President won on the rules and conceded on the platform to neutralize the ideological fervor of the opposition.

On the rules, the Kennedy forces proposed a rule releasing delegates from their preconvention commitments on the Presidency. Once again, most delegates were liberals, and Kennedy supporters hoped that, if freed, most liberals would vote for Kennedy and their ideology rather than the President. The Kennedy proposal was defeated soundly, 1,936.42 to 1,390.58. Kennedy then withdrew from the race. But, in an effort to avoid embarrassing defeats on the platform, Carter forces allowed Kennedy to address the convention, and the Senator gave one of his most eloquent addresses, assuring liberal Democrats that "the dream shall never die."[21] The delegates then approved minority platform planks on economic policy proposed by Kennedy, including an antirecession jobs program, a housing program, and a promise to prioritize fighting unemployment over fighting inflation. Seeking to avoid roll calls on the economic issues, the Carter forces agreed to the latter plank before the balloting, and lost on the other two. The result was a platform that could hardly have satisfied liberal Democrats more, even had Kennedy been the nominee.

President Carter won renomination on the first ballot by a vote of 2,129.02 to 1,150.48 for Kennedy. If Carter won the nomination in 1976 only because liberal Democrats were divided, in 1980 he won renomination only because he was the sitting President.

Kennedy endorsed Carter without enthusiasm. Plagued by recession and the hostage crisis, his party as divided as Ford's had been four years before, President Carter was defeated for re-election by Republican Ronald Reagan.

CONCLUSION

Tables 5.7 and 5.8 illustrate the mirror-image similarity of the geographic and ideological divisions in the two nominating contests involving a challenge to an incumbent President. Across party lines, most of the states that supported challenger Kennedy in the Democratic Party had supported President Ford in the Republican Party. Most of the states that supported challenger Reagan in the Republican Party would support President Carter in the Democratic Party. Though a number of states, most of them classified as "moderate" in the 1964–1972 alignment of states, supported both Presidents, the states supporting the two challengers, Reagan the conservative Republican and Kennedy the liberal Democrat, are almost mutually exclusive.

The challenges to the Presidents within their own parties in 1976 and 1980 both reflected the ideological polarization that had already occurred between the parties. Neither challenge would have been so strong had it not come from the majority faction in the nominating politics of each party, the conservative Republicans and liberal Democrats. Neither President could have overcome the challenge without the advantages of incumbency. Each President came away from his convention with a badly divided party, and only lukewarm support from his recent intraparty opponents, and neither President could win the ensuing election.

Both challenges, and the initial nomination of Jimmy Carter, also reflected the short-term results of reform and party decay. None of the nomination campaigns discussed here could have taken place without weakening party leaders and party-based delegate selection processes and the development of participatory delegate selection processes in both parties.

But these were indeed short-term results. The ideological polarization between the parties and the opening of both parties to participatory nominating politics would, in surprisingly short order, promote a revival of political parties, however altered their form.

TABLES

Table 5.1

Support for Ford and Reagan at 1976 Republican National Convention, by 1964–1972 Ideological Alignment of States

	Ideological Alignment of States, 1964–1972		
	liberal	*moderate*	*conservative*
Ford	Connecticut	Alaska	Florida
	D.C.	Delaware	Kansas
	Massachusetts	Hawaii	Mississippi
	Michigan	Illinois	North Dakota
	Minnesota	Iowa	
	New York	Kentucky	
	Oregon	Maine	
	Pennsylvania	Maryland	
	Rhode Island	New Hamphsire	
	Wisconsin	New Jersey	
		Ohio	
		Vermont	
		West Virginia	
Reagan	Washington	California	Alabama
		Colorado	Arizona
		Missouri	Arkansas
		Montana	Georgia
		South Dakota	Idaho
		Texas	Indiana
			Louisiana
			Nebraska
			Nevada
			North Carolina
			Oklahoma
			South Carolina
			Tennessee
			Utah
			Virginia
			Wyoming

G = .87

See Chapter 1 and Table 1.19 for ideological alignment of states according to voting behavior in 1964–1972 Presidential elections.

Derived from *National Party Conventions, 1831–1996* (Washington, D.C.: Congressional Quarterly, 1997), p. 251.

Table 5.2
**1976 Republican Presidential Nomination by Patterns of Support for
Previous Convention Candidates**

1st Ballot				
	By delegation support for **1952 Republican Presidential nomination**			
	Eisenhower	*Other*	*Taft*	*National*
Ford	**61**	15	50	**53**
Reagan	38	**85**	50	47

	By delegation support for **1964 Republican Presidential nomination**				
	Rockefeller	*Scranton*	*Other*	*Goldwater*	*National*
Ford	**81**	89	**73**	37	**53**
Reagan	18	11	27	**63**	47

	By delegation support for **1968 Republican Presidential nomination**				
	Rockefeller	*Other*	*Nixon*	*Reagan*	*National*
Ford	**86**	76	40	11	**53**
Reagan	14	24	**60**	89	47

Delegations sorted by plurality support for the Republican Presidential nomination at indicated conventions.
Derived from *National Party Conventions*, pp. 239–251.

Table 5.3

Outcome of 1976 Democratic Presidential Primaries, by 1964–1972 Ideological Alignment of States

	Ideological Alignment of States, 1964–1972		
	liberal	*moderate*	*conservative*
Winner			
Carter	D.C.	Illinois	Arkansas
	Michigan	Kentucky	Florida
	Pennsylvania	New Hampshire	Georgia
	Wisconsin	Ohio	Indiana
		South Dakota	North Carolina
		Texas	Tennessee
		Vermont	
Brown		California	Nevada
		Maryland	
Wallace			Alabama
Church	Oregon	Montana	Idaho
			Nebraska
Jackson	Massachusetts		
	New York		
Favorite Sons	Rhode Island	New Jersey	
& Other		West Virginia	

$G = -.10$

See Chapter 1 and Table 1.19 for methodology of ideological alignment of states.
Candidates listed in the order of their delegate strength at the convention.
Derived from *Presidential Elections, 1789–1996* (Washington, D.C.: Congressional Quarterly, 1997), pp. 186–190.

Table 5.4

Liberal Democrats versus Carter: Projected Winners in 1976 Democratic Primaries, Combining Presidential Preference Votes of Liberal Democrats

	Ideological Alignment of States, 1964–1972		
	liberal	*moderate*	*conservative*
Pluralities	*D.C.	California	Idaho
for	Massachusetts	Maryland	Nebraska
liberal	*Michigan	Montana	Nevada
Democrats	Oregon	*New Hampshire	
	*Pennsylvania		
	Rhode Island		
	*Wisconsin		
Pluralities		*Illinois	*Arkansas
for		*Kentucky	*Florida
Carter		*New Jersey	*Georgia
		*Ohio	*Indiana
			*North Carolina
			*Tennessee

G = .77

See Chapter 1 and Table 1.19 for methodology of ideological alignment of states. Derived from *Presidential Elections*, pp. 186–190.

* Primaries actually won by Carter.

Table 5.5
**Mean Vote for Candidates in 1976 Democratic Presidential Primaries,
by 1964–1972 Ideological Alignment of States**

MEAN VOTE FOR CANDIDATES IN DEMOCRATIC PRIMARIES						
	By 1964–1972 ideological alignment of states					
	liberal	*moderate*	*conservative*	*Non-South*	*South*	*National*
Carter	**31**	**37**	**50**	**35**	**63**	**40**
Udall	21	10	3	12	4	10
Brown	4	10	6	9		7
Wallace	7	8	14	7	21	10
Church	9	9	15	13	1	13
Jackson	8	2	6	5	7	5
MEAN VOTE (WITH LIBERAL DEMOCRATS COMBINED)						
Carter	31	37	**50**	35	**63**	40
Liberal Democrats	**57**	**49**	34	**54**	14	**46**
Wallace	7	8	14	7	21	10

See Chapter 1 and Table 1.19 for explanation of ideological alignment of states.
Udall, Brown, Church, Jackson, Bayh, Harris, Shriver, Humphrey, Kennedy, and
Shapp combined to create cumulative vote for liberal Democrats.
Derived from *Presidential Elections*, pp. 186–190.

Table 5.6

1980 Democratic Presidential Primaries, by 1964–1972 Ideological Alignment of States

WINNERS OF PRIMARIES BY IDEOLOGICAL ALIGNMENT OF STATES			
	liberal	*moderate*	*conservative*
Carter	Oregon	Illinois	Alabama
	Wisconsin	Kentucky	Arkansas
		Maryland	Florida
		Montana	Georgia
		New Hampshire	Idaho
		Ohio	Indiana
		Texas	Kansas
		Vermont	Louisiana
		West Virginia	Nebraska
			Nevada
			North Carolina
			Tennessee
Kennedy	Connecticut	California	New Mexico
	D.C.	New Jersey	
	Massachusetts	South Dakota	
	New York		
	Pennsylvania		
	Rhode Island		

$G = -.81$

MEAN VOTE IN PRESIDENTIAL PREFERENCE PRIMARIES, BY 1964–1972 IDEOLOGICAL ALIGNMENT OF STATES						
	liberal	*moderate*	*conservative*	*Non-South*	*South*	*National*
Carter	42	**51**	**59**	**49**	**60**	**52**
Kennedy	**51**	40	28	41	27	38

See Chapter 1 and Table 1.19 for explanation of ideological alignment of states. Derived from *Presidential Elections*, pp. 191–197.

Table 5.7
Cross Partisan Patterns of Support in Preconvention Challenges to Presidents, 1976–1980

	1980 (D)	
1976 (R)	*Kennedy*	*Carter*
Ford	Connecticut	Alaska
	D.C.	Delaware
	Maine	Florida
	Massachusetts	Hawaii
	New Jersey	Illinois
	New York	Iowa
	North Dakota	Kansas
	Pennsylvania	Kentucky
	Rhode Island	Maryland
	Vermont	Michigan
		Minnesota
		New Hampshire
		Ohio
		Oregon
		West Virginia
		Wisconsin
Reagan	Arizona	Alabama
	California	Arkansas
	New Mexico	Colorado
	South Dakota	Georgia
		Idaho
		Indiana
		Louisiana
		Mississippi
		Missouri
		Montana
		Nebraska
		Nevada
		North Carolina
		Oklahoma
		South Carolina
		Tennessee
		Texas
		Utah
		Virginia

G = .53
Derived from *National Party Conventions*, pp. 249–251.

Table 5.8
Cross Partisan Ideological Patterns: Delegations for Challengers to the President, by 1964–1972 Ideological Alignment of States, 1976–1980

	liberal	*moderate*	*conservative*
For	Connecticut	Maine	North Dakota
Kennedy	D.C.	New Jersey	
versus	Massachusetts	Vermont	
Carter	New York		
(D-1980)	Pennsylvania		
	Rhode Island		
For		California	Arizona
Both		South Dakota	New Mexico
Challengers			
For	Washington	Colorado	Alabama
Reagan		Missouri	Arkansas
versus		Montana	Georgia
Ford		Texas	Idaho
(R-1976)			Indiana
			Louisiana
			Mississippi
			Nebraska
			Nevada
			North Carolina
			Oklahoma
			South Carolina
			Tennessee
			Utah
			Virginia
			Wyoming

G = .91
See Chapter 1 and Table 1.19 for explanation of ideological alignment of states.
States not listed voted for both Presidents.
Derived from *National Party Conventions*, pp. 249–251.

NOTES

1. John H. Aldrich, *Why Parties? The Origin and Transformation of Party Politics in America* (Chicago: University of Chicago Press, 1995), pp. 97–125.

2. See Joel H. Silbey, "Beyond Realignment and Realignment Theory," in Byron E. Shafer, ed., *The End of Realignment? Interpreting American Electoral Eras* (Madison: University of Wisconsin Press, 1991), pp. 3–23.

3. Earl Black and Merle Black, *The Vital South: How Presidents Are Elected* (Cambridge: Harvard University Press, 1992), pp. 213–240.

4. See Nelson W. Polsby, *The Consequences of Party Reform* (Oxford: Oxford University Press, 1983), and Austin Ranney, *Curing the Mischiefs of Faction: Party Reform in America* (Berkeley and Los Angeles: University of California Press, 1975).

5. Nelson W. Polsby and Aaron Wildavsky, *Presidential Elections: Contemporary Strategies of American Electoral Politics* (New York: The Free Press, 1991), pp. 42–96.

6. Theodore H. White, *The Making of the President 1972* (New York: Atheneum Publishers, 1973), pp. 195–198.

7. Gerald R. Ford, *A Time to Heal: The Autobiography of Gerald R. Ford* (New York: Harper and Row, 1979), p. 66. Mr. Ford defines himself as a "liberal" on foreign policy because he was an internationalist. "Internationalism versus isolationism" shaped the factional politics of the Republican Party in the early days of Ford's political career, and Ford himself was a supporter of Wendell Willkie and Arthur Vandenburg when he was breaking into politics. See Chapter 3 for a discussion of the internationalist-versus-isolationist debate within the Republican Party between 1940 and 1952.

8. Ibid., pp. 63–123.

9. Jules Witcover, *Marathon: The Pursuit of the Presidency 1972–1976* (New York: Viking Press, 1977), p. 92.

10. Ibid., p. 47.

11. Ibid., p. 51.

12. Ibid., pp. 408–414.

13. Data for Presidential primaries is drawn or derived from *Presidential Elections, 1789–1996* (Washington, D.C.: Congressional Quarterly, 1997). Data for conventions is derived or drawn from *National Party Conventions, 1831–1996* (Washington, D.C.: 1997).

14. Witcover, pp. 443–503.

15. Ibid., pp. 473–486.

16. Ibid., p. 500.

17. Much of the discussion concerning the race for the 1976 Democratic Presidential nomination is drawn from Witcover, pp. 105–370. See *Presidential Elections, 1789–1996*, pp. 186–190 for data on primaries.

18. See Witcover, pp. 105–118.

19. The Gallup Poll, November 22, 1979, reported in George H. Gallup, *The Gallup Poll: Public Opinion 1979* (Wilmington, Del.: Scholarly Resources, 1980), p. 280.

20. Byron E. Shafer, *Bifurcated Politics* (Cambridge: Harvard University Press, 1988), pp. 100–107.

21. David Broder, "Democrats," in David Broder, Lou Cannon, Haynes Johnson, Martin Schram, and Richard Harwood, *The Pursuit of the Presidency 1980* (New York: G.P. Putnam's Sons, 1980), p. 199.

Ideological Homogenization and Party Revival

The period of 1964–1972 is widely recognized as one of critical change in American parties and elections, but it is widely understood as a time of dealignment and party decay rather than as a time of realignment and party revival. As outlined in Chapter 5, the decade or so thereafter provided mounting evidence of the decline of political parties.

Although my argument has been that the electoral change of 1964–1972 should be understood as one of realignment and party revival, the evidence of party decay in that period cannot be discounted. Indeed, it is central to the point of the realignment/party revival thesis. The parties in decay after 1964–1972 are the political parties born in the nineteenth century. Their decline was a necessary first step in the development of new party institutions that followed. Viewed in that context, party decay and party revival are not mutually exclusive, and dealignment is realignment by other means.

Party change since 1964–1972 is based on two concurrent and related processes: the ideological polarization between the parties, and party reform. To review, ideological polarization was the result of the growing power of ideologues and issue activists in both parties. The issue activists, in turn, pushed party reform that opened up both parties to popular participation in their nominating processes. These participatory processes certainly weakened the nineteenth-century party structures and further increased the power of issue activists in both parties. The power of issue activists led to candidate-centered nomination campaigns in which the priority of issues took precedence over concern for the party.

Yet, as issue activists gained power in party affairs, they were no longer on the outside looking in. The one-time insurgents and their political descendants had become the new party elite, and they were consolidating their power. As political parties became their instruments, the interests of the party became their concern. This process was reinforced by ideological polarization. The Republican Party became a conservative party, the Democratic Party became a liberal party, and issue activists in both parties became increasingly self-interested in partisan victory at the polls. Though factionalism continued, the range of disagreement on issues within each party decreased, party unity increased, and more ideological and nationalized parties developed.

Starting around 1980, with the nomination, election, and Presidency of Ronald Reagan, the emergence of these new parties became more evident. In the two decades since, stability and consensus have marked the nominating politics of both parties, displacing the instability and internal conflict of the realigning period.

THE IDEOLOGICAL HOMOGENIZATION OF THE REPUBLICAN PARTY

The challenge by Ronald Reagan in 1976 almost certainly cost President Ford and the Republicans the election that year. But when Reagan announced for the Republican Presidential nomination in 1980, he was not regarded as a disloyal maverick, as one might expect for a candidate who had challenged his own party's incumbent President. Rather, he was the candidate of his party's majority conservative faction, and the presumptive front-runner. With strong support from party leaders, he was in a position to unite the party from the right. Reagan's position in early 1980 illustrates how decisive leadership of a majority faction of activists had become in nominating politics. The translation of factional leadership into party leadership without Reagan paying any measurable price for his challenge four years before and the relative ease with which Reagan proceeded to the Republican Presidential nomination illustrate the new rule of the nominating game: A candidate who can unite, or come close to uniting, the majority ideological faction of his party in the primaries will secure the nomination in advance of the convention. In fact, Reagan came very close to clinching the nomination without a serious fight, and might have done so, had he not been upset in the Iowa precinct caucuses by George Bush of Texas.

Reagan could count on a base of conservative support that amounted, even at the outset, to a majority of Republican primary voters in most states. On the other hand, moderate Republicans faced an elimination contest within their own ranks, among Bush, Senate Minority Leader Howard Baker, and Representative John B. Anderson of Illinois. John B. Connally of Texas tried to bridge the factions by presenting himself to moderates as the only Republican who could beat Reagan and to conservatives as the only Republican who could beat the Democrats. The contest, then, matched an almost united majority against a divided minority.

The division among moderate Republicans explains the behavior of both Reagan and Bush at the Nashua debate that probably decided the New Hampshire primary, and possibly the nomination. When Reagan, "paying for this microphone," demanded that the bilateral debate with Bush be turned into a multicandidate meeting, he knew that he was offering a stage to candidates who would take votes mostly from Bush. Bush, by his uncharacteristically graceless attempt to refuse admittance to the rest of the field, only facilitated Reagan's purpose.[1] Three days later, Reagan won the primary with 50 percent of the vote, to only 23 percent for Bush, 13 percent for Baker, and 10 percent for Anderson.[2]

Bush was in a position very much like Udall in 1976, but worse. Like Udall, Bush had established himself as the front-runner's leading opponent but had not united his own faction. Yet, unlike Udall, Bush did not find his electoral base in the majority faction of his party. Even if moderate-to-liberal Republicans had united behind Bush, he could not have beaten Reagan. And, to make matters worse, moderates and liberals did not unite quickly. Bush won primaries only in the northeast quadrant, and not as many as he should have there, because Anderson survived the early primaries and lingered, taking liberal Republican votes from Bush. (See Table 6.1.)

Thus, while Bush won Massachusetts narrowly, Reagan won Vermont, where GOP moderates should win primaries; Anderson ran a strong second in both contests, and in fact, won the composite Presidential preference vote of the two states.

Reagan proceeded to eliminate Connally in South Carolina, beat Bush by almost 2–1 in Florida, and, for all practical purposes, eliminate Anderson in Illinois. Bush got his hoped for one-on-one showdown in Pennsylvania and won narrowly. But ideology outweighed favorite son status when Reagan narrowly defeated Bush in Texas, effectively eliminating him. Altogether, Reagan won thirty-one out of the thirty-five primaries he entered, with 61 percent of the total vote. Perhaps the best indication of the Reagan sweep is that he won an overwhelming majority of the delegates in New York, once the base for the liberal Republicanism of Thomas E. Dewey and Nelson Rockefeller.

Very early in the 1980 Republican primary campaign, it looked briefly as if an ideological showdown between the Main Street faction supporting Reagan and the Wall Street faction may yet occur. Former President Gerald Ford was urged to run by moderate Republicans, and seriously considered doing so, even signing papers authorizing the filing of delegate slates pledged to him in the Ohio primary. But he did not want to interfere with the Bush campaign and never entered the race.[3] For his part, Bush hung on in the race beyond his defeat in Texas, until he won the Michigan primary and lost the Oregon primary on the same day. Even after scoring a victory, Bush counted delegates and withdrew.

The fact that Bush withdrew even on the day he won a primary while Ford declined to run in 1980 stands in contrast to the divisive end game of the 1964 campaign, when Rockefeller withdrew to support Scranton in an eleventh hour stop-Goldwater campaign. In 1980 Reagan was no longer perceived as being out of the Republican mainstream, as Goldwater was perceived to be in 1964, and moderate-to-liberal Republicans found it much easier to accept the inevitability of Reagan's nomination. Nor were they unwilling to support Reagan as the party's nominee, in contrast to the fact that liberal Republicans never lined up behind Goldwater sixteen years before.[4]

With the nomination decided well in advance of its meeting, the Republican convention in 1980 was a ceremony, not a decision-making assembly. Reagan was nominated on the first ballot by a nearly unanimous vote. He added George Bush to the ticket as his running mate and led a united Republican Party to victory in November.

Republicans since Reagan

Since Reagan, campaigns for contested Republican Presidential nominations have followed the 1980 pattern: An overwhelming conservative majority in primaries and caucuses, and a clear early front-runner who stumbled, only to recover and clinch the nomination well before the convention.

In 1988, the early front-runner was Vice President Bush. The 1988 campaign for the Republican Presidential nomination would not be unimportant in party affairs; the candidacy of the Reverend Pat Robertson would greatly enhance the standing of the Christian right, advancing further still the ideological polarization between the parties.[5]

Robertson was well organized far in advance of the 1988 campaign, enough so that his presence eventually eliminated Representative Jack F. Kemp of New York, the coauthor of the tax cut so central to

Reaganomics. In the Iowa precinct caucuses, Robertson placed a surprising second, behind only Senate Minority Leader Robert Dole. That is where Bush, finishing third, stumbled.

Well organized at the grass roots for precinct caucuses, Robertson lacked a broad enough base to compete seriously for the nomination in the primaries, which soon narrowed to Bush and Dole. Bush recovered with a victory in the New Hampshire primary. Dole won South Dakota but would not win another contest. Bush won his "fire wall" victory in South Carolina, swept the south and New England on Super Tuesday three days later, then eliminated Dole with a decisive victory in the Illinois primary. He had clinched the nomination four months before the convention. Though Bush and Dole were both moderates when compared with Robertson, both could count on support from conservatives, and there was almost no ideological divide to their vote in the primaries. Bush ran best in the northeast quadrant, where moderate Republicans historically have won primaries, and in the south, where conservative Republicans have won.

Four years later, as incumbent President, Bush stumbled again, this time in the New Hampshire primary, winning by a disappointing 53 percent to 37 percent over Pat Buchanan. Thereafter, President Bush swept the primaries, and his renomination was secure by Super Tuesday in March. The battle between Bush and Buchanan certainly fits the Wall Street versus Main Street mold historically found in Republican nominating contests, but it was hardly an ideological showdown. Buchanan is an ultraconservative on cultural issues, but his economic nationalism has a working-class appeal that breaks down clear ideological categorizations. Once again, there was almost no ideological divide to the vote in the Republican primaries.[6]

The same pattern is observed yet again in 1996. The front-runner, Senator Dole, lost in New Hampshire to Buchanan and in Arizona to Malcolm S. Forbes, Jr. He never lost again. Like Bush in 1988, Dole won a decisive contest in South Carolina, then swept primaries in New England, the south, and the Great Lakes region over the next three weeks to secure the nomination. As in 1988 and 1992, there was little ideological distinction in the pattern of the vote in the Republican primaries.[7]

Table 6.2 illustrates the ideological homogenization of the vote in Republican Presidential primaries since 1988.

THE IDEOLOGICAL HOMOGENIZATION OF THE DEMOCRATIC PARTY

The race for the Democratic Presidential nomination in 1984 followed a pattern similar to all the recent Republican contests. There was little difference in ideology among the leading candidates, and the front-runner, after early setbacks, recovered to win the nomination handily.

Former Vice President Walter F. Mondale, the early front-runner, might have united the party without a contest had he won the New Hampshire primary. He had a list of endorsements from party and interest group leaders that rivaled Muskie's in 1972. But when Senator Gary Hart of Colorado placed second in the Iowa precinct caucuses, he picked up a rapid momentum that, within a week's time, brought him to victory in New Hampshire. The contest among Mondale, Hart, and Jesse Jackson that followed, although not polarized ideologically, was more than personal; its roots could be traced in the factional history of the Democratic Party. Mondale was the candidate of the party regulars, drawing the base of his support from party organizations in the large industrial states of the north. Jimmy Carter endorsed Mondale, bringing with him remnants of the old Carter administration and party leaders from the south. Hart had emerged as the candidate of the reform faction of the party. Jackson's base was predominantly black and represented an emerging faction of the party, the "Rainbow Coalition."[8]

The nonideological structure to the contest between Mondale and Hart is illustrated by the distribution of victories in the primaries. Whereas Hart won all of the primaries in his home region of the west, Mondale won most, but by no means all, of the primaries in both the northeast quadrant and the south. Jackson ran strongest in the south and urban areas of the north, where black voters are numerous. The fact that Mondale and Hart were not drastically different in their ideological appeal, and the racial component of the vote for Jackson, neutralized ideology as a factor in the vote in the primaries, as measured at the state level (see Table 6.3).

After New Hampshire, Hart pushed his lead with victories in Massachusetts and Florida; Mondale reassumed the lead by winning Georgia, Illinois, New York, and Pennsylvania. Hart survived by winning Ohio and Indiana, while Mondale took North Carolina and Maryland the same day. On the final day of primaries in June, Mondale won in New Jersey, while Hart won in California.

Mondale's lead was by no means overwhelming when he proclaimed himself the nominee apparent after winning the New Jersey primary. The difference was made for him by the new "superdelegates" that had been added in the party rules. These superdelegates were appointed by party organizations, largely favorable to Mondale, to supplement delegates selected in primaries and participatory caucuses. Indeed, the opportunity to challenge Mondale still existed before the convention. Hart and Jackson might have combined to challenge Mondale delegates won on a winner-take-all basis at the district level in Illinois, New York, Pennsylvania, and

New Jersey, as a violation of proportional representation requirements. Whether the challengers would have had the votes is certainly not clear. But it is also irrelevant: The ideological polarization that had existed within the party when the issue was civil rights or Vietnam was no longer there. The 1984 convention was not only a convention of Democrats; it was a convention of liberal Democrats.

The 1988 and 1992 contests for the Democratic Presidential nomination, like the Democratic primaries of 1976, involved multicandidate fields, with eliminations within each faction of the party. Nevertheless, the candidate who, like Carter in 1976, emerged as the front-runner out of the early maze went on to clinch the nomination before the convention.

In 1988, Gary Hart appeared to be the front-runner until the scandal with Donna Rice drove him from the race. After he re-entered, his candidacy never recovered. Had it not been for his personal troubles, he almost certainly would have been able to unite liberal Democrats and win the nomination, and the single front-runner model would have applied. As it is, the crowded field evolved. Jesse Jackson was running again, and in the crowd, he was the early front-runner in the polls. Senator Paul Simon of Illinois and Governor Michael Dukakis of Massachusetts were the liberal Democrats in the race. Backed by the party in Chicago, Simon appeared to have potential as the candidate of the party regulars; Dukakis had a more middle-class, reform base to his support. Three moderate Democrats were making the race: former Governor Bruce Babbitt of Arizona, Senator Albert Gore of Tennessee, and Representative Richard Gephardt of Missouri. Thus, early on, Jackson would hold the Rainbow Coalition; Simon and Dukakis would compete for other liberals; and Babbitt, Gore, and Gephardt would compete for the centrist vote.

The major alteration in the rules for 1988 was the geometric expansion of Super Tuesday to fourteen primaries in the south and border states. This change reflected a determination among moderate Democrats to exercise more early influence on the nominating process by placing the south early on the delegate selection calendar. If a moderate could win the south, build momentum as the front-runner, and go on to the nomination as Jimmy Carter had in 1976, the Democrats might hope to regain the Presidency.

Gephardt and Gore both survived the earlier primaries and caucuses to compete on Super Tuesday. Gore survived by delaying any serious campaigning until reaching the south, a strategic decision that probably aided Gephardt to do so well in the earlier contests. Gephardt, campaigning on a note of trade protection, won the Iowa precinct caucuses, then placed second in the New Hampshire primary, behind Dukakis. Next, Gephardt won the South Dakota primary.

Going into Super Tuesday, there was a four-cornered race across the south among Dukakis, Gephardt, Gore, and Jackson. The results were splintered, defeating the purpose the designers had for the multiprimary day. Dukakis, running well in metro areas, won the megastates of Texas and Florida, as well as Massachusetts and Rhode Island in New England; Gore, assembling impressive support from southern party leaders, won North Carolina, Tennessee, Kentucky, Oklahoma, and Arkansas; Jackson, sweeping the black vote, won across the deep south, in Georgia, Alabama, Mississippi, and Louisiana; and Gephardt, nearly finished, won only his home state of Missouri. Gore had done reasonably well, but no better than Dukakis and Jackson. He did not come out of the south as the front-runner, and he had not gained the momentum he needed. Up north, he would be beaten, badly, placing behind both Dukakis and Jackson in Wisconsin and New York.

After winning the New York primary, Dukakis was a strong front-runner, opposed only by Jackson. Jackson had run well in the south and in Illinois, Wisconsin, and New York; but he had carried only the five deep south states, and only by his strength among black voters. His candidacy, with a solid but nonexpanding base, counted on a multi-candidate field. When it became a two-way race, Jackson was finished as a real contender for the nomination. Dukakis swept the remaining primaries, except D.C., and his nomination became a certainty.

For 1988, at least, the Super Tuesday plan had backfired, for three reasons. First, moderate Democrats were not themselves united before Super Tuesday and split their vote in the south. Had the vote for Gore and Gephardt been united on a single candidate, that candidate would have won six out of ten southern primaries on Super Tuesday. Second, Jackson swept the black vote, an important element of the Carter coalition in 1976. Without the black vote, no moderate Democrat could replicate the Carter coalition. Finally, in the new, more polarized party system, the Democratic electorate in the south had become more liberal, as conservatives moved to the Republican Party.[9]

An ideological dimension can be observed in the vote in the 1988 Democratic primaries. Except for black voters, more liberal Democrats supported Dukakis; Gore lost everywhere outside the south but ran strongest among moderate Democrats. Jackson was nearly isolated to the black vote, but that was solid for him. As a result of his dependable base, Jackson ran second to Dukakis in the north, and second to Gore in the south (see Table 6.4).

Nevertheless, the ideological differences among the candidates were not great and are certainly overstated by the division of the vote in the Democratic primaries. Neither Gore nor Gephardt was George Wallace in disguise. They might have been moderate within the spectrum of the

Democratic Party, but both were liberals on a bipartisan ideological spectrum. Indeed, both had voting records that drew a rating of 70 from Americans for Democratic Action (ADA); from the Committee on Political Education (COPE) of the AFL-CIO, Gore enjoyed a rating of 86, Gephardt a rating of 80. The 1988 Democratic primaries had been fought among candidates who were liberal, more liberal, and less liberal; but there were no conservatives. Candidates like George Wallace were no longer Democrats, and neither were the voters who had supported the likes of Wallace.

In 1992, in contrast to 1988, Super Tuesday would serve its purpose, to the benefit of Governor Bill Clinton of Arkansas. Clinton in 1992 found himself in almost exactly the same competitive position as Jimmy Carter in 1976; Clinton was the only moderate Democrat in the field, running against four candidates who were more liberal: former Senator Paul Tsongas of Massachusetts, Senator Bob Kerrey of Nebraska, Senator Tom Harkin of Iowa, and former Governor Jerry Brown of California. The only difference between Clinton's position in 1992 and Carter's in 1976 worked to Clinton's advantage: In 1992, there was no conservative like George Wallace to contend with. Not only was there no Wallace to Clinton's right, there was also no Jesse Jackson to compete for African American voters.

Even before the election year began, Clinton was generally regarded as the front-runner. As the national chair of the centrist Democratic Leadership Council, he had a strong claim to the support of moderate Democrats. Three events strengthened his position and created the possibility that he might clinch the nomination without a serious contest. First, Governor Mario M. Cuomo of New York, who enjoyed strong support among liberal Democrats, announced that he would not enter the primaries. Second, Governor L. Douglas Wilder of Virginia, a black moderate Democrat who had earlier announced his candidacy, withdrew. Had he remained in the race, he would have taken many black votes that Clinton needed to win, particularly on Super Tuesday in the south. Finally, with Cuomo and Wilder out, and Clinton enjoying the united support of party moderates, a group of leading New York Democrats in the House jumped on the bandwagon and endorsed the Arkansas governor.[10] The endorsement gave Clinton legitimacy among the party's liberals, and he was already developing momentum, well before the primaries.

Then came Gennifer Flowers. For a few days, about a week before the New Hampshire primary, Clinton appeared to be in a free-fall. However, after his appearance on CBS' 60 Minutes with Hillary, he recovered to place second in New Hampshire, behind Tsongas. The victory established the Tsongas candidacy, but Clinton survived, and he could claim regained momentum as the "comeback kid."

The factional politics of the Democratic Party is an important explanation of how Clinton survived a scandal that was objectively more serious than the one that eliminated Gary Hart in 1988. There was speculation in the media during the free-fall period that Clinton would have to withdraw if he did not do well in New Hampshire. Then, the speculation went, another moderate Democrat such as Gore, Gephardt, or Senator Lloyd M. Bentsen of Texas, would enter the race to carry the flag for the centrist constituency in the party.[11] Such speculation never was based on a realistic assessment of the situation. Clinton might have been eliminated had he not placed at least second in New Hampshire, but he would not have been replaced by a new candidate because the filing deadlines for almost all of the later primaries had already passed. Because the overwhelming majority of delegates are now chosen in primaries, Clinton was the only candidate available for moderate Democrats. Therefore, there was no real pressure on Clinton to withdraw to make way for another candidate to represent the cause. In 1988, by contrast, there were any number of liberal Democrats waiting to benefit from the demise of Gary Hart, and voters inclined to support Hart could easily find an alternative.

Super Tuesday came soon after New Hampshire. Here Clinton could count on victory for the two reasons cited earlier: First, whereas Jesse Jackson had been a factor in 1988, now Wilder was out of the race; second, whereas moderate Democrats had been split between Gore and Gephardt in 1988, now they were united behind Clinton. On Super Tuesday, Clinton won all six primaries across the south by landslide margins, including Texas and Florida.

Clinton won Michigan and Illinois a week later and New York two weeks after that. The nomination was his.

There was an apparent ideological component to the vote in the Democratic primaries. Again, like Jimmy Carter in 1976, Clinton won at least partly because moderate Democrats were united while liberal Democrats were divided. Tsongas scored three of his four victories in the northeast quadrant, and Brown one of his two. But Clinton, who ran strongest in the south and won most of the west, won most of the northeast quadrant as well. The consensus on his nomination, even before it was clinched, reached far across factional lines. (See Table 6.5.)

THE NEW NOMINATING EQUILIBRIUM

The new American party system emerging at the end of the twentieth century is more polarized ideologically than the party system born in the nineteenth century, while the new parties themselves are internally more homogenized ideologically. It should not be surprising that these

new parties practice new and continuously changing nominating pro-
cedures for their national leadership, yielding a new pattern of outcomes in Presidential nominations. There are five observations of recent
nominating contests that have been consistent enough to be projected
as patterns of party development, at least into the near-term future.
Much of what is observed here agrees with what party decay theorists
have observed. However, these observations should leave an impression of a dialectical process of party decay and renewal, rather than a
linear process of decline.

1. *Presidential nominations are now participatory processes,* a reality that
is unlikely to be reversed in form, even if it is neutralized to some degree
in practice. Nomination processes are candidate-centered, rather than
party-centered, much as elections themselves have become. The vast
majority of convention delegates are now chosen in primaries; most of
the rest are chosen in caucus/convention systems that are participatory
and structured around candidate competition rather than party leadership or loyalty. These open nominating systems, then, are manipulated
by more ideological issue activists, whose first concerns are issues and
candidates rather than the party.

2. *Primaries decide Presidential nominations, conventions ratify them.* Not
since 1952 has a national convention gone beyond one ballot to select a
nominee. Not since 1976 has there been a serious contest for the nomination at a convention. Not since 1980 has there been any doubt whatever as to who would be nominated for the Presidency when the
convention met. As late as 1960, John F. Kennedy was winning primaries in order to persuade the party leadership to nominate him at the
convention; the convention was still the party's. Now candidates enter
primaries to win enough delegates to seize the nomination before the
convention meets. Conventions have become ceremonial affairs, campaign inaugurations, and four-day advertisements, hardly worthy of
media coverage.

3. *Campaign reform has had an influence on nominating politics in both
parties, but not necessarily the influence intended by reformers.* Certainly,
requirements for participatory delegate selection have promoted the
growth of primaries and delegate-centered caucuses, although as discussed later, even that has not had the impact intended. But proportional representation, for example, has had, since 1972, almost no
impact on the outcomes of nominations. It was widely expected that
proportional representation would make it more difficult for any candidate to obtain a majority of the delegates to a convention, leading to
more-open conventions; this was particularly anticipated in 1976. But
in 1976, and in every campaign thereafter, early victories and momentum for the front-runner winnowed out the opposition, and the nomination was effectively settled before the convention. Campaign finance

reform was expected to have a democratizing impact; what Federal matching funds have in fact done is make it easier for candidates with access to money to raise more money. Front-runners with money today are able to discourage opposition and limit the nomination contest even more than party leaders of the old umbrella parties could once discourage opposition to the party's choice, if there was one.

Both proportional representation and campaign finance reform have had much more influence on who runs rather than on who wins once the running starts. Proportional representation played a role in expanding the early fields of candidates and in building the now common strategy of running in almost every primary. A candidate no longer has to win to earn a share of the delegates, and he or she almost has to run everywhere to avoid being crowded out of the race. These large early fields have not, however, stopped the winnowing process; indeed they have increased its decisiveness. Candidates need to win primaries to stay in the race. Before reform, there were fewer candidates in the primaries, but more candidates still active at the convention, than there are now.

Federal matching funds and crowded fields of candidates have created longer campaigns, and particularly the now widely recognized "invisible primary" that determines front-runners and eliminates candidates even before the election year begins, quite contrary to the intention of the Democratic reform, which restricted delegate selection to the election year.[12] Sometimes even potentially major candidates are eliminated before a vote is cast, as was the case with former Vice President Dan Quayle who, in 1995, saw the money being raised by another conservative Republican, Senator Phil Gramm of Texas, and who at the same time was being squeezed out in his home state of Indiana by Senator Richard Lugar.[13] Other potentially important candidates, who almost certainly would have gathered convention delegates before reform, have been discouraged from putting the time and money necessary into such complex campaigns. We shall never know, empirically, whether Governor Mario Cuomo of New York or Senator Sam Nunn of Georgia would have been nominated or elected in 1988 or 1992.

4. *The early front-runner, if one is identified, is most likely to be nominated.* This would seem ironic and is the result of a dialectical process. Reform opened up the nominating system; the participatory process created more primaries and a longer campaign. At first, this led to a series of upsets in Presidential nominations, through 1976. Then, the accumulation of primaries promoted front loading, as states competed for influence; the long crowded calendar made early organization and financing all the more important. Now, even established party leaders must have campaign organizations ready to go early, as only insurgents had to in

the days of Barry Goldwater and George McGovern. There no longer is an open path to the guerilla-like sneak attacks of the Goldwater and McGovern campaigns. Early upsets in Iowa and New Hampshire always seem to occur, but when they do, the surprise winner does not have the resources to hold off the early front-runner, who comes back to win. Thus, we are back pretty much where we started: A clear front-runner, if one can be identified, is more likely than any other candidate to win the nomination. This general rule describes the nominations of Ronald Reagan in 1980, Walter Mondale in 1984, George Bush in 1988, and Robert Dole in 1996. To a lesser degree, it might be applied to Bill Clinton in 1992.

The 2000 presidential campaign—as it is unfolding at this writing a year in advance of the conventions—provides a case in point of the power of a well-financed front-runner with party backing. Governor George W. Bush of Texas, having raised a record $37 million to date, is already single-handedly winnowing the field and is hopeful of winning the Republican presidential nomination with little or no contest. He is in a stronger position at the moment than the front-runner for the Democratic nomination, Vice President Albert Gore, who apparently faces a fight in the primaries against former Senator Bill Bradley of New Jersey. But both Bush and to a lesser extent Gore are being treated as nominees apparent in the media, months in advance of the first caucus or primary. That treatment may not turn out to be accurate, but it is a reflection of the fact that in recent campaigns, identifiable front-runners have prevailed in nomination contests.

It is, of course, not always the case that a clear early front-runner is identified. Larry Bartels has classified three typologies of nominating campaigns.[14] The first is the front-runner against the field, described earlier. The second is the one-on-one race between two leading candidates, which has not happened since Carter and Kennedy in 1980. The third is the crowded field, which occurred in the Democratic primaries of 1976, 1988, and 1992. However, in each of these cases, the first candidate to emerge as the front-runner, even if seriously challenged in the interim, went on to the nomination.

Bartel's classification of nominating campaigns, based on primaries, is not unlike the earlier classification of nominations by William Keech and Donald Matthews, which was based more on the convention decision.[15] For reasons previously discussed, the convention no longer decides, but that fact makes their classifications all the more instructive about what has happened to preconvention politics.

First, Keech and Matthews describe *consensual* nominations, in which there is a single candidate identified as the front-runner before the primaries and who never faces serious opposition. This occurs more frequently in the party in the White House, of course, particularly when the incumbent President is seeking renomination, but it occurs in the party out of the White House as well. Second, *semiconsensual* nominations are those in which a front-runner emerges early and faces vigorous opposition during the primaries before finally securing the nomination. The semiconsensual nominee is not a unanimous choice but is broadly acceptable across factions of the party. Finally, the *nonconsensual* nomination seriously divides the party along factional lines, sometimes doing telling damage after the convention.

The nominations classified by Keech and Matthews through 1976 are listed in Table 6.6, along with an application of these classifications to nominations since that time. Keech and Matthews recognized what most observers of party politics at that time did not, that the vigorous campaigns in the Presidential primaries did not necessarily do damage to the party. Indeed, they pointed out, the 1976 primaries built a consensus in the Democratic Party that had not previously existed, leading to the nomination and election of Jimmy Carter. That observation has almost become the rule. Though contested nominations up to that time were polarizing and nonconsensual as often as not, there has not been a nonconsensual nomination in either party since 1980. Using the Keech and Matthews analysis, as they revised it slightly after 1976 to recognize the reality of consensus emerging during the primaries, consensual nominations are apparently becoming the rule, even in the party not in the White House. This is a reflection of the fact that the factional conflict within parties before the 1964–1972 realignment has been replaced by ideological polarization between the parties, ideological homogenization within the parties, and generally greater party unity.

5. *Ideological homogenization within the parties has had as much or more to do with the new nominating system as reform.* Goldwater's activists seized the Republican Party before, not after, reform. Reform could not have been passed in the first place had not a coalition of liberal Democrats already had the convention majority to do it in 1968. Ideological polarization between the parties was already well advanced before the impact of reform was felt, and the increased ideological homogenization within the parties has done much to shape nominating politics since then.

Ideological homogenization has certainly promoted preconvention consensus building and contributed to nominations being decided early. Opposing candidates withdraw once a front-runner is established partly because they are out of money, but partly also because their ideological differences with the front-runner are not that great. The losers' supporters generally do not find it that difficult to support the winner at the convention and in the election. Indeed, considerations of money and ideology are not mutually exclusive. If ideological differences among the leading candidates in the primaries were greater, issue activists would be out raising money for their candidate, or for a new candidate, in a last ditch effort to stop the front-runner. Thus, Robert Dole found it relatively easy to withdraw in favor of George Bush, compared with Nelson Rockefeller, who, when he withdrew, could not bring himself to back Barry Goldwater; instead, Rockefeller and his supporters promoted a hopeless eleventh-hour campaign for William Scranton. On the Democratic side, for example, Paul Tsongas could withdraw in favor of Bill Clinton in 1992, pleading lack of funds, despite the fact that he had won several primaries and still had a base of support. And Gary Hart could carry on against Walter Mondale in name only in 1984, without attempting a serious stand at the convention. But both Mo Udall in 1976 and Ted Kennedy in 1980 found it necessary to contest Jimmy Carter all the way to the convention, and had the support to do so, even though their real chances for the nomination were gone. And although he swept the contested primaries in 1960, John F. Kennedy had to overcome Lyndon B. Johnson, Adlai E. Stevenson, and W. Stuart Symington at the convention.

The front loading of primaries has often been cited as a cause of the early clinching of nominations.[16] Indeed, in 2000, an even more front loaded schedule of primaries is expected to determine nominations early again. Certainly, front loading has to do with the fact that the nomination race is decided so early, after only a few weeks in recent years. But it has little to do with the fact that conventions no longer nominate. The last convention to take more than one ballot to nominate, in 1952, was twenty years before reform, and thirty-six years before any serious front loading of primaries occured. And although the contest was decided at several conventions between 1952 and 1976, never since 1952 has any convention displaced the preconvention front-runner.

Front loading, indeed, is only a factor in deciding nominations because of the decreased ideological differences and factional conflict within the parties. If the current front loaded primaries were being contested between Harry Truman and Richard Russell, or Jimmy Carter and Ted Kennedy, or Gerald Ford and Ronald Reagan, or between Nelson Rockefeller and Barry Goldwater, or Dwight D. Eisenhower and Robert Taft, the battle would still go all the way to the convention. But such extreme ideological differences within each party have seldom been observed since the realignment of 1964–1972.

There is still conflict between party leaders and issue activists in nominating contests and at conventions. The Christian Right and movement conservatives are critical of the Republican establishment for not being conservative enough, and the Rainbow Coalition is critical of the Democratic establishment for not being progressive enough. These ideological movements can be counted on to have a presence at their party's convention, often behind a candidate, such as Pat Robertson and

Jesse Jackson in 1988 or Pat Buchanan and Jerry Brown in 1992.[17] But that candidate has no chance at the nomination. The conflict over the platform, between party leaders, now focused on winning the election, and activists, still focused on issues, is a family conflict among liberals in the Democratic Party and conservatives in the Republican Party. Although the front-runner can help or hurt his or her chances in the coming election by how he or she handles the conflict, the nomination is not in jeopardy.

Finally, although the distinction between issue activists and party leaders is still a useful one, increasingly party leaders have gained their position with the support of issue activists rather than party professionals; and increasingly, issue activists are party leaders. Presidents are not only nominated by issue activists, they take issue activists to the White House. The Republican Congress elected in 1994 and the elevation of Newt Gingrich to the House Speakership are examples of issue activists becoming party leaders. Certainly that process creates some role conflict, both between politicians with conflicting agendas and within individuals torn by competing priorities. But this new style of leadership, and the role conflict it brings with it, is testimony to the emerging, ideologically homogenized political party.

CONCLUSION

The new, more nationalized and ideologically homogenized political parties, aggregating internally more harmonious interests than the nineteenth-century parties, are more unified than the nineteenth-century parties, a fact that has been apparent in changing patterns of Presidential nominations since the ideological polarization between the parties of the 1960s.

The evidence presented here suggests that factional realignment within parties is as important to the study of the party system as is electoral realignment between the parties. The "realignment at the top" in Presidential elections was as much an intraparty realignment as it was an interparty realignment. But neither realignment was recognized as it happened because it took so long to spread to the "bottom." The secular spread of realignment from the top to the bottom and its relationship to split-ticket voting and divided government is the subject of Chapter 7.

TABLES

Table 6.1
1980 Republican Presidential Primaries

WINNERS OF PRIMARIES, BY 1964–1972 IDEOLOGICAL ALIGNMENT OF STATES		
	liberal	*moderate*	*conservative*

	liberal	*moderate*	*conservative*
Reagan	New York	Illinois	Alabama
	Oregon	Maryland	Florida
	Wisconsin	New Hampshire	Georgia
		Texas	Indiana
		Vermont	Louisiana
			Nebraska
			North Carolina
			Tennessee
Bush	Connecticut		
	D.C.		
	Massachusetts		
	Michigan		
	Pennsylvania		

See Chapter 1 and Table 1.19 for methodology of ideological alignment of states.

MEAN VOTE IN PRESIDENTIAL PREFERENCE PRIMARIES					
By 1964–1972 ideological alignment of states					
	liberal	*moderate*	*conservative*	*Non-South*	*South*	*National*
---	---	---	---	---	---	---
Reagan	33	**45**	**68**	**44**	**65**	**52**
Bush	**44**	29	19	32	24	29
Anderson	18	17	6	18	3	12

Figures represent mean percentage of the vote in Presidential preference primaries. All primaries included until Bush withdrew on May 26.

Derived from *Presidential Elections, 1789–1996* (Washington, D.C.: Congressional Quarterly, 1997), pp. 191–197.

Table 6.2
Republican Presidential Primaries, 1988–1996, by 1964–1972 Ideological Alignment of States

	By 1964–1972 ideological alignment of states					
	liberal	*moderate*	*conservative*	*Non-South*	*South*	*National*
1988						
Bush	**71**	**47**	**54**	**53**	**57**	**55**
Dole	17	34	24	30	22	26
Robertson	6	11	15	10	15	12
1992						
Bush	**71**	**67**	**69**	**69**	**68**	**69**
Buchanan	23	24	24	23	26	24
1996						
Dole	**55**	**49**	**49**	**50**	**51**	**50**
Buchanan	23	22	24	22	26	23
Forbes	10	14	16	14	13	14

See Chapter 1 and Table 1.19 for methodology of ideological alignment of states. Figures represent mean percentages of the vote in Republican primaries. All primaries included until the front-runner clinched the nomination in the delegate count.
Derived from *Presidential Elections*, pp. 204–227.

Table 6.3
1984 Democratic Presidential Primaries, by 1964-1972 Ideological Alignment of States

WINNERS OF PRESIDENTIAL PRIMARIES			
	liberal	*moderate*	*conservative*
Mondale	New York	Illinois	Alabama
	Pennsylvania	Maryland	Georgia
		New Jersey	North Carolina
		West Virginia	Tennessee
Hart	Connecticut	California	Florida
	Massachusetts	New Hampshire	Idaho
	Oregon	Ohio	Indiana
	Rhode Island	South Dakota	Nebraska
	Wisconsin	Vermont	New Mexico
			North Dakota
Jackson	D.C.		Louisiana

$G = -.14$
See Chapter 1 and Table 1.19 for methodology of ideological alignment of states.

MEAN VOTE IN PRESIDENTIAL PRIMARIES						
	By 1964–1972 ideological alignment of states					
	liberal	*moderate*	*conservative*	*Non-South*	*South*	*National*
Mondale	34	35	34	35	**33**	34
Hart	**38**	**37**	**39**	**41**	29	**38**
Jackson	19	13	17	14	24	16

Figures represent mean percentage of the vote in Presidential primaries.
Derived from *Presidential Elections*, pp. 198–203.

Table 6.4

1988 Democratic Presidential Primaries, by 1964–1972 Ideological Alignment of States

WINNERS OF PRESIDENTIAL PRIMARIES			
	liberal	*moderate*	*conservative*
Dukakis	Connecticut	California	Florida
	Massachusetts	Maryland	Idaho
	New York	Montana	Indiana
	Oregon	New Hampshire	Nebraska
	Pennsylvania	New Jersey	New Mexico
	Rhode Island	Ohio	
	Wisconsin	Texas	
		Vermont	
		West Virginia	
Jackson	D.C.		Alabama
			Georgia
			Louisiana
			Mississippi
			Virginia
Gore		Kentucky	Arkansas
			North Carolina
			Oklahoma
			Tennessee
Gephardt		Missouri	
		South Dakota	
Simon		Illinois	

G = .46

See Chapter 1 and Table 1.19 for methodology of ideological alignment of states.

MEAN VOTE IN PRESIDENTIAL PRIMARIES						
	By 1964–1972 ideological alignment of states					
	liberal	*moderate*	*conservative*	*Non-South*	*South*	*National*
Dukakis	**54**	**43**	**31**	**50**	19	**41**
Jackson	34	22	29	26	33	28
Gore	6	9	26	8	**33**	15
Gephardt	2	14	7	8	8	8
Simon	2	7	2	5	1	4

Figures represent mean percentage of the vote in Presidential primaries.
Derived from *Presidential Elections,* pp. 204–211.

Table 6.5
1992 Democratic Presidential Primaries, by 1964–1972 Ideological Alignment of States

WINNERS OF PRESIDENTIAL PRIMARIES			
	liberal	*moderate*	*conservative*
Clinton	D.C.	California	Alabama
	Michigan	Illinois	Arkansas
	Minnesota	Kentucky	Florida
	New York	Montana	Georgia
	Oregon	New Jersey	Idaho
	Pennsylvania	Ohio	Indiana
	Washington	Texas	Louisiana
	Wisconsin	West Virginia	Mississippi
			Nebraska
			New Mexico
			North Carolina
			Oklahoma
			South Carolina
			Tennessee
Tsongas	Massachusetts	Maryland	
	Rhode Island	New Hampshire	
Brown	Connecticut	Colorado	
Kerrey		South Dakota	

G = –.71
See Chapter 1 and Table 1.19 for methodology of ideological alignment of states.

MEAN VOTE IN PRESIDENTIAL PRIMARIES						
	By 1964–1972 ideological alignment of states					
	liberal	*moderate*	*conservative*	*Non-South*	*South*	*National*
Clinton	**41**	**48**	**62**	**45**	**65**	**51**
Tsongas	25	17	11	19	14	17
Brown	25	16	11	20	9	17
Kerrey	1	6	1	3	1	3

Figures represent mean percentage of the vote in Presidential primaries.
Derived from *Presidential Elections*, pp. 212–219.

Table 6.6
Party Conflict and Consensus in Presidential Nominations

Nonconsensual	Semiconsensual	Consensual
1912 (R)**		
1912 (D)		
1916 (R)		1916 (D)**
1920 (D)*		
1920 (R)		
1924 (D)		1924 (R)**
	1928 (R)*	
	1928 (D)	
	1932 (R)**	
	1932 (D)	
		1936 (D)**
		1936 (R)
1940 (R)	1940 (D)**	
		1944 (D)**
		1944 (R)
1948 (R)	1948 (D)**	
1952 (D)*		
1952 (R)		
	1956 (D)	1956 (R)**
	1960 (D)	1960 (R)*
1964 (R)		1964 (D)**
1968 (D)*	1968 (R)	
1972 (D)		1972 (R)**
1976 (R)**		1976 (D)
1980 (D)**		1980 (R)
	1984 (D)	1984 (R)**
	1988 (D)	1988 (R)*
		1992 (R)**
		1992 (D)
		1996 (D)**
		1996 (R)

William R. Keech and Donald R. Matthews, *The Party's Choice* (Washington, D.C.: Brookings Institution, 1977). Between 1936 and 1972 classifications of nominations are drawn directly from Keech and Matthews. Before and since that time, nominations are classified by the author according to their theory.

*Incumbent party.

**Incumbent party, President an active candidate. In 1952 and 1968, Presidents were on the ballot for one or more Democratic primaries but did not formally seek renomination.

NOTES

1. Lou Cannon and William Peterson, "GOP," in David Broder, Lou Cannon, Haynes Johnson, Martin Schram, and Richard Harwood, *The Pursuit of the Presidency 1980* (New York: G.P. Putnam's Sons, 1980), pp. 141–143.

2. All data on Presidential primaries is drawn from *Presidential Elections, 1789–1996* (Washington, D.C.: Congressional Quarterly, 1997), pp. 191–227.

3. Cannon and Peterson, "GOP," in David Broder, et al., *The Pursuit of the Presidency 1980*, p. 148.

4. Theodore H. White, *The Making of the President 1964* (New York: Atheneum, 1965), p. 337.

5. See Jack W. Germond and Jules Witcover, *Whose Broad Stripes and Bright Stars? The Trivial Pursuit of the Presidency 1988* (New York: Warner, 1989), pp. 63–165, for a discussion of the contest for the Republican Presidential nomination in 1988. See also Gerald M. Pomper, "The Presidential Nominations," in Gerald M. Pomper, Ross K. Baker, Walter Dean Burnham, Barabara G. Farah, Marjorie Randon Hershey, Ethel Klein, and Wilson Carey McWilliams, *The Election of 1988: Reports and Interpretations* (Chatham, N.J.: Chatham House, 1989), pp. 33–71.

6. See Ross K. Baker, "The Presidential Nominations," in Gerald M. Pomper, F. Christopher Arterton, Ross K. Baker, Walter Dean Burnham, Kathleen A. Frankovic, Marjorie Randon Hershey, and Wilson Carey McWilliams, *The Election of 1992: Reports and Interpretations* (Chatham, N.J.: Chatham House, 1993), pp. 39–73.

7. See William G. Mayer, "The Presidential Nominations," in Gerald M. Pomper, Walter Dean Burnham, Anthony Corrado, Marjorie Randon Hershey, Marion R. Just, Scott Keeter, Wilson Carey McWilliams, and William G. Mayer, *The Election of 1996: Reports and Interpretations* (Chatham, N.J.: Chatham House, 1997), pp. 21–76.

8. There has, in fact, always been a rainbow coalition within the Democratic Party, but historically it has been found within the party regular faction. As the Rainbow Coalition associated with Jesse Jackson has served the function of mobilizing previously disenfranchised voters into the party and organizing them politically, so did the party machine in the industrial cities in decades past. In the case of the Rainbow Coalition, the voters are disproportionately black and poor or working class, whereas the voters mobilized by the urban machines were disproportionately immigrant and poor or working class.

9. Earl Black and Merle Black, *The Vital South: How Presidents Are Elected* (Cambridge: Harvard University Press, 1992), pp. 241–271. See also Charles D. Hadley and Harold W. Stanley, "The Southern Super Tuesday: Southern Democrats Seeking Relief from Rising Republicanism," in William G. Mayer, ed., *In Pursuit of the White House: How We Choose Our Presidential Nominees* (Chatham, N.J.: Chatham House, 1996), pp. 158–189.

10. Gwen Ifill, "Pragmatism Is a Big Winner as Clinton Gains in New York," *New York Times*, January 21, 1992, p. A19.

11. Clifford Krauss, "Capitol Hill Starts Rounding Up the Usual Suspects," *New York Times*, February 14, 1996, p. A17. See also, "Democrat Sees Draft Scenario," *New York Times*, February 16, 1996, p. 26.

12. Arthur T. Hadley, *The Invisible Primary* (Englewood Cliffs, N.J.: Prentice-Hall, 1976).

13. Emmett H. Buell, Jr., "The Invisible Primary," in William G. Mayer, ed., *In Pursuit of the White House: How We Choose Our Presidential Nominees* (Chatham, N.J.: Chatham House, 1996), p. 3.

14. Larry M. Bartels, *Presidential Primaries and the Dynamics of Public Choice* (Princeton, N.J.: Princeton University Press, 1988), pp. 166–171.

15. William R. Keech and Donald R. Matthews, *The Party's Choice* (Washington, D.C.: The Brookings Institution, 1977), pp. 157–213 and pp. 251–264.

16. See, for example, Mayer, "The Presidential Nominations," in Pomper, et al., *The Election of 1992*.

17. Byron E. Shafer, *Bifurcated Politics* (Cambridge: Harvard University Press, 1988), pp. 183–225.

Ideological Polarization and the Two-Tier Party System: Split-Ticket Voting, Divided Government, and Realignment in American Politics

Although the nonideological and decentralized character of American political parties has historically combined with the separation of powers to make a responsible party system highly unlikely in the United States, unified control of the Presidency and Congress has been the rule more often than not. Divided government has, however, been the rule for about the last four decades and is often cited as evidence of party decay. But, ironically, the last previous period of frequently divided government came in the heyday of the nineteenth-century political parties, just before the realignment of 1896.

The argument presented in this chapter is that the split-ticket voting and divided government of the last four decades is a function of the realignment of the 1960s, and may even be more a sign of party revival than party decay. The two-tier party system of the late twentieth century has featured "realignment at the top and dealignment at the bottom," in the words of James Q. Wilson.[1] As discussed in the previous chapters, realignment at the top is associated with ideological polarization between the major parties. Dealignment at the bottom is associated with two factors. First, the increased power of incumbency has produced candidate-centered elections for the United States House of Representatives, with decreased turnover in response to national electoral trends. This has been widely recognized by observers of American elections and often cited as evidence of party decay. Second, and less widely recognized, has been the uneven spread of ideological polarization from the top to the bottom. While ideological polarization between the parties in Presidential nominations and elections was rather sudden between 1964 and 1972, it occurred hardly at all in Congress or Congressional elections at that time. Since then, split-ticket voting has not been equally common everywhere. Rather, it had an ideological structure to it, increasing most in the south, where conservative Democrats were running for re-election to the House. Then, the Congressional election of 1994 demonstrated that ideological polarization between the parties had finally spread to the bottom. The party system since the 1960s then might better be understood as "critical realignment at the top, secular realignment at the bottom." Although still operating within the constitutional separation of powers, the parties emerging at the end of the twentieth century resemble the responsible party model to a degree that is almost unAmerican.[2]

This chapter begins with a case study of Congressional voting on civil rights in the context of the Presidential and Congressional elections of 1964. Using that experience as a model, the balance of the chapter examines the relationship between ideological polarization between the parties and split-ticket voting between the Presidency and Congress.

CIVIL RIGHTS, THE POLITICS OF REALIGNMENT, AND SPLIT-TICKET VOTING

The Civil Rights Bill of 1964 passed by a vote of 290–130 in the House of Representatives, and 73–27 in the Senate, with bipartisan majorities in both houses. Only among southern Democrats in both houses was there majority opposition to the bill. See Table 7.1.[3]

What is particularly notable about the bill, apart from its obvious importance for society at-large, is evidence it offers about changing alignments between the parties, both in Congress and in the electorate, and about the pattern of split-ticket voting that has produced divided government more often than not since that time.

First, of course, most of the opposition to the Civil Rights bill came from southern Democrats. Entering the debate on the bill that summer, Jim Crow was still alive and living almost entirely within the Democratic Party. Senator Ralph Yarborough of Texas was the only southern Democrat to vote for the bill in the Senate. In the House, only seven out of ninety-three southern Democrats supported the bill. In addition to Yarborough, four of the seven in the House were Texans, probably reflecting the strong push given to the bill by President Johnson.[4] All eight of the southern Democrats who voted for the bill won their elections in the Democratic landslide the following November. Senator Yarborough defeated Republican George Bush. Representative Ross Bass of Tennessee was elected to the Senate seat vacated by the death of Estes Kefauver. Bass defeated Republican Howard Baker, who was making his first bid for the Senate. Claude Pepper of Florida, already a veteran, continued his long career on the Hill. Jack Brooks of Texas would go on to vote for the impeachment of President Nixon on the House Judiciary Committee and would stay in the House until he was finally defeated for re-election in the Republican victory of 1994. Henry B. Gonzalez of Texas would survive to serve a long tenure as the chair of the House Banking Committee. The bill's other supporters among southern Democrats in the House were Richard Fulton of Tennessee, Jake Pickle of Texas, and Albert Thomas of Texas.

Second, on the Congressional roll calls on the Civil Rights bill, the Republicans still looked like the party of Lincoln. In both houses, the Republican majorities for the bill were larger than the Democratic majorities. This, of course, is because of the split between northern Democrats, who were collectively the strongest supporters of the bill, and southern Democrats. But the Republican majorities for civil rights in the summer of 1964 were overwhelming.

The vote on the Civil Rights bill took place just as the Republican Party was falling into the hands of its conservative, Main Street faction. Indeed, the civil rights vote would indicate that it was not only conservatives in general, but far right ideologues who were taking over the party at its national convention in San Francisco. When he was about to win the Republican presidential nomination, Senator Barry Goldwater of Arizona was one of only six Republicans to vote against the bill in the Senate, along with Bourke Hickenlooper of Iowa, Norris Cotton of New Hampshire, Edward Mechem of New Mexico, John Tower of Texas, and Milward Simpson of Wyoming. Senate Minority Leader Everett M. Dirksen, a conservative Republican who had long supported the late Robert A. Taft, and who was now endorsing Goldwater for president, played a decisive role in ushering the bill through the Senate with Republican support.[5] Thus, not only did liberal Republicans support the Civil Rights bill in Congress, so did most conservative Republicans. This fact was hardly apparent when the Republican National Convention voted to reject the minority plank on Civil Rights only two weeks later.

The Civil Rights vote in Congress represents perhaps the last opportunity to see American parties as they were before the ideological polarization of the 1964–1972 period. If we look at that moment frozen in time, both parties have within them ideological factions that cross party lines in both directions. Almost all northern Democrats are liberals, and they constitute a majority of their party on the hill. The south is conservative as ever, yet still solidly Democratic. And, the Republican Party, still almost entirely absent in the south, still lives under an umbrella that covers both liberals and conservatives.

Change in the party system in 1964 was more visible in the behavior of the electorate in response to the Goldwater nomination, particularly with regard to split-ticket voting. Continuity was certainly more obvious than change in the 1964 election. The majority party since the New Deal won by a landslide to retain both the Presidency and Congress. Indeed, the result left President Johnson with a governing coalition that enabled him to proceed with the Great Society. But the once Democratic solid south was closely contested in the Presidential election while remaining strongly Democratic in the Congressional election. Although split-ticket voting had increased dramatically in the postwar years, in 1964 it reached new heights, and it took on an ideological pattern that would produce divided government more often than not for the remainder of the century.

This pattern is visible in the relationship between the Civil Rights vote in Congress and split-ticket voting in November. In 1964, there were split outcomes between the Presidency and the House in one-third of all Congressional districts, as high a figure as was ever recorded up to that time. And, the 88 percent re-election rate for House incumbents was lower than in any subsequent Congressional election.[6] These results, however, reflected more than the coattails President Johnson offered to Democrats in his landslide election. Although thirty-five Republican incumbents lost their seats, 78 percent of all Republicans running for re-election to the House won. And, while almost all Democratic incumbents were winning re-election in districts carried by the President, many southern Democrats had to overcome a regional tide for Goldwater to win. The overall result was that while a majority of Congressional districts with Republican incumbents split their tickets, the rate of split-ticket outcomes was much higher in districts where the Republican had voted for the Civil Rights bill. And, while the rate of split-ticket outcomes was almost zero in districts where incumbent Democrats had voted for the Civil Rights bill, it was nearly 30 percent in districts where Democrats running for re-election had voted against the bill, the latter grouping almost entirely in the south. All together, in 117 of the 147 Congressional districts that produced split outcomes between the Presidency and the House, incumbents who disagreed with their party's nominee for President on civil rights were running for re-election. Split-ticket outcomes are less frequent in open seats and where incumbents of both parties agree with their party's Presidential nominee on civil rights. (See Table 7.2.)

The same pattern carries over to the Senate. All six incumbent Senators who were the beneficiaries of split tickets to win re-election disagreed with their party's Presidential nominee on civil rights: Democrat John Stennis of Mississippi, and Republicans John Williams of Delaware, Hiram Fong of Hawaii, Roman Hruska of Nebraska, Hugh Scott of Pennsylvania, and Winston Prouty of Vermont.

TOWARD A MODEL OF SPLIT-TICKET VOTING IN THE TWO-TIER PARTY SYSTEM

If the vote on the Civil Rights Act of 1964 can be generalized as an indicator of ideology in electoral politics, the preceding discussion and the data offered in Table 7.2 would certainly be evidence of a relationship between ideological polarization and split-ticket voting. Just as much evidence appears for the relationship between incumbency advantages in Congressional elections and split-ticket voting between the Presidency and the House. But incumbency advantage has been much more recognized in the literature than ideological polarization, creating a picture of dealignment as electoral chaos.[7] The argument presented here is that dealignment has been realignment by other means and represents electoral order more than disorder.

The overwhelming reality of Congressional elections since the 1960s has been the rate at which incumbents are re-elected to the House of Representatives—consistently over 90 percent. It would make intuitive sense to conclude that incumbency advantage, by itself, would explain much of the split-ticket voting between Presidential and Congressional elections. As incumbents construct solid electoral bases of support in their districts, election results become less variable, and less correlated with the vote for President. The result is the "two-tier" party system.

Elections for the House have been analyzed as national events and as local events. As national events, Congressional elections have been tied to Presidential coattails in Presidential election years, and to a "surge and decline" in the vote, forecasting the loss of seats for the President's party in mid-term elections.[8] Congressional elections in mid-term years have been observed to reflect voter responses to Presidential performance and the economy, with the two variables often related closely.[9]

But in the "two-tier" party system, Presidential coattails have become shorter, resulting in more frequently divided government. With the increased success of incumbents running for reelection, there has been less fluctuation in the membership and party composition of the House, resulting in apparently institutionalized control of the House of Representatives by the Democrats until 1994. Party-line voting has seemed to persist in Congressional elections beyond its decline in Presidential elections, and voters almost unanimously vote for House incumbents of their own party.[10] With the decline in coattails and the increase in seniority in the House, the "surge and decline" pattern became less pronounced.[11] The advantages of incumbency (and the advantage of perceived advantages) became great enough to discourage serious challenges.[12] In short, elections for the House became more candidate-centered, incumbent-specific, and local.

Split-ticket voting to the advantage of incumbents in the House has been widely attributed to the fact that, as Tip O'Neill often put it, "all politics is local" in Congressional elections. According to this reasoning, national and international issues are salient for voters in Presidential elections, and often those issues are more symbolic and ideological than the relatively local issues that are salient to Congressional elections. When voting for the House, the electorate is more focused on who brings home the "pork," that is, economic issues and interests. This argument is consistent with the observation by Lloyd Free and Hadley Cantril that American voters are ideologically conservative and operationally liberal.[13] According to this interpretation, majorities since the 1960s have voted for Republican Presidents on ideological grounds, while defending their more narrow economic interests by voting for incumbent Democrats for the House.

This might explain why the ideological polarization found in Presidential elections was not spread evenly to Congressional elections, at least until 1994. Some analysts have attributed the difference in outcomes of Presidential and Congressional elections in the same year to a decisive minority of "sophisticated voters" who split their tickets for the purpose of electing a divided government. With two ideologically extreme national parties, voters split their tickets to balance the result of the Presidential election in order to limit government power and to obtain policy moderation.[14]

If these explanations of split-ticket voting were satisfactory, ticket splitters would be found to be mostly nonpartisan political moderates, and Congress would be governed by centrist coalitions. The data presented in this chapter would tend to indicate, to the contrary, that split-ticket voting has been most common for most of the last thirty years among historically conservative Democrats and has produced generally conservative governing coalitions in Congress. With increased incumbency advantages in Congressional elections, partisan loyalties remained relatively stable and historic coalitions that predated the electoral change of the 1960s were somewhat more persistent than in Presidential elections. Particularly in the south, which shifted toward the Republicans in Presidential elections, conservative Democrats continued to win re-election to the House. In the northeast quadrant, which shifted toward the Democrats in Presidential elections, a smaller number of liberal Republicans continued to win re-election to the House. Thus, in the "two-tier" party system, the ideological polarization between the Presidential parties advanced far more quickly than between the Congressional parties. This difference is treated hypothetically in the current study as offering a significant explanation for split-ticket voting between the Presidency and the House, and for the increased incidence of divided government. Using Wilson's language, ideological polarization promoted "realignment at the top" in the 1960s; the relative absence of ideological polarization in Congressional elections resulted in a long period of what Wilson called "dealignment at the bottom," and what is analyzed in the current study as "secular realignment at the bottom."

Data and Analysis

The ideological polarization/realignment theory presented here treats the 1968 Presidential election as the model election in American politics for nearly three decades thereafter. According to the model, the Nixon voter would continue to vote the Republican ticket for President and Congress; the Humphrey voter would vote the Democratic ticket. The split tickets would be produced by conservative Democrats voting for George Wallace in 1968, who later would tend to vote Republican for President and Democratic for Congress. These expectations are supplemented by the observation that re-election rates to the House of Representatives are so high across party lines that incumbents of both parties are generally safe, regardless of other electoral trends. The resulting model yields three empirical predictions about split-ticket voting. The first is predicted by the model at the aggregate level. The next two focus on the relationship between incumbents running for re-election to the House and Senate and their party's Presidential ticket.[15]

1. *There will be a very strong positive relationship between the vote for George Wallace and split-ticket voting.* The states that voted for Wallace in the 1968 Presidential election will be the states yielding the highest rates of split outcomes between Presidential and Congressional elections. States that cast the lowest percentages of their vote for Wallace will produce the least split-ticket voting. Most of the House and Senate incumbents in states where Wallace won or ran very well, mostly in the south, will be conservative Democrats.

2. *The correlation between the vote for President and the vote for the Senate and House will be higher in states and Congressional districts with open seats than in states and districts with incumbents running for re-election. Districts*

ADA position more than two-thirds of the time are classified as "liberals"; those who oppose the ADA position more than two-thirds of the time are classified as "conservatives." Those with scores in the middle are classified as "moderates." The hypothesis, then, predicts that correlations between Presidential and House or Senate elections would be relatively high in cases where there is an open seat or where liberal Democrats or conservative Republicans are running for re-election. In seats where conservative Democrats or, to a lesser degree, liberal Republicans are running for re-election, the correlations would be lower, and the frequency of split-ticket voting higher.

IDEOLOGY, INCUMBENCY, AND SPLIT-TICKET VOTING: THE HOUSE

Data comparing electoral outcomes between the Presidency and Congress in Presidential election years tend to support the ideological polarization/realignment model of split-ticket voting and divided government. Table 7.3 shows state-level correlations between the vote for President and the aggregate vote for the House of Representatives since 1896. It reveals a pattern very similar to the direction of electoral change in Presidential elections over the same period, which was illustrated in Table 1.3. State-level correlations showed a long-term stability in Presidential elections between 1896 and 1944, followed by a period of secular realignment, then critical realignment between 1964 and 1972, and a period of relative stability since 1972. Similarly, correlations between the Presidential and Congressional vote are consistently high and positive between 1896 and 1944, fluctuate wildly at reduced levels between 1948 and 1960, then are generally negative between 1964 and 1972. Since 1976, correlations between the vote for President and the House are positive again, but never at levels as high as the 1896–1944 period.

The ideological polarization/realignment model of split-ticket voting suggests that these similar patterns are not coincidental. They reflect electoral change in Presidential elections that is not replicated quickly in Congressional elections, particularly in the south. Secular realignment in Presidential elections between 1948 and 1960 is accompanied by almost no electoral change in Congressional elections over the same period; critical realignment in Presidential elections after 1964 is accompanied by a very slow secular change in Congressional elections during the same period. Thereafter, secular realignment in Congressional elections is very much in the same direction as electoral change in Presidential elections, but it takes nearly three decades to become critical in its dimensions.

with open seats will also be carried by the same party in Presidential
Congressional elections more frequently than is generally the case in states
districts with incumbents running for re-election.

3. *Among states and Congressional districts where incumbents are runn*
for re-election to the Senate or House, the ideological positions of the candid
will be strongly related to party line and split-ticket voting. The correlat
between the vote for President and the vote of the Senate or House v
be higher, and the same party will carry the state or district m
frequently, where the Congressional incumbent and the party's Pre
dential nominee are in similar ideological positions. Where the incu
bent is in ideological disharmony with the party's President
nominee, the correlation will be lower, split-ticket voting and divid
results will occur more frequently.

The expectation behind this model is that ideological polarizati
between the Presidential parties will begin to play a major role in t
1964–1972 period. The realignment of states in Presidential electio
during that period is predicted to define the geographic structure
split-ticket voting since that time. Accordingly, the states that shift
most from the Democrats toward the Republicans in Presidential ele
tions, in the "L" of the south and west, would initially be expected
show the most split-ticket voting since 1964. However, since much
the west shifted to the Republicans in both Presidential and Congre
sional elections during the Eisenhower years, split-ticket voting an
divided results will be most common in the south, where the Republ
can nominee for President frequently has won while conservative Den
ocrats have retained their seats in the House, and to a lesser degree, i
the Senate. The states in the northeast quadrant might be expected
similarly, to produce the most split-ticket voting to the benefit of libera
Republicans running for Congress, as was the case in 1964. But thi
expectation is somewhat neutralized by the reality that Republican
dominated Presidential elections between 1968 and 1988.

The theoretical basis behind this model is consistent with finding
from survey data of increased ideological and issue-based voting start
ing in the 1960s, and of greater ideological voting in Presidential elec
tions than in Congressional elections.[16] The hypothesis presented her
assumes, incumbency advantages aside, an aggregate ideological ratio
nality to split-ticket voting. The model is important because it predicts
that as ideological polarization between the parties spreads to Congress, as Democrats become more liberal and Republicans more conservative, the frequency of split-ticket voting and divided government will
be reduced.

The ideological positions of Senators and Representatives running for
re-election are indicated by the ratings of Americans for Democratic
Action (ADA) most recent to any given election. Those who support the

The relationship between Presidential and Congressional election coalitions in the states is illustrated in Tables 7.4 and 7.5. Between 1896 and 1944, the coalitions of states for President and the House in Presidential election years are uniform. The most partisan states, for both parties, tend to support their normal party's Presidential and House candidates. The "L" pattern is clear: The northeast quadrant is heavily Republican, and the south is solidly Democratic. Divided results tend to occur only in the most closely contested states.

After 1964, there is, of course, a greater difference between the coalition of states found in Presidential and Congressional elections, indicating the increase in split-ticket voting. But that increase is not random. Split-ticket voting is no longer concentrated in the most closely contested states. Rather, it seems concentrated in states historically the most Democratic that have become among the most Republican in Presidential elections. The "L" pattern is again clear, if almost reversed: The solidly Republican states are found in the west; solidly Democratic states are weighted toward the northeast quadrant. In the south, states are voting Republican for President and Democratic for Congress.

Table 7.6 compares Congressional election coalitions in Presidential election years between 1896 and 1944 with the post-1964 period. Chapter 1 in general, and Table 1.3 in particular, presented evidence of a very sharp critical realignment of coalitions of states in Presidential elections between 1964 and 1972. No such critical realignment is found in Congressional elections at the same time. Instead, there is much more stability across time in Congressional election coalitions. There is evidence of secular realignment, a product of electoral change in the New Deal. By 1964 the Democrats have gained majorities of House seats in a number of states in the northeast quadrant, most of them solidly Republican states in the system of 1896. But there is little evidence of realignment in the south in Congressional elections. The solid south, gone in Presidential elections after 1964, is still Democratic and nearly solid in Congressional elections. It is in these states, as Table 7.5 indicates, that the predisposition to split-ticket outcomes is greatest.

The Wallace Vote and Split-Ticket Voting

This finding is consistent with the expectation that split-ticket voting between the Presidency and the House will generally be greatest where George Wallace ran strongest in the 1968 Presidential election. Table 7.7 illustrates the state-level relationship between the vote for Wallace for President in 1968 and split-ticket voting. The prediction is confirmed for three Presidential elections since 1968: 1972, 1984, and 1988. It is not found to be the case in 1976, 1980, 1992, or 1996.

Table 7.7 also compares split-ticket results between the north and south generally, and across the 1964–1972 ideological alignment of states. This comparison reveals evidence that is similar to the findings based on the Wallace vote. State-level data indicate that split-ticket results are much greater in the south than elsewhere and that ideology is a major factor in split-ticket voting in 1972, 1984, and 1988. There is little difference between split-ticket results in the north and south, and ideology is at best a minor factor in split-ticket voting in 1976, 1980, 1992, and 1996.

These uneven findings, however, tend to support the ideological polarization/realignment model. For all three of the elections in which split-ticket results are most common in the states carried by Wallace or where he runs particularly well, the Democratic nominee is a northern liberal. For all four of the other elections, the Democratic nominee is either Jimmy Carter or Bill Clinton, both moderate Democrats from the south. Thus, in 1972, 1984, and 1988, southern voters who voted for incumbent moderate-to-conservative Democrats for the House rejected the liberal Democrat who was running for President and voted Republican at the top of the ticket. In 1976, 1980, 1992, and 1996, southerners who were comfortable with the incumbent Democrat in the House were also more likely to support the moderate Democrat who was running for President. In the latter four cases there was a much smaller ideological gap between the Presidential and Congressional nominees on the Democratic ticket.

Ideology, Incumbency, and Split-Ticket Voting

The ideological polarization/realignment model of split-ticket voting gains further support from data at the Congressional-district level. Table 7.8 reports the relationship between the Democratic Presidential vote and the Democratic House vote at the Congressional-district level, and Table 7.9 does the same for the Republican vote. Both tables compare split-ticket voting where incumbents are running for re-election to the House with open seats and subdivide the ideology of the incumbents according to voting records in the House.

Generally, the relationships found between the Presidential and Congressional vote are consistent with the ideological polarization/realignment model of split-ticket voting. On the whole, split-ticket voting is more common in Congressional districts with incumbents running for re-election than in open-seat districts. Among incumbents, split-ticket voting is higher where the incumbent Representative is ideologically out of step with the party's national ticket.

The mean difference between the Democratic Congressional vote and the Democratic Presidential vote is smallest in districts where no incumbent is running for re-election. The correlations between the Democratic votes are highest in districts with open seats and where incumbent liberal Democrats are running for re-election. The same correlations are lower or negative where incumbent moderate-to-conservative Democrats are running for re-election. In each election, the Democratic nominee for President runs much further behind incumbent conservative Democrats than he does incumbent liberal Democrats.

The relationships are similar, although not as consistent or clear, for Republican candidates. In every election, correlations between the Republican Presidential vote and the Republican Congressional vote are highest in districts where no incumbent is running for the House. Correlations are generally higher where incumbent moderate-to-conservative Republicans are running for re-election than in districts where liberal Republican incumbents are on the ballot. In every election, the Republican nominee for President generally runs well behind moderate-to-liberal Republican incumbents, while polling a vote much closer to conservative Republican incumbents. The lesser degree in the pattern of split-ticket voting among Republicans appears to be explained by three observations: First, polling data historically demonstrates that Republican self-identifiers vote the party line much more frequently than Democrats. An examination of the distribution of ideological leanings of incumbents of both parties reveals that, throughout the period since 1968, Republicans have been much more uniformly conservative than Democrats have been liberal. Indeed, the data for liberal Republicans are drawn from so few cases as to be relatively insignificant statistically. Finally, because the Republicans dominated Presidential elections between 1968 and 1988, and the Democrats controlled the House for all of that period (and some years before and after), Democrats have been disproportionately the beneficiaries of incumbency advantages and split-ticket voting for the House.

Table 7.10 illustrates the relationship among partisanship, ideology, and split-ticket voting, correlating the vote for President with the Congressional vote, across party lines. Table 7.10 categorizes House incumbents, assuming ideological polarization between the parties in the House of Representatives. "Partisan ideologues" are conservative Republicans and liberal Democrats, according to ADA scores. "Ideological misfits" are conservative Democrats and liberal Republicans by the same measure. Those with ADA scores between 33 and 67 are rated as "moderates."

The data presented in Table 7.10 lend further support to the ideological polarization/realignment model. For all elections between 1972 and 1996, the correlations between the Presidential vote and the Congressional vote for both parties are higher for districts with open seats and for districts where partisan ideologues are running for re-election to the House than for districts where the House incumbents are moderates or ideological misfits. Almost without exception, the correlation between the Presidential vote and the Congressional vote for each party is lowest, or even negative, where ideological misfits are running for re-election to the House.

The data presented in Table 7.11, showing the percentage of split outcomes in the Congressional districts, also indicate that incumbency advantage and ideological position shape the pattern of split-ticket voting in Presidential and Congressional elections. Incumbency by itself cannot explain the increase in split-ticket voting over the last three decades. Calculated in the aggregate, across party lines, divided results are no more common where incumbent partisan ideologues, liberal Democrats and conservative Republicans, are up for re-election, than in Congressional districts with open seats. Much higher rates of divided results are found where moderates and ideological misfits of both parties are running for re-election.

For all elections except 1976, split results are much more common where incumbents are running for re-election than in open seats and where ideological misfits are running for re-election than where partisan ideologues are running. Also for all elections except 1976, when Jimmy Carter was elected, split results are more common where moderate-to-conservative Democrats are running for re-election to the House than where liberal Democrats are running. Split results are also always more common where moderate-to-liberal Republicans are running for re-election to the House than where incumbent conservative Republicans are running.

The exceptions found for the 1976 election are important to this analysis, which anticipates a relationship between the ideological position of the Presidential nominees and Congressional incumbents on the one hand and split-ticket voting on the other. It makes sense, accordingly, to expect the elections of 1976 and 1980, with Jimmy Carter at the head of the Democratic ticket, to reveal a somewhat different ideological pattern to split-ticket than other elections since 1968. In both 1976 and 1980, Carter ran as a centrist and encountered his most persistent opposition in the primaries from liberal Democrats. Though the Democratic nominee for President runs strongest in Congressional districts where liberal Democrats are up for re-election in every other Presidential election, in 1976 and 1980 the vote for Carter is rather consistent across the ideological spectrum. Unlike the other elections since 1972, the difference between the vote for Jimmy Carter and the vote for Democratic incumbents is approximately the same, regardless of the ideological position of the House incumbent.

The differences in the pattern of split-ticket voting between the 1976 and 1980 elections on the one hand and all other elections since 1968 on the other seem related to the ideological position of the Presidential nominees. Carter is more of a centrist than the other Democrats running for President since 1968. The differences from the pattern are greater in 1976 when Carter is running against President Gerald Ford, a moderate Republican, than they are in 1980, when Carter is facing Ronald Reagan. Finally, it is no surprise that Carter of Georgia won ten of the eleven states of the south in 1976 and ran relatively well in the south in 1980. In those elections, moderate-to-conservative Democrats running for re-election to the House in the south are running in districts where their party's nominee for President is much stronger than in other elections between 1968 and 1988. The ideological pattern to split-ticket voting found in 1972 re-emerges intact in 1984 and persists thereafter.

What is surprising in the data presented here is that the 1976 and 1980 elections do not stand apart more than they do. The important observation is that the correlation between the Presidential vote and the Congressional vote is higher where liberal Democrats are running for re-election to the House than where moderate-to-conservative Democrats are running for *every* election since 1972, and that, for every election, the correlation is higher where partisan ideologues of both parties are running for re-election to the House than where moderates and ideological misfits are running. These observations include even 1976 and 1980.

The relationship between the ideological position of House incumbents and split-ticket voting in Presidential elections is not primarily one of coattails. Instead, it is mostly a matter of where Presidential nominees are likely to do well. Rates of re-election to the House have consistently remained over 90 percent, until 1980, regardless of party and ideology of the incumbent (see Table 7.12). Treating the fate of the House incumbents as almost a constant, the Presidential vote is an ideological variable. Republican Presidential nominees do better in Republican districts and where conservatives of both parties are running for re-election to the House; Democratic Presidential nominees do better in Democratic districts and where liberals of both parties are running for re-election. Once again, the ideological polarization of the national parties plays into this expectation. As Tables 7.8 and 7.9 illustrate, the vote for House incumbents across districts is not structured ideologically; House incumbents tend to win with over 60 percent of the vote. The Presidential vote is structured ideologically, as shown in both tables. It is this ideological structure, more than coattails, that shapes split-ticket voting between the Presidency and the House. Incumbency advantages sustained pre-1964 party coalitions in elections for the House, even in the face of "realignment at the top," particularly where conservative Democrats were running for re-election in the south. Starting in 1980, when Ronald Reagan was elected President, incumbency advantages for members of the House begin to take an ideological slant, as the re-election rate among conservative Democrats begins to decline. This change in electoral pattern, however, does not have a decisive impact on Congressional elections until 1994.

IDEOLOGY, INCUMBENCY, AND SPLIT-TICKET VOTING: THE SENATE

Split-ticket outcomes between the Presidency and the Senate follow similar patterns to split-ticket outcomes between the Presidency and the House. The data drawn from Presidential and Senate elections offer further support for the realignment/ideological polarization model of split-ticket voting, although it is more qualified.

First, there has been a significant increase in split-ticket outcomes between the Presidency and the Senate in the last half of the twentieth century, as there has been for the House. Table 7.13 shows a very similar pattern of correlations between the vote for President and the United States Senate to the correlations between the Presidential and House vote in Table 7.3. The correlations are high and positive through 1944, generally lower for the next twenty years, generally negative during the 1964–1972 realignment, and positive since then, but never so high as they were before 1944. Table 7.14 demonstrates that between 1916, the first Presidential election year with popular elections for the U.S. Senate and 1944, partisan coalitions of states in Presidential and Senate elections were uniform, as was the case in comparing Presidential and House coalitions. The most-partisan states tended to vote the party line; the most-competitive states split tickets with greater frequency. During this period, the "L" states of the south and west were Democratic, as they were in Presidential and House elections, the south solidly so. Between 1896 and 1944, not one state found in a party coalition in Presidential elections is found in the other party's coalition in elections for the Senate. In the period since 1964, there is a much greater predisposition to split-ticket outcomes between the Presidency and the Senate, and almost no apparent relationship between the two coalitions of states.

Second, there is an apparent relationship between electoral change in Presidential elections and the predisposition to split tickets between the Presidency and the Senate, much as there is between the Presidency and the House. As illustrated in Table 7.15, the states that tend to vote Republican for President and Democratic for the Senate since 1964 are mostly "L" states of the south and west that were Democratic in the system of 1896 and have trended Republican since the 1960s. And the two states that have tended to vote Democratic for President and

Republican for the Senate are both northeastern states among the most Republican in the country in the system of 1896, which have trended Democratic since the 1960s.

As is the case in elections for the House, there is almost no general relationship between the coalition of states in Senate elections before 1944 and the coalition found after 1964. A comparison of Table 7.16 with Table 7.6 would indicate, however, that there was more change in Senate elections than in House elections between the two periods. In elections for the Senate, like the House, the direction of electoral change is geographically the same as it is in Presidential elections but less pronounced. The states that have shifted most from the Democrats toward the Republicans are "L" states of the south and west; the states that have shifted most from the Republicans toward the Democrats are mostly in the northeast quadrant. But, again like the House, there is more stability in the coalition of states for the Senate than there is in Presidential elections. More than half of the most-Democratic states in Senate elections since 1964 are also "L" states that have long since gone Republican in Presidential elections.

The fact that there is more evidence of electoral change in Senate elections since the 1964–1972 period than in House elections is an important ingredient to understanding the relationship between realignment in Presidential elections and split-ticket voting. Whereas in the House the rate of re-election of incumbents has never been under 92 percent in any Presidential election year since 1972, in the Senate the general rate of re-election of incumbents in the same years has been 81 percent. In the Senate, like the House, incumbency has sustained pre-1964 electoral coalitions longer than they persisted in Presidential elections, but not to nearly the same extent. Senate races receive much more national attention and money than House races generally do, and challengers in Senate races enjoy much higher name recognition than challengers for the House. Thus, while the re-election of incumbents to the House can be considered almost a constant in comparison with electoral trends in Presidential elections, the re-election or defeat of Senators is very much a variable. Although Senators start re-election campaigns with great advantages, and win much more often than not, incumbency does not protect them from national electoral change nearly as much as it does Representatives. The result is that even though incumbency by itself is not much of a factor in split-ticket voting between the Presidency and the Senate, realignment in Presidential elections and the ideology of Senators do appear to be reasonably important, although the evidence is not as compelling as it is in House elections.

Table 7.17 illustrates these points. First, as was the case in the relationship between Presidential and House elections, split-ticket results between the Presidency and Senate have been most common since 1972 in the five states George Wallace carried in the 1968 Presidential election. Also, as was the case with House elections (see Table 7.7) ideology seems to be a factor in this relationship. In the 1976, 1980, 1992, and 1996 elections, when southern moderate Democrats are running for President, there is almost no difference between Presidential-Senate split tickets in the states Wallace carried than elsewhere in the country. In 1972, 1984, and 1988, however, when northern liberals are the Democratic nominees for President, nine of the eleven Senate races in Alabama, Arkansas, Georgia, Louisiana, and Mississippi result in split tickets, always with moderate-to-conservative Democrats winning re-election to the Senate while the Republican carries the state in the Presidential election.

Second, since 1972, split-ticket results have been least common in states where the Senators running for re-election have been conservative Republicans and most common where moderate-to-conservative Democrats have run for re-election. Again, the data is not as unambiguous as it is for the relationship between voting for President and the House, but ideological polarization between the parties has certainly given structure to split-ticket voting between the Presidency and Congress.

Finally, however, unlike the House, there is no greater tendency toward split-ticket voting when Senators are running for re-election than when a Senate seat is open. This seems largely to be explained by greater incumbency advantages in the House, which tend to protect Representatives from larger electoral forces. This difference in incumbency advantage also explains why electoral change in Senate elections has moved at a faster pace than electoral change in House elections. While split-ticket outcomes between the Presidency and the House have been generally more frequent in the south than the rest of the country, the south does not stand out in split-ticket outcomes between the Presidency and the Senate. Republicans began to win Senate seats in the south in larger numbers sooner than they won House seats, starting with John Tower of Texas in 1961 and Howard Baker of Tennessee in 1966. Thus, as a general trend, conservative Democrats in the south began losing Senate seats before they lost House seats, and the ideological structure to split-ticket voting between the Presidency and Senate has not been as pronounced as between the House and Senate. The net result is that ideological polarization between the parties, even if it was not as extreme in the Senate as it would later become in the House, emerged earlier in the Senate. In 1980, when Ronald Reagan was elected President, the Republicans won the Senate, but not the House, in a year of unusually long coattails.

THE 1994 CONGRESSIONAL ELECTION:
REALIGNMENT AT THE BOTTOM

Evidence of split-ticket voting between the Presidency at the "top" and the House and Senate at the "bottom" confirms the reality of incumbent-specific, candidate-centered, Congressional elections. Nevertheless, that reality alters the pace of electoral change, not its direction. For most of the last thirty years, Republicans have benefited from "realignment at the top" to win the Presidency. "Dealignment at the bottom" retained control of the House for the Democrats, and usually the Senate too, for most of that time. But even while the Democrats retained partisan control on the hill, a conservative coalition governed Congress more frequently than not. Ironically, in the 1990s, the tables turned. Democrat Bill Clinton was elected President in 1992, and two years later the Republicans won both houses of Congress. When President Clinton was re-elected in 1996, the Republicans retained Congress. It was divided government upside down.

In 1994 the Republican Party won control of both houses of Congress for the first time since 1952, when Dwight D. Eisenhower was elected President. Not once during the Republican domination of Presidential elections between 1968 and 1988 did they win control of Congress, and for only six of those years did they enjoy a majority in the Senate. In 1994 also, the Republicans secured control of both houses of Congress at a midterm election for the first time since 1946. Finally, in 1994, the Republicans won a majority of House seats from the south for the first time since Reconstruction. Nationally, the Republicans won 230 seats in the House of Representatives to 204 for the Democrats, and 1 Independent. In the Senate, the Republicans won 53 seats, to 47 for the Democrats.[17]

These results, by themselves, suggest uncommon electoral change and present the possibility for a profound change in governance. For the first time in four decades, Republicans would have an opportunity to set the legislative agenda. They were well positioned to claim a mandate to do so, having presented their Contract with America during the campaign. The outgoing Speaker of the House, Democrat Thomas Foley of Washington, had been defeated for re-election in his own Congressional district, and the new Speaker, Republican Newt Gingrich of Georgia, became the center of attention on Capitol Hill.

As with any election, the evaluation of electoral change in the 1994 Congressional election must consider evidence of continuity found in the results. Two patterns consistently found in recent Congressional elections persisted in 1994.

First, contrary to impressions left by the Republican victory, incumbency advantage retained a considerable presence across party lines: 90

percent of all incumbents seeking reelection to the House won, including 84 percent of incumbent Democrats. These re-election rates were the lowest since the post-Watergate election of 1974, but generally consistent with the pattern of incumbency advantage found in Congressional elections since 1950.[18]

Second, as has been the case in every midterm election since 1934, the President's party lost seats in the House of Representatives. What was surprising in 1994 was the magnitude of the loss. The Democrats lost fifty-four seats from their 1992 level, more than any President's party had lost at the midterm since the Republican seizure of both houses of Congress in 1946, when the Democrats lost fifty-five seats. The Democratic decline surpassed the Republican losses of 1958 and 1974 (each forty-eight seats) and the Democratic losses of 1966 (forty-seven seats).

The question is not why the Democrats lost seats, which was normal and expected, but why so many. One of the central debates in the literature on Congressional elections focuses on what variables best predict the losses suffered by the President's party at the midterm.

The Congressional Election as Referendum

One explanation treats the midterm election as a referendum on the President's performance in office and ties the outcome closely to the condition of the economy.[19] The Democratic landslides of 1958 and 1974 would certainly seem to support the referendum theory. Both midterm elections occurred in the midst of economic recessions, and the 1974 election was dominated by the Watergate affair. In 1994, no such recession or political disaster was in the equation, and a milder loss of seats for the Democrats would seem to be predicted by the referendum theory. Moreover, if the midterm election is a referendum on Presidential performance and the economy, we would expect, if only by chance, that the President's party would gain seats at least occasionally. Instead, when the President's party loses, say, fifteen seats or less, the White House and party leaders spin the result as a favorable reflection on the President. The problem is clear: No theory oriented to a case-by-case treatment can explain a phenomenon that occurs in almost every case. Thus, although the referendum theory might help explain the magnitude of seat change at a given election, it cannot explain why the President's party loses so consistently in midterm elections.

Surge and Decline Theory

A second body of theory seeking to explain seat change in the House at midterm elections places each Congressional election in the context of a relevant string of elections. Two propositions stand out in this analysis. First, each party has a "normal vote" in Congressional elections, which can be influenced by short-term forces. Second, there is a "surge and decline" tendency that explains why the President's party loses seats at the midterm election, and the extent of the loss: The winning party in the preceding Presidential election enjoyed short-term advantages that added to its number of House seats. These advantages are not replicated at the midterm, putting the party's "extra" House seats in special jeopardy. Thus, the President's party enters the midterm campaign at a structural disadvantage relative to its position two years before.[20]

Different versions of "surge and decline" theory emphasize different structural advantages enjoyed by the winning party at a Presidential election, including Presidential coattails,[21] the quality and quantity of turnout in midterm elections,[22] and the differing patterns of voting behavior found in Presidential and Congressional elections. Whatever the emphasis, "surge and decline" theory posits that, all things being equal, the greater the margin of victory and related gains in the House in a Presidential election, the greater the losses for the President's party at the following midterm election.[23]

In 1992, when Democrat Bill Clinton was elected President, he polled only 43 percent of the popular vote, and the Democrats actually lost ten seats in the House. The "surge and decline" thesis, like referendum theory, would have predicted only mild Democratic losses in the House in 1994. James E. Campbell, who has authored and revised the "surge and decline" analysis, has admitted that his model predicted a Democratic loss of between eighteen and twenty-two House seats.[24] Thus, though the "surge and decline" model, offering as it does greater systemic and historical perspective, might produce the better of the two general explanations of the magnitude of seat change in the House of Representatives at the midterm election, neither theory approached a satisfactory explanation for the 1994 outcome.

Realignment?

Because explanations built on short-term forces oriented to a "normal vote" seem to underestimate the Republican gains of 1994, an examination of longer-term forces is indicated. Walter Dean Burnham revived the resilient concept of realignment when he pronounced the 1994 Congressional election as the most compelling realigning election since the Congressional elections of 1894, which heralded the emergence of the system of 1896.[25] A comparison of the Republican coalition in the 1994 Congressional elections with the coalition in their last previous midterm sweep of both Houses of Congress in 1946, offers some support for Burnham's observation. The following analysis focuses on states as units of analysis, so that it is easily comparable to the analysis of Presidential elections in Chapter 1.

The Republican coalition of states found in the 1994 Congressional election emerged very slowly, over a period of about forty years. Meanwhile, the Republican coalition of 1946 has disappeared almost entirely, so that the partisan coalitions of states in the two elections show no resemblance to each other. Only fourteen of the forty-seven states participating in both elections produce a majority for the same party in their vote for the House of Representatives in the two elections.[26] (See Tables 7.18 and 7.19.)

Table 7.18 indicates secular realignment between 1946 and 1994, rather than the sort of sudden shift associated with critical realignment. Although Republicans were gradually gaining in the south in Congressional elections starting in the 1960s, they did not win a majority of seats in the House, either across the south or nationally, until 1994. Then, in a shift that proved decisive, the Republicans won a majority of House seats, both in the south and across the country. But the suddenness of the shift is more apparent than real. As Table 7.18 indicates, the Republican coalition in elections for the House has resembled 1994 more than the 1946 election since 1980, when Ronald Reagan was elected President. The gradual electoral change between 1946 and 1994 is illustrated in Table 7.20: In almost all the states where Republicans made the steadiest and greatest gains over that period of time, mostly in the south, they do not achieve majorities of the vote until 1994. More important to the analysis of realignment, the direction, geographic distribution, and long-term magnitude of electoral change demonstrated in Table 7.20 all look very much the same as electoral change in Presidential elections illustrated in Chapter 1, Table 1.18.

The Senate

Conveniently for this analysis, the same seats were filled in the Republican midterm victory of 1994 as in the Republican mid-term victory of 1946. Tables 7.21 and 7.22 indicate the same general pattern of secular realignment in Senate races between 1946 and 1994 as was found in races for the House of Representatives. The Republican vote found in the 1946 Senate elections correlates negatively at the state level with the Republican vote in the 1994 Senate elections. For each election after 1946, the resemblance with 1994 increases while the resemblance with 1946 decreases. Once again, the south is the most strongly Democratic region in 1946 and has moved most noticeably toward the Republicans by 1994.

Two-Tier Coalitions

The data just presented would indicate that what James Q. Wilson calls "dealignment at the bottom" is more like secular realignment at the bottom. And while the data in this chapter, combined with Chapter 1, would certainly indicate a two-tier party system in the last half of the twentieth century, electroal change has certainly not been chaotic. Rather, the direction of electoral change in Congressional elections has been much the same as it has been in Presidential elections, although without the critical dislocations of the 1960s. On both tiers, in both Presidential and Congressional elections, the Republicans have made their greatest gains over the last half of the twentieth century in the "L" states of the south and west, and the Democrats have made their greatest gains in the northeast quadrant. Table 7.23 sorts the Republican gains in the House of Representatives between 1946 and 1994 according to the patterns of electoral change in Presidential elections over the past century, as presented in Chapter 1. What appears is a convergence between party coalitions in Presidential and Congressional elections, generally consistent with the ideological polarization between the parties.

CONVERGENCE AND THE 1996 ELECTION

President Clinton won re-election in 1996 with 50 percent of the popular vote to 41 percent for Republican Robert Dole. The President carried thirty-one states with 379 electoral votes to 159 electoral votes for Dole. Meanwhile, the Republicans retained control of Congress, losing eleven seats in the House while actually gaining two in the Senate.

It was an election very much like recent elections. There was nothing new in the fact that the election resulted in divided government. This has been the case most of the time since 1954. There was nothing new in the fact of split-ticket voting, an increasing force in American politics over the same period of time.

It was an election very much like recent elections, except that a Democrat was elected President for only the third time in more than three decades, and a Democratic President was re-elected for the first time in five decades. It was an election very much like recent elections, except that the Republicans won both houses of Congress, which had not happened for nearly half a century before 1994, and the Republicans retained both houses, which had not happened in seven decades.

In most recent elections, divided government had produced a Republican President and a Democratic Congress. The reversal to a Democratic President and a Republican Congress is important to our understanding of electoral change and stability in the 1996 election.

Coalitions of States

The political geography that had dominated Presidential elections since the 1964–1972 period persisted in 1996, almost entirely undisturbed. All of the states that President Clinton carried were in the northeast quadrant, or on the Pacific rim, where Democrats have run strongest for three decades. Mr. Dole kept his base in the "Republican L" of the south and interior west. Once again, the Presidential election of 1996 presented a mirror image to the political map of 1896, in which what is now the "Republican L" voted for Democrat William Jennings Bryan.

What was new in 1996, traced to 1994, was that for the first time in a Presidential election year, the mirror image political geography now applied in the Congressional election as well. Realignment of the coalition of states "at the top" had spread to the bottom. In particular, the south, Republican in Presidential elections but lingering Democratic in Congressional elections, was now Republican at the Congressional level. Thus, an important structural characteristic of split-ticket outcomes in American elections had been neutralized.

Between 1964 and 1992, the south's tendency to vote Republican for President and Democratic for Congress had been the most common element behind split-ticket voting. This swing vote in the south produced a conservative governing coalition: a Republican President with a decisive swing vote of conservative Democrats in Congress.

After 1996, however, that pattern is gone. Split-ticket outcomes apparently remain more frequent than they were in the system of 1896; but they are less frequent than they have been in recent decades. Second, in the split-ticket voting of 1996, there is little relationship to ideological polarization or historic patterns of electoral change. Rather, the swing voter now is where he or she might be expected to be: in the center. And the swing states and districts are those that are closely contested in both Presidential and Congressional elections.

The new pattern is a political geography more structured to voting a party ticket. Unlike most of the last three decades, the most-Republican states in the Presidential election tend to be the most-Republican states in the Congressional election—the "L" states of the south and west. And, the most-Democratic states in the Presidential election are the most-Democratic in the Congressional election—most of which are in the northeast quadrant. (See Table 7.24.)

THE NEW CONGRESS AND THE PARTY SYSTEM

What is genuinely new about Congress since the 1994 Congressional election can be summarized in three observations. First, the Republicans control both houses of Congress for the first time in over four decades. Second, the legislative agenda set by the Republicans, starting with the Contract with America, has been self-consciously ideological and partisan. Finally, of greatest importance to this inquiry, the parties in Congress have become as polarized ideologically as the national parties have been in recent Presidential elections. The Congressional parties have become almost unAmerican in the extent to which they are coming to resemble the responsible party model.

It is important to note that the conservative majorities in Congress are not new. Rather, conservative majorities in Congress have been the rule, rather than the exception, for the last half of the twentieth century. Since 1954, when the Democrats began their long monopoly on majorities in the House of Representatives, liberal Democrats have controlled Congress only twice: after the Johnson landslide in 1964 and after the Watergate landslide of 1974. But, until 1994, the conservative majority was never partisan. Instead, it was composed of the "conservative coalition" of Republicans and southern Democrats.

Many conservative Democrats from the south in Congress remained with their party largely because of advantages in seniority and committee positions associated with being in the majority. A few switched parties after the 1994 elections, because they are more ideologically at home in the Republican Party, because they could read electoral trends in their own states and districts, and because the advantage associated with being in the majority was no longer found in the Democratic caucus. In so doing, they followed the lead, most notably, of Senator Richard Shelby of Alabama, who had been counted as a "Republican" vote long before he made it official.

Thus, victories for the conservatives in Congress were also nothing new. The conservative coalition was, in fact, essential to passing the Reagan administration economic program and tax cuts in 1981. Indeed, in every session of Congress since the election of 1966, the conservative coalition has always won the overwhelming majority of roll calls on which it appeared.[27]

However, the conservative coalition has appeared with decreasing frequency in recent years, while party unity and ideological polarization between the parties in Congress have both generally increased since 1972, as Democrats have become more liberal and Republicans even more decidedly conservative. (See Table 7.25.) The appearance of the conservative coalition is actually rather infrequent in 1964, when a majority of Republicans joined a majority of northern Democrats in voting for the Civil Rights Bill. Over the next eight years, however, the conservative coalition appears more frequently. Then, as the parties become more polarized ideologically, the frequency of the appearance of the conservative coalition declines. Nevertheless, its victory rate increases, reflecting the reality of divided government as an interbranch conservative governing coalition for most of the last three decades.

Table 7.26 illustrates the ideological polarization of the parties in the House and Senate, according to ratings of the voting records by Americans for Democratic Action (ADA) at three well-spaced points since 1964. The first is 1964, the year of the Civil Rights Act and the nomination of Barry Goldwater for the Presidency; the second is 1980, just before the election of Ronald Reagan to the Presidency; and the third is 1996, just before the re-election of President Clinton. The same trends emerge generally. Ideological polarization seems to be a much more linear trend in the Senate, reflecting the earlier victories of conservative Republicans in Senate races in the south, and the incumbency advantages of conservative Democrats in the House. But by 1996, the parties are clearly polarized along ideological lines in both the House and Senate.

As important as the analysis presented here is the data showing the disappearance of ideological misfits in both parties, first of liberal Republicans rather quickly after 1964, then of conservative Democrats more gradually and recently. In 1996, according to voting records, no incumbent in the House was a liberal Republican, and only five were conservative Democrats. In the Senate in 1996, there were no liberal Republicans or conservative Democrats. To the extent that ideological factionalism within parties is an important ingredient of split-ticket voting, as illustrated in Tables 7.7 through 7.11 and Table 7.17, we can expect that the increasing ideological homogeneity within the parties will promote a decline in split-ticket voting.

The 1994 election, then, did not necessarily leave behind a Republican majority that will thrive in the long term. But the 1994 election was no accident, either. It amounted to a final step in a long secular realignment that may yet prove to result in still another critical realignment. The 1994 election is historically important more for the electoral coalitions and the ideologically polarized political parties it left behind than for its particular outcome.

This analysis suggests that realignment, with its periodically large shifts in electoral coalitions punctuating eras of relative electoral stability, remains an important variable for observers of American politics to study. In recent years, ideological polarization and electoral dealignment have promoted divided government, but that may be more transitional than a long-term phenomenon. It is certainly premature to conclude that the American political system has become "postpartisan."[28] With "realignment at the top" spreading to the "bottom," we may yet see the emergence of revitalized political parties appropriate to the changing society in which they develop.

TABLES

Table 7.1
Vote in Congress: Civil Rights Bill of 1964

	Yea	Nay
House of Representatives	290	130
Democrats	152	96
Northern Democrats	145	10
Southern Democrats	7	86
Republicans	138	34
Senate	73	27
Democrats	46	21
Northern Democrats	45	1
Southern Democrats	1	20
Republicans	27	6

Congressional Quarterly Almanac 1964 (Washington, D.C.: Congressional Quarterly, 1965), pp. 86 and 606.

Table 7.2

Civil Rights Vote by Incumbents and Split-Ticket Results in 1964 Presidential and Congressional Elections

	Incumbents in House of Representatives	
	Democrats	*Republicans*
Civil Rights Vote by Incumbent		
Yea	2 (N=137)	74 (N=125)
Nay	29 (N=82)	53 (N=32)

Split-Ticket Outcomes:
  Democrats for and Republicans against the Civil Rights Act: 12% (N=169)
  Republicans for and Democrats against the Civil Rights Act: 57% (N=207)
  All Incumbents: 36% (N=380)
  Open Seats: 26% (N=43)

Figures are percentages of districts with divided result between President and House. Alabama is excluded because President Johnson was not on the ballot. Four incumbents were not recorded on civil rights vote.

Derived from *Congressional Quarterly Almanac 1964* (Washington, D.C.: Congressional Quarterly,1965).

Table 7.3

State-Level Correlations of Vote for President and House of Representatives, 1896–1996

Election	Democratic	Republican
1896	.88	.94
1900	.97	.98
1904	.97	.98
1908	.93	.96
1912	.95	.64
1916	.93	.96
1920	.75	.69
1924	.94	.90
1928	.81	.82
1932	.88	.89
1936	.85	.91
1940	.90	.94
1944	.93	.94
1948	−.23	.94
1952	.83	.82
1956	.73	.86
1960	.37	.70
1964	−.19	−.29
1968	−.20	.80
1972	−.04	.02
1976	.59	.61
1980	.31	.22
1984	.45	.44
1988	.32	.30
1992	.19	.14
1996	.50	.74

Correlations are Pearson's r.

Derived from *Presidential Elections* (Washington, D.C.: Congressional Quarterly, 1997), pp. 102–127; and the biannual *Almanac of American Politics*, currently coauthored by Michael Barone and Grant Ujifusa, and published by *National Journal*. (The full citation for the *Almanac* appears in note 15 of this chapter.)

Table 7.4
State Electoral Behavior in Presidential Election Years: Partisan Vote for President and House of Representatives, 1896–1944

President	House of Representatives		
	Republican	Competitive	Democratic
Republican	Connecticut Illinois Iowa Kansas Maine Massachusetts Michigan Minnesota New Jersey North Dakota Oregon Pennsylvania Rhode Island South Dakota Vermont Wisconsin		
Cyclical/ Competitive	California Idaho Indiana New Hampshire Ohio Utah Washington West Virginia Wyoming	Nebraska New York	Colorado Delaware Maryland Missouri
Democratic		Montana	Alabama Arizona Arkansas Florida Georgia Kentucky Louisiana Mississippi Nevada New Mexico North Carolina Oklahoma South Carolina Tennessee Texas Virginia

G = .99

States classified in party coalitions in Presidential elections voted for the indicated party, with percentages higher than the national vote for that party, in most elections in the period. All states not fitting in either party coalition are classified as cyclical/competitive. For Congressional elections, states that elect a majority of Representatives from one party in most elections in the period are classified in that party coalition.

Table 7.5
State Electoral Behavior in Presidential Election Years: Partisan Vote for President and House of Representatives, 1964–1996

President	House of Representatives		
	Republican	*Competitive*	*Democratic*
Republican	Alaska	Colorado	Alabama
	Arizona	Montana	Florida
	Idaho	Nevada	Georgia
	Kansas		Indiana
	Nebraska		Louisiana
	New Hampshire		Mississippi
	New Mexico		New Jersey
	South Dakota		North Carolina
	Utah		North Dakota
	Virginia		Oklahoma
	Wyoming		South Carolina
			Texas
Cyclical/ Competitive	Delaware	Illinois	Arkansas
	Iowa	Maine	California
	Vermont	Ohio	Connecticut
			Kentucky
			Michigan
			Missouri
			Oregon
			Tennessee
			Wisconsin
Democratic			Hawaii
			Maryland
			Massachusetts
			Minnesota
			New York
			Pennsylvania
			Rhode Island
			Washington
			West Virginia

G = .62
See Table 7.4 for partisan classification of states.

Table 7.6
Change in Congressional Election Coalitions in Presidential Election Years 1896–1996

	1964–1996		
	Republican	Competitive	Democratic
1896–1944			
Republican	Idaho	Illinois	California
	Iowa	Maine	Connecticut
	Kansas	Ohio	Indiana
	New Hampshire		Massachusetts
	South Dakota		Michigan
	Utah		Minnesota
	Vermont		New Jersey
	Wyoming		North Dakota
			Oregon
			Pennsylvania
			Rhode Island
			Washington
			West Virginia
			Wisconsin
Competitive	Nebraska	Montana	New York
Democratic	Arizona	Colorado	Alabama
	Delaware	Nevada	Arkansas
	New Mexico		Florida
	Virginia		Georgia
			Kentucky
			Louisiana
			Maryland
			Mississippi
			Missouri
			North Carolina
			Oklahoma
			South Carolina
			Tennessee
			Texas

G = .27
See Table 7.4 for partisan classification of states.

Table 7.7

Split-Ticket Results in Presidential and Congressional Elections, by Three Variables: The Wallace Vote, Sectionalism, and the 1964–1972 Ideological Alignment of States, 1972-1996

	1972	1976	1980	1984	1988	1992	1996
WALLACE VOTE IN 1968							
States Wallace carried:	79	15	21	68	65	38	32
29%–34%	65	18	35	58	53	20	20
18%–24%	66	30	49	52	40	28	30
10%–15%	36	33	38	41	33	23	22
Under 10%	34	28	26	36	22	19	27
SECTIONALISM							
South	69	23	34	58	52	26	26
Non-South	36	28	31	39	26	21	26
1964–1972 IDEOLOGICAL ALIGNMENT OF STATES							
liberal	34	27	27	37	24	21	31
moderate	43	26	35	42	25	16	24
conservative	58	27	31	52	52	32	26
NATIONAL	44	27	31	44	33	23	26

Figures of percentages of Congressional districts producing split outcomes betweeen the Presidency and the House of Representatives. States are divided into the following five categories according to the Wallace vote: States Wallace carried in 1968 (Alabama, Arkansas, Georgia, Louisiana, and Mississippi); states where Wallace placed second to Nixon, polling between 29% and 34% of the vote (Florida, North Carolina, South Carolina, and Tennessee); other states where Wallace polled between 18% and 24% (Kentucky, Texas, and Virginia); states where Wallace polled 10% to 15%, approximately his national vote; and states where Wallace polled less than 10% of the vote. Southern states are the eleven states of the Confederacy. The 1964–1972 ideological alignment of states is introduced in Chapter 1, and in Table 1.19.
Derived from *The Almanac of American Politics*.

Table 7.8

Democratic Ticket Voting by Ideological Position of House Incumbent, in Presidential and House Elections, 1972–1996

Elections	Democratic Incumbents			Open Seats	All Seats
	liberals	*moderates*	*conservatives*		
1972	N=80	N=54	N=44	N=57	N=379
President	50	42	33	35	39
House	66	65	65	48	51
Difference	(16)	(23)	(32)	(13)	(15)
r	.66	.26	.32	.52	.52
1976	N=115	N=65	N=32	N=51	N=386
President	56	53	54	53	51
House	67	66	69	59	56
Difference	(12)	(13)	(15)	(6)	(5)
r	.74	.62	.29	.72	.66
1980	N=100	N=71	N=39	N=42	N=383
President	48	44	44	42	42
House	65	61	64	51	51
Difference	(17)	(17)	(20)	(9)	(9)
r	.74	.32	.58	.86	.65
1984	N=135	N=49	N=18	N=26	N=367
President	49	41	35	38	41
House	65	62	59	46	50
Difference	(16)	(21)	(24)	(8)	(9)
r	.73	.50	.50	.69	.69
1988	N=145	N=36	N=6	N=30	N=360
President	54	43	34	44	46
House	69	66	69	50	53
Difference	(15)	(23)	(35)	(6)	(7)
r	.71	.37	−.17	.71	.64
1992	N=144	N=40	N=6	N=87	N=401
President	49	41	34	46	44
House	62	60	64	54	52
Difference	(13)	(19)	(30)	(8)	(8)
r	.64	.28	.45	.82	.66
1996	N=114	N=39	N=3	N=50	N=410
President	63	49	32	49	50
House	69	62	56	49	50
Difference	(6)	(13)	(24)	(0)	(0)
r	.87	.52	.64	.92	.82

Figures are mean percentages of the vote for President and the House. Correlation is Pearson's *r* between vote for President and the House at the Congressional-district level. Ideological classification of House incumbents determined by ADA ratings of voting record: Ratings over 67 are "liberal"; ratings under 33 are "conservative." All others are "moderate."
Derived from *The Almanac of American Politics*.

Table 7.9
Republican Ticket Voting by Ideological Position of House Incumbent, in Presidential and House Elections, 1972–1996

Elections	Republican Incumbents			Open Seats	All Seats
	liberals	*moderates*	*conservatives*		
1972	N=4	N=23	N=117	N=57	N=379
President	59	61	67	65	61
House	69	63	64	50	47
Difference	(10)	(2)	(3)	(15)	(14)
r	−.41	.60	.45	.50	.55
1976	N=1	N=18	N=104	N=51	N=386
President	59	54	55	47	49
House	68	67	63	39	44
Difference	(9)	(13)	(8)	(8)	(5)
r		−.15	.18	.76	.66
1980	N=9	N=21	N=100	N=42	N=383
President	47	50	57	49	50
House	68	67	68	48	47
Difference	(21)	(17)	(11)	(1)	(3)
r	−.08	.35	.34	.86	.65
1984	N=3	N=29	N=107	N=26	N=367
President	48	61	67	61	59
House	66	67	68	53	49
Difference	(18)	(6)	(1)	(8)	(10)
r	.91	.67	.58	.68	.69
1988	N=6	N=32	N=105	N=30	N=360
President	45	55	61	55	53
House	69	67	67	48	47
Difference	(24)	(12)	(6)	(7)	(6)
r	.24	.54	.63	.81	.64
1992	N=3	N=13	N=107	N=87	N=401
President	39	37	43	35	37
House	68	63	60	43	45
Difference	(29)	(26)	(17)	(8)	(8)
r	−.93	.54	.51	.78	.65
1996	N=0	N=13	N=190	N=50	N=410
President		37	47	42	40
House		58	61	49	48
Difference		(21)	(14)	(8)	(8)
r		.55	.58	.91	.82

Figures are mean percentages of the vote for President and the House. Correlation is Pearson's *r* between vote for President and the House at the Congressional-district level. Ideological classification of House incumbents determined by ADA ratings of voting record: Ratings over 67 are "liberal"; ratings under 33 are "conservative." All others are "moderate."
Derived from *The Almanac of American Politics*.

Table 7.10
Ideology and Split-Ticket Voting across Party Lines between Presidential and House Elections, 1972–1996

Election	All Districts	Open Seats	Partisan Ideologues	Moderates	Ideological Misfits
1972	N=379	N=57	N=197	N=77	N=48
Democrats	.52 (12)	.52 (13)	.78 (8)	.34 (15)	.07 (33)
Republicans	.55 (14)	.50 (15)	.79 (9)	.41 (17)	.12 (30)
1976	N=386	N=51	N=219	N=83	N=33
Democrats	.66 (5)	.72 (6)	.71 (1)	.57 (6)	.39 (14)
Republicans	.66 (5)	.76 (8)	.70 (2)	.56 (7)	.35 (15)
1980	N=383	N=42	N=200	N=92	N=48
Democrats	.65 (9)	.86 (9)	.71 (7)	.40 (11)	.45 (15)
Republicans	.65 (3)	.86 (1)	.78 (0)	.37 (5)	.06 (10)
1984	N=367	N=26	N=242	N=78	N=21
Democrats	.69 (9)	.69 (8)	.80 (8)	.41 (11)	−.19 (19)
Republicans	.69 (10)	.69 (9)	.80 (9)	.40 (12)	−.20 (19)
1988	N=360	N=30	N=250	N=68	N=12
Democrats	.64 (7)	.71 (6)	.78 (7)	.13 (7)	−.77 (6)
Republicans	.64 (6)	.81 (7)	.78 (6)	.15 (6)	−.76 (5)
1992	N=401	N=87	N=251	N=53	N=9
Democrats	.66 (8)	.82 (8)	.75 (9)	.09 (12)	−.57 (15)
Republicans	.65 (8)	.78 (8)	.77 (9)	.06 (4)	−.80 (1)
1996	N=410	N=50	N=304	N=52	N=3
Democrats	.82 (0)	.92 (0)	.89 (2)	.17 (6)	.64 (24)
Republicans	.82 (8)	.91 (7)	.88 (9)	.12 (1)	.94 (15)

Ratios are Pearson's *r* at the Congressional-district level. Numerals in parentheses are the mean absolute difference between the party vote for President and the House at the Congressional-district level. "Partisan ideologues" are liberal Democrats and conservative Republicans; "Ideological misfits" are conservative Democrats and liberal Republicans. "Moderates" are moderates of both parties. All classified according to ADA ratings.
Derived from *The Almanac of American Politics*.

Table 7.11
Split Outcomes between Presidency and House, 1972–1996

Election	1972	1976	1980	1984	1988	1992	1996
All contested seats	38	29	33	40	32	24	26
Incumbents	40	29	35	42	33	24	27
Democrats	70	34	50	69	50	23	10
Republicans	2	20	9	2	10	27	39
Liberal Democrats	54	37	50	62	41	13	2
Moderate Democrats	81	31	53	88	83	45	31
Conservative Democrats	86	31	57	72	83	100	67
Liberal Republicans	0	0	33	33	83	67	
Moderate Republicans	4	11	5	3	16	46	85
Conservative Republicans	2	21	6	2	4	23	37
Open Seats	30	31	21	20	27	24	22
Partisan Ideologues	30	28	28	31	17	17	23
Moderates	56	32	42	61	55	35	44
Ideological Misfits	81	25	59	79	86	63	67
South	54	24	37	51	55	30	27
Non-South	34	31	34	37	26	19	26

All entries are percentages of split outcomes between the Presidential election and the House election, by Congressional district.
Derived from *The Almanac of American Politics.*

Table 7.12
Re-election Rates to the House, by Party and Ideology, 1972–1996

Election	1972	1976	1980	1984	1988	1992	1996
All contested seats	97	97	92	95	98	94	94
Democrats	96	97	88	94	97	94	98
Republicans	98	96	98	97	99	95	91
Liberal Democrats	96	96	94	96	99	94	99
Moderate Democrats	96	95	81	94	100	92	97
Conservative Democrats	95	100	87	72	83	100	67
Liberal Republicans	100	100	100	100	100	100	
Moderate Republicans	96	100	100	97	93	92	92
Conservative Republicans	98	95	98	98	98	95	91

All figures are percentages of incumbents running for re-election in contested
districts who won.
Derived from *The Almanac of American Politics*.

Table 7.13
Correlations between Vote for President and the U.S. Senate, 1916–1996

Election	Democratic	Republican
1916	.90	.89
1920	.73	.61
1924	.91	.87
1928	.59	.62
1932	.81	.78
1936	.79	.87
1940	.86	.79
1944	.93	.90
1948	−.14	.93
1952	.62	.57
1956	.59	.66
1960	.30	.60
1964	−.20	−.19
1968	−.12	.59
1972	−.09	−.18
1976	.16	.29
1980	.48	.52
1984	.38	.36
1988	.15	.16
1992	.42	.03
1996	.61	.65

Correlations are Pearson's *r* at the state level.

Table 7.14
State Electoral Behavior in Presidential Election Years: Partisan Vote for President and Senate, 1916–1944

President	Senate		
	Republican	*Competitive*	*Democratic*
Republican	Indiana		
	Kansas		
	Maine		
	Michigan		
	Pennsylvania		
	South Dakota		
	Vermont		
Cyclical/	California		Idaho
Competitive	Colorado		Illinois
	Connecticut		Maryland
	Delaware		Massachusetts
	Iowa		Missouri
	Minnesota		New York
	Nebraska		Rhode Island
	New Hampshire		Utah
	New Jersey		Wyoming
	North Dakota		
	Ohio		
	Oregon		
	West Virginia		
	Wisconsin		
Democratic		Washington	Alabama
			Arizona
			Arkansas
			Florida
			Georgia
			Kentucky
			Louisiana
			Mississippi
			Montana
			Nevada
			New Mexico
			North Carolina
			Oklahoma
			South Carolina
			Tennessee
			Texas
			Virginia

G = .98

See Table 7.4 for partisan classification of states in Presidential elections. States are classified in a party coalition for the Senate if one party won a majority of Senate elections in the state between 1916 and 1944.

Table 7.15
State Electoral Behavior in Presidential Election Years: Partisan Vote
for President and Senate, 1964–1996

President	Senate		
	Republican	*Competitive*	*Democratic*
Republican	Arizona	Colorado	Alabama
	Idaho	Florida	Georgia
	Indiana	Mississippi	Louisiana
	Kansas	Texas	Montana
	New Hampshire		Nebraska
	New Mexico		Nevada
	North Carolina		New Jersey
	Oklahoma		North Dakota
	South Carolina		South Dakota
	Utah		Virginia
	Wyoming		
Cyclical/	Kentucky	California	Arkansas
Competitive	Ohio	Delaware	Connecticut
		Iowa	Illinois
		Maine	Michigan
		Missouri	Oregon
		Vermont	Tennessee
			Wisconsin
Democratic	Pennsylvania	Minnesota	Maryland
	Rhode Island	New York	Massachusetts
			Washington
			West Virginia

G = .23
See Table 7.4 for partisan classification of states in Presidential elections. State
classified in a party coalition for the Senate if one party won a majority of Senate
elections in the state between 1964 and 1996.

Table 7.16
**Change In Coalition of States in Elections for the U.S. Senate
1916–1996**

	1964–1996		
	Republican	*Competitive*	*Democratic*
1916–1944			
Republican	Indiana	California	Connecticut
	Kansas	Colorado	Michigan
	New Hampshire	Delaware	Nebraska
	Ohio	Iowa	New Jersey
	Pennsylvania	Minnesota	North Dakota
		Maine	Oregon
		Vermont	South Dakota
			West Virginia
			Wisconsin
Competitive			Washington
Democratic	Arizona	Missouri	Alabama
	Idaho	New York	Arkansas
	Kentucky	Florida	Georgia
	New Mexico	Mississippi	Illinois
	North Carolina	Texas	Louisiana
	Oklahoma		Maryland
	Rhode Island		Massachusetts
	South Carolina		Montana
	Utah		Nevada
	Wyoming		Tennessee
			Virginia

G = −.13
States are classified in a party coalition if that party won a majority of elections
for the U.S. Senate during the period. States where no party won a majority of
elections are classified as competitive.

Table 7.17
Split-Ticket Outcomes in Presidential and Senate Elections,
1972–1996

	1972, 1984–1988	1976–1980, 1992–1996	Total
All Seats (N=232)	51	32	40
Incumbents (N=172)	51	32	41
Conservative Democrats (N=9)	80	50	67
Moderate Democrats (N=35)	83	30	49
Liberal Democrats (N=46)	72	32	48
Conservative Republicans (N=58)	21	27	24
Moderate Republicans (N=14)	36	67	43
Liberal Republicans (N=9)	43	0	33
Independents (N=1)	100		100
Open Seats (N=60)	50	33	38
Ideological Misfits (N=18)	58	33	50
Moderates (N=49)	61	35	47
Partisan Ideologues (N=104)	41	29	35
South (N=53)	52	29	40
Non-South (N=179)	50	33	40
By state vote for Wallace:			
39%–66% (N=24)	82	23	50
29%–34% (N=19)	25	36	32
18%–24% (N=20)	40	30	35
10%–15% (N=56)	52	23	34
2%–9% (N=113)	49	39	43

All entries are percentages of states with split outcomes between the Presidential election and the Senate election. Senators are classified by ideology according to the score they receive for their voting record from Americans for Democratic Action (ADA). Those with ratings over 67 are classified as "liberal." Those with ratings under 33 are classified as "conservative." Those with ratings between 33 and 67 are classified as "moderate." "Partisan ideologues" are liberal Democrats and conservative Republicans; conservative Democrats and liberal Republicans are "ideological misfits." All others are "moderates."

Table 7.18
Correlation of Republican Vote for House in All Congressional Elections with 1946 and 1994

Congressional Election	With 1946	With 1994
1946	1.00	.02
1948	.98	.00
1950	.97	.03
1952	.97	.00
1954	.96	.05
1956	.93	.09
1958	.93	.11
1960	.94	.15
1962	.84	.15
1964	.68	.23
1966	.76	.27
1968	.73	.32
1970	.56	.35
1972	.41	.40
1974	.44	.40
1976	.49	.25
1978	.34	.30
1980	.23	.38
1982	.37	.44
1984	.42	.45
1986	.28	.35
1988	.20	.43
1990	.26	.40
1992	.12	.69
1994	.02	1.00

Correlations are Pearson's r at the state level.

Table 7.19
Majorities in State Delegations in the House of Representatives, 1946 and 1994

	1994		
	Republican	*Even Split*	*Democratic*
1946			
Republican	Colorado	Connecticut	California
	Delaware	Illinois	Massachusetts
	Idaho	Maine	Michigan
	Indiana	Vermont	Minnesota
	Iowa		Missouri
	Kansas		New York
	Nebraska		North Dakota
	Nevada		Oregon
	New Hampshire		Pennsylvania
	New Jersey		South Dakota
	Ohio		West Virginia
	Washington		
	Wisconsin		
	Wyoming		
Even Split	Utah		Montana
Democratic	Arizona	Maryland	Alabama
	Arkansas		Louisiana
	Florida		Mississippi
	Georgia		Rhode Island
	Kentucky		Texas
	New Mexico		Virginia
	North Carolina		
	Oklahoma		
	South Carolina		
	Tennessee		

G = −.05

Table 7.20
**Change in Republican Vote for House of Representatives, by State,
1946–1994 (Mean Percentages for Multiple Years)**

State	1946	1948–1962	1964–1978	1980–1992	1994	Net Change
South Carolina		5	33	45	57	+57
Georgia		10	27	32	55	+55
Arkansas	2	16	52	45	52	+50
Alabama	8	8	35	35	56	+48
Texas	5	13	29	42	53	+48
Mississippi		3	26	34	42	+42
Florida	19	24	43	47	51	+32
Arizona	33	46	51	62	61	+28
Tennessee	30	31	45	43	55	+25
Virginia	33	32	45	52	55	+22
Oklahoma	41	37	42	42	58	+17
Delaware	57	50	56	44	73	+16
North Carolina	39	34	42	46	54	+15
Utah	52	51	52	57	63	+11
New Mexico	48	42	48	54	58	+10
Idaho	56	51	58	53	65	+9
New York	45	50	45	46	51	+6
Kentucky	54	40	43	45	59	+5
Colorado	56	49	49	54	60	+4
Kansas	60	56	61	56	63	+3
Maryland	48	45	42	40	51	+3
Nevada	59	45	30	48	61	+2
Indiana	55	52	49	49	57	+2
Wyoming	56	56	51	67	56	0
California	52	49	48	48	51	−1
New Hampshire	62	58	59	57	60	−2
Illinois	56	50	50	47	54	−2
Montana	49	48	48	48	46	−3
Nebraska	68	60	59	67	64	−4
Iowa	62	57	49	52	58	−4
Ohio	57	53	54	49	53	−4
Missouri	52	43	40	44	48	−4
New Jersey	60	52	47	49	55	−5
Connecticut	57	49	46	50	51	−6
Michigan	61	50	47	45	52	−9
Washington	58	56	44	45	49	−9

(continued)

Table 7.20   (continued)

State	1946	1948–1962	1964–1978	1980–1992	1994	Net Change
Minnesota	59	50	47	44	49	−10
Wisconsin	66	53	46	50	54	−12
Pennsylvania	58	50	47	49	46	−12
Maine	63	58	51	57	50	−13
Massachusetts	54	46	36	28	39	−15
Rhode Island	45	38	34	52	30	−15
West Virginia	50	43	36	32	34	−16
Vermont	64	62	65	66	48	−16
North Dakota	72	63	61	31	54	−18
Oregon	65	59	58	38	38	−27

Table 7.21
Correlation of Republican Vote in Presidential and Senate Elections with 1946 and 1994 Senate Elections

Election	Senate Elections With		Presidential Elections With	
	1946	1994	1946	1994
1944			.90	−.43
1946	1.00	−.43		
1948			.86	−.39
1952	.84	−.38	.57	−.18
1956			.68	−.27
1958	.66	−.33		
1960			.43	−.05
1964	.45	−.26	−.62	.45
1968			.51	−.09
1970	.32	−.01		
1972			−.55	.35
1976	.24	.14	.17	.23
1980			−.10	.27
1982	.11	.36		
1984			−.21	.38
1988	.14	.49	−.38	.49
1992			−.49	.23
1994	−.43	1.00		
1996			−.41	.32

Correlations are Pearson's r at the state level.

Table 7.22
Coalition of States in Senate Elections, 1946 and 1994

	1994	
	Republican	Democratic
1946		
Republican	Delaware	California
	Indiana	Connecticut
	Maine	Massachusetts
	Michigan	Nebraska
	Minnesota	Nevada
	Missouri	New Jersey
	Montana	New York
	North Dakota	Wisconsin
	Ohio	
	Pennsylvania	
	Utah	
	Vermont	
	Washington	
Democratic	Arizona	Maryland
	Florida	New Mexico
	Mississippi	Virginia
	Rhode Island	West Virginia
	Tennessee	
	Texas	
	Wyoming	

G = −.04

Table 7.23
Realignment in Presidential and Congressional Elections

Electoral Change in Presidential Elections, 1896–1996	Electoral Change in House Elections, 1946–1994		
	Republican/ Democratic	Electoral Stability/ Mixed Results	Democratic/ Republican
Republican/ Democratic	Maine Massachusetts Minnesota Pennsylvania Rhode Island Vermont	Connecticut Illinois Iowa Michigan New Jersey New York	
Electoral Stability	North Dakota Oregon South Dakota West Virginia Wisconsin	California Colorado Kansas Kentucky Maryland Missouri New Hampshire Ohio Washington	Delaware New Mexico
Democratic/ Republican		Idaho Indiana Montana Nebraska Nevada Wyoming	Alabama Arizona Arkansas Florida Georgia Mississippi North Carolina Oklahoma South Carolina Tennessee Texas Utah Virginia

G = .85

Table 7.24
Coalitions of States in 1996 Presidential and House Elections

President	House of Representatives		
	Democratic	*Even Split*	*Republican*
Democratic	California	Arkansas	Iowa
	Connecticut	Illinois	Louisiana
	Delaware	Maryland	New Jersey
	Hawaii	Vermont	
	Maine		
	Massachusetts		
	Michigan		
	Minnesota		
	New York		
	Rhode Island		
	West Virginia		
Competitive	Missouri		Arizona
	Oregon		Florida
	Pennsylvania		Kentucky
	Wisconsin		Nevada
			New Hampshire
			New Mexico
			Ohio
			Tennessee
			Washington
Republican	North Dakota		Alabama
	Texas		Alaska
			Colorado
			Georgia
			Idaho
			Indiana
			Kansas
			Mississippi
			Montana
			Nebraska
			Oklahoma
			South Carolina
			South Dakota
			Utah
			Virginia
			Wyoming

G = .76

"Competitive" states in the Presidential election were carried by Clinton with less than his national percentage of the vote. States classified in Congressional election according to majorities of seats in the House of Representatives.

Derived from *Presidential Elections, 1789–1996* (Washington, D.C.: Congressional Quarterly, 1997), p. 127, and Michael Barone and Grant Ujifusa, *The Almanac of American Politics 1998* (Washington, D.C.: National Journal, 1997).

Table 7.25
The Conservative Coalition and Party Loyalty in the House And Senate, 1964–1996

Year	Conservative Coalition Appearance	Party Unity Voting	Partisan Ideologues
House of Representatives:			
1964	11 (67)	55	57
1968	22 (63)	35	56
1972	25 (79)	27	61
1976	17 (59)	36	65
1980	16 (67)	38	58
1984	14 (75)	47	71
1988	8 (82)	47	76
1992	10 (88)	64	80
1996	11 (100)	56	69
Senate:			
1964	17 (47)	36	56
1968	25 (80)	32	56
1972	29 (63)	36	54
1976	26 (58)	37	61
1980	20 (75)	46	56
1984	17 (94)	40	71
1988	10 (97)	42	60
1992	14 (87)	53	58
1996	12 (97)	62	80

"Conservative Coalition" represents the percentage of roll calls on which the conservative coalition appeared that year. The conservative coalition appears when a majority of Republicans and southern Democrats vote in opposition to a majority of northern Democrats. The numbers in parentheses represent the percentage of roll calls that the conservative coalition won when it appeared.

"Party Unity" roll calls appear when a majority of Democrats vote in opposition to a majority of Republicans.

For purposes of this table, "Partisan Ideologues" are classified according to voting records on conservative coalition roll calls. Representatives and Senators who vote with the conservative coalition more than 67 percent of the time are classified as "conservative." Those who vote with the conservative coalition less than 33 percent of the time are classified as "liberal." Those with conservative coalition scores between 33 and 67 are classified as "moderate." Partisan ideologues are conservative Republicans and liberal Democrats.

Congressional Quarterly.

Table 7.26
Ideological Polarization between the Parties in Congress, 1964–1996

	liberals	moderates	conservatives
Senate			
1964			
Democrats	35	10	19
Republicans	6	9	21
G = .57			
1980			
Democrats	21	32	6
Republicans	3	11	27
G = .80			
1996			
Democrats	43	4	0
Republicans	0	6	47
G = 1.00			
House			
1964			
Democrats	125	32	47
Republicans	7	19	150
G = .92			
1980			
Democrats	116	87	68
Republicans	6	24	128
G = .84			
1996			
Democrats	140	53	5
Republicans	0	15	220
G = .996			

Senators and Representatives are sorted by ideology according to ratings of their voting records by Americans for Democratic Action (ADA). Ratings over 67 are "liberal"; ratings under 33 are "conservative"; and ratings between 33 and 67 are "moderate."

NOTES

1. The notion of a two-tier party system comes from the work of Everett Carll Ladd. See especially, Ladd with Charles D. Hadley, *Transformations of the American Party System* (New York: Norton, 1978) and Ladd, "Like Waiting for Godot: The Uselessness of 'Realignment' for Understanding Change in Contemporary American Politics," in Byron E. Shafer, ed., *The End of Realignment? Interpreting American Electoral Eras* (Madison: University of Wisconsin Press, 1991), pp. 24–36. James Q. Wilson introduced his theory of dealignment in Wilson, "Realignment at the Top, Dealignment at the Bottom," in Austin Ranney, ed., *The American Elections of 1984* (Durham, N.C.: American Enterprise Institute/Duke University Press, 1985), pp. 277–310.

2. The use of the term "unAmerican" here is not meant to be an ideological judgment, as if Joseph McCarthy were using it. Instead it reflects the approach of one of the better textbooks in comparative politics I remember reading as an undergraduate. In his classic text on the British political system, Douglas V. Verney argued that British government could only be expected to be "unAmerican" because it was, after all, British. The point here, then, is that American political parties are developing now along institutional patterns that are historically unAmerican. See Douglas V. Verney, *British Government and Politics: Life without a Declaration of Independence* (New York: Harper and Row, 1976).

3. All data on the Civil Rights Act of 1964 and the Presidential and Congressional elections of that year are drawn or derived from *Congressional Quarterly Almanac 1964* (Washington, D.C.: Congressional Quarterly, 1965).

4. See Theodore H. White, *The Making of the President 1964* (New York: Atheneum, 1965), pp. 162–189.

5. Ibid., pp. 184–186.

6. Harold W. Stanley and Richard G. Niemi, eds., *Vital Statistics on American Politics*, 4th ed. (Washington, D.C.: Congressional Quarterly, 1994), pp. 128–129.

7. See, in particular, Ladd, "Political Parties and Presidential Elections in the Postindustrial Era," in Harvey L. Schantz, *American Presidential Elections: Process, Policy, and Political Change* (Albany: State University of New York Press, 1996), pp. 189–210.

8. Angus Campbell, "Surge and Decline: A Study of Electoral Change," *Public Opinion Quarterly* 24 (1960): 397–418. See also James E. Campbell, "Explaining Presidential Losses in Midterm Congressional Elections," *Journal of Politics* 47 (1985): 1140–1157; "Predicting Seat Gains from Presidential Coattails," *American Journal of Political Science* 30 (1986): 165–183; and "The Revised Theory of Surge and Decline," *American Journal of Political Science* 31 (1987): 965–979.

9. See Gerald H. Kramer, "Short-Term Fluctuations in U.S. Voting Behavior," *The American Political Science Review* 65 (1971): 131–143; Donald R. Kinder and D. Roderick Kiewiet, "Economic Discontent and Political Behavior: The Role of Personal Grievances and Collective Economic Judgments in Congressional Voting," *American Journal of Political Science* 23 (1979): 495–527; and Edward R. Tufte, "Determinants of Outcomes in Mid-Term Congressional Elections," *The American Political Science Review* 69 (1975): 812–826.

10. Barbara Hinckley, *Congressional Elections* (Washington D.C.: Congressional Quarterly, 1981). See also Walter Dean Burnham, "Insulation and Responsiveness

in Congressional Elections," *Political Science Quarterly* 90 (1975): 411–435 and David R. Mayhew, "Congressional Elections: The Case of the Vanishing Marginals," *Polity* 6 (1974): 295–317.

11. See James E. Campbell, "Explaining Presidential Losses," "Predicting Seat Gains," and "The Revised Theory."

12. Gary C. Jacobsen, "Strategic Politicians and the Dynamics of U.S. House Elections," *The American Political Science Review* 83 (1989): 773–794; and *The Electoral Origins of Divided Government: Competition in U.S. House Elections, 1946–1988* (Boulder: Westview Press, 1990); "The Effects of Campaign Spending on U.S. House Elections: New Evidence for Old Arguments," *American Journal of Political Science* 34 (1990): 334–363.

13. Lloyd A. Free and Hadley Cantril, *The Political Beliefs of Americans* (New Brunswick, N.J.: Rutgers University Press, 1967).

14. See, for example, Morris P. Fiorina, *Divided Government*, 2nd ed. (Boston: Allyn and Bacon, 1996).

15. For the analysis in this chapter, Congressional election data and Presidential election data at the Congressional-district level are drawn from: Michael Barone, Grant Ujifusa, and Douglas Matthews, *The Almanac of American Politics 1974* (Boston: Gambit, 1973); Barone, Matthews, and Ujifusa, *The Almanac of American Politics 1976* (New York: E.P. Dutton, 1975); Barone, Matthews, and Ujifusa, *The Almanac of American Politics 1978* (New York: E.P. Dutton, 1977); Barone, Matthews, and Ujifusa, *The Almanac of American Politics 1980* (New York: E.P. Dutton, 1979); Barone and Ujifusa, *The Almanac of American Politics 1982* (Washington, D.C.: Barone and Co., 1981); Barone and Ujifusa, *The Almanac of American Politics 1984* (Washington, D.C.: National Journal, 1983); Barone and Ujifusa, *The Almanac of American Politics 1986* (Washington, D.C.: National Journal, 1985); Barone and Ujifusa, *The Almanac of American Politics 1988* (Washington, D.C.: National Journal, 1987); Barone and Ujifusa, *The Almanac of American Politics 1990* (Washington, D.C.: National Journal, 1989); Barone and Ujifusa, *The Almanac of American Politics 1992* (Washington, D.C.: National Journal, 1991); Barone and Ujifusa, *The Almanac of American Politics 1994* (Washington, D.C.: National Journal, 1993); Barone and Ujifusa, *The Almanac of American Politics 1996* (Washington, D.C.: National Journal, 1995); Barone and Ujifusa, *The Almanac of American Politics 1998* (Washington, D.C.: National Journal, 1997). Congressional election data prior to 1972 are drawn or derived from *Congressional Quarterly's Guide to U.S. Elections* (Washington, D.C.: Congressional Quarterly, 1997).

16. See Angus Campbell, Philip E. Converse, Warren E. Miller, and Donald E. Stokes, *The American Voter* (New York: Wiley, 1960), for the classic survey research on American voting behavior in the 1950s. Findings of greater issue sophistication are presented in a replication to that study, Norman H. Nie, Sidney Verba, and John R. Petrocik, *The Changing American Voter* (Cambridge, Mass.: Harvard University Press, 1979). See also Gerald Pomper, "From Confusion to Clarity: Issues and American Voters, 1956–1968," *The American Political Science Review* 66 (1972): 415–428. For findings of relatively strong ideological voting in Presidential elections, see Teresa E. Levitin and Warren E. Miller, "Ideological Interpretations of Presidential Elections," *The American Political Science Review* 73 (1979): 751–780.

17. See Clyde Wilcox, *The Latest American Revolution? The 1994 Elections and Their Implications for Governance* (New York: St. Martin's Press, 1995), particularly pp. 1–3

for division of seats in House and Senate, and Walter Dean Burnham, "Realignment Lives: The 1994 Earthquake and Its Implications," in Colin Campbell and Bert A. Rockman, eds., *The Clinton Presidency: First Appraisals* (Chatham, N.J.: Chatham House, 1996), pp. 363–395.

18. Wilcox, pp. 11–14.

19. See, in addition to sources already cited, Samuel Kernell, "Presidential Popularity and Negative Voting: An Alternative Explanation of the Mid-Term Congressional Decline of the President's Party," *The American Political Science Review* 71 (1977): 44–66 and James E. Campbell, *The Presidential Pulse of Congressional Elections* (Lexington, Ky.: The University Press of Kentucky, 1993).

20. See James Campbell, *Presidential Pulse*, pp. 36–62.

21. James Campbell, *Presidential Pulse*.

22. See particularly Angus Campbell, "Surge and Decline: A Study of Electoral Change," *Public Opinion Quarterly* (1960): 397–418.

23. James E. Campbell, *Presidential Pulse*, pp. 85–196; "Explaining Presidential Losses in Midterm Congressional Elections," and "Predicting Seat Gains from Presidential Coattails."

24. Wilcox, p. 11.

25. See Walter Dean Burnham, "Realignment Lives: The 1994 Earthquake and Its Implications."

26. Louisiana instituted a nonpartisan runoff system for Congressional elections after 1976 and is excluded from the analysis of partisan elections.

27. Stanley and Niemi, *Vital Statistics on American Politics*, p. 216.

28. See Joel H. Silbey, "Beyond Realignment and Realignment Theory: American Political Eras, 1789–1989," in Byron E. Shafer, ed., *The End of Realignment? Interpreting American Political Eras* (Madison: University of Wisconsin Press, 1991), pp. 3–23.

8

Race and Class in the Post–New Deal Order

Observations of a decline in the New Deal electoral order have often included concurrent observations of a decline in its class-based partisan coalitions. Explanations for the decline of voting by social class have included structural change associated with postindustrial modernization, affluence, and the politics of racial polarization. However they differ, these explanations seem to agree on the increased salience of "cultural" issues or the "social issue." What was once an "end-of-ideology" resulting from the resolution of economic class conflict has become a new ideological polarization articulated on the social agenda, focusing on issues like race, the environment, and abortion. The previous chapters of the current work support the argument that racial issues have been decisively important to realignment in American politics since the 1960s.

Certainly social class was the organizing principle behind the electoral coalitions of the New Deal era. Just as certainly, cultural issues relating to modernization versus traditionalism in general, and race in particular, have been central to electoral conflict throughout American history. Clearly, issues of race and class have cut across electoral coalitions in American politics.

Voting behavior across lines of race and class is a particularly important subject if, as argued in the previous chapters, ideological polarization is shaping a new party system in American politics. American political culture has been generally observed to feature a very low level of class consciousness.[1] This characteristic of American politics has frequently been cited as an important factor in a two-party system featuring two umbrella parties that are not very distinct ideologically. The parliamentary democracies of other advanced capitalist societies are based in political cultures that contain somewhat stronger levels of class consciousness, more ideological and programmatic political parties, and multiparty systems. This general relationship between class consciousness and party systems presents an interesting question: How would ideologically polarized parties function, in the relative absence of a strong class consciousness and class-based coalitions, in the American democracy of the twenty-first century?

The purpose of this chapter is to examine the dynamics of race and class in the post–New Deal electoral order. The broader issues concerning the relationship among race, class, and the new party system are addressed in Chapter 10.

IDEOLOGICAL POLARIZATION AND THE "INVERSION OF THE NEW DEAL ORDER"

Everett Carll Ladd first observed what he called the "inversion of the New Deal order" during the period of pronounced electoral change in the early 1970s.[2] Although he has since conceded that his observation was an "over extrapolation" of trends in his polling data, at least a relative decline in the class basis of party coalitions has come to be generally accepted by Ladd and other scholars as a central characteristic of post–New Deal electoral politics.[3] Ladd attributed this decline to postindustrial modernization: "The composition of the American party coalitions has been transformed, from what it was in the New Deal era because of the transformation of conflict which has occurred with the entry into a sociopolitical setting most aptly described as postindustrial."[4]

Ladd argued that because of affluence and the changing structure of the work force, voting behavior is less oriented to the economic interests of social class than it was during the New Deal era. Arguments along this line fit well into the "end-of-ideology" model presented by Daniel Bell at about the same time.[5] According to this line of reasoning, modern capitalist societies have developed service economies that are technologically advanced and, in the aggregate, affluent. In such societies, service delivery and information have replaced material production as the central focus of economic activity. With affluence achieved, the objective conditions for the resolution of economic problems are in place; and the resolution of economic problems implies the decline of class conflict, an increase in working-class conservatism, and the rise of the politics of consensus.[6] As Ladd and Hadley put it,

> As a result of technological changes, the wealth of society has been enlarged to a point where a majority of the population is beyond subsistence concerns. Because of affluence thus construed, a mass public can partake of values previously limited only to a few. . . .
>
>   The dramatic growth of mass prosperity . . . contributed to a pervasive sense that deep political divisions were being eroded throughout the United States and the rest of the developed world. The fundamental problems had been resolved, the fundamental antagonisms had been removed.[7]

This is not to say that the postindustrial thesis actually concludes that social class is irrelevant or that political conflict will disappear. Rather, new classes are being formed, restructuring political conflict along lines that transcend narrow economic conceptions of class. The emerging class system described by postindustrial theorists is a technocratic one. For David Apter, postindustrial society features three classes, defined by their relationship to technology: the technologically competent, the technologically obsolete, and the technologically superfluous.[8]

Apter's "technologically competent" seems to resemble what has been more generally referred to as a "new middle class," reaching positions of power and influence because of their education, technical expertise, and access to information.[9] Not so concerned with economic interests as the industrial middle class, the new middle class is able to "partake of values previously limited to only a few" and is relatively liberal on social and cultural issues, such as civil rights, women's rights, consumer affairs, and the environment. It is this new middle class who prioritizes the "post-materialist" values, such as the environment, human rights, and libertarian attitudes toward personal choices, as discussed by Ronald Inglehart.[10]

Apter's "technologically obsolete" portrays a working class with rapidly changing interests. Economically comfortable, the working class is nevertheless not secure; indeed, it can be said to be declining, along with the decline of manufacturing employment in the postindustrial economy. Having a lot to lose economically, perceiving themselves as socially threatened, these working class voters are increasingly conservative on social and cultural issues.[11] Thus, Ladd and

Hadley argued that "the distinctive feature of postindustrialism" is a "working class which is middle class and conservative."[12]

The increasing conservatism of the working class and the increasing liberalism of the middle class, to the extent that these changes can be observed, do not represent a simple "inversion" or reversal of the roles. Instead, the ideological transformation of the social classes illustrates the increasing salience of social and cultural issues on the public agenda in postindustrial society. As with previous alignments, the current electoral period seems well defined by a public agenda featuring cross-cutting issues. In this case, ideological polarization can be indicated along two dimensions: the economic and the sociocultural.[13]

Thus, affluence and a decline in class antagonism on economic issues, even if they can be established, have not led to a decline of ideological polarization. The reverse may even be the case, because differences on cultural issues, such as race, or the environment, or abortion, may be more difficult to resolve and are certainly more difficult to compromise. As Walter Dean Burnham put it:

> So long as these cultural struggles are intense "world-view" conflicts, there is one thing that cannot be done with them. They cannot be treated in a "more-or-less" fashion . . . as if they were equivalent to conflicts over tariffs, taxes, or minimum wages. They inherently involve not questions of more-or-less, but either-or.[14]

Whereas Ladd tied the decline in class-based voting and the increase in ideological polarization on cultural issues to affluence and postindustrial modernization, others have linked both to race and racial issues in American politics. James Sundquist, in his early work on realignment, demonstrated that in geographic areas where blacks are numerous, whites tend to vote less along class lines, a finding confirmed later by Robert Huckfeldt and Carol Weitzel Kohfield.[15] Racial issues have been central to the splintering of the New Deal coalition not only with regard to the growth of the Republican vote in the south but also with regard to the decline of the Democratic vote among working-class whites.[16]

Observations of ideological polarization and electoral change attributed to a number of cultural issues on the one hand, and observations tracing these processes to racial issues are not necessarily mutually exclusive. Norman H. Nie, Sydney Verba, and John R. Petrocik presented increased ideological voting as one of the more important characteristics of *The Changing American Voter*.[17] Their finding, based on survey research and altering previous findings developed with University of Michigan data, followed upon similar conclusions offered by Gerald Pomper and by Nie and Kristi Andersen, and anticipated the later findings of Teresa E. Levitin and Warren E. Miller concerning Presidential elections.[18] All this work concluded that American voters, at least partly in response to more polarized issue positions taken by the candidates of the two major parties, were becoming more ideological and were more "sophisticated" at tying issue positions together among a variety of cultural issues. Edward G. Carmines and James A. Stimson found not only increased issue constraint, or a "bundling" of a variety of issues with race, but an increased identification by American voters of Democrats as racial liberals and Republicans as racial conservatives since 1964.[19]

This identification by voters fits with reality, according to voting records in Congress. Carmines and Stimson also found increased polarization between the political parties in Congress on Civil Rights roll calls starting about the same time.[20] Prior to 1964, there was little difference between national Democrats and Republicans on civil rights. Then in 1964 came the almost simultaneous events marking a turning point: the passage of the Civil Rights Act, and the nomination of Senator Barry Goldwater of Arizona for the Presidency by the Republicans. The Civil Rights Act passed with bipartisan support, with opposition being almost entirely limited to southern Democrats. The Republican Party, on the Civil Rights roll calls, still looked like the party of Lincoln, as a higher proportion of Republicans than Democrats nationally supported passage. But Goldwater was one of only six Republican Senators to vote against the bill.[21] His nomination marked the seizure of the Republican Party by its conservatives, and his campaign marked the critical stage in the movement of the south into the Republican electoral fold. This electoral realignment, its roots in factional struggles within the parties, and its spread to the parties in Congress are all discussed in previous chapters.

Electoral change in the south alone would have been enough to reverse the national pattern of support for the parties, effectively ending the New Deal party system. But as issues on the civil rights agenda were taken beyond the crusade against white supremacy in the south, and as racial issues gained salience in the north, the splintering of the New Deal coalition spread beyond the south, and the major parties became polarized on race issues. In 1965, as with the Civil Rights Bill the year before, most Republicans in both houses of Congress voted for the Voting Rights Act, which was directed largely at southern states. But by 1968, a majority of Congressional Democrats voted for Housing Rights, while a majority of Republicans voted against the bill, which had as much impact in the north as in the south.

Thomas Byrne Edsall and Mary D. Edsall provide an excellent account of events after 1964 that altered many white attitudes on race.[22] Riots in majority black inner-city neighborhoods, starting with Watts in

1965, moving through Detroit in 1967, and climaxing with the violence after the assassination of Martin Luther King in 1968, created images many whites feared, and led many whites to "bundle" race with crime. Though these riots were more spontaneous expressions of frustration and anger than political demonstrations, younger blacks were organizing people in their own neighborhoods and on college campuses for political action that appeared to many whites to be more extreme than the Civil Rights movement associated with King and the Southern Christian Leadership Conference. At the same time, King himself was developing an agenda that focused increasingly on economics, class, and poverty.[23] As affirmative action, welfare rights, and busing and housing rights took center stage on the civil rights agenda, racial polarization in electoral politics increased, and the white working-class base of the New Deal coalition weakened. Perhaps the first clear sign for the potential of a backlash against civil rights among white working-class Democrats came in the Democratic Presidential primaries of 1964, when Governor George C. Wallace of Alabama polled 25 percent of the vote in Wisconsin, 34 percent in Indiana, and 43 percent in Maryland, all against favorite sons standing in for President Johnson. That pattern of support for Wallace carried through the 1968 Presidential election, when he was a third-party candidate, into 1972, when he won Democratic primaries not only in Florida, Tennessee, and North Carolina but also in Maryland and Michigan, his campaign ended only by the assassination attempt that left him paralyzed.[24]

Indeed, the electoral politics of racial polarization and the decline of class-based coalitions were particularly visible in metropolitan areas, where three out of every four Americans lived by 1970. Consistent with the findings of Sundquist in the south and Huckfeldt and Kohfield in the north, white working-class voters who lived in urban and suburban areas near concentrations of blacks were apparently trending Republican in their voting behavior. Edsall and Edsall particularly take note of the decline of the Democratic vote among labor-union voters in Macomb County, Michigan, in response to the Detroit riots of 1967 and the busing issue, and the racial polarization of voting in Chicago in response to protests for open housing, and in New York in response to organized efforts for welfare reform.[25]

Many Republicans stood ready to take advantage of the changing dynamic of the race issue. Kevin Phillips, in his forecast of an "emerging Republican majority," saw the shift of the south toward the Republicans and the weakening of working-class ties to the Democratic coalition in the north as the cornerstones of realignment at the time.[26] Republicans would benefit by the decreasing salience of the economic issues that shaped the New Deal agenda, and the increasing salience of social issues bundled around race.

As Carmines and Stimson would explain the party politics:

> Every party alignment embodies a more or less explicit issue agenda ...
> the set of policy conflicts around which the struggle for power has been
> fought. The winning party naturally seeks to maintain the salience and
> centrality of the current agenda. . . .
>
> Not so with the existing minority. Its ultimate goal is to upset the
> dominant party alignment, including the issue basis on which it has been
> constructed.[27]

Thus, since the 1960s, Democrats have sought to construct campaigns
around the economy, in the confidence that they could win if working-
class whites voted their class interests. Republicans have trumpeted
social issues bundled around race in their effort to solidify their developing strength in the south and to draw working-class whites in the
north. Before the 1972 campaign, President Nixon focused much of his
attention to politics on removing George Wallace from the race or
getting him to run in the Democratic primaries rather than as a third-
party candidate, where he would appeal to this realigning portion of
the electorate.[28] Thereafter, Ronald Reagan and George Bush used
rhetoric laced with racial code.[29] In short, Presidential campaigns since
the 1964–1972 period have consistently amounted to "It's the economy,
stupid," versus the Willie Horton commercial.

This chapter examines the dynamics of race and class in the post–
New Deal party system, focusing on electoral coalitions in metropolitan
areas and across the regions of the country.

RACE AND CLASS IN THE POST–NEW DEAL
PARTY SYSTEM: METHODOLOGY

The following analysis tests two hypotheses regarding the decline in
class-based electoral coalitions in the post–New Deal party system. The
first is the proposition that the "inversion of the New Deal order" is
associated with affluence and postindustrial modernization, as argued
by Ladd and Burnham and consistent with the theories of Bell, Apter,
and Inglehart. The second is the proposition that the racial polarization
of the electorate is behind the decline in class-based voting by whites,
as argued by Edsall and Edsall, Carmines and Stimson, and Huckfeldt
and Kohfield.

The two arguments are, of course, not necessarily mutually exclusive;
but standing alone, each presents a different understanding of social
and political change. The first presents an "end-of-ideology" model of
consensus on economic issues in an environment of affluence. Cultural
issues dominate the political agenda because fundamental economic

issues have been resolved. The second argument presents a model of social and ideological polarization based not only on fault lines between races and subcultures in a diverse society but also on economic insecurity and inequality. According to this polarization model, a large number of working-class whites are more conservative than during the New Deal period not because they are middle class and comfortable, but because they are economically insecure: They perceive the Democratic Party as promoting a civil rights agenda that advances the economic interests of blacks at their expense.

In this chapter, I examine the question of whether the "inversion of the New Deal order" has been a reality in elections since the 1960s. To the extent that it has, the data are examined for evidence of support or refutation of each of the models. This research does not investigate self-conscious motivations behind voter choice reported in survey data. Rather, my interest is in empirical observations of patterns found in aggregate electoral data.

Because we are looking for the presence or absence of inversion of the New Deal order, class-based voting is defined to exist where Democrats run stronger among working-class and poor voters, and Republicans run stronger among middle-class and wealthy voters.

The central focus of this analysis is the relationship between social class and voting behavior. The previous chapters have focused on electoral coalitions using state-level data. However, although states are excellent for observing and analyzing national electoral change generally, they do not serve well for the analysis of class-based coalitions. Thus, in this chapter, the Congressional district is the unit of analysis. At that level, general relationships between median income and voting behavior can be inferred.

Census data compiled by *Congressional Quarterly* provides the central basis for the data observations made in this chapter.[30] Voting behavior is operationalized in this analysis as the Democratic and Republican percentages of the vote for President in each Congressional district for each Presidential election between 1968 and 1996. Social class is operationalized as median income for each district, reported on an index, to be explained in what follows. Survey research has consistently revealed since 1976 that Republicans do better among upper-income voters, and Democrats do better among lower-income voters, thus indicating that Ladd's "inversion" either did not occur or that it was a temporary phenomenon.[31] However, polling data that reports voting behavior by levels of income is potentially misleading because income levels and the cost of living are very different in different areas of the country. For the purposes of a consistent base from which to use income as an indicator of social class, Congressional districts are blocked into regions, and median income for each district is calculated on an index.

The mean median income for each region is assigned a value of 100, with the median income of each district calculated relative to that mean. Thus, districts with above-average median incomes will have income index figures over 100; those below average will be below 100 on the income index. Congressional districts are divided roughly into quintiles for each election according to their income index scores derived from the nearest census data, and classified as affluent, upper middle class, middle class, working class, and poor. Of course, the general expectation remains that Republicans will do better in higher-income districts, and Democrats better among lower-income districts, but exceptions to that rule may provide clues as to the conditions under which we will find inversions of class-based electoral coalitions.

Regions are defined by urban Congressional districts that are adjacent to each other and centered on each other geographically, economically, politically, and by communications media. An urban Congressional district is one in which 75 percent or more of the population lives in urban and suburban areas. Congressional districts falling entirely or mostly within metropolitan areas are easiest to block together in regions. For all the elections covered here, there are metropolitan regions centered on Boston/Providence, New York, Philadelphia, Baltimore-Washington, DC, Miami, Houston, Dallas-Fort Worth, Atlanta, Cleveland, Detroit, Indianapolis, Milwaukee, Chicago, St. Louis, Minneapolis-St. Paul, Denver, Los Angeles, and the San Francisco Bay Area.

Congressional districts in which 50 to 75 percent of the population lives in urban areas are classified in metropolitan regions if they are mostly within political subdivisions, such as counties, that are part of the region, or if they are linked by media markets primarily to a single region. For example, the current 5th Congressional District of Connecticut, in the northwest part of the state, is tied to both the New York and Hartford-New Haven media markets. Because it is in Connecticut, and a majority of its people live in New Haven County, Connecticut 5 is classified in the Southern New England region. The 4th Congressional District of Connecticut, however, is clearly within the New York Metropolitan Area, despite the state line. Almost all its people live in the New York suburbs of Fairfield County, and the district is entirely within the New York media market.

Congressional districts that cannot be placed clearly in any particular metropolitan region, including rural districts (those with less than 50 percent of the population living in urban areas), are assigned income index scores relative to the mean median income of the districts in their state.

Median income is isolated for the purposes of this study from occupational level and education, which together make up the more general concept of socioeconomic status (SES). This is necessary because of our interest in examining the relationship between postindustrial modernization and the decline of class-based electoral coalitions. Postindustrial modernization is operationalized as the composition of the work force in each Congressional district. If the hypothesized decline of class-based voting is associated with modernization, we would expect to find that among districts with more than 75 percent of the work force employed in white collar and service occupations, class-based coalitions, measured by the relationship between median income and voting behavior, are weaker than among districts in which more than 25 percent of the work force is employed in industrial and manufacturing occupations. These percentages are selected because they reflect approximately the same percentages as are found in the national work force.

The relationship between voting behavior and social class is also tested, controlling for race and diversity in urban regions. Congressional districts in which the population is more than 85 percent white are classified as "white." The figure of 85 percent is selected because that is the percentage of the national population that is white and non-Hispanic according to the 1990 Census. Districts between 50 and 85 percent white are classified as "mixed." If the black and Hispanic population of a district combine to greater than 15 percent, the district is also classified as "mixed." Districts with black or Hispanic pluralities and white minorities are classified as "Black" or "Hispanic" accordingly. Differences in voting behavior by class and race are compared, and the tendency of whites to vote according to social class is analyzed. Polling data over the years have provided evidence of increasing racial polarization in American party coalitions, and increasing partisan polarization among white voters on racial issues. The same data have indicated a strong relationship between increasing racial polarization and declining class polarization among whites in voting behavior.[32] The purpose of the current analysis is to look for replication of these findings in aggregate electoral data at the Congressional-district level. The focus is on districts sorted in metropolitan regions where racial polarization between heavily minority-populated central cities and largely white suburbs is a continuing and increasing reality. If, until the 1960s, the degree of electoral polarization on racial issues could be illustrated largely by differences in voting patterns between the south and the rest of the country, that is no longer the case. Since then, racial polarization and the polarization of the electorate on racial issues is increasingly indicated by the urban-suburban divide in metropolitan areas. Research interest in metropolitan electoral coalitions is timely, because in the 1990s, for the first time, a majority of votes in national elections have been cast in suburbs.

RACE AND CLASS IN PRESIDENTIAL ELECTIONS, 1968–1996

According to polling data going back to 1952, voting behavior by social class and race can be understood with two simple observations. First, working-class and poor Americans vote Democratic in greater numbers than middle-class and wealthy Americans. And second, African Americans vote more Democratic than whites.[33] Taken as a whole, these data would seem to yield little reason to study inversion, but they hardly explain the dynamics of race and class in the electorate as simply as it would seem. Aggregate electoral data at the Congressional-district level indicates a more ambiguous but also more revealing pattern in voting behavior by race and class.

Evidence of inversion was stronger in the 1968 and 1972 Presidential elections than it has been since, and as Ladd has since acknowledged, was not as persuasive as he then thought. Indeed, polling data generally has indicated some restoration of class polarization in the electorate since 1972. Nevertheless, electoral change in the direction of inversion among white voters did occur, and it has remained more persistent than polling data would suggest.

In 1968 Vice President Hubert H. Humphrey, the Democratic nominee for President, averaged 47 percent of the vote in Congressional districts with median incomes over $11,000, districts that ranked roughly in the highest quintile of income across the country.[34] In districts in the lowest quintile, with median incomes under $8,000, Humphrey averaged only 36 percent of the vote. Four years later, a similar class pattern emerged in the Democratic vote for George McGovern. Meanwhile, in 1972, President Nixon, the Republican incumbent, actually ran strongest in Congressional districts that ranked in the lowest quintile for median income, averaging 66 percent of the vote. Taken at face value, these results seem to present strong evidence of the "inversion of the New Deal order" observed by Ladd. (See Table 8.1.)

As argued earlier, these data should not be taken at face value, because of differences in the cost of living from one region to another across the country. The top-down class coalitions for the Democrats in 1968 and 1972, and the bottom-up coalition for Nixon in 1972, both indicated when accounting for median income in raw dollars, are certainly misleading. The south generally had lower median incomes than the rest of the nation, exaggerating the estimate of lower-income votes for George Wallace in 1968 and for Nixon in 1972. When the income index is used to control for cost of living differences, the inversion is mildly reversed. (See Table 8.2.)

However, the evidence of inversion should not be discounted entirely. Before 1968, Republican strength with upper-income voters and Democratic strength with lower-income voters were revealed using absolute dollars, even given the regional differences in the cost of living.[35] And, after 1972, relative Democratic strength at lower incomes re-emerged, whether measured in absolute dollars or by the income index. (See Table 8.3.) Accordingly, the 1968 and 1972 votes reveal weaker class-based voting not only when compared with the New Deal age elections before that, but even when compared with elections since. The 1968 and 1972 data indicate, if not an "inversion," at least some flattening of the class basis of the vote. Thereafter, even as class-based electoral coalitions are restored to some extent, only the lowest-income Congressional districts vote significantly more Democratic that other districts. Since 1980, the difference in the Democratic vote between the fourth and fifth quintile districts on the income index is greater than the difference among the top four quintiles. This indicates that the "flattening" of the New Deal order has persisted, with working-class districts generally closely contested in Presidential elections, whereas only the poorest districts can be found reliably in the Democratic coalition.

The ambiguity of the evidence of the inversion or flattening of class-based electoral coalitions presents a number of questions central to the analysis of the post–New Deal party system. First, of course, is the question of the extent to which inversion or flattening of class-based coalitions can be found across Presidential elections since 1968. Second, to the extent that there is a reduction in class-based voting, how is it to be explained? This chapter examines two hypotheses tracing inversion to affluence and postindustrial modernization on the one hand, and the politics of racial polarization on the other.

Class-Based Voting and Postindustrial Modernization

If Ladd was correct that the "inversion of the New Deal order" is associated with postindustrialism, those Congressional districts with the greatest share of the work force in white collar and service employment would be expected to exhibit collectively less class-based voting than those districts with the largest proportions of the work force engaged in blue collar occupations. In fact, for seven of the eight Presidential elections since 1968, the reverse appears to be the case. (See Table 8.4.)

In 1968 and 1972, when evidence of a general inversion was strongest, class distinctions in voting behavior appear much greater in districts with 75 percent or more of the work force in white collar and service occupations than in districts where more than 25 percent of the work force is blue collar. Starting in 1976, class-based voting in blue collar districts recovers, but only in 1984 does it surpass the class-based voting in districts with the greatest white collar and service employment.

If the expectations of Ladd, Apter, and Burnham were to be verified, we would expect to find that among Congressional districts with 75 percent or more of the work force white collar and service occupations, strong Democratic support would be found in both upper- and lower-income districts, and stronger Republican support among middle-income districts. Instead, in these districts, there is little evidence of a numerically significant upper-income vote for the Democrats. However, among these districts, there is much stronger middle-class support for the Democrats, and poor and working-class districts are strongly Democratic. Rather than an inversion in the districts with postindustrial employment patterns, in most Presidential elections since 1968, the Democrats are weakest in upper-income districts and strongest in lower-income districts. What is interesting, however, is that the Democrats carry the middle-income postindustrial districts in every Presidential election since 1968. Meanwhile, the blue collar districts follow national patterns of class-based voting closely. Thus, postindustrial modernization seems to help the Democrats in most elections at every income level, but it does not reduce class-based voting. The Democrats are still generally strongest at the lower incomes.

Class-Based Voting and Race

Polls conducted by the University of Michigan Center for Political Studies, the Gallup Poll, and the *New York Times* have consistently found that at least since 1964, partisan differences in voting behavior by race have been greater than differences by social class, whether the latter variable is measured by occupation or income. Aggregate electoral data at the Congressional-district level presented in the current study confirm these findings. For every Presidential election since 1968, the partisan differences between Congressional districts where 85 percent or more of the population is white and districts where at least a plurality of the population is black are much greater than the differences between Congressional districts that rank in the top and bottom quintiles of median income. (See Table 8.5.)

In fact, the data presented in Table 8.5 underestimate the degree to which racial differences in partisan voting behavior outweigh class differences. Table 8.6 presents differences in voting by median income for only those Congressional districts in which whites make up 85 percent or more of the population. Among these districts, class differences in party choice seem to disappear in 1968 and 1972, thereafter to return with only modest differences between the most affluent and poorest white districts. Between 1968 and 1996, the difference between the vote in the top quintile of white districts and the lowest quintile, by median income, is never more than 8 percentage points (in 1988). Differences between the Presidential vote in white and black vote districts, presented on Table 8.5, is never less than the 19 percentage points in the Republican vote for 1992, and are usually closer to between 25 and 40 percentage points. Finally, the vote for President among even the poorest of the predominantly white Congressional districts is more Republican than the total national vote in seven of the eight Presidential elections since 1968. The lone exception is 1988, in which the mean vote for President in the lowest-income white Congressional districts is 53 percent Republican, very close to the national average.

Finally, Table 8.7 offers a control for social class between the almost all white Congressional districts and the districts with black pluralities and majorities. All the districts included in Table 8.7 range from the poorest white districts to the wealthiest black districts, all of which rank below the national median income for each election between 1968 and 1996. For each election, among these districts with little income variability, the difference between the partisan vote in white and black districts is almost as great as in Table 8.5, where all districts, from upper to lower income, are included. In no case is the racial difference in party choice among these poor and working-class districts less than the 16 percentage points in the Republican vote in 1992, and it usually is around 25 percentage points.

It would appear from the evidence that race and racial issues have much to do with the decline in class-based voting where it is found among white voters, and that postindustrial modernization has little to do with it. It is not simply a matter, as Ladd once argued, of the working class becoming middle class in the postindustrial society. Poor and working-class whites, whose income does not qualify them as "middle class," have generally followed voting patterns much more similar to middle-class and affluent whites than they are to working-class and poor blacks. Though working-class whites vote as if there is some difference in interest between themselves and more-wealthy whites, they also vote as if they perceive much more differences between themselves and blacks generally.

The result is a flattening of the New Deal class electoral order among white voters, as illustrated in Tables 8.5 and 8.6. But after 1972 there is no inversion, and there is no general indication of a top-bottom coalition against the middle, as foreseen by Burnham, using Apter's model of a technocratic postindustrial class system. Indeed, the top-bottom observation, which contributes to the inversion model, is just about half true. Among largely white Congressional districts in which blue collar employment amounts to more than 25 percent of the work force, there has been a strong tendency toward flattening of the class structure of the vote. In lower-income blue collar districts, the Democratic vote between 1968 and 1996 is not much higher than in upper-income blue collar districts. For every election between 1968 and 1988, these blue collar districts with homogeneously white populations vote Republican from top to bottom of the median income scale, and in the Democratic victories of 1992 and 1996, these districts are closely contested from top to bottom. In these districts, the "bottom" is voting with the "top."

The same observation is not found among upper-income white districts with heavy white collar and service employment. Taken as a whole, these upscale districts have voted Republican in every Presidential election between 1968 and 1996, and more heavily Republican than lower-income districts with postindustrial employment patterns. Because there are so few of these districts in the data between 1968 and 1984, conclusions about class-based coalitions in those elections must be tentative. But the increase in white collar and service employment yields reliable data since 1988, and it indicates that class-voting is stronger in districts with heavy white collar and service employment than among blue collar districts, even those with homogeneously white populations. Thus, as demonstrated in Table 8.8, the expectation of an increased Republican vote in blue collar areas is upheld. The concurrent expectation of upper-income voters trending Democratic is not.

Evidence for the "top" half of the top-bottom coalition occurs in pockets too small to emerge clearly in data at the Congressional-district level. This is not simply a statistical anomaly; it is that upscale liberal neighborhoods are too small to dominate Congressional districts. The blue collar workers of Cambridge, Massachusetts, are more numerous than the members of the Harvard intellectual community in the 8th Congressional District, which over the past fifty years has elected Democrats John F. Kennedy, Tip O'Neill, and Joseph P. Kennedy III to the House. Blue collar workers, blacks, and middle-class suburbanites are more numerous in the 3rd Congressional District around New Haven, Connecticut, than are Yale professors. Thus, the argument here is not that there is no upscale liberal component to the electorate; only that their number and influence has been overestimated, while the Republican trending blue collar vote is large enough to appear, even at the Congressional-district level, going back to 1968.

The clearest exception demonstrates this rule. There is no better example of an upscale liberal urban Congressional district in the country than the "silk-stocking district" on the east side of Manhattan, which runs from the southern tip of Harlem down to Greenwich Village. Not only is the silk-stocking district very liberal and very Democratic, it provides a case that supports the expectation of a growing Democratic vote among upper-income voters in the post–New Deal party system. The district always ranks among the highest nationally in median family income, and in the 1990 census it had the highest average household income in the country. It is also of more than passing interest that the district's population is overwhelmingly white. It is the district Theodore H. White once called "the perfumed stockade," with heavy vested interests in art, the performing arts, and literature.[36] Yet the silk-stocking district has consistently voted Democratic for President in the post–New Deal period, which was not always the case. A Republican district in the New Deal age, the silk-stocking district was nevertheless notably liberal Republican. The east side of Manhattan elected Kenneth F. Simpson, an early supporter of Wendell L. Willkie, to the House in 1940. When Simpson died in office, he was succeeded by Joseph Clark Baldwin, an even more liberal Republican who lost a primary to Frederic R. Coudert in 1946. After Coudert served for six terms, the silk-stocking district elected John V. Lindsay, another liberal Republican, three times. Lindsay was elected Mayor on the Republican and Liberal Party lines in 1965, and re-elected on the Liberal line after losing the Republican primary in 1969. Sensing the ideological polarization between the parties, Mayor Lindsay switched parties and unsuccessfully sought the Democratic Presidential nomination in 1972.

Soon after Lindsay went to City Hall, the silk-stocking district elected Edward I. Koch, a reform liberal Democrat who had driven Tammany boss Carmine De Sapio from politics in the 1961 municipal primary. Koch, the first Democrat elected to the House from the silk-stocking district since 1936, was habitually re-elected until he was elected Mayor for the first of three terms in 1977. The House seat then returned to Republican hands. Its occupant was S. William Green, a patrician liberal Republican in the Lindsay mold. Unlike Lindsay, however, he had to fight for re-election every two years, and in 1984, the east side was the only Congressional district in the nation to vote for Democrat Walter F. Mondale for President while electing a Republican to the House. Green finally lost the seat in 1992, to Carolyn Maloney, a Democrat who still holds it.

Table 8.9 illustrates the electoral position of the east side of Manhattan in Presidential elections in the New York Metropolitan Area. The silk-stocking district votes almost as Democratic as the low-income minority majority districts in Harlem, the South Bronx, and Bedford-Stuyvesant, while middle-income districts tend to vote more Republican, giving the appearance of the "top-bottom" coalition. But the east side makes up only one Congressional district and is an exception to the rule. The silk-stocking district aside, median income is apparently tied to voting behavior, with upper-income districts, mostly in the suburbs, voting more Republican, and lower-income districts, mostly in cities, more Democratic. Certainly, some flattening of the New Deal order appears in the New York metro area, as it does across the country.

But this certainly does not amount to inversion or a top-bottom coalition. The silk-stocking district is unique, not only in New York, but nationally. No other Congressional district in the country presents such a district-wide example of upscale Democratic voting.

Table 8.10 indicates that the general pattern found in the New York Metropolitan Area is replicated among urban and suburban Congressional districts nationally. As has been previously and consistently demonstrated by polling data, aggregate electoral data at the Congressional-district level show that urban districts are outliers in the extent that they have voted more Democratic than suburban and exurban districts. In every Republican victory in a Presidential election since 1968, only urban Congressional districts collectively voted Democratic, while the suburbs consistently voted Republican.

Certainly race is a major factor. The national differences in the vote between homogeneously white Congressional districts and black plurality or majority districts are found again in metropolitan areas. For every election since 1968, the electoral pattern reflects the *de facto* isolation of blacks in inner cities, where the only majority black Congressional districts in metropolitan areas are found. Not only are urban districts the most Democratic, but the vote in urban white Congressional districts resembles the vote in suburban white districts much more than it does the vote in urban black Congressional districts. (See Table 8.11.) And class-based voting is much stronger in cities in every election since 1968 than it is in suburbs. Indeed, across suburban white Congressional districts, there seems to be almost no class distinction in partisan voting behavior. (See Table 8.12.)

Race, Class, and the Decline of the New Deal Order

The aggregate electoral data just presented corroborate polling data over three decades that have shown an increased racial polarization in the electorate. At the same time, these data indicate that the flattening of the class-based voting of the New Deal age is greater than polling data would indicate. Chapter 2 addressed the splintering of the elements of the New Deal coalition within the Democratic Party as the civil rights issue gained salience on the policy agenda. So long as economic issues addressing class interests were paramount, the white south, white working-class voters in the north, and blacks had reason to remain under the Democratic umbrella, however uncomfortable they might have been with each other. But as the racial issue came to the fore, that uneasy coalition came undone—and has remained undone—even in elections won by the Democrats.

Table 8.13 examines trends among the base elements of the old Democratic coalition of the New Deal in Presidential elections since

1968. Table 8.13 indicates that since 1968 only blacks have remained solidly a part of the Democratic coalition in Presidential elections. White working-class voters, so central to the Democratic majority arising out of the New Deal realignment, have since that time voted very similarly to the national electorate. Indeed, in no Presidential election since 1968 have northern white working-class Congressional districts collectively cast a majority of their votes for the Democratic nominee. Finally, white southerners, once solidly Democratic, are now among the most Republican voters in the country. This evidence is consistent with the state-level analysis of realignment over the past century presented in Chapter 1.

Democrat Bill Clinton recovered sufficiently in the south and among white working-class voters in the north to win the Presidency in 1992 and 1996. But in neither election did he succeed in restoring the New Deal Democratic coalition. Although competitive in the south, Clinton lost his home region both times, carrying only four of the eleven southern states in each election. He did as well as he did largely because of the black vote. Even given the choice of the southern Democrat, white southerners voted Republican in both elections.

Mr. Clinton also won a plurality of votes from non-southern white working-class Congressional districts in both elections. But, even with a campaign strategy built on the reminder "It's the economy, stupid," Clinton did not do as well in these districts as he did across the country. As the Democratic share of the national popular vote increased steadily, from 41 percent in 1984 to 50 percent in 1996, the Democratic vote in non-southern white working-class districts improved only from 42 percent in 1984 to 46 percent in 1996. Indeed, the vote for Clinton in these districts in 1992 and 1996 does not even quite match Mondale in 1984 and Dukakis in 1988, respectively. Compared with national trends, the Democratic vote in non-southern white working-class Congressional districts actually declines slightly in the Clinton elections. The Clinton victories, thus, were accomplished despite the continuing decline of the New Deal Democratic coalition, not because of its renewed strength.

CONCLUSION

The analysis of this chapter does not support the argument that there has been an inversion of the New Deal order, because working-class voters remain generally more Democratic than middle-class and upper-income voters. But there has been a racial polarization of the vote that has seen an increase in Republican support among white voters all the way up and down the class hierarchy, and a near unanimity among

African American voters for Democratic candidates. The white work-ing-class and southern voters often called "Reagan Democrats" have not returned to the Democratic coalition. They might just as well be called "Wallace Democrats" or "Nixon Democrats" on the basis of their voting behavior in the post–New Deal party system. Non-southern white working-class voters have become genuine swing voters in the last thirty years, moved by cross-cutting economic and cultural issues. White southern voters, on the other hand, are generally no longer Democrats of any description: They have become part of the Republican base in the same period, first in Presidential elections and more recently in Congressional elections. The shift in their voting behavior did not come with Ronald Reagan but with the ideological polarization of the 1964–1972 period, starting with issues of race. Nor was the electoral change of that time a short-term accident. The resulting coalitions have persisted and matured and are continuing to shape the American party system at the turn of the twenty-first century.

TABLES

Table 8.1
Vote of Congressional Districts in Presidential Elections, by Median Income, 1968–1972

1968	Nixon (R)	Humphrey (D)	Plurality
Over $11,000	45	47	2 D
$10,000–$10,999	45	46	1 D
$9,000–$9,999	45	43	2 R
$8,000–$8,999	43	42	1 R
Under $8,000	35	36	1 D
National	43	43	—
1972	Nixon (R)	McGovern (D)	Plurality
Over $11,000	61	39	22 R
$10,000–$10,999	59	41	18 R
$9,000–$9,999	61	39	22 R
$8,000–$8,999	62	38	24 R
Under $8,000	66	34	32 R
National	61	38	23 R

Percentages are means of Presidential vote at the Congressional-district level.
Derived from the biannual *Almanac of American Politics*, now coauthored by Michael Barone and Grant Ujifusa and published by *National Journal*, cited completely in note 15 of Chapter 7.

Table 8.2
Vote of Congressional Districts in Presidential Elections, by Income Index, 1968–1972

1968	Nixon (R)	Humphrey (D)	Plurality
Over 107	45	40	5 R
100–107	44	44	—
95–99	45	42	3 R
89–94	40	43	3 D
Under 89	39	44	5 D
National	43	43	—

1972	Nixon (R)	McGovern (D)	Plurality
Over 107	66	34	32 R
100–107	62	38	24 R
95–99	63	37	26 R
89–94	60	40	20 R
Under 89	59	41	18 R
National	61	38	23 R

Figures represent mean Presidential vote at the Congressional-district level.

Electoral data derived from *The Almanac of American Politics.* Demographic and economic data at the Congressional-district level drawn or derived from *Congressional Districts in the 1970s* (Washington, D.C.: Congressional Quarterly, 1973); *Congressional Districts in the 1980s* (Washington, D.C.: Congressional Quarterly, 1983); and *Congressional Districts in the 1990s* (Washington, D.C.: Congressional Quarterly, 1993). In subsequent tables, the latter three sources will be cited collectively as *Congressional Quarterly.*

Table 8.3

Mean Vote of Congressional Districts in Presidential Elections, by Median Income and Income Index, 1976–1996

Vote of Congressional Districts in Presidential Elections by Median Income			
1976	*Carter (D)*	*Ford (R)*	*Plurality*
Over $23,000	46	53	7 R
$20,000–$22,999	48	50	2 R
$18,000–$19,999	50	48	2 D
$16,000–$17,999	53	45	8 D
Under $16,000	61	38	23 D
National	50	48	2 D
1980	*Reagan (R)*	*Carter (D)*	*Plurality*
Over $23,000	53	37	16 R
$20,000–$22,999	52	39	13 R
$18,000–$19,999	51	41	10 R
$16,000–$17,999	50	44	6 R
Under $16,000	42	54	12 D
National	51	41	10 R
1984	*Reagan (R)*	*Mondale (D)*	*Plurality*
Over $23,000	61	39	22 R
$20,000–$22,999	60	39	21 R
$18,000–$19,999	59	40	19 R
$16,000–$17,999	60	39	21 R
Under $16,000	51	48	3 R
National	59	41	18 R
1988	*Bush (R)*	*Dukakis (D)*	*Plurality*
Over $43,000	57	43	14 R
$36,000–$42,999	54	46	8 R
$32,000–$35,999	56	44	12 R
$28,000–$31,999	51	48	3 R
Below $28,000	47	53	6 D
National	53	46	7 R
1992	*Clinton (D)*	*Bush (R)*	*Plurality*
Over $43,000	42	39	3 D
$36,000–$42,999	43	37	6 D
$32,000–$35,999	41	39	2 D
$28,000–$31,999	45	37	8 D
Under $28,000	51	35	16 D
National	43	37	6 D

(continued)

Table 8.3 (continued)

Vote of Congressional Districts in Presidential Elections by Median Income

1996	Clinton (D)	Dole (R)	Plurality
Over $43,000	50	40	10 D
$36,000–$42,999	50	40	10 D
$32,000–$35,999	47	43	4 D
$28,000–$31,999	49	40	9 D
Under $28,000	56	36	20 D
National	50	41	9 D

Vote of Congressional Districts in Presidential Elections by Income Index

1976	Carter (D)	Ford (R)	Plurality
Over 108	45	54	9 R
101–108	49	49	—
96–100	50	48	2 D
88–95	52	47	5 D
Under 88	58	41	17 D
National	50	48	2 D

1980	Reagan (R)	Carter (D)	Plurality
Over 108	55	35	20 R
101–108	53	39	14 R
96–100	51	41	10 R
88–95	50	43	7 R
Under 88	43	50	7 D
National	51	41	10 R

1984	Reagan (R)	Mondale (D)	Plurality
Over 108	63	36	27 R
101–108	62	37	25 R
96–100	59	40	19 R
88–95	58	42	16 R
Below 88	48	52	4 D
National	59	41	18 R

1988	Bush (R)	Dukakis (D)	Plurality
Over 113	60	40	20 R
101–113	57	43	14 R
95–100	53	46	7 R
85–94	54	46	8 R
Under 85	40	59	19 D
National	53	46	7 R

(continued)

Table 8.3   (continued)

Vote of Congressional Districts in Presidential Elections by Income Index			
1992	*Clinton (D)*	*Bush (R)*	*Plurality*
Over 113	39	42	3 R
101–113	41	40	1 D
95–100	43	38	5 D
85–94	42	38	4 D
Under 85	57	28	29 D
National	43	37	6 D
1996	*Clinton (D)*	*Dole (R)*	*Plurality*
Over 113	46	45	1 D
101–113	47	43	4 D
95–100	49	40	9 D
85–94	47	42	5 D
Under 85	63	29	34 D
National	50	41	9 D

Figures represent mean Presidential vote at the Congressional-district level.
Electoral data drawn from *The Almanac of American Politics*. Economic and demographic
data derived from *Congressional Quarterly*.

Table 8.4
Vote of Congressional Districts in Presidential Elections, by Income Index and Work Force Composition 1968–1996

1968, 75 percent or more white collar and services			
	Nixon (R)	*Humphrey (D)*	*Plurality*
Over 107	48	42	6 R
100–107	34	54	20 D
95–99	35	60	25 D
89–94	36	60	24 D
Under 89	22	77	55 D
1968, more than 25 percent blue collar			
	Nixon (R)	*Humphrey (D)*	*Plurality*
Over 107	45	39	6 R
100–107	44	43	1 R
95–99	45	42	3 R
89–94	39	43	4 D
Under 89	40	44	4 D

(continued)

Table 8.4 (continued)

1972, 75 percent or more white collar and services

	Nixon (R)	McGovern (D)	Plurality
Over 107	63	37	26 R
100–107	52	48	4 R
95–99	43	57	14 D
89–94	46	54	8 D
Under 89	28	72	44 D

1972, more than 25 percent blue collar

	Nixon (R)	McGovern (D)	Plurality
Over 107	67	33	34 R
100–107	62	38	24 R
95–99	64	36	28 R
89–94	61	39	22 R
Under 89	59	41	18 R

1976, 75 percent or more white collar and services

	Carter (D)	Ford (R)	Plurality
Over 107	44	55	11 R
101–107	52	48	4 D
96–100	62	37	25 D
88–95	57	41	16 D
Under 88	60	39	21 D

1976, more than 25 percent blue collar

	Carter (D)	Ford (R)	Plurality
Over 107	46	53	7 D
101–107	49	49	—
96–100	50	48	2 D
88–95	51	47	4 D
Under 88	58	40	18 D

1980, 75 percent or more white collar and services

	Reagan (R)	Carter (D)	Plurality
Over 107	56	33	23 R
101–107	47	43	4 R
96–100	36	53	17 D
88–95	37	51	14 D
Under 88	40	53	13 D

(continued)

Table 8.4 (continued)

1980, more than 25 percent blue collar

	Reagan (R)	Carter (D)	Plurality
Over 107	54	38	16 R
101–107	53	39	14 R
96–100	51	40	11 R
88–95	51	40	11 R
Under 88	43	52	9 D

1984, 75 percent or more white collar and services

	Reagan (R)	Mondale (D)	Plurality
Over 107	63	36	27 R
101–107	52	47	5 R
96–100	38	61	23 D
88–95	43	57	14 D
Under 88	56	44	12 R

1984, more than 25 percent blue collar

	Reagan (R)	Mondale (D)	Plurality
Over 107	64	36	28 R
101–107	63	37	26 R
96–100	60	40	20 R
88–95	59	40	19 R
Under 88	52	48	4 R

1988, 75 percent or more white collar and services

	Bush (R)	Dukakis (D)	Plurality
Over 113	60	40	20 R
101–113	55	45	10 R
95–100	48	52	4 D
85–94	41	59	18 D
Under 85	26	74	28 D

1988, more than 25 percent blue collar

	Bush (R)	Dukakis (D)	Plurality
Over 113	60	40	20 R
101–113	59	41	18 R
95–100	54	45	9 R
85–94	56	44	12 R
Under 85	44	55	11 D

(continued)

Table 8.4 (continued)

1992, 75 percent or more white collar and services

	Clinton (D)	Bush (R)	Plurality
Over 113	39	41	2 R
101–113	42	38	4 D
95–100	49	33	16 D
85–94	58	29	29 D
Under 85	73	18	55 D

1992, more than 25 percent blue collar

	Clinton (D)	Bush (R)	Plurality
Over 113	40	42	2 R
101–113	40	42	2 R
95–100	42	39	3 D
85–94	40	39	1 D
Under 85	53	31	22 D

1996, 75 percent or more white collar and services

	Clinton (D)	Dole (R)	Plurality
Over 113	46	45	1 D
101–113	51	39	12 D
95–100	57	33	24 D
85–94	63	29	34 D
Under 85	78	16	62 D

1996, more than 25 percent blue collar

	Clinton (D)	Dole (R)	Plurality
Over 113	45	44	1 D
101–113	44	46	2 R
95–100	47	42	5 D
85–94	46	44	2 D
Under 85	59	32	27 D

Figures represent percentages of the Presidential vote at the Congressional-district level.

Electoral data drawn from *The Almanac of American Politics*. Economic and demographic data derived from *Congressional Quarterly*.

Table 8.5
Electoral Polarization by Race in Class: Vote in Congressional Districts in Presidential Elections, 1968–1996

Democratic Vote for President

Income Index	1968	1972	1976	1980	1984	1988	1992	1996
Top Quintile	40	34	45	35	36	40	39	46
Bottom Quintile	44	41	58	50	48	59	57	63
Difference	4	7	13	15	12	19	18	17

Race								
White	42	36	47	38	37	43	39	45
Black	70	77	72	72	69	70	71	76
Difference	28	41	25	34	32	27	32	31

Republican Vote for President

Income Index	1968	1972	1976	1980	1984	1988	1992	1996
Top Quintile	45	66	54	55	63	60	42	45
Bottom Quintile	39	59	41	43	52	40	28	29
Difference	6	7	13	12	11	20	14	16

Race								
White	47	64	51	53	62	57	40	43
Black	24	23	26	23	31	30	21	20
Difference	23	41	25	30	31	27	19	23

Congressional districts are sorted roughly into quintiles on the income index. For race, "white" Congressional districts with populations more than 85 percent white. "Black" districts are those with black populations that represent a plurality or majority of the total.

Electoral data drawn from *The Almanac of American Politics*. Economic and demographic data derived from *Congressional Quarterly*.

Table 8.6
Presidential Vote in White Congressional Districts, by Median Income Index, 1968–1996

1968	Nixon (R)	Humphrey (D)	Plurality
Over 107	48	42	6 R
100–107	48	42	6 R
95–99	47	42	5 R
89–94	47	42	5 R
Under 89	47	43	4 R
National	43	43	—
1972	Nixon (R)	McGovern (D)	Plurality
Over 107	64	36	28 R
100–107	65	35	30 R
95–99	64	36	28 R
89–94	64	36	28 R
Under 89	64	36	28 R
National	61	38	23 R
1976	Carter (D)	Ford (R)	Plurality
Over 107	43	56	13 R
101–107	49	50	1 R
96–100	48	50	2 R
88–95	49	49	—
Under 88	48	50	2 R
National	50	48	2 D
1980	Reagan (R)	Carter (D)	Plurality
Over 107	56	34	22 R
101–107	53	38	15 R
96–100	52	39	13 R
88–95	52	39	13 R
Under 88	54	39	15 R
National	51	41	10 R
1984	Reagan (R)	Mondale (D)	Plurality
Over 107	64	35	29 R
101–107	62	37	25 R
96–100	61	39	22 R
88–95	60	39	21 R
Under 88	62	38	24 R
National	59	41	18 R

(continued)

Table 8.6 (continued)

1988	Bush (R)	Dukakis (D)	Plurality
Over 113	61	39	22 R
101–113	58	42	16 R
95–100	54	45	9 R
85–94	56	44	12 R
Under 85	53	47	6 R
National	53	46	7 R
1992	Clinton (D)	Bush (R)	Plurality
Over 113	38	43	5 R
101–113	39	41	2 R
95–100	41	39	2 D
85–94	39	40	1 R
Under 85	41	37	4 D
National	43	38	5 D
1996	Clinton (D)	Dole (R)	Plurality
Over 113	44	46	2 R
101–113	45	44	1 D
95–100	47	41	6 D
85–94	45	44	1 D
Under 85	46	41	5 D
National	50	41	9 D

Figures represent mean percentage of the Presidential vote in Congressional districts with 85 percent or more white populations.

Electoral data drawn from *The Almanac of American Politics*. Economic and demographic data derived from *Congressional Quarterly*.

Table 8.7
Presidential Vote by Racial Composition in Poor and Working-Class Congressional Districts, 1968–1996

1968	Nixon (R)	Humphrey (D)	Plurality
White	47	42	5 R
Black	20	77	57 D
Difference	27	35	
1972	Nixon (R)	McGovern (D)	Plurality
White	64	36	28 R
Black	21	79	58 D
Difference	43	43	
1976	Carter (D)	Ford (R)	Plurality
White	49	49	—
Black	30	69	39 D
Difference	19	20	
1980	Reagan (R)	Carter (D)	Plurality
White	53	39	14 R
Black	28	68	40 D
Difference	25	29	
1984	Reagan (R)	Mondale (D)	Plurality
White	61	39	22 R
Black	37	63	26 D
Difference	24	24	
1988	Bush (R)	Dukakis (D)	Plurality
White	57	43	14 R
Black	31	69	38 D
Difference	26	26	
1992	Clinton (D)	Bush (R)	Plurality
White	40	38	2 D
Black	70	22	48 D
Difference	30	16	
1996	Clinton (D)	Dole (R)	Plurality
White	46	42	4 D
Black	75	21	54 D
Difference	29	21	

Electoral data drawn from *The Almanac of American Politics*. Economic and demographic data derived from *Congressional Quarterly*.

Table 8.8
Vote of White Congressional Districts in Presidential Elections, by Median Income Index and Work Force Composition, 1968–1996

1968, 75 percent or more white collar and services

	Nixon (R)	Humphrey (D)	Plurality
Over 107	48	42	6 R
95–99	21	76	55 D
89–94	36	60	24 D

1968, more than 25 percent blue collar

	Nixon (R)	Humphrey (D)	Plurality
Over 107	47	42	5 R
100–107	46	44	2 R
95–99	47	42	5 R
89–94	45	42	3 R
Under 89	48	39	9 R

1972, 75 percent or more white collar and services

	Nixon (R)	McGovern (D)	Plurality
Over 107	37	63	26 R
95–99	34	66	32 D
89–94	42	58	16 D

1972, more than 25 percent blue collar

	Nixon (R)	McGovern (D)	Plurality
Over 107	65	35	30 R
100–107	62	38	24 R
95–99	64	36	28 R
89–94	63	37	26 R
Under 89	66	34	32 R

1976, 75 percent or more white collar and services

	Carter (D)	Ford (R)	Plurality
Over 107	42	57	15 R
96–100	58	38	20 D
88–95	60	39	21 D
Under 88	44	54	10 R

1976, more than 25 percent blue collar

	Carter (D)	Ford (R)	Plurality
Over 107	44	56	12 R
101–107	49	49	—
96–100	48	50	2 R
88–95	48	50	2 R
Under 88	49	50	1 R

(continued)

Table 8.8 (continued)

1980, 75 percent or more white collar and services

	Reagan (R)	Carter (D)	Plurality
Over 107	58	32	26 R
96–100	34	53	19 D
88–95	36	52	16 D
Under 88	60	34	26 R

1980, more than 25 percent blue collar

	Reagan (R)	Carter (D)	Plurality
Over 107	54	36	18 R
101–107	52	38	14 R
96–100	52	39	13 R
88–95	53	38	15 R
Under 88	53	40	13 R

1984, 75 percent or more white collar and services

	Reagan (R)	Mondale (D)	Plurality
Over 107	65	34	31 R
96–100	40	59	19 D
88–95	44	56	12 D
Under 88	66	34	32 R

1984, more than 25 percent blue collar

	Reagan (R)	Mondale (D)	Plurality
Over 107	64	36	28 R
101–107	62	37	25 R
96–100	61	39	22 R
88–95	62	38	24 R
Under 88	61	38	23 R

1988, 75 percent or more white collar and services

	Bush (R)	Dukakis (D)	Plurality
Over 113	61	39	22 R
101–113	57	43	14 R
95–100	50	50	—
85–94	48	52	4 D
Under 85	48	52	4 D

1988, more than 25 percent blue collar

	Bush (R)	Dukakis (D)	Plurality
Over 113	59	41	18 R
101–113	58	42	16 R
95–100	54	44	10 R
85–94	56	44	12 R
Under 85	53	47	6 R

(continued)

Table 8.8 (continued)

1992, 75 percent or more white collar and services

	Clinton (D)	Bush (R)	Plurality
Over 113	37	42	5 R
101–113	40	40	—
95–100	48	33	15 D
85–94	48	37	11 D
Under 85	47	35	12 D

1992, more than 25 percent blue collar

	Clinton (D)	Bush (R)	Plurality
Over 113	38	43	5 R
101–113	39	41	2 R
95–100	40	39	1 D
85–94	39	40	1 R
Under 85	42	37	5 D

1996, 75 percent or more white collar and services

	Clinton (D)	Dole (R)	Plurality
Over 113	44	46	2 R
101–113	49	41	8 D
95–100	57	32	25 D
85–94	52	38	14 D
Under 85	54	33	21 D

1996, more than 25 percent blue collar

	Clinton (D)	Dole (R)	Plurality
Over 113	44	43	1 D
101–113	43	46	3 R
95–100	45	42	3 D
85–94	44	44	—
Under 85	47	40	7 D

Figures represent mean percentages of vote for President among Congressional districts that are 85 percent or more white in population.

Electoral data drawn from *The Almanac of American Politics*. Economic and demographic data derived from *Congressional Quarterly*.

Table 8.9
Presidential Elections in the New York Metropolitan Area: The Silk-Stocking District and Voting by Median Income Index in Other Congressional Districts

1968	Nixon (R)	Humphrey (D)	Plurality
Manhattan, East Side	10	89	79 D
Over 107	50	44	6 R
100–107	47	45	2 R
95–99	41	51	10 D
89–94	29	67	38 D
Under 89	32	61	29 D

1972	Nixon (R)	McGovern (D)	Plurality
Manhattan, East Side	42	58	16 D
Over 107	62	38	24 R
100–107	63	37	26 R
95–99	58	42	16 R
89–94	55	45	10 R
Under 89	38	62	24 D

1976	Carter (D)	Ford (R)	Plurality
Over 112	45	54	9 R
Manhattan, East Side	65	34	31 D
109–111	45	54	9 R
101–108	49	51	2 R
96–100	60	39	21 D
88–95	61	38	23 D
Under 88	68	31	37 D

1980	Reagan (R)	Carter (D)	Plurality
Over 112	55	34	21 R
Manhattan, East Side	36	52	16 D
109–111	58	34	24 R
101–108	54	37	17 R
96–100	42	49	7 D
88–95	43	49	6 D
Under 88	33	61	28 D

(continued)

Table 8.9 (continued)

1984	Reagan (R)	Mondale (D)	Plurality
Over 112	63	36	27 R
Manhattan, East Side	39	60	21D
109–111	66	33	33 R
101–108	62	38	24 R
96–100	43	56	13 D
88–95	49	51	2 D
Under 88	32	68	36 D

1988	Bush (R)	Dukakis (D)	Plurality
Over 132	63	37	26 R
Manhattan, East Side	35	65	30 D
114–131	56	44	12 R
101–113	57	43	14 R
95–100	54	46	8 R
85–94	27	73	46 D
Under 85	29	71	42 D

1992	Clinton (D)	Bush (R)	Plurality
Over 132	39	46	7 R
Manhattan, East Side	70	23	47 D
114–131	43	42	1 D
101–113	43	42	1 D
95–100	50	37	13 D
85–94	77	18	59 D
Under 85	71	22	49 D

1996	Clinton (D)	Dole (R)	Plurality
Over 132	48	43	5 D
Manhattan, East Side	70	23	47 D
114–131	53	38	15 D
101–113	55	35	20 D
95–100	59	32	27 D
85–94	82	14	68 D
Under 85	80	14	66 D

For each election, the silk-stocking district, the East Side of Manhattan, is listed where it ranks on the Median Income Index, as derived from census data. Figures represent the mean Presidential vote at the Congressional-district level.
Electoral data drawn from *The Almanac of American Politics*. Economic and demographic data derived from *Congressional Quarterly*.

Table 8.10
Presidential Vote in Metropolitan Congressional Districts, 1968–1996

1968	Nixon (R)	Humphrey (D)	Plurality
Urban	36	53	17 D
Metro	46	45	1 R
Suburban	45	41	4 R
Exurban	45	42	3 R
National	43	43	—
1972	Nixon (R)	McGovern (D)	Plurality
Urban	51	49	2 R
Metro	62	38	24 R
Suburban	62	38	24 R
Exurban	64	36	28 R
National	61	38	23 R
1976	Carter (D)	Ford (R)	Plurality
Urban	58	40	18 D
Metro	46	52	6 R
Suburban	47	51	4 R
Exurban	49	50	1 R
National	50	48	2 D
1980	Reagan (R)	Carter (D)	Plurality
Urban	40	52	12 D
Metro	54	37	17 R
Suburban	54	37	17 R
Exurban	66	28	38 R
National	51	41	10 R
1984	Reagan (R)	Mondale (D)	Plurality
Urban	47	53	6 R
Metro	62	37	25 R
Suburban	61	38	23 R
Exurban	63	36	27 R
National	59	41	18 D
1988	Bush (R)	Dukakis (D)	Plurality
Urban	40	60	20 D
Metro	54	46	8 R
Suburban	57	43	14 R
Exurban	57	42	15 R
National	53	46	7 R

(continued)

Table 8.10 (continued)

1992	Clinton (D)	Bush (R)	Plurality
Urban	59	28	31 D
Metro	43	37	6 D
Suburban	41	38	3 D
Exurban	39	41	2 R
National	43	38	5 D
1996	Clinton (D)	Dole (R)	Plurality
Urban	65	28	37 D
Metro	52	39	13 D
Suburban	49	41	8 D
Exurban	44	45	1 R
National	50	41	9 D

Classification of Congressional districts:

Urban = Congressional district in which at least 75 percent of the population is classified in the census as "urban," and in which a single central city provides more than half of the total population.

Metro = Congressional district in which at least 75 percent of the population is classified in the census as "urban," and in which the population from the central city is greater than any other locality in the district.

Suburban = Congressional district in which at least 75 percent of the population is classified in the census as "urban," in which the population of the central city is less than half the total of the district, and in which the population from at least one suburban locality is greater than that of the central city portion of the district.

Exurban = Congressional district in which at least 50 percent but not more than 75 percent of the population is classified in the census as "urban."

Electoral data drawn from *The Almanac of American Politics*. Economic and demographic data derived from *Congressional Quarterly*.

Table 8.11
Presidential Vote by Racial Composition in Urban and Suburban Congressional Districts, 1968–1996

1968	Nixon (R)	Humphrey (D)	Plurality
Suburban, white	46	45	1 R
Urban, white	41	50	9 D
Urban, black	24	70	46 D
1972	Nixon (R)	McGovern (D)	Plurality
Suburban, white	63	37	26 R
Urban, white	58	42	16 R
Urban, black	23	77	54 D
1976	Carter (D)	Ford (R)	Plurality
Suburban, white	45	53	8 R
Urban, white	50	48	2 D
Urban, black	74	25	49 D
1980	Reagan (R)	Carter (D)	Plurality
Suburban, white	54	36	18 R
Urban, white	49	40	9 R
Urban, black	22	72	50 D
1984	Reagan (R)	Mondale (D)	Plurality
Suburban, white	63	37	26 R
Urban, white	56	43	13 R
Urban, black	30	70	40 D
1988	Bush (R)	Dukakis (D)	Plurality
Suburban, white	58	42	16 R
Urban, white	53	47	6 R
Suburban, black	25	75	50 D
Urban, black	25	75	50 D
1992	Clinton (D)	Bush (R)	Plurality
Suburban, white	39	39	—
Urban, white	44	38	6 D
Suburban, black	74	19	55 D
Urban, black	76	17	59 D
1996	Clinton (D)	Dole (R)	Plurality
Suburban, white	47	42	5 D
Urban, white	50	41	9 D
Suburban, black	80	16	64 D
Urban, black	81	14	67 D

See Table 8.5 for an explanation of racial classifications of Congressional districts, and Table 8.10 for an explanation of urban/suburban classifications.
Electoral data drawn from *The Almanac of American Politics*. Economic and demographic data derived from *Congressional Quarterly*.

Table 8.12
Presidential Voting by Median Income Index and Racial Composition of Congressional Districts in Cities and Suburbs, 1968–1996

1968 Presidential Election

Urban	Nixon (R)	Humphrey (D)	Plurality
Over 107	44	40	4 R
100–107	33	54	21 D
95–99	39	49	10 D
89–94	35	57	22 D
Under 89	29	63	34 D

Suburban	Nixon (R)	Humphrey (D)	Plurality
Over 107	48	43	5 R
100–107	44	46	2 D
95–99	45	44	1 R
89–94	39	52	13 D
Under 89	42	51	9 D

Urban/White	Nixon (R)	Humphrey (D)	Plurality
Over 107	45	44	1 R
100–107	41	52	11 D
95–99	39	53	14 D
89–94	35	61	26 D
Under 89	37	50	13 D

Suburban/White	Nixon (R)	Humphrey (D)	Plurality
Over 107	48	43	5 R
100–107	43	47	4 D
95–99	48	41	7 R
89–94	41	50	9 D
Under 89	42	52	10 D

1972 Presidential Election

Urban	Nixon (R)	McGovern (D)	Plurality
Over 107	65	35	30 R
100–107	53	47	6 R
95–99	58	42	16 R
89–94	48	52	4 D
Under 89	34	66	32 D

Suburban	Nixon (R)	McGovern (D)	Plurality
Over 107	65	35	30 R
100–107	61	39	22 R
95–99	63	37	26 R
89–94	55	45	10 R
Under 89	62	38	24 R

(continued)

Table 8.12   (continued)

1972 Presidential Election (continued)

Urban/White	Nixon (R)	McGovern (D)	Plurality
Over 107	64	36	28 R
100–107	54	46	8 R
95–99	56	44	12 R
89–94	47	53	6 D
Under 89	67	33	34 R

Suburban/White	Nixon (R)	McGovern (D)	Plurality
Over 107	64	36	28 R
100–107	60	40	20 R
95–99	66	34	32 R
89–94	59	41	18 R
Under 89	62	38	24 R

1976 Presidential Election

Urban	Carter (D)	Ford (R)	Plurality
Over 107	47	52	5 R
101–107	49	50	1 R
96–100	55	42	13 D
88–95	56	42	14 D
Under 88	69	30	39 D

Suburban	Carter (D)	Ford (R)	Plurality
Over 107	44	54	10 R
101–107	50	48	2 D
96–100	49	50	1 R
88–95	56	43	13 D
Under 88	51	48	3 D

Urban/White	Carter (D)	Ford (R)	Plurality
Over 107	39	60	21 R
101–107	48	53	5 R
96–100	51	46	5 D
88–95	62	36	26 D

Suburban/White	Carter (D)	Ford (R)	Plurality
Over 107	44	54	10 R
101–107	49	49	—
96–100	47	51	4 R
88–95	46	54	8 R
Under 88	46	52	6 R

(continued)

Table 8.12   (continued)

1980 Presidential Election

Urban	Reagan (R)	Carter (D)	Plurality
Over 107	54	36	18 R
101–107	51	41	10 R
96–100	43	48	5 D
88–95	41	50	9 D
Under 88	28	66	38 D

Suburban	Reagan (R)	Carter (D)	Plurality
Over 107	55	34	21 R
101–107	51	39	12 R
96–100	54	38	16 R
88–95	46	46	—
Under 88	53	41	12 R

Urban/White	Reagan (R)	Carter (D)	Plurality
Over 107	62	27	35 R
101–107	51	41	10 R
96–100	46	43	3 R
88–95	38	51	13 D

Suburban/White	Reagan (R)	Carter (D)	Plurality
Over 107	55	34	21 R
101–107	52	38	14 R
96–100	56	38	18 R
88–95	45	46	1 D
Under 88	58	36	22 R

1984 Presidential Election

Urban	Reagan (R)	Mondale (D)	Plurality
Over 107	61	39	22 R
101–107	60	40	20 R
96–100	51	48	3 R
88–95	47	53	6 D
Under 88	35	65	30 D

Suburban	Reagan (R)	Mondale (D)	Plurality
Over 107	63	36	27 R
101–107	60	39	21 R
96–100	59	40	19 R
88–95	54	46	8 R
Under 88	61	39	22 R

(continued)

Table 8.12   (continued)

1984 Presidential Election (continued)

Urban/White	Reagan (R)	Mondale (D)	Plurality
Over 107	68	31	37 R
101–107	63	37	26 R
96–100	54	46	8 R
88–95	44	56	12 D

Suburban/White	Reagan (R)	Mondale (D)	Plurality
Over 107	63	36	27 R
101–107	62	38	24 R
96–100	63	37	26 R
88–95	55	45	10 R
Under 88	65	35	30 R

1988 Presidential Election

Urban	Bush (R)	Dukakis (D)	Plurality
Over 113	51	49	2 R
101–113	54	46	8 R
95–100	50	50	—
85–94	40	60	20 D
Under 85	27	72	45 D

Suburban	Bush (R)	Dukakis (D)	Plurality
Over 113	61	39	22 R
101–113	56	44	12 R
95–100	52	47	5 R
85–94	55	44	11 R
Under 85	53	47	6 R

Urban/White	Bush (R)	Dukakis (D)	Plurality
Over 113	53	47	6 R
101–113	59	41	18 R
95–100	51	49	2 R
85–94	43	56	13 D
Under 85	44	56	12 D

Suburban/White	Bush (R)	Dukakis (D)	Plurality
Over 113	60	40	20 R
101–113	56	44	12 R
95–100	56	44	12 R
85–94	65	35	30 R
Under 85	51	49	2 R

(continued)

Table 8.12   (continued)

1992 Presidential Election

Urban	Clinton (D)	Bush (R)	Plurality
Over 113	48	35	13 D
101–113	43	38	5 D
95–100	47	35	12 D
85–94	59	28	31 D
Under 85	71	19	52 D

Suburban	Clinton (D)	Bush (R)	Plurality
Over 113	38	42	4 R
101–113	41	38	3 D
95–100	45	34	11 D
85–94	44	35	9 D
Under 85	44	35	9 D

Urban/White	Clinton (D)	Bush (R)	Plurality
Over 113	45	37	8 D
101–113	36	43	7 R
95–100	49	36	13 D
85–94	55	28	27 D
Under 85	48	34	14 D

Suburban/White	Clinton (D)	Bush (R)	Plurality
Over 113	38	41	3 R
101–113	40	38	2 D
95–100	41	35	6 D
85–94	34	43	9 R
Under 85	40	37	3 D

1996 Presidential Election

Urban	Clinton (D)	Dole (R)	Plurality
Over 113	51	41	10 D
101–113	50	41	9 D
95–100	54	37	17 D
85–94	65	27	38 D
Under 85	78	16	62 D

Suburban	Clinton (D)	Dole (R)	Plurality
Over 113	46	45	1 D
101–113	50	39	11 D
95–100	52	37	15 D
85–94	51	38	13 D
Under 85	49	39	10 D

(continued)

Table 8.12   (continued)

1996 Presidential Election (continued)			
Urban/White	*Clinton (D)*	*Dole (R)*	*Plurality*
Over 113	48	44	4 D
101–113	44	47	3 R
95–100	56	35	21 D
85–94	62	27	35 D
Under 85	57	30	27 D
Suburban/White	*Clinton (D)*	*Dole (R)*	*Plurality*
Over 113	46	44	2 D
101–113	50	40	10 D
95–100	49	39	10 D
85–94	40	48	8 R
Under 85	44	43	1 D

Figures represent mean vote for President among indicated Congressional districts. "White" Congressional districts have populations 85 percent or more white.

Urban = Congressional district in which at least 75 percent of the population is classified in the census as "urban," and in which a single central city provides more than half of the total population.

Suburban = Congressional district in which at least 75 percent of the population is classified in the census as "urban," in which the population of the central city is less than half the total of the district, and in which the population from at least one suburban locality is greater than that of the central city portion of the district.

Electoral data drawn from *The Almanac of American Politics*. Economic and demographic data derived from *Congressional Quarterly*.

Table 8.13
The Base of the New Deal Democratic Coalition in Presidential Elections, 1968–1996

Election	National Democratic Vote	Southern Whites	Non-South White Working Class	National Blacks
1968	43	28 (−15)	43 (0)	70 (+27)
1972	38	25 (−13)	37 (−1)	77 (+39)
1976	50	51 (+1)	49 (−1)	72 (+22)
1980	41	40 (−1)	41 (0)	72 (+31)
1984	41	33 (−8)	42 (+1)	69 (+28)
1988	46	35 (−11)	47 (+1)	70 (+24)
1992	43	36 (−7)	41 (−2)	71 (+28)
1996	50	41 (−9)	46 (−4)	76 (+26)

Figures represent mean Democratic vote for President at the Congressional-district level. "White" Congressional districts have populations at least 85 percent white. Southern districts are from the eleven states of the Confederacy. Black districts have black populations larger than the Anglo-Saxon white population. Working-class districts are those found in the fourth quintile on the income index.
Electoral data drawn from *The Almanac of American Politics*. Economic and demographic data derived from *Congressional Quarterly*.

NOTES

1. See the Introduction for an initial discussion of the relationship between class consciousness and the party system, and for citations on the low level of class consciousness found in the American political culture.

2. See, for example, Everett Carll Ladd, "Liberalism Upside Down: The Inversion of the New Deal Order," in William Crotty, ed., *The Party Symbol: Readings on Political Parties* (San Francisco: W. H. Freeman and Company, 1980). See also Everett Carll Ladd, with Charles Hadley, *Transformations of the American Party System: Political Coalitions from the New Deal to the 1970s* (New York: Norton, 1975), and Everett Carll Ladd, "Like Waiting for Godot: The Uselessness of 'Realignment' for Understanding Change in Contemporary American Politics," in Byron E. Shafer, ed., *The End of Realignment? Interpreting American Electoral Eras* (Madison: University of Wisconsin Press, 1991), pp. 24–36.

3. See Ladd, "Like Waiting for Godot" and Ladd, "Political Parties and Presidential Elections in the Postindustrial Era," in Harvey L. Schantz, *American Presidential Elections: Process, Policy, and Political Change* (Albany: State University of New York Press, 1996), pp. 189–210.

4. Ladd, with Charles D. Hadley, p. 182.

5. See Daniel Bell, *The Coming of Postindustrial Society: A Venture into Social Forecasting* (New York: Basic Books, 1973). See also Bell, *The End of Ideology: On the Exhaustion of Political Ideas in the Fifties* (New York: The Free Press, 1960) and *The Cultural Contradictions of Capitalism* (New York: Basic Books, 1976).

6. See, for example, Bell, *The End of Ideology*; Seymour Martin Lipset, *Political Man* (New York: Doubleday, 1960); Robert E. Lane, *Political Ideology: Why the American Common Man Believes What He Does* (New York: The Free Press, 1962); Lane, "The Fear of Equality," *The American Political Science Review* 53 (1959): 35–51; Lane, "The Politics of Consensus in an Age of Affluence," *The American Political Science Review* 59 (1965): 874–895; and Herbert McClosky, "Consensus and Ideology in American Politics," *The American Political Science Review* 58 (1964): 361–382.

7. Ladd, with Hadley, p. 201.

8. David Apter, "Ideology and Discontent," in Apter, ed., *Ideology and Discontent* (London: The Free Press, 1964).

9. See Daniel Bell, *The Winding Passage* (New York: Basic Books, 1980) and Everett Carll Ladd, "Pursuing the New Class: Social Theory and Survey Data," in B. Bruce Biggs, *The New Class?* (New Brunswick, N.J.: Transaction Books, 1979).

10. See Ronald Inglehart, "Post-Materialism in an Environment of Insecurity," *The American Political Science Review* 75 (1981): 880–900; Inglehart, *The Silent Revolution: Changing Values and Political Styles among Western Publics* (Princeton, N.J.: Princeton University Press, 1977); and Inglehart, "The Silent Revolution in Europe: Intergenerational Change in Postindustrial Societies," *The American Political Science Review* 64 (1971): 991–1017.

11. Walter Dean Burnham, "American Politics in the 1970s: Beyond Party?" in Jeff Fishel, ed., *Parties and Elections in an Anti-Party Age* (Bloomington: Indiana University Press, 1978); Kevin Phillips, *The Emerging Republican Majority* (New Rochelle, N.Y.: Arlington House, 1969); and Richard Scammon and Ben Wattenburg, *The Real Majority* (New York: Coward-McCann, 1970).

12. Ladd, with Hadley, p. 195.

13. The concept of cross-cutting issues in previous realignments is well developed in Walter Dean Burnham, *Critical Elections and the Mainsprings of American Politics* (New York: Norton, 1970), and James L. Sundquist, *The Dynamics of the American Party System: Alignment and Realignment of Political Parties in the United States* (Washington, D.C.: Brookings Institution, 1983). See also Burnham, "American Politics in the 1970s"; Jerome M. Clubb, William H. Flanigan, and Nancy H. Zingale, *Partisan Realignment: Voters, Parties and Government in American History* (Beverly Hills: Sage Library, 1990); Ladd, "Liberalism Upside Down"; Ladd, with Hadley; Norman H. Nie, Sidney Verba, and John R. Petrocik, *The Changing American Voter* (Cambridge, Mass.: Harvard University Press, 1976).

14. Walter Dean Burnham, *Critical Elections*, p. 141.

15. Sundquist, *Dynamics*; Robert Huckfeldt and Carol Weitzel Kohfield, *Race and the Decline of Class in American Politics* (Urbana: University of Illinois Press, 1989).

16. Thomas Byrne Edsall, with Mary D. Edsall, *Chain Reaction: The Impact of Race, Rights, and Taxes on American Politics* (New York: Norton, 1992).

17. Nie, Verba, and Petrocik.

18. Gerald Pomper, "From Confusion to Clarity: Issues and the American Voter, 1956–1968," *The American Political Science Review* 66 (1972): 415–428; Norman H. Nie and Kristi Andersen, "Mass Belief Systems Revisited: Political Change and Attitude

Structure," *Journal of Politics* 36 (1974): 541–591; and Teresa Levitin and Warren E. Miller, "Ideological Interpretations of Presidential Elections," *The American Political Science Review* 73 (1979): 751–771.

19. Edward G. Carmines and James A. Stimson, *Issue Evolution: Race and the Transformation of American Politics* (Princeton, N.J.: Princeton University Press, 1989).

20. Ibid.

21. See Chapter 7 for a discussion of the passage of the Civil Rights Act of 1964.

22. Edsall, with Edsall, pp. 47–73.

23. See, for example, Gerald D. McKnight, *The Last Crusade: Martin Luther King, Jr., the FBI, and the Poor People's Crusade* (Boulder, Colo.: Westview Press, 1998), and Adam Fairclough, "Was Martin Luther King a Marxist?" in E. Eric Lincoln, *Martin Luther King, Jr.: A Profile* (New York: Hill and Wang, 1984), pp. 228–242.

24. See Dan T. Carter, *The Politics of Rage: George Wallace, the Origins of the New Conservatism, and the Transformation of American Politics* (Baton Rouge: Louisiana State University Press, 1995), pp. 195–450. Data on Presidential primaries are taken from *Presidential Elections, 1789–1996* (Washington, D.C.: Congressional Quarterly, 1997), pp. 176–177.

25. Edsall, with Edsall, pp. 47–98.

26. Phillips.

27. Carmines and Stimson, pp. 5–6.

28. Carter, pp. 324–414.

29. Edsall, with Edsall, pp. 172–214.

30. Data are drawn from the following sources: *Congressional Districts in the 1970s* (Washington, D.C.: Congressional Quarterly, 1973); *Congressional Districts in the 1980s* (Washington, D.C.: Congressional Quarterly, 1983); *Congressional Districts in the 1990s* (Washington, D.C.: Congressional Quarterly, 1993). Data are also drawn from the biannual *Almanac of American Politics*, originally authored by Michael Barone, Grant Ujifusa, and Douglas Matthews. More recent editions are coauthored by Barone and Ujifusa and published by National Journal. Most socioeconomic data are drawn from the Congressional Quarterly sources, and electoral data are drawn from the *Almanac*.

31. I refer particularly to the University of Michigan National Election Studies, the Gallup Poll, and the CBS/*New York Times* exit polls.

32. In addition to the survey data alread cited, I refer to Carmines and Stimson; Edsall, with Edsall; Huckfeldt and Kohfield; and David G. Lawrence, *The Collapse of the Democratic Presidential Majority* (Boulder, Colo.: Westview Press, 1987), particularly Chapters 4 and 5.

33. These observations are reported uniformly in the University of Michigan National Elections Studies, the Gallup Poll, and the CBS/*New York Times* Poll.

34. For ease of reference, the term "quinitile" is used in this text, although it is more approximate than precise. The grouping of Congressional districts is roughly in quintiles according to both income and income index, but consideration is given to where there seem to be "breaks" in the data when classifying districts.

35. Although the New Deal period was certainly marked by an unusual degree of class-based voting, the Democratic solid south, with its generally lower incomes, may have even exaggerated the appearance of the class basis of the New Deal coalition.

36. See Theodore H. White, *The Making of the President 1964* (New York: Atheneum, 1965), pp. 66–72.

9

Realignment and the Study of American Elections

The previous chapters have provided evidence that American political parties are not in decline, and that realignment remains a useful concept in electoral analysis. Certainly American political parties as they were structured in the nineteenth century and persisted into the twentieth have decayed as institutions. But the revival of political parties seems to be a reality at the turn of the twenty-first.

The realignment of the 1964–1972 period was defined as dealignment by most political scientists, because most of its evidence portrayed the decay of a party system more than a century old. Fewer voters were identifying with either major party, more voters were splitting their tickets, and divided government was becoming a more frequent result of American elections. But the realignment of that time was, neverthe-less, the most profound realignment in American history. The south, once the solid base of the Democratic coalition, shifted dramatically toward the Republicans, suddenly in Presidential elections and more slowly in Congressional elections. The decay of the political parties of the old order contained the seeds of the birth of the ideologically polarized parties of the new order.

This chapter comments on the continuing usefulness of realignment theory. Chapter 10 describes American political parties at the turn of the twenty-first century and evaluates the new party system for its impact on American democracy.

REALIGNMENT AND THE STUDY OF AMERICAN ELECTIONS

I have argued in the previous chapters that reports of the "end of realignment" have been at least premature and exaggerated and that realignment remains a useful concept for political scientists, journalists, and other observers of American elections. This analysis does not take issue with the common characterization of the electoral change that reached critical proportions in the 1964–1972 period as "dealignment." But it does argue that dealignment should be understood as realignment by other means.

In Chapter 1, I concluded that observers had failed to understand the realignment of the 1964–1972 period for what it was because, ironically, they had rendered the concept of realignment, developed to give historical perspective to the analysis of elections, ahistorical. Those who failed to find realignment in that time period were looking for a realignment that would look just like those of the past. In particular, the New Deal realignment served as a model. Those who were "waiting for Godot" expected realignment to embody a checklist that included a mobilized electorate, new electoral coalitions, and a new majority party, resulting in unified government, a new governing coalition, and a new policy agenda. However, given the structural change that was taking place in our party system, and given the fact that there were great differences even among previous realignments, such a citing was hardly likely and should not have been the standard by which realignment is defined.

Chapter 1 criticized such a "checklist" approach to the definition of the concept of realignment. Nevertheless, if we are to move from this critique to a conclusion that realignment remains a useful analytical tool, we must derive a conceptual definition that is broad enough to cover the variations in previous realignments, while being precise enough to retain meaning. If, as was argued in Chapter 1, a rigid definition of realignment is out of place because previous realignments also differed from each other, salvation of the concept requires finding certain characteristics of previous realignments in common.

It is not likely that all the variables on a checklist will produce evidence of radical change at every realignment; indeed, this has never been the case. On the other hand, even those who argue that realignment is no longer or never was a useful concept should concede that there has been systemic change in the electoral environment about every third decade for nearly two centuries. This phenomenon needs to be explained, if not by the concept of realignment, then by some better idea. This book has been motivated by the argument that realignment has been and remains a useful concept, worthy of salvation. The problem with the checklist definition is that it sets the bar too high, so high that very fundamental systemic electoral change reached critical proportions in the 1964–1972 period without being observed, or was observed as if the change was chaotic. What happened in political science is very much what has often happened in other sciences at times of paradigm change. Because the new observations did not fit the prevailing model, they were either dismissed or analyzed as random.[1]

Even if the concept of realignment, as understood by those "waiting for Godot," fails to observe fundamental electoral change in some of its forms, we should not seek a concept that overreacts to minor or short-term shifts. The concept of realignment should be simple and rigorous, capable of identifying fundamental change in the electoral environment without imagining it.

In Chapter 1, I argued that realignment should be understood contextually, in terms of the system change it represents. Toward that end, realignment should be defined along two dimensions that provide an umbrella for the checklist items without rigid requirement that all of them be satisfied in every realignment cycle. First, realignment involves a persistent systemic change in the electoral environment producing a new *pattern* of electoral outcomes. Realignments will produce new cleavages and coalitions, or a new normal majority, or both. Second, the result of these electoral outcomes will be a new and persistent governing coalition, yielding a new policy agenda.

Table 9.1 presents the concept of realignment according to this understanding. The checklist items are grouped under the two dimensions. The table evaluates change in the political system according to the linkage between elections and policy. The first dimension—a new pattern of electoral outcomes—is the input dimension. The second dimension—the new governing coalition and policy agenda—is the output dimension. The table also makes a general evaluation of whether each checklist item and each dimension are satisfied during each of the periods commonly recognized as realigning in the development of the American party system, including the 1964–1972 period. Although no realignment has ever satisfied every item on the checklist, every realignment has satisfied both of these dimensions. Moreover, a persistent change along both of these dimensions has been observed only during realigning periods.

Table 9.1 addresses whether each electoral era associated with re-alignment was marked by significant coalition change and a new majority party. Each era saw one or the other to a degree sufficient to alter the electoral environment fundamentally. The development of new majorities did not always occur by the same process. In some cases, like the New Deal realignment, a new majority party displaced the old; in one realignment, 1896, a majority party emerged out of a previously competitive balance; and in some cases, like 1964–1972, the old majority coalition declined without the emergence of a new majority party. The early realignments brought the birth of new parties in name and form, but the Democrats and the Republicans have been the two major parties since the 1850s.

Every realignment has brought with it a new governing coalition and policy agenda. In some cases the governing coalition was characterized by generally unified government in the hands of the majority party, in others divided government produced the new governing coalition.

Chapter 1 discussed realignments since 1896 in detail. The following discussion summarizes previous realignments for the purposes of con-structing Table 9.1.

The first party system, matching the Federalists against the Demo-cratic-Republicans (or Jeffersonian Republicans), turned on the realign-ment of 1800, when Thomas Jefferson was elected President. There was no radical shift in party coalitions: Federalists were strongest in New England and the Jeffersonians in the south both before and after 1800. But starting with the Presidential election of 1800, there was a uniform shift in the electorate toward the Jeffersonians, resulting in a new majority party, governing coalition, and policy agenda. Starting with the Louisiana Purchase and continuing through the construction of a canal system and wilderness roads, the federal government promoted westward expansion and the development of a national economy. By the 1820s and the "Era of Good Feeling" under President James Monroe, the Democratic-Republicans had achieved electoral hegemony in na-tional elections. The Federalists had died out, and the Democratic-Re-publican Party under Monroe provided an umbrella that covered John Quincy Adams and the New Englanders, Henry Clay and the leading proponents of nation-building, and John C. Calhoun and the south. It was a remarkable but uneasy coalition that could not long persist.

It collapsed in the Presidential election of 1824, which was decided in the House, where Henry Clay was Speaker. The House chose John Quincy Adams for President over Andrew Jackson, who had won a plurality of popular and Electoral votes. Over the next decade, the supporters of Jackson coalesced as the Democratic Party. More than a loose coalition, the Democrats produced the institutional structure of the nineteenth-century mass political party, starting with the Democratic National Convention that renominated President Jackson and nominated Martin Van Buren of New York for Vice President for the 1832 elections. Supporters of Adams and Clay emerged as the opposition party, the Whigs, which likewise institutionalized a national alliance. The electoral coalitions were not vastly different from the coalitions of the Jeffersonians and the Federalists. The Democrats were strongest in the south and west and in rural areas. The Whigs had their strongest support in the northeast and urban areas. But the Democrats regularly won national elections. With the Democrats commanding a normal majority, the Whigs adopted the strategy of an opposition umbrella party, seeking to crack the Democratic coalition, in 1836 by nominating regional candidates for the Presidency and in 1840 by promoting William Henry Harrison as a cider-drinker with rural appeal.[2]

The Jacksonian policy agenda was a reaffirmation of Jeffersonianism mixed with radical democratization. President Jackson went further than Jefferson could have imagined in promoting a states' rights agenda when he forced the closing of the second National Bank and appointed Roger Taney to replace John Marshall as Chief Justice of the United States. At the same time, Jackson enhanced the power of the Presidency and protected the power of the national government by facing down South Carolina on nullification and pushing the removal of the Cherokee Indians across the Mississippi River. The westward push to Texas and California was completed under Jackson's protégé, James K. Polk.

When the issue of slavery could no longer be compromised or ignored, and with the Civil War approaching, the Republican Party was born in the 1850s. The Republicans won the Presidency most of the time starting in 1860, but they had to battle for a closely contested Congress. Nevertheless, a persistent governing coalition facilitated rapid industrialization, capital accumulation, and the development of a modern commercial economy.

As detailed in Chapter 1, the electoral coalitions of the realignment of 1860, not very different from those that predated them, persisted for a century—the Democratic base in the south and the Republican base in the northeast. Even in the Republican realignment of 1896 and the Democratic realignment of 1932, there was little change in electoral coalitions, regardless of which party was in the majority. Whereas the realignment of 1896 saw some shifting of the west between the Democrats of William Jennings Bryan and the Republicans, in the New Deal realignment of 1932, the new Democratic majority was much more the product of a consensus shift across the electorate than coalition change.

THE REALIGNMENT OF 1964–1972

The electoral change of 1964–1972, by contrast, merits classification as the most compelling realignment in American history, marked as it is by an unprecedented change in the coalitions of the two parties, as well as by a new governing coalition and policy agenda.

On the input dimension, the coalition change centered on the breakup of the historically Democratic solid south, and the shift of the region toward the Republicans in Presidential elections, as discussed in Chapter 1. Realignment in the south was, in turn, the result of decisive factional struggles in both parties, won by liberals in the Democratic Party and by conservatives in the Republican Party, as outlined in Chapters 2 through 6. The issue of race, historically the most enduring in American politics, shaped nathional realignment in the 1964–1972 period. As presented in Chapter 7, the Congressional vote on the Civil Rights Act of 1964 still revealed the factional divisions within both parties, but thereafter, the Democrats came to be identified as the pro–civil rights party, and the Republicans, whose nominee for President in 1964 opposed the Civil Rights Act, as the anti–civil rights party. As Chapter 8 illustrates, national coalition change also involved an increasing racial polarization of the vote and decreasing class polarization.

However dramatic it was, coalition change did not result in a new majority party across the branches of the national government. Instead, divided government has been the rule since 1968, usually with a Republican President and a Democratic Congress. This pattern of electoral outcomes has been the result of "realignment at the top, dealignment at the bottom," in the words of James Q. Wilson. The electoral shift of the south toward the Republicans in Presidential elections was not immediately replicated in Congressional elections, as Democrats continued to win re-election to the House and Senate.

The fact that no new national majority party was established in the 1964–1972 realignment did not, however, prevent the emergence of a new governing coalition. As discussed in Chapter 7, the Congressional winners in the south were disproportionately conservative Democrats, who became the swing vote in Congress. Their electoral base historically also became the swing vote in the national electorate. These southern conservative Democrats voted in large numbers for George Wallace in 1968. Then, in four of five Presidential elections between 1972 and 1988, they voted Republican for President and Democratic for the House. Only in 1976 did enough of them break for Jimmy Carter to elect a Democratic President. Thus the governing coalition, while bipartisan, was a conservative one.

Policy Change and the Realignment of 1964–1972

Observers who missed realignment in the 1964–1972 period would appear to gain support from the apparent absence of a new policy agenda associated with the Nixon administration. But that absence is, indeed, more apparent than real. Viewed in the realignment context, although the Nixon administration avoided radical policy departures, it did mark a real change in ideological direction, reflecting the conservative governing coalition then taking hold.

President Nixon most publicly shifted course in foreign policy, with his adaption of *realpolitik*, in playing off the Soviet Union and China to negotiate *détente*. But his global grand strategy probably had less to do with realignment than his more subtle or less public shifts on civil rights and the economy.

Foreign policy is, however, closely connected to the Watergate affair, which was a reflection of the ideological polarization of the time. It was more than a personal scandal, not only because of its constitutional importance, but also because in addition to whatever character flaws Nixon brought to the event, he and his inner circle saw themselves as engaged in a culture war. The formation of the White House plumbers' unit was a response to national security leaks, particularly the publication of the Pentagon Papers, and opposition to the Vietnam War. Nixon's willingness to authorize extreme measures, such as opening citizens' mail, compiling a White House enemies list, use the IRS on political opponents, or to form the plumbers, was as much the product of an ideology through which he saw himself engaged in a confrontation against an unAmerican and illegitimate counterculture.[3] No doubt, Watergate warped electoral outcomes in 1974 and 1976, diminishing the appearance of realignment.

Of course, there is ambiguity in the domestic policies of the Nixon administration, not surprising for a time when direction was changing. This was particularly evident on the issue of civil rights, so important to the realignment. Even as the United States Supreme Court was approving busing as a means to school desegregation, President Nixon was taking a public position against busing and keeping his promise to appoint strict constructionists to the Federal courts. And, even as President Nixon was issuing an executive order for affirmative action, he was ordering the Justice Department not to go beyond the strict requirements of the law in enforcing civil rights.[4] Indeed, the presence of affirmative action on the policy agenda served a political purpose for Republicans, creating a divide between two cornerstone constituencies of the New Deal Democratic coalition, labor and the civil rights movement. Moreover, during much of his first term, Nixon still had George Wallace to contend with, and his strategy was to draw the Wallace constituency through the issues "bundled" with race without making explicit appeals to racism.[5] By the time he ran for re-election in 1972, President Nixon had the support of a solid, but Republican south. Not only did he sweep the south, it was his strongest section of the country in a record national landslide.

President Nixon drew less attention on economic issues, but he did nothing less than dismantle the postwar economic policy regime. The construction of American prosperity in the years after World War II required a new wave of massive federal government policy innovation. The result had been a social bargain that would endure uninterrupted in the United States and other advanced democratic capitalist polities for a generation: The public sector would provide social investments and fiscal stimulus; the private sector would profit; and the mass population would benefit with increased employment and real incomes.[6] The postwar international economic system was constructed around the Bretton Woods agreement of 1944, which put the world on the dollar standard. By 1947 the United States supplemented that with the Marshall Plan to rebuild Europe. At home, Congress adopted Keynesian economics with the Employment Act of 1946. By the 1960s, the federal government was using budgets that would roughly balance at "full employment."

The structure of an affluent society was developed on three fronts in the generation after World War II, all based on promoting economic growth through public investment and private profit. First, the Cold War produced a policy of "military Keynesianism" that promoted the development of a military-industrial complex that became a central feature of the American economy. Second, the national government took the lead in the construction of a social infrastructure that would promote profits and jobs. The centerpiece was the Federal Highway Act of 1956, which fueled the sprawl of suburbs in metropolitan areas. The result was an economy built around automobiles, oil, and highways. By the 1960s, the automobile and highway industries accounted for one out of every six businesses and almost one of every five American jobs.[7] Finally, affluence was extended by the welfare state. Much of the welfare state, including Social Security, unemployment insurance, and Medicare, was designed initially to support middle-class life. Later, as economic growth provided the revenues to redistribute income incrementally, the Great Society declared War on Poverty. Between 1959 and 1973, the proportion of Americans living in poverty was reduced by half, from 22 percent to 11 percent.[8]

To a large extent because of the success of the Bretton Woods/Keynesian policy regime, changes in the structure of the international economy made its collapse inevitable. By the time Richard M. Nixon took office, the Vietnam War had fueled a major inflation; the automobile culture had rendered the United States dependent on foreign oil; and the United States was a competitor, rather than the dominant force, in international trade. The United States was running a negative balance of trade, corporate rates of profit had been declining since 1966, and the American economy went into recession in 1970. In an effort to restore the balance of trade, Nixon floated the dollar on August 15, 1971.[9]

Just as he was declaring himself a Keynesian, President Nixon had in practice dismantled the Bretton Woods system and abandoned the full employment budget. The dollar, previously frozen in official value by the Bretton Woods treaty, now plummeted in real value. The resulting oil embargo of 1973 ended the long postwar economic expansion, and with it, the social bargain. In the new stagflationary economy, fiscal policy was no longer effectively available to the federal government as a means of stimulating economic growth. The effort to restore corporate rates of profit and economic growth would now involve a set of policies that would redistribute wealth upward.

The conservative movement gained strength in the 1970s and coalesced around a number of issues. The end of the social bargain created a zero-sum politics on economic issues, which reduced working-class support for the welfare state and increased support for the tax revolt, which in turn laid the political ground for Reaganomics. Economic and cultural issues were married in the increased opposition to affirmative action. And, finally, abortion became the new central issue of the cultural debate between proponents of modern and traditional values. With its decision in *Roe v. Wade* in 1973, the United States Supreme Court not only recognized abortion rights but stimulated an invigorated pro-life movement.[10]

During the stagflation and oil shocks of the 1970s, even the Democratic President, Jimmy Carter, could not reinvest in social programs or avoid rising interest rates. He thus lost the support of liberals in his own party (see Chapter 5) while conservatives asserted their power within the Republican Party, leading to the nomination and election of Ronald Reagan to the Presidency in 1980.

President Reagan took new and bold policy initiatives, but he was responding to a set of electoral realities and a public policy agenda, both nearly a decade old. The economic growth of the 1980s was not as consistently high as the 1960s, and it did not spread affluence. Rather, Reaganomics was based on an upward redistribution of wealth by shifting the tax burden. Despite the market rhetoric of the Reagan administration, economic growth was promoted by massive federal budget deficits related to the tax cuts and a renewed military Keynesianism. Meanwhile, American personal incomes had stopped growing as early as 1973, and the proportion of the population living in poverty increased from 11 percent to about 14 percent in 1990.[11] If the Reagan administration had accomplished anything beyond short-term economic growth, it was a fundamentally political objective: The accumulated federal budget deficits and national debt of the 1970s and 1980s would severely constrain the federal government in economic policy well into the next century. The achievement of this political objective, in turn, laid the foundation for the Republican Contract with America in general, and welfare reform in particular, after the 1994 Congressional election.

While the Reagan Presidency represents the great strides in accomplishing conservative policy objectives, it was Nixon who reversed policy direction, dismantled the New Deal regime, and ended the social bargain. His vigorous efforts to rein in the executive branch bureaucracy and impound funds from Great Society programs was aborted by Watergate. But by the time he was forced to resign, the policy corner had been turned. More important to realignment analysis, the new electoral environment was well established and could not be shaken, even by Watergate.

Discussion

Certainly, the Nixon administration does not fit the model of radical policy change timed with electoral change. Certainly, Nixon had no grand design to dismantle the social bargain, and his brand of welfare reform, the Family Assistance Plan, was a distinctly more liberal proposal than the welfare reform that passed Congress a quarter century later.[12]

But the expectation that realignment must be associated with a grand policy design has the same flaw as the checklist conception of realignment: It is ahistorical. Only two realignments were marked by the rapid emergence of a new policy regime immediately following a critical election: the election of Abraham Lincoln in 1860 followed by the Civil War, and the election of Franklin D. Roosevelt in 1932 followed by the New Deal. Even Lincoln and Roosevelt were Presidents responding to crisis with policies unanticipated in their campaigns for the Presidency. Lincoln would have preferred to avoid civil war, and he had no early intention of freeing the slaves. Roosevelt ran for President promising to balance the budget, and later developed the New Deal largely through trial and error. Both the radicalism and timing of policy change in the realignment process have been overrated. Jacksonianism was essentially Jeffersonianism renewed. The policy agenda of the Progressive Era did not take hold until the Presidency of Theodore Roosevelt, well after the realigning election of William McKinley. Nor did Nixon anticipate his shift in economic

policy during the 1968 campaign. In responding to the new international economy, President Nixon was no different from previous
Presidents associated with realignment who were also responding to
fundamental change in their political and policy environments.

Thus, although electoral realignment may be "rooted in the electorate," in the words of Walter Dean Burnham, it should not be understood
as necessarily the independent variable in the analysis of political
change. Making that determination would require a broader theoretical
discussion of pluralist, elitist, and class analyses of power in American
society. Moreover, the very point of this book has been that the periodic
sea changes in American elections serve as demarcations of broader
political change, but the historic meaning of each realignment should
be understood largely in its own terms. Realignment is an important
concept, then, for at least two reasons. First, realignments are evidence
of waves of economic modernization, shifts in the issue agenda of
American politics, and broader change in the political system. Second,
realignment remains a useful concept for more-focused analysis of
American elections.

THE LAST REALIGNMENT AND THE NEXT

Presidential elections since the 1960s have been marked by an increased defection from party-line voting, particularly among Democrats, which seems related to the ideological polarization between the
parties. Each party counts on a base of about 40 percent of the vote, with
a large fluid vote of about 20 percent. The vote for Humphrey in 1968,
McGovern in 1972, Carter in 1980, Mondale in 1984, and Clinton in 1992
ranges between 38 and 43 percent and seems to represent the Democratic base. Similarly, the vote for Goldwater in 1964, Nixon in 1968,
Bush in 1992, and Dole in 1996 ranges between 38 and 43 percent and
seems to represent the Republican base.

The balance of the electorate, however, has not been composed primarily of independents who are ideological moderates, drifting between the two parties. Rather, the swing voters have been influenced
by cross-cutting economic and cultural issues that historically accom-
pany realignment in American politics.[13] For most of the period since
the 1960s, the "decisively large minority" of swing voters has been
relatively conservative on cultural issues, such as race and abortion,
and relatively liberal on economic issues. These populist voters are the
"Reagan Democrats" who constituted the decisive swing vote in Presidential elections between 1968 and 1988. Disproportionately southern,
white, male, and working class, they were important to the electoral
coalitions of George Wallace and Richard M. Nixon as well as Ronald

Reagan, although enough of them returned to the Democratic fold to elect Jimmy Carter in 1976. These conservative Democrats also were pivotal to the "realignment at the top, dealignment at the bottom," usually voting Republican for President and Democratic for Congress from the 1960s to the 1990s. However, Congressional elections since 1994 and the Presidential election of 1996 seem to reveal that these voters are now voting the Republican line for both President and Congress. In short, they are no longer swing voters. In terms of voting behavior, if not party identification, they are Republicans.

The new and apparently growing swing vote seems more genuinely moderate in political attitudes, leaning toward libertarian positions on both economic and cultural issues. These small-government voters, thus, tend to be fiscal conservatives who are environmentalists, pro-choice on abortion, and relatively liberal on civil rights. Historically liberal Republicans, these voters gave relatively strong support to John B. Anderson in 1980 and Ross Perot in 1992 and 1996. Large numbers of them voted for President Clinton on the Democratic line in 1996, but Republican for Congress.

These voters are apparently moderates who find Republicans to be too dogmatic on the right, and Democrats too dogmatic on the left. It is ironic that whereas moderates have historically been more supportive of an electoral status quo more than "extremists" of the left or right, much of the discontent with government and the political status quo in the 1990s is now located in the center of the American ideological spectrum. This irony is made more profound by the fact that although American third parties have in the past been found on the ideological fringes, the electoral base of a potential third party, such as the Reform Party, is currently found among moderates.

This change in the complexion of the swing vote, from the populist to the libertarian, or from the "Reagan Democrat" to the "soccer mom," contains the seeds of a potential realignment at the turn of the twenty-first century. This realignment would not necessarily mean that most voters had themselves been "realigned" to new partisan habits. Rather, there would be more stable partisan bases to electoral coalitions in an ideologically polarized party system: a large and perhaps growing independent vote in the ideological middle, surrounded by liberal Democrats and conservative Republicans. The partisan voters would vote the party ticket more than has been the case in the post–New Deal party system, while the independent moderates would divide similarly in Presidential and Congressional elections. Less frequently divided government would be the result.

However, even if there is periodicity to electoral change, as realignment theory suggests, there is no inevitability to election outcomes. Certainly, party and policy elites are presented by the electoral context of the turn of the twenty-first century with both opportunities and dangers. Though there is some evidence of a developing realignment, the actions of elites, and policy outcomes, will determine electoral winners and losers and whether a stable partisan majority will actually emerge in the near-term future.

If there are core beliefs to be found in the new moderate center, they might be simplified in two motivations: advocacy of small, limited government, both on economic and cultural issues. Although hard data are not yet voluminous or clear, reflections from anecdotal and electoral evidence would suggest that the new moderates want government out of their bedrooms as well as their pocketbooks and wallets.

Thus, Republicans who perceive a mandate to cut taxes and government programs are probably right in a general sense, so long as they do not go to extremes. But, Republicans who wish to win future elections would do well not to use their Congressional majority to expand governmental authority into areas of private personal conduct.

Meanwhile, Democrats would do well to abandon arbitrary defense of large bureaucratic programs of the welfare state. Rather, Democrats who want to win elections and who continue to believe that government remains the central instrument for the resolution of economic problems need to design new programs to replace, rather than supplement, the old. In a structurally low-growth economy with a large public debt, competition for public investment in social programs is a zero-sum game, and there is no policy alternative. Democrats will not only have to persuade the new moderates that a social program is preferable to a tax cut; they will also have to show how to pay for new programs by cutting the old. Democrats, then, need to avoid being put in the position of defending particular government programs that may have been appropriate to an earlier time, and instead, design new programs more fitting to the twenty-first century. For example, the Clinton administration failed to achieve comprehensive national health insurance at least partly because the proposal was not comprehensive enough. Instead of replacing Medicare and Medicaid with a comprehensive insurance program paid for partly by cuts in old programs, the administration proposed still another bureaucratic structure designed to appeal to vested interests who remained opposed to public health insurance in any case. Similarly, when the Republicans proposed welfare reform, Democrats in Congress did little more than defend the status quo, rather than present a serious alternative welfare system.

Policy outcomes, of course, feed back to shape a changing electoral environment. If the Republicans are right in their free market philosophy, and cuts in taxes and spending can be shown to result in a new wave of economic growth that actually benefits most Americans, they may yet assemble a stable governing majority. If not, the outcome is likely to be an undisguised upward redistribution of wealth, and middle-class fears of economic insecurity will be realized. If, as Everett Carll Ladd observed, the New Deal coalition collapsed partly because white working-class Americans became middle-class and conservative, an observation generally supported in Chapter 8, what would happen if middle-class Americans become working class again?

Of course, such speculation is confused in the short term by the definition of incumbency in a continuing divided government. Whereas the political parties present voters with polarized choices on social and cultural issues, the electorate remains retrospective on the economy, crediting incumbents in good times, punishing them in bad times. Voters seem to focus that credit or blame on the President, thus explaining the resiliency of President Clinton in relatively good economic times. This is not a sign of polarization on economic issues but an electoral response to the business cycle. What cannot be foreseen at this writing is the timing of the business cycle, and how it will influence the political cycle. The next realignment may well be shaped by economic events, as previous realignments were by a depression in the 1890s, the Great Depression of the 1930s, and the end of the social bargain in the 1970s.

However, the ideological polarization of the parties on social and cultural issues, traced to the 1964–1972 realignment, does seem to be an established reality in American politics for the long term. This new reality seems likely to shape the electoral environment and the party system well into the twenty-first century.

TABLE

Table 9.1
The Dimensions of Realignment: Electoral Change and Policy Change

Realignment Characteristic	1800	1824–1832	1854–1860	1892–1900	1928–1936	1964–1972
Input: Electoral Outcomes						
Coalition Change	-	-	x	x	-	x
New Majority Party*	x	x	-	x	x	-
Displacement	x	-	-	-	x	-
Emergence	-	-	-	x	-	-
Decline	-	-	x	-	-	x
New Parties	-	x	x	-	-	-
Voter Mobilization	-	x	x	-	x	-
New Issue Cleavages	-	x	x	x	x	x
Ideological Polarization	-	-	-	-	-	x
Output: New Governing Coalition/Policy Agenda						
New Governing Coalition						
Unified Government	x	x	-	x	x	-
Divided Government	-	-	x	-	-	x
New Policy Agenda	x	x	x	x	x	x

Table evaluates whether qualitative change along named dimension was persistent during each electoral era. See related text in this chapter, and detailed discussion in Chapter 1, supporting this argument.

* Displacement = Displacement of old majority party with new majority.

Emergence = New majority party emerges from competitive electoral environment.

Decline = Decline of majority party without emergence of new majority party.

New Parties = New major parties develop during realignment.

NOTES

1. For the classic discussion of paradigm change, see T. S. Kuhn, *The Structure of Scientific Revolutions* (Chicago: University of Chicago Press, 1962).

2. Louis Hartz presented an excellent discussion on the importance of the "Tippecanoe and Tyler, too" campaign as a model for the electoral strategy of American opposition parties. After the failure of the Federalists in the early nineteenth century, starting with the Whig campaign for Harrison, American opposition parties made it a habit to attempt to usurp the issue positions of the majority party. In later years, supporters of Robert Taft and Barry Goldwater would refer to this phenomenon, in their own time and party, as "me, too" Republicanism. See Louis Hartz, *The Liberal Tradition in America* (New York: Harcourt, Brace and World, 1955), pp. 89–113.

3. See Theodore H. White, *Breach of Faith* (New York: Atheneum, 1975), pp. 80–187.

4. See Thomas Byrne Edsall, with Mary D. Edsall, *Chain Reaction: The Impact of Race, Rights, and Taxes on American Politics* (New York: Norton, 1992), pp. 74–98.

5. See Dan T. Carter, *The Politics of Rage: George Wallace, the Origins of the New Conservatism, and the Transformation of American Politics* (Baton Rouge: Louisiana State University Press, 1995), pp. 324–414.

6. See John Cornwall, *Economic Breakdown and Recovery: Theory and Policy* (Armonk, N.Y.: M.E. Sharpe, 1994), and Richard B. DuBoff, *Accumulation and Power: An Economic History of the United States* (Armonk, N.Y.: M.E. Sharpe, 1989), particularly pp. 93–168.

7. DuBoff, pp. 102–104.

8. Harold W. Stanley and Richard G. Niemi, eds., *Vital Statistics on American Politics*, 4th ed. (Washington, D.C.: Congressional Quarterly, 1994), p. 381.

9. See Marc Allan Eisner, *The State of the American Economy* (Englewood Cliffs: Prentice Hall, 1995), pp. 268–272, and Peter Gourevitch, *Politics in Hard Times: Comparative Responses to International Economic Crises* (Ithaca, N.Y.: Cornell University Press, 1986), pp. 208–214.

10. *Roe v. Wade* 410 U.S. 113 (1973).

11. Stanley and Niemi, p. 381.

12. See Richard M. Nixon, *RN: The Memoirs of Richard Nixon* (New York: Grosset and Dunlap, 1978), pp. 426–428.

13. See Walter Dean Burnham, *Critical Elections and the Mainsprings of American Politics* (New York: Norton, 1970), and James L. Sundquist, *The Dynamics of the Party System: Alignment and Realignment of Political Parties in the United States*, rev. ed. (Washington, D.C.: Brookings Institution, 1983).

10

Conclusion: The Party System and American Democracy at the Turn of the Twenty-First Century

The recent impeachment of President Bill Clinton provided the occasion for special interest in comparing American democracy with parliamentary democracies, and particularly for comparing the American party system with party systems in parliamentary democracies. The American President, unlike prime ministers elsewhere, cannot be removed from office by a simple vote of no confidence. The Constitution of the United States requires impeachment by a majority in the House of Representatives and conviction by a vote of two-thirds of the Senate. This difference is founded not only on the constitutional separation of powers but also on the reality that political parties do not govern in the United States. The President of the United States is not the leader of a parliamentary majority party or coalition as is the prime minister, premier, or chancellor in parliamentary democracies. Even without the separation of powers, it has usually been doubtful whether the President could govern, even when his party held majorities in Congress, because of the nature of American political parties themselves, which historically have been more like factional systems than rational-acting, unified organizations.

Nevertheless, throughout the impeachment process, even defined as it was by the American constitutional system, members of both political parties acted as if they were members of parliamentary parties. In the House particularly, votes in committee and on the floor were almost entirely along party lines, almost as if the issue were one of confidence rather than of impeachment. That is, their voting behavior was almost unAmerican!

The analysis presented in the previous chapters offers an explanation for the partisan polarization in Congress over impeachment. It indicates that rather than a linear decline of parties, a new party system has emerged in about the last third of the twentieth century. Certainly, the nineteenth-century political parties, founded in the days of Jackson and Lincoln, have declined, but they have been replaced not by nonpartisan competing interests and electoral chaos but by a new party system that is almost unAmerican in the degree of ideological polarization between the parties. Chapter 1 illustrated change in party coalitions in the electorate; Chapters 2 through 6 discussed the dynamics of change within the parties. Chapter 7 analyzed the ideological polarization between the parties in Congress in recent years. The parties that began to emerge in the 1964–1972 realignment are now maturing to the point that we can predict the form that American political parties will take in the twenty-first century.

The purpose of this chapter is to discuss the political parties now emerging and to evaluate their impact on American democracy.

STABILITY AND CHANGE IN THE AMERICAN PARTY SYSTEM

Certainly, there are elements of stability, even in the changing party system. First, the American party system has always been and apparently remains a two-party system. With American legislatures at the national and state levels elected from single-member districts, the creation of a two-party system in the nineteenth century was highly likely, once parties began to organize, and its maintenance ever since even more likely. With Democrats and Republicans dominating the state legislatures, states have structured election laws to maintain the two-party system by making the introduction of independent candidates and third parties so difficult as to be nearly impossible.

Nevertheless, even this cornerstone characteristic of the historic American party system is operating under deeply altered conditions. Since the 1964–1972 realignment, producing ideologically polarized major parties, third parties have, for the first time in American history, emerged in the ideological center. The Presidential campaigns of John Anderson and Ross Perot, and the governorships of James Longley and Angus King in Maine, Lowell P. Weicker in Connecticut, and the election of Jesse Ventura of the Reform Party as Governor in Minnesota are all indications of the potential of a centrist third party. Such a party may yet emerge, particularly in states where there is a history of third parties and where access to the ballot is relatively easy. Although we are not yet at the point of a decline of the two-party system, so long as the two major parties continue to drift toward ideological extremes, that potential exists.

A second historic characteristic of American parties that is unlikely to change is the fact that both major parties are Lockean liberal parties, dedicated to the ideological proposition that a good society is one based upon individual liberty and private property. As such, Democrats and Republicans alike support capitalism and republican government without room for controversy. Both parties, then, express the limits of the mainstream American political culture; on these points even the most liberal Democrats and conservative Republicans agree. Neither major party is a class-conscious labor party. Even the new ideologically polarized parties fit within these limits on the ideological spectrum, and it should be no surprise that the new ideological polarization between the parties is articulated in terms of social and cultural issues, more than in terms of economic or class issues. As Chapter 8 demonstrated, racial polarization in American electoral coalitions is much greater than class polarization, and indeed, class differences among white Americans in voting behavior are rather small.

Elements of Change in the New Party System

The American political parties born in the nineteenth century were umbrella parties. As Chapters 2 and 3 illustrated, the parties were factional systems that were vehicles for interest aggregation. The factions had a strong geographic and ideological base, and the parties were highly decentralized, with power residing at the state and local levels. Each party's umbrella covered the ideological spectrum of American politics. Thus, the parties were patronage oriented rather than issue oriented, with the power to provide jobs for followers resting mostly in the hands of state and local party leaders, and at the national level in the hands of the President.

The political parties emerging at the turn of the twenty-first century, by contrast, are much more ideologically homogeneous, issue oriented, and nationalized. This pattern of party development is, as Chapters 4 through 6 illustrated, closely related to the outcomes of factional struggles within the parties and electoral realignment. The more ideological faction of each party, the conservative Republicans and liberal Democrats, won the factional struggles of the 1960s, resulting in more issue-oriented appeals by candidates and a more ideologically polarized electorate. The result was more ideological and nationally centralized parties than had been seen in the American experience. Each party's umbrella is ideologically exclusive and cohesive. Where the American party system once featured a party that was relatively liberal on social and cultural issues and relatively conservative on economic issues (the Republicans) and a party that was relatively conservative on social and cultural issues and relatively liberal on economic issues (the Democrats), it now features a conservative party (the Republicans) and a liberal party (the Democrats).

This ideological polarization seems to explain the reversal in the partisan coalition of states illustrated in Chapter 1. The most culturally conservative states, in the "L" of the south and west, have moved toward the Republicans, while the most liberal states, mostly in the northeast quadrant, have moved toward the Democrats.

Social Change and Party Development

If the shift in the nature of American parties was only the result of electoral change, it might be argued that still another realignment might reverse the recent changes. This is not likely to happen, because nationalization and centralization in party development are associated with broader patterns of political and socioeconomic modernization that extend beyond electoral change.

First, party decay theorists are correct to point out the weakening of parties as institutions associated with political reforms starting in the late nineteenth century. By reducing the scope of the appointment powers of elected executives, civil service reform produced an increasing disconnect between election results and appointment to public administrative office. As a result of a reform made in the name of "good government" over the past century, there has been at least some reduction in the linkage between elections and policy, as more policy is made by a professionalized public administration. This reduction in the power of the spoils system was particularly damaging to the political party as a governing tool at the local level, as urban machines declined in power over the decades thereafter.

Primaries were also introduced around the turn of the twentieth century and reduced the power of party leaders in making nominations for elective office. The post-1968 reforms, such as the further expanse of Presidential primaries and proportional representation in the delegate selection process, have become an essential ingredient of the party system since the 1964–1972 realignment and have further weakened party leaders. As discussed in Chapters 4 through 6, these reforms greatly increased the power of issue activists in determining party nominations.

Candidate-centered campaigns have been very much the product of these reforms and of the post-Watergate campaign finance reforms. Candidates for the Presidency now use primaries not to persuade party leaders to nominate them but to secure control of the nominating convention before it meets. As a result, candidates owe their nominations not to party leaders but to the issue activists who are so important to early fund-raising and conducting a campaign in the caucuses and primaries.

Second, beyond the narrow perspective of politics, broader socioeconomic modernization has weakened the social foundations of the nineteenth-century political party. Increasing geographic mobility, particularly in the latter half of the twentieth century, has weakened personal ties to communities and weakened political parties at their local roots. The Federal Highway Act not only promoted use of the automobile in daily commutation to and from work, it also promoted a pattern in which Americans lived in one place and worked in another. Suburban sprawl and the decay of inner cities, particularly in the older industrial urban areas, combined with reform movements to weaken urban party organizations. Increasingly, Americans in recent decades have come to live in social networks rather than in geographically stable communities.

Increasingly, as well, communication and political mobilization of voters have become a function of mass media, particularly television, rather than locally based political parties. This, of course, serves to feed the money driven candidate-centered campaign and to further advance the power of nationally organized issue activists.

As argued in previous chapters, all of this results in the decline of the nineteenth-century political party, but it does not necessarily mean that parties are disappearing or becoming irrelevant. Rather, political reform and social change have produced a new political party, more national in its organization, more ideologically homogenized and issue oriented, which articulates interests more and aggregates interests less than the nineteenth-century party did. Where the factions within American political parties prior to the 1960s were based largely in geographic sections of the country, today's factions within political parties are competing interest groups focused on national issues, such as race, abortion, the environment, education, labor relations, business regulation, and the economy. Even groups that advocate policy-making at the state level on these issues are seeking national decisions in that direction.

Institutionally, the national political party is developing as a "service" party, coordinating House and Senate campaigns, advertising, and fund-raising for campaigns.[1] The growth of a party role in raising "soft" money, not covered by the regulations of campaign finance reform, is only an example of the reality that national party organization has developed ahead of the law. The nationalization of parties is further strengthened by increasing ideological differences between the major parties, and decreasing ideological difference among the factions within parties.

ELITE REALIGNMENT AND PARTY CHANGE

The factional struggles and electoral realignment of the 1964–1972 period promoted a realignment among party elites who found themselves isolated in their historic parties. This elite realignment, although limited in scale, served to reinforce the ideological polarization between the parties. It also reflected the outcome, in practice, of a debate among party leaders about the proper function of political parties in American democracy: Should we have two parties, both of which span the ideological spectrum and offer an umbrella to a broad variety of interests, as the parties born in the nineteenth century did? Or should political parties be "responsible" parties, representing clear issues and ideological positions, offering clear and distinct choices to the electorate?

Senator Barry Goldwater of Arizona presented an ideological vision of responsible political parties that was rare, but not unique, prior to the 1964–1972 realigning period. When he withdrew his candidacy in favor of Vice President Nixon at the 1960 Republican National Convention, his instruction to "grow up, conservatives" was an admonition more than an encouragement. Goldwater's message to conservative Republicans in that year was that if they were dissatisfied with the party ticket and platform in 1960, they should nevertheless not withhold support from their party in some fit of pique. Rather, they should support the party vigorously now, then work to "take this party back" before the next national convention. This, of course, is what his supporters did, in the name of his Presidential candidacy, by 1964. Indeed, as asserted in Chapter 1, the important outcome of the 1964 Presidential election, from the point of view of its lasting impact, was not Goldwater's defeat, but his victory. His nomination left the Republican Party as the conservative party in American politics.

Barry Goldwater was a self-conscious advocate of the responsible party. He thought it would be as good for the country as for his party if liberals could be driven from the Republican Party to the Democratic

Party, where they belonged. At the same time, he thought, conservative Democrats should leave their party and join the Republicans. This would present voters with the clear choice that should be presented in a democracy. His nomination for the Presidency had the long-term effect of moving the party system in the direction of that vision.

Goldwater was not the first major party leader to advocate movement toward a responsible party system. Twenty years before Goldwater's time, his notion of ideologically coherent responsible parties had been shared, at least in theory, by the two national leaders of the major parties, and had they lived, they might have acted on their shared view. In the spring and summer of 1944, as President Franklin D. Roosevelt was preparing to run for a fourth term, and after Wendell L. Willkie had been defeated for renomination for President in the Republican primaries, the two planned to meet to discuss what they might do to produce a deliberate realignment of the party system along ideological lines. FDR, according to the account of his aide, Samuel Rosenman, was enthusiastic. The President instructed Rosenman to set up a meeting with Willkie, commenting:

> I think the time has come for the Democratic Party to get rid of its reactionary elements in the South and to attract the liberals in the Republican Party. Willkie is the leader of those liberals. He talked . . . about a coalition of the liberals in both parties, leaving the conservatives in both parties to join together as they see fit. I agree with him one hundred percent and the time is now—right after the election.[2]

Willkie indicated his interest in a meeting. "Both parties are hybrids," Willkie told Rosenman. According to Rosenman, Willkie was interested in a realignment of the parties, "between all the liberal forces on the one hand and all the conservative forces on the other. You tell the President that I'm willing to devote almost full time to this."[3]

Because both FDR and Willkie preferred to wait until after the election to meet, no meeting ever took place. Willkie died before the election at the age of 52, after a series of heart attacks, and Roosevelt died in office the following year, no action having been taken.

Willkie's foe within the Republican Party, Governor Thomas E. Dewey of New York, himself a moderate-to-liberal Republican, took issue with Willkie on the desirability of a responsible party system. Dewey believed in the umbrella parties, both because he believed they served a diverse society like the United States better than a responsible party system would, and because he believed it was in the best interests of the Republican Party to broaden its own umbrella in order to assemble electoral majorities. Dewey delivered a series of lectures in which he argued, consistent with the impression of the New Deal period, that if the parties were neatly divided by ideology, the more liberal of the two parties would win every national election.[4]

What Dewey opposed, Goldwater advocated, and FDR and Willkie could only dream of has slowly become the reality since the realignment of 1964–1972, although not with the uniform results Dewey feared. When Goldwater was the Republican nominee for President in 1964, he was endorsed by Senator J. Strom Thurmond of South Carolina, the Dixiecrat who became a Republican and serves in the Senate as of this writing. Representative John Bell Williams, Democrat of Mississippi, also backed Goldwater, and later switched parties. In the 1970s, three prominent liberal Republicans—Mayor John V. Lindsay of New York, Representative Ogden Reid of New York, and Representative Donald Riegle of Michigan—became Democrats. Mayor Lindsay was an unsuccessful candidate for the Democratic Presidential nomination in 1972; Reid was re-elected as a Democrat but unsuccessfully sought the Democratic and Liberal nominations for Governor in 1974; Riegle went on to a long career in the Senate. Also in the 1970s, former Governor John B. Connally of Texas, a moderate-to-conservative Democrat and protégé of Lyndon B. Johnson, became a Republican in support of President Nixon. Connally would wage an expensive unsuccessful campaign for the Republican Presidential nomination in 1980, gambling all on the South Carolina primary and losing to Ronald Reagan.

In the 1980s and 1990s, a number of conservative Democrats would follow the examples of Thurmond, Williams, and Connally and switch to the Republican Party. Representative Phil Gramm of Texas would rise to prominence in the Senate before his aborted campaign for the Republican Presidential nomination in 1996. Senator Richard Shelby of Alabama and Senator Ben Nighthorse Campbell of Colorado led another wave of moderate-to-conservative Democrats into the Republican Party after the Congressional election of 1994.

This process of elite realignment is the product of electoral realignment. These politicians have switched parties not because the factions where they have found their electoral bases have disappeared, but because those factions have found a new partisan home. If anything, American society is becoming more diverse, and competing interests continue to multiply. Both parties still reside under umbrellas, but the umbrellas no longer overlap. As the diversity of the American electorate grows and ideological polarization between the parties develops, the ideological diversity within the parties is decreasing. The interests within each party are much more coherent ideologically than they were before 1964.

American political parties today are ideologically polarized in precisely the manner once argued to be unlikely and undesirable. The questions remain whether this development represents a step in the direction of a responsible party system in the United States, and whether American democracy could thrive in such a system.

TOWARD A RESPONSIBLE PARTY SYSTEM?

Political scientists have generally agreed about the importance of political parties to democracy. E. E. Schattschneider expressed the consensus with his oft-cited remark that "democracy is unthinkable save in terms of parties."[5] There has been disagreement, however, about both the possibility and desirability of a responsible party system in the United States.

As long ago as 1950, the American Political Science Association Committee on Political Parties, speaking as much or more as citizens than political scientists, advocated reforms to develop a responsible party system in the United States.[6] Their work followed upon that of Schattschneider and laid the groundwork for subsequent political scientists who would advocate reform in the direction of the responsible party model.[7]

Advocates of a responsible two-party system have done excellent comparative analysis of party systems and presented a strong normative argument for responsible parties. But they have not demonstrated the possibility of a responsible party system in the United States. Meanwhile, critics of the responsible party model have made the same error as theorists who see only party decay and the end of realignment: Their analysis is ahistorical, superimposing the nineteenth-century political party on the twenty-first century. Critics seem to assume, incorrectly, that if the nineteenth-century umbrella party is in decline, it cannot be replaced in the United States by any other form of party.

The emergence of a conservative party and a liberal party in American politics leads to speculation that the historic umbrella parties will be replaced by a responsible party system, not unlike those found in parliamentary democracies. It is a question of continuing analytic interest to political scientists, as well as a normative issue for those concerned about the outlook for American democracy in the twenty-first century.

A responsible party system exhibits the following three requisite characteristics:

1. *A responsible party system requires a functional, if not constitutional, fusion of powers between the executive and legislative branches.* In short, a responsible party system produces party government. The constitutional separation of powers makes this characteristic of responsible parties very problematic for the United States. In the American experi-

ence, policy-making has taken on a responsible party appearance periodically, usually during periods of critical realignment.

The possibility of a responsible party system and party government is reduced further by the bicameralism of the American Congress. Whereas the American system is a Presidential democracy, with powers separated between the executive and legislative branches, the United Kingdom is the purest example of parliamentary democracy with a responsible party system, marked by a fusion of powers, in which the executive leadership of the government, the prime minister and cabinet, is the political leadership of the majority in the House of Commons. The prime minister and cabinet are themselves members of the House of Commons, and govern with its confidence. They serve terms of five years or less, so long as they maintain the support of the parliamentary majority. Finally, the British system is functionally unicameral: The House of Lords has become a symbolic appendage of the Parliament. In such a system, responsible parties can govern, or offer a loyal opposition to the government, and the executive has the votes in the legislature to deliver on its policy programs.

Periods of gridlock in policy-making in recent years have been commonly associated with divided government in the separation-of-powers system. Historically, however, there is no such necessary association. Certainly, unified government has been associated with policy-making efficiency during realigning periods such as with the Democratic majorities of the New Deal. And, just as certainly, divided government has sometimes led to policy stasis. But divided government has also often been productive. The reforms of the aptly named Progressive Era were often the product of bipartisan progressive majorities in Congress under both Republican and Democratic Presidents. The bipartisan foreign policy for two decades after World War II by definition did not require united government. The Federal Highway Act during the Eisenhower administration was a public works project of record dimensions that did nothing less than redesign the American community after passing with nearly unanimous support from both parties in Congress. The civil rights legislation of 1957–1965 was the product of a bipartisan liberal majority. Finally, Reaganomics passed a Democratic Congress with conservative majorities in both houses. All but Reaganomics were examples drawn from periods when the ideological spectrum of both major political parties spanned from liberal to conservative. Even Reaganomics required the support of conservative Democrats to pass. In all these cases, bipartisan ideological or centrist majorities were assembled.

The party system has changed, in government as in the electorate, as illustrated in Chapter 7. As "realignment at the top" has spread to the "bottom," that is, as the realignment in Presidential elections has spread over a thirty-year period to Congressional elections, the political parties in Congress have become ideologically polarized. Divided government now, unlike cases of divided government in much of American history, is government divided between ideologically polarized parties, and thus, is associated more definitively with gridlock. The result is that unified government will probably be more important to legislative productivity in the future than it has been in the past. The Clinton economic package of 1993, for example, passed only with a strict enforcement of party loyalty among the Democrats in Congress. Since then, with the exception of welfare reform, divided government, now with a Democratic President and a Republican Congress, has left behind a decrease in legislative productivity. The government shutdown in 1995 is a dramatic example of the association between partisan ideological polarization and policy paralysis. Even the budget deals since then disguise the fact that controversies involving the budget in the longer term, Social Security and Medicare, and any prospective tax cut, were not addressed, resulting in a "pork" bill to the perceived advantage of incumbents of both parties. The important policy decisions were left to another day when, the leaders of each party hope, they will control both the Presidency and Congress. As argued in Chapter 7, the new similarity between Presidential election and Congressional election coalitions makes it likely that elections will result in unified government more frequently than has been the case over the past thirty years. Quietly, even in the face of the separation of powers, the ideological polarization of the major parties may yet be producing at least an approximation of responsible parties and party government in the twenty-first century.

2. *Responsible parties present clear ideological or programmatic alternatives, can govern when in the majority, and can offer organized loyal opposition when in the minority.* American political parties have not fit the responsible party model, with the possible infrequent exception of electoral moments known as critical realignments. Instead, American parties are historically umbrella parties, nonideological coalitions of factions with diverse interests.

Critics of the responsible party model have pointed out that spatially distinct programmatic and ideological political parties are contrary to the American experience and are in any case not a prerequisite to a "responsible electorate."[8] Indeed, according to critics, ideological polarization has been an important ingredient of party decay, not the sort of party development that would seem to be necessary for a responsible party system to emerge.[9]

The previous chapters, however, have demonstrated that what has declined is not the American political party, *per se*, but the locally-based, nonideological umbrella party born in the nineteenth century. What is emerging is a party system featuring two ideologically homogenized political parties offering the electorate much more polarized choices than has generally been the American experience. Historically, the function of umbrella parties has been interest aggregation, more than interest articulation, which has been the function of interest groups rather than parties. But with liberal Democrats and conservative Republicans each the dominant factions in their parties, and with liberal interest groups operating almost entirely within the Democratic Party and conservative interest groups operating almost entirely within the Republican Party, parties at the turn of the twenty-first century are increasingly engaged in interest articulation.

The ideological polarization between the major parties, however, is much more advanced on issues couched in social and cultural terms, such as race or abortion, than on economic issues. The low level of class consciousness in American political culture leaves the system still without a labor party. Both parties are ideologically classic liberal and capitalist political parties, a fact that is not likely to change in the foreseeable future. Within that context, the Democrats remain the party more likely to support government intervention in the economy, and more likely to support it at the national level. The Republicans remain the party less likely to support government intervention, and when they do, more likely to support it at the state level. It remains easier to compromise economic issues, as Walter Dean Burnham observed. But two trends may change that. First, economic issues are themselves discussed more in cultural terms. The debates about welfare reform, for example, were laden with references to moral responsibility and racial stereotypes. Second, as advanced capitalist societies develop structurally low-growth economies with rapid technological change increasing structural unemployment, economic issues will become more of the sorts of either-or issues that social and cultural issues are; in a lower-growth economy, economic issues become more zero-sum and harder to compromise. Even if both parties are capitalist parties, then, economic choices will become inherently more extreme, and lend themselves to ideological polarization.

The nationalization of American political parties facilitates the development of responsible parties, as discussed in Chapters 4 through 7. The decentralized umbrella parties prior to 1964 tended to nominate candidates who did not represent clear ideological alternatives. In northeastern states, both the Democrats and Republicans nominated relatively liberal candidates; in the south, both parties (where the Republicans functioned) tended to nominate conservatives. In the more nationalized and ideologically polarized parties of the post–New Deal period, ideologically motivated issue activists have come to control nominations in candidate-centered caucuses and primaries. As a result, Republican nominees at every level of office tend to be the more conservative in every region of the country, and Democratic nominees tend to be the more liberal. The result is a national articulation of more distinct interests and issue alternatives in campaigns both for the Presidency and for Congress.

3. *In a responsible party system, the executive and legislative branches have fundamentally the same electoral base.* The American separation-of-powers system not only separates executive from legislative policy-making processes, it separates electoral processes and staggers elections, making possible the incidence of divided government, which was the subject of Chapter 7. With Presidential elections set every four years, elections for the House of Representatives every two years, and elections of one-third of the U.S. Senate every two years, the constitutional system of staggered elections separates electoral results temporally, as well as geographically. Since 1789, American voters have never voted in what the British electorate has at least every five years: a national general election.

Responsible party systems in parliamentary governments create an electoral and governing marriage between the executive and legislative "branches" whether they are constitutionally fused or not. That is, the prime minister and the parliament rely upon each other to stay in office, requiring a governing coalition that links the two to each other and to the electorate.

The debate during the recent impeachment process illustrates how unusual the American political system is among advanced democracies. The defenders of President Clinton argued that his conduct did not rise to the "constitutional" level of impeachment. Such an argument would be irrelevant in a parliamentary motion of no confidence, which is by definition political. But in a parliamentary democracy, the removal of the executive generally means either the selection of a new one by the majority, or the closing of the parliament, followed by a national election.

Although staggered elections separate the electoral foundations of the executive and legislative branches in American government, unified government has usually been the rule, anyway. Indeed, American political parties have briefly, if temporarily, resembled responsible parties, during periodic critical realignments. The previous chapters have presented the case for two propositions that, if true, would lead American parties to resemble responsible parties more frequently in the twenty-first century. First, the resolution of factional struggles in both major parties and an associated critical realignment in Presidential elections between 1964 and 1972 left in their wake an ideologically polarized party system at the national level. Second, secular realignment since that time has created party coalitions in Congressional elections very similar to the ones that emerged in Presidential elections in the 1964–

1972 period. Borrowing from and editing the language of James Q. Wilson, Chapter 7 referred to this process as "critical realignment at the top, secular realignment at the bottom."

For three decades after 1964, ideological polarization between the Democrats and Republicans in Presidential elections was not matched in Congressional elections. The south, for most of that time, violated its historic voting habits by supporting Republicans in Presidential elections, but continued to vote Democratic for the House and Senate. Electoral change in the south in Congressional elections was slow in coming, but it did evolve. Finally, in 1994, the Republicans won majorities in both houses of Congress for the first time in fifty years. More important, the Republicans ran for the House of Representatives on a national platform, the "Contract with America." Self-consciously conservative, the contract was promoted by virtually all Republican candidates for the House and particularly by Newt Gingrich. When the Republicans won the House, and he was installed as Speaker, Gingrich set himself up almost as if he were Prime Minister of the United States. His political fall since that time does reduce this trend toward nationalized and ideologically polarized parties. Indeed, the impeachment of President Clinton was continuing evidence of developing partisanship in the American Congress, which is almost parliamentary in its dimensions.

The analysis here and in the previous chapters indicates that, at the least, a responsible party system can no longer be discounted as impossible in the United States. The constitutional constraints against it have not been eliminated, nor are they likely to be. We have a new party system that increasingly resembles the responsible party model, but we do not have party government. That is, we have a party system that is increasingly appropriate to a parliamentary democracy, but we do not live in a parliamentary democracy.

The constitutional constraints, however, important as they are, do not change the fact that the ideological polarization in the American party system is something brand new, and it will have a telling impact on the political life of American democracy.

THE PARTY SYSTEM AND AMERICAN DEMOCRACY IN THE TWENTY-FIRST CENTURY

If Schattschneider was right in his claim that "democracy is unthinkable save in terms of parties," the condition of American democracy will depend to a large degree on the condition of its political parties and the party system.

The great advantage of umbrella parties in a complex democracy such as the United States is that they aggregate interests and facilitate the construction of electoral and governing majorities. In a two-party system, umbrella parties shape and legitimize public debate and at the same time build political consensus. This has worked well more often than not in a society that is so demographically diverse.

Nevertheless, the decline of the umbrella parties, and their replacement by a closer approximation to responsible parties, will not necessarily harm American democracy, and may even bring some benefit. The following discussion is based on three assumptions. First, based on the observations and analysis presented here, it is already an accomplished reality that American political parties of at least the early twenty-first century will resemble the responsible party model more than they will the historic umbrella party. Second, the constitutional structure of the American separation of powers will remain fundamentally in place. Just as certainly, however, the processes of party change presented here invite a discussion of the possibility and desirability of a responsible party system in the United States. Finally, the increasing momentum of social and economic change in a postindustrial society makes it imperative to confront the issues we face; failure to do so will be more destabilizing than the political conflict that accompanies vigorous public debate.

Evaluating party systems (as with larger social systems) does not lead to a simple conclusion that one system is good and one bad. Rather, it is a matter of balancing the advantages and disadvantages of the systems being compared. In the case of the declining umbrella parties in American politics and the ideologically polarized parties emerging in their place, it is a matter, at least initially, of balancing the value of consensus against the value of conflict.

It may sound strange to refer to the "value" of conflict, but the reference is intentional. The umbrella parties have generally marshaled conflict well enough to build consensus, but this has often been achieved by arbitrarily limiting dissent and avoiding conflict that might have been engaged with a better policy result.

The tendency to limit dissent is not primarily the result of the American party system. Rather, it is the product of a classic Lockean liberal political culture, in which, in the words of Louis Hartz, Americans "refuse to pay their critics the compliment of an argument."[10] The party system, then, is not the cause of stifling dissent, but an instrument by which it is done. This is not all bad, of course. If the party system is to legitimize public debate, it must render some debate illegitimate. But the American party system, both the umbrella party system of the nineteenth century and the emerging polarized system, is ideologically the narrowest of any advanced democratic capitalist system. There are no major communist, socialist, or fascist parties in the United States, nor even a labor party, as there are in all other advanced democracies.

The new American party system does not promise to alter this fact. Ideological polarization between the parties in the United States simply means that the parties have come to occupy neatly the opposite sides within the American ideological spectrum. Both major parties are fundamentally classic liberal parties, advocating a society based on individual liberty, private property, and capitalism; the liberal party is more likely to favor "modern" values and government intervention in the economy, while the conservative party is more likely to favor "traditional" values and the free market.

Though this characteristic of our party system facilitates political consensus and moderation, it does so too often by limiting debate arbitrarily and denying access to the ballot to parties and interests on the ideological fringes. Ideological extremism can often be a serious problem, particularly when a movement is violent, but moderation for its own sake is not necessarily the answer. Indeed, the notion that some ideologies are moderate and "reasonable" often stifles debate that the public might benefit from hearing. At certain times, such as during the Red Scare after World War I, or during the height of McCarthyism, this enforcement of a mainstream ideology is overt and visible. Perhaps precisely because classic liberalism is so deeply woven in the political culture, in more normal times, few Americans take note of the legal and institutional mechanisms that are designed to discourage political parties that dissent from the ideological consensus.

Umbrella parties have at times achieved the appearance of consensus by avoiding rather than addressing and resolving conflict. During times of social instability, ideological hegemony and the system of two umbrella parties may actually stifle debate so much as to threaten the political order. There are conflicts in American society that require attention, and they will get it, either through democratic politics or through politics by other means. When there is no legitimate access for marginalized groups, such as has at times been the case for labor or racial minorities, political violence is often the result. This is sometimes because the marginalized group has no choice but to take to the streets, and just as often because the marginalized group is the victim of official violence, or of private violence tolerated by the authorities. Violence against labor activists and African Americans and violent responses by them (the latter usually more publicized) are scattered throughout American history.[11]

Of course, the most destabilizing example of political violence in American history is the Civil War. The causes of that war are found throughout the fabric of antebellum America, but the major political parties at the time were incapable of being the vehicle through which policy elites might intervene for peace. Neither the Democrats nor the Whigs could resolve their factional conflicts about slavery enough to take a useful position to the electorate. By 1860, the Democratic Party split apart over slavery, the Whigs had folded, and the Republicans had emerged as an extreme anti-slavery party. No genuine interest aggregation remained possible, and it was no longer possible, if it ever had been, to assemble an electoral or governing majority that could resolve the slavery issue. One of the strategies of managing the slavery issue had been to keep it off the agenda as much as possible, for which umbrella parties functioned well, or to compromise in such a fashion as to delay the inevitable need to find a stable resolution. Thus, initially, umbrella parties kept the peace by avoiding or compromising the issue; later they lost the peace through their inability to confront it in the electoral arena.

The Civil War is the clearest example establishing the fact that the ideological hegemony of classic liberalism in American political culture in general, and the umbrella parties in particular, have served to cover what is the very deep cultural divide in American society. This divide has appeared, ever since the first American elections, in the coalitions between parties, as discussed in Chapter 1; it has defined the factional struggles within parties, as illustrated in Chapters 2–5; and it has been central to electoral realignment since the 1964–1972 period. Whereas prior to the 1964–1972 realignment, the cultural divide cut across party lines, in electoral politics it is now articulated in largely partisan terms. The question is whether the political institutions of American democracy, including the newly polarized political parties, can at once engage controversial issues and resolve conflict. Can the new American party system stimulate debate and preserve national unity at the same time?

Conflict, Consensus, and Change in the New Party System

Conflict is not by definition contrary to national unity; indeed, conflict is necessary to democracy. When unity is preserved by avoiding conflict, that unity becomes an artificial consensus that is soon destabilized by the issues ignored. During previous electoral realignments, American society and the party system went through relatively brief periods of heightened conflict, articulated largely through the political parties. These realigning periods were then followed by policy resolution and more extended periods of electoral stability and political consensus. During the consensus periods, the umbrella parties would come to resemble each other so much on the issues that critics of the policy agenda would charge that the parties had become "tweedledum-tweedledee" or "me, too" parties with, in the words of George Wallace, "not a dime's worth of difference" between them. This would describe the political parties of the 1850s, 1880s, 1920s, and 1950s, just before periods of critical realignment.

The pattern of party change since the 1964–1972 realignment, however, has been different. For the first time, the political parties have not genuinely converged on the issues. Certainly, the election of Bill Clinton to the Presidency is owed in large part to his appeal to the ideological center. But, while moderate Democrats gained some ground in their own party, the center of gravity in the Republican Party was becoming even more conservative.

So far, this persistent ideological polarization between the parties has produced a pronounced bitterness in the tenor of public discourse. The sharp polarization over civil rights was followed closely by the divisiveness of the Vietnam War, then by Watergate. The effective freeze on the take-home income of Americans since 1973, along with the increasing difference between rich and poor may not have increased class consciousness generally, but it did increase the vigor of public debate about the economy, at least until the period of growth and the achievement of an officially balanced federal budget in the 1990s. Finally, over the past twenty-five years or so, the public agenda has increasingly focused on abortion, "family" values, and "culture wars," the sorts of "either-or" issues cited by Burnham. Today's political rhetoric too often leaves the general impression that speakers on either side believe themselves to be morally superior to their adversaries. Such an attitude hardly facilitates the open debate so essential to democratic life.

The sometimes vicious discord of political debate in recent years would seem to present a normative argument against the continuing emergence of ideologically polarized parties. But this conclusion is valid only if we consider national unity a value to be maximized, even at the expense of the healthy conflict that is central to democratic politics. To function in the public interest, the political process must be capable of addressing the most controversial of issues, even, and indeed especially, when their resolution will entail vigorous conflict along the way.

Polarizing Issues in American Politics

When the issues on the public agenda lend themselves relatively easily to consensus, the umbrella parties have functioned well. But the dominant issues of the twenty-first century are likely to remain a combination of "either-or" cultural issues and zero-sum economic issues. The experience of American history and the ideological polarization between the parties in recent years combine to make it appear likely that candidates of the two parties will continue to articulate the divide between traditional and modern values in American culture. What is less clear is whether the electoral arena will serve as a forum for addressing the economic issues of the twenty-first century.

Historically, there has been a strong political consensus in the United States on capitalism and economic growth. Economic growth has itself fed political consensus. With a growing pie, competing interests could negotiate over the costs and benefits of new policies with only the increments of growth at stake. The period of the social bargain for the generation after World War II was one of bipartisan governance at least partly because growth facilitated consensus.

That consensus collapsed in the realignment of 1964–1972 initially over issues that were expressed in cultural terms: civil rights and Vietnam. Then, as argued in Chapter 9, economic issues became zero-sum issues as the social bargain was dismantled by the end of the Bretton Woods system, the oil shocks, and stagflation.

At this writing, economic growth is reasonably strong (between 3 and 4 percent annually), but economic issues remain zero-sum issues. It would be convenient and dramatic for the analysis presented in this book to argue that the zero-sum economic debate in a period of growth is merely a reflection of the new partisan ideological polarization in American politics; the problem with that assertion would be that it would be inaccurate.

The zero-sum nature of the economic issues at the turn of the twenty-first century is attributable to the fact that they are issues of rapid structural change associated with postindustrial modernization and globalization. There is little consensus (or even understanding) about these issues, and the pace of change will make them increasingly difficult to resolve, well into the twenty-first century. Today's economy will only become more fluid, replacing the old with the new in technological innovation, information flows, and global investment.

Under conditions of such rapid structural change, economic growth is no longer so highly correlated with the actual economic well-being of most citizens as it was in the days of the social bargain. The postindustrial economy features pockets of economic growth and pockets of decay, each associated with change and innovation. There is a growth in relatively high-paying knowledge jobs and relatively low-paying service jobs, along with a decline in middle income manufacturing jobs, all associated much more with structural change than with the business cycle. This process exacerbates the division between rich and poor, and threatens the security of the middle class. Class polarization, historically so foreign to American political culture, may yet become a general reality in American politics in the twenty-first century.

Historically, from slavery to civil rights to affirmative action, the most consistently polarizing issue in American politics has been race. As the twenty-first century dawns, Americans have yet to solve the problem of race relations. No longer primarily an issue of north and south in American politics, the great racial barrier is found along the urban-suburban divide in metropolitan areas, discussed in Chapter 8. Most African Americans today are working class or middle class, in or moving toward the mainstream of American life. At the same time, most poor Americans are white. But African Americans are disproportionately poor and disproportionately populate a growing urban underclass, particularly in older cities with declining industrial infrastructures. The presence of this underclass contributes to the fact that one American child in five today lives in poverty, which does not bode well for the American economy when they become adults. If class polarization does not become central to the coalitions of American politics in the twenty-first century, racial polarization may prove to have been the barrier, as it has been in the past.

The Next Realignment: Legitimizing the New Party System

Whether the issue is macroeconomics, or income security, or health care, or civil rights, or the environment, or education, the political parties at the turn of the twenty-first century are internally relatively united on programmatically or ideologically distinct alternatives: The Democrats are more likely to favor government intervention in the economy and modern values; the Republicans are more likely to favor the free market and traditional values. In no previous American party system have the major parties remained so distinguishable on economic issues for such an extended period of time.

The solution to the discord of recent times is not a return to the umbrella parties of the nineteenth century. Structural change in society at-large, the dynamic of nominating politics, and the nature of the issue agenda, all make that unlikely, even if it were desirable. The question is how to move from polarized partisan electoral politics to governance, given that twenty-first century political parties are likely to be ideological vehicles. Bipartisan governing coalitions were central to governing with umbrella parties. With ideological parties, policy-making will require either some approximation of party government or appeals by both parties beyond their electoral bases to the middle of the road. Despite the discouraging bitterness of politics in recent years, both party government and partisan appeals to moderates are more likely now than at any time since the realignment of 1964–1972, and both would represent hopeful signs for American democracy.

Party government is more likely now than it has been through most of American history for two reasons. First, the parties are more ideologically polarized than they were before the 1964–1972 realignment. Prior to then, even unified government usually did not mean party government because of the factional divisions within each party. Now, unified government is more likely to translate into control by a relatively unified majority. Second, because of factors of realignment, explored earlier and in Chapters 7 and 9, unified control of the elected branches of government by one party will be more frequent in the next generation than they have been in the past generation. Starting in the 1990s, Presidential election and Congressional election coalitions have become quite similar, and unified partisan majorities have become more likely. Even if American voters are more retrospective than ideological in their voting behavior, they have clear issue-oriented choices attached to the parties and can evaluate alternatives in that context, both from the point of view of policy preferences and performance in office.

The second route to stable governance through an ideological party system is the appeal to the middle of the road. Observers of recent American politics might be discouraged about that prospect. But electoral realignment has changed the options party elites face. So long as conservative Democrats held the balance of power in the national electorate and in the Congress, the swing voter was generally rather conservative, looking for an ideological appeal. Making an appeal to moderates was thus unwise for the Republicans and both difficult and costly for the Democrats. For most of the last three decades, mounting personal attacks on the opposition paid dividends, particularly for the Republicans seeking to win over conservative Democrats by isolating liberals. Now, however, the swing voter is a genuine moderate, ready to respond to parties and candidates appealing for their votes. It may be that liberal Democrats and conservative Republicans control nominations, but to assemble electoral and governing majorities, both will have to appeal beyond their base to the moderates, and will have some hope of doing so successfully. Thus, party nominees in general elections will once again be likely to dash for the center, even if their starting points are further apart than they once were, and there is good reason to hope that campaigns will become less acrimonious than they have been recently.

Certainly both mass media and money in politics have done more to exacerbate highly personal conflict in recent years than to promote an intelligent discussion of the issues or to facilitate political consensus. Television has the tendency to emphasize the dramatic over the important, the personal over the structural, and image over issues. Money spent on television in recent campaigns seems to emphasize negative advertising, with candidates working hard to define their opponents. Polling data indicate that most Americans are turned off by attack ads in general, but that the attacks in particular cases nevertheless work, especially if there is no response. The attack ads may, in fact, discourage voter turnout. Many of the attack ads have been paid for by money from issue activists rather than either candidates or political parties, and promoted as issue ads, the expense does not count against campaigns. Thus, campaigns become both more costly and more negative.

The most salient issue having to do with campaign finance at this writing is the problem of soft money, raised by political parties with the result of helping campaigns circumvent candidate-centered campaign finance laws. Passed mostly during the Watergate period, campaign finance reform in the 1970s was a practical application of the assumption that American political parties were in decline, and that campaigns were constructed around candidates whose spending should be limited. These reforms and the decision of the United States Supreme Court in *Buckley v. Valeo* (1976) have had the effect of promoting Political Action Committees, and turning campaigns into de facto candidate-centered corporations whose financial assets and obligations outlived the election for which they were formed. This process not only recognized but advanced the decline of the nineteenth-century parties. It also encouraged the development of the twenty-first century parties. With candidate campaigns heavily regulated, the role of parties in fund-raising increased markedly, particularly with the involvement of national committees and House and Senate campaign committees. Thus, the nationalization of parties increased along with ideological polarization, as discussed in detail earlier.

If campaign finance reform is to be effective at stimulating public debate during election campaigns, it should encourage party development. Thus, efforts to regulate soft money should not strangle donations to parties; rather, such efforts should set reasonable limits and reporting standards for giving to parties. Although *Buckley v. Valeo* puts up some legal barriers, nothing could democratize American elections more than increased public financing of campaigns.

Mass media and money certainly have magnified the bitterness of electoral campaigns, but they are the instruments of political elites, rather than the cause of the problem. Not enough consideration has been given to ideological polarization as a cause of negative campaigning. Given ideological polarization between the parties and the alignment of the electorate, campaigns since the 1964–1972 period would have become more negative regardless of the changing technologies of mass communications, just as campaigns have been periodically harsh and negative throughout American history. Even with the advance of television and money, had the major parties continued generally to nominate two moderates for public office, the campaigns themselves would have remained moderate and conducive to consensus.

Now, the potential for a more graceful tenor of campaign rhetoric exists, even with the ideologically polarized parties as they are, brought on by the next wave of realignment. For some thirty years, conservative Democrats, slowly realigning from one party to the other, were the swing voters. Now they are Republicans and are being replaced as the swing vote by political moderates. Candidates will still have to appeal to partisan ideologues to win nominations. But they will then have to appeal to the moderates, or lose general elections. Thus, the new, ideologically polarized party system will not, in the long term, tear at the fabric of American democracy. Although it is too soon to tell, realignment of the early twenty-first century may yet produce the first American responsible party system.

CONCLUSION

American political parties have persisted for so long precisely because they have so frequently been capable of change in a changing polity. Nationalized and ideologically polarized political parties are probably here for the foreseeable future, and there will be plenty of time for party and policy elites, and for voters, to practice working with them. Certainly nothing like parliamentary responsible parties and party government will emerge in the United States anytime soon, but the parties of the twenty-first century will not much resemble the American parties of the nineteenth century either. More than the declining political parties did, the new political parties are likely to resemble responsible parties. If so, they will represent an opportunity to achieve the sort of issue-oriented process of conflict and consensus-building that has previously been characteristic of American politics only periodically, during times of critical realignment.

NOTES

1. Paul Beck and Frank Sorauf, *Party Politics in America*, 7th ed. (New York: HarperCollins, 1992), pp. 467–468.

2. Ellsworth Barnard, *Wendell Willkie: Fighter for Freedom* (Marquette, Mich.: Northern Michigan University Press, 1966), pp. 480–481.

3. Ibid., p. 481.

4. Thomas E. Dewey, *Thomas E. Dewey on the Two-Party System* (New York: Doubleday, 1966).

5. E. E. Schattschneider, *Party Government* (New York: Rinehart, 1942), p. 1.

6. American Political Science Association Committee on Political Parties, *Toward a More Responsible Two Party System* (New York: Rinehart and Co., 1950).

7. See, for example, Schattschneider; and James L. Sundquist, *Constitutional Reform and Effective Government*, rev. ed. (Washington, D.C.: Brookings Institution, 1992). See also Paul Christopher Manuel and Anne Marie Cammisa, *Checks and Balances? How a Parliamentary System Could Change American Politics* (Boulder: Westview Press, 1999).

8. See V. O. Key, *The Responsible Electorate* (Cambridge: Harvard University Press, 1966) and Evron M. Kirkpatrick, "Toward a More Responsible Party System: Polit-

ical Science, Policy Science, or Pseudo Science?" *The American Political Science Review* 65 (1971): 965–990.

9. See particularly William Crotty, *American Parties in Decline*, 2nd ed. (Glenview, Ill.: Scott, Foresman, 1984), and Nelson Polsby, *The Consequences of Party Reform* (Oxford: Oxford University Press, 1983).

10. Louis Hartz, *The Liberal Tradition in America* (New York: Harcourt, Brace and World, 1955), pp. 58–59.

11. See Patricia Cayo Sexton, *The War on Labor and the Left* (Boulder, Colo.: Westview Press, 1991), particularly pp. 162–180.

Epilogue: The Y2K Election

Since the periodicity of critical realignments has been remarkably precise, the theory presented in the previous chapters can be subjected to something of a test in relatively short order. The critical elections that have marked the realigning turning points have occurred exactly every thirty-six years since 1860: in 1896, 1932, and if the definition asserted in this book is correct, in 1968. If that remarkable consistency should continue, we can expect another realigning election in 2004.

Of course, history is not actually as neat as the categories historians and social analysts create to understand it. Realignments reach critical proportions over relatively brief periods of time, spanning two or three elections, like 1896–1900, 1928–1936, or 1964–1972. The elections between these periods do not offer stasis, either. Rather, they exhibit relative electoral stability marked by secular realignment. If the periodic nature of the process holds, we are on the eve of yet another critical realignment.

This epilogue discusses the coming election of 2000 as a laboratory for the theory of realignment and party change presented in this book.

THE PRESIDENTIAL NOMINATIONS

A year before their national conventions for the 2000 Presidential election, both major political parties seem poised to nominate moderates for the Presidency: Vice President Albert Gore or former Senator Bill Bradley for the Democrats, and Governor George W. Bush of Texas for the Republicans. This fact alone might seem to refute the observations of ideological polarization between the parties made in this book. But the emergence of moderates as the front-runners for their party's Presidential nomination is not as important as the fact that Gore, Bradley, and Bush are all about as close to the center of the ideological spectrum as candidates can get in either party and still win the nomination. Gore and Bradley are moderate liberals: That is, they are not liberal Democrats, but they are liberals nonetheless. George W. Bush, like his father, is a moderate conservative: He is not a conservative Republican, but he is a conservative nonetheless.

Democrats like Gore and Bradley and a Republican like Bush could easily be found in the Democratic and Republican parties before and during the 1964–1972 realignment. But their ideological positions in their respective parties would have been very different than they are now. Where today, moderate Democrats like Gore or Bradley (or President Clinton) would be found to the right of most other Democrats, and a moderate Republican like Bush is to the left of most Republicans, up through the 1964–1972 period, politicians like Gore, Bradley, Clinton, and Bush would have been in the center not only of the national ideological spectrum but of the spectrum of their own parties; there would have been Democrats and Republicans alike who were much more liberal and more conservative than the moderates.

Getting down to cases and personalities, Figure E.1 (page 322) presents an impressionistic sketch of party leaders on the ideological spectra of the parties in the 1964–1972 period, and a similar sketch for both parties at the present time. In 1964–1972, we find liberal Democrats such as George McGovern, Eugene McCarthy, and Robert F. Kennedy; we find Hubert H. Humphrey, who was by that time a more moderate-to-liberal Democrat, and Lyndon B. Johnson close to the ideological center. And, we find George C. Wallace, the conservative Democrat who still represented a significant constituency in the Democratic Party as late as 1972, according to his showing in the Presidential primaries.

In 1964–1972, we also find Nelson Rockefeller, the liberal Republican who still hoped to become President; Richard M. Nixon, moving to the right, but still near the center of the national ideological spectrum; and both Barry Goldwater and Ronald Reagan, the movement candidates of conservative Republicans at that time. Both Goldwater and Reagan were then considered to be outside the Republican mainstream, but the mainstream of the party was already moving toward Reagan by 1968. As Chapter 4 pointed out, Reagan was the much bigger threat to Nixon at the 1968 convention than Rockefeller was, and Nixon knew it and acted accordingly.

Today, we find Gore and Bradley near the center of the national ideological spectrum. Within their party we find more liberal Democrats, such as Edward M. Kennedy, Jesse Jackson, and Senator Paul Wellstone of Minnesota, who almost ran for President himself but has endorsed Bradley instead. And we find Bush near the center, with a number of more conservative Republicans who are opposing him, perhaps in futility, for the GOP nomination.

Thus in 1964–1972, the ideological spectra of both parties still spanned the national spectrum. Today, the ideological spectrum of each party tends to end where the other's begins. It makes for a structurally very different electoral environment, and a party system that, by the standards of our history, is almost unAmerican for its degree of ideological polarization. And, ideological polarization between the parties has come to mean ideological homogenization within the parties. It is in the context of this electoral environment and party system, both born in the 1964–1972 realignment, that the election must be viewed.

The Democrats

There are two ways to look at Al Gore as a candidate for the Presidency. First as the Vice President of the United States, he seems to be the heir apparent to President Clinton. The nomination should be his for the asking, but apparently it is not yet secure. Second, if Al Gore were not Vice President, he would at best be one candidate in a very large field, and probably a long shot at that, as he was in 1988. It is best to remember that Jimmy Carter and Bill Clinton, both moderate Democrats, won their nominations only because the liberals in the party were divided in the primaries. Thus, although there is very little difference between Gore and Bradley, the discontent with Gore, such as it is, comes mostly from liberal Democrats, and it is apparently from them that Bradley is finding his support and his rather impressive funding to date. And it is because Bradley finds his support among party liberals that he has a chance to derail Gore.

Vice President Gore is in a position very much like Vice President Bush was in the 1988 Republican primaries, and very much like the incumbent Presidents who were challenged in the primaries of 1976 and 1980 (see Chapters 5 and 6). That is, Gore may have a solid claim among the minority moderate-to-conservative faction of the Democratic Party. But the majority of the vote in the primaries, and the majority of the delegates at the convention, will be liberal Democrats, torn between their ideology and their Vice President.

Whether he becomes their first choice or not, it is precisely because Vice President Gore is so acceptable to liberal Democrats that the field of opponents he faces has been limited to Bradley. Jesse Jackson, Paul Wellstone, and Bob Kerrey all considered making the race and opted out. Ironically, had there been enough opposition to Gore from the party's liberals, a number of them might have entered the race, and like Carter and Clinton, Gore would have faced a divided field; in that case, he probably would have won the nomination with little trouble. Bradley has a shot largely because he has Gore one-on-one.

It has been a common argument, and one with some validity, that while for a time after 1972 insurgent candidates could make their mark in the early primaries and take the lead later, now the front loading of primaries works to the advantage of the early front-runners. However, in Chapter 6, I argued that the ideological polarization between the parties was producing an ideological homogenization within the parties; and that this ideological homogenization had as much or more to do with the success of early consensus candidates as front loading. In 2000, the front loading is even more intense, but it alone will not save Al Gore. If Gore can score impressive victories early, the race will be over and the nomination his; but if Bradley can even come close to Gore in the Iowa precinct caucuses and New Hampshire primary, he will have the opportunity to win New York and California only a few weeks later. If that should happen, a long contest, perhaps all the way to the convention like days gone by, will be in store. Indeed, if Bradley can win Iowa, New Hampshire, New York, and California, Gore will need to win the Florida and Texas primaries just to save himself from elimination.

The ideological differences between Gore and Bradley, of course, are simply not that extreme. Whatever differences there are seem to be more a matter of style (and not even much on that count) than of substance. Whether its nominee is Albert Gore or Bill Bradley, the Democratic Party will have no trouble uniting for the general election campaign. And whoever is the nominee, the Democratic Party will remain the liberal party of the United States.

The Republicans

Governor George W. Bush of Texas should not be the nominee apparent of the Republican Party, but he is. At this writing, he has raised by far the most money of all the candidates for the Presidency in either party. But what is more interesting, and more important to the analysis of party change, is the fact that although Bush is a moderate Republican, party leaders on the whole, including most GOP conservatives, are lining up to endorse him. It is not surprising that Republican Governors should, almost en masse, side with Bush. Republican Governors, who must govern as executives and are generally less ideological in approach than legislators, have historically supported moderates, from Dewey to Eisenhower to Rockefeller to Ford to Vice President Bush in 1988. What is more important is that the Republican Congressional leadership has united behind George W. Bush and is moving to coordinate the party's Congressional campaign with its Presidential campaign in 2000. It is almost as if the Republican Party were organized on the "responsible" party model, with George W. Bush as its parliamentary leader; it is almost as if Bush were running for prime minister.

This could not have happened if Bush, even as a party moderate, were not at least acceptable, with some degree of mutual comfort, to most conservative Republicans. The Republican Party was able to develop an early consensus on Nixon in 1960, but Nixon was at the center of both the Republican and national ideological spectrum at the time. The consensus George W. Bush enjoys now is not unlike the consensus for his father in 1988, only apparently stronger. It is evidence of the ideological homogenization of the Republican Party.

The nomination of Governor Bush is not a certainty, of course. Much could happen to derail it. But most of the opposition to his nomination seems currently to come from more-conservative Republicans. Steve Forbes, who presented himself as a pro-choice candidate in the 1996 Presidential primaries, has learned his lesson and is making his appeal now to social conservatives. He has the money to conduct a campaign against Bush, if he survives the early delegate selection contests and chooses to make the fight. Gary Bauer is seeking to unite the Christian right around his candidacy, has done well in fund-raising, and may well become one of the early candidates left standing for the primaries. Pat Buchanan is running another guerilla campaign, organizing at the grass roots until he is alone in the field with Bush and Forbes. Senator Orrin Hatch of Utah, a conservative Republican to be sure, is nevertheless presenting himself as a potential President who could overcome the rancor of recent political seasons to build a bipartisan governing coalition between the White House and Congress. It is a measure of the rightward drift of the Republican Party that Hatch should seek to present himself with the image of a moderate. Surprisingly, former Vice President Dan Quayle seems to have failed already in the "invisible primary" and has been eliminated before the election year actually arrives on the calendar. Representative John Kasich of Ohio, after an exploratory campaign, has already withdrawn and endorsed Bush.

A relatively moderate Republican could also survive, as something of a maverick, to oppose Bush in the primaries. This seems to be the approach of Senator John McCain of Arizona, who hopes to finesse Iowa and gain a showdown with Bush in New Hampshire. A strong showing there and a victory in the Arizona primary might set McCain up to battle Bush in the later primaries. Ironically, Elizabeth Dole, former cabinet secretary and President of the Red Cross, and wife of the Republican nominee for President in 1996, is apparently presenting herself as the outsider's alternative to George W. Bush. Lamar Alexander of Tennessee, like Bush a southern moderate Republican, has been squeezed out of the field at this writing; he had little money and no constituency to call his own and no way to distinguish himself from the Texas Governor.

Interestingly, Bush is in a strong position not only to clinch the nomination early, but for a more extended contest, if necessary. Of course, he has the money for a long campaign. But he also is well positioned ideologically in the field of Republican candidates. Forbes, Bauer, Buchanan, Hatch, and Alan Keyes are all going after the votes of social conservatives, while Bush may well unite GOP moderates. Thus, Bush is in the same position as Democrats Jimmy Carter and Bill Clinton were when they first ran against a crowded field of liberals, except that Bush has the added advantage of being the front-runner. And, should McCain or Dole emerge as the leading challenger to Bush in the primaries, Bush would probably win over most of the conservatives to his candidacy.

Bush, then, will probably emerge as the Republican nominee. If Bush is upset, the Republican nominee for President will still either be a moderate conservative or a more conservative candidate than Bush. Nelson Rockefeller is dead, no Republican carries the Rockefeller mantle, and most voters who would have at one time supported Rockefeller have long since deserted the GOP. The Republican Party is the conservative party of the United States.

A Third Party?

Until the 1964–1972 realignment, major political parties in the United States were umbrella parties, appealing across the ideological spectrum. Third parties were founded on the ideological fringes and usually survived, if at all, only until the leaders with whom they were associated passed from the scene or until their issue preferences and voters were absorbed by one or both of the major parties. After the 1964–1972 realignment, for example, most of the support for George Wallace drifted toward the Republican Party, very quickly in Presidential elections, only slowly in Congressional elections (see Chapters 1 and 7).

The Reform Party is a new third party in a new electoral environment. With ideologically polarized major parties, the Reform Party seems to appeal to a fundamentally centrist electoral coalition. Governor Jesse Ventura of Minnesota, elected on the Reform Party line in 1998, has said that the Reform Party appeals to a new swing voter in American politics who tends to be a fiscal conservative and a social liberal. These are the voters, identified in Chapter 9, who supported John B. Anderson for President in 1980 and Ross Perot in 1992 and 1996. Perot could be the Reform Party nominee again, although this is less likely after the recent Reform Party national convention, which changed party leadership and moved its headquarters. Ventura seems to be the rising star in the party now, although he continues to maintain that he will not run for President in 2000. Ventura has sounded out former Governor Lowell P. Weicker of Connecticut about running, and Weicker has expressed interest. Weicker is a one-time liberal Republican (whose supporters would have once voted for Rockefeller) who was elected Governor on the A Connecticut Party (ACP) line in 1990.

But something interesting is happening to the Reform Party. As ultraconservative Republicans become more frustrated about the waning possibility of denying George W. Bush the GOP nomination in 2000, Senator Robert C. Smith of New Hampshire and Pat Buchanan have apparently begun to consider running for President as independents. At this writing, Smith has reportedly settled on being the nominee of the United Taxpayers' Party. But Buchanan may yet seek the Reform Party nomination. The Reform Party, then, now seems to be developing a tent that would include Weicker, Ventura, Perot, and Buchanan. Thus for the first time in American history, a statistically significant third party may be becoming an umbrella party, even as the major parties become more ideological, an interesting reversal of electoral and institutional roles.

But if the Reform Party should nominate a movement conservative for the Presidency, it will probably go the way of previous third parties: It will lose its potential moderate voters, and see its remaining constituency swallowed up (or, more accurately, re-swallowed) by the Republican Party. If, on the other hand, the Reform Party becomes a genuine centrist party, it may well survive well beyond the life expectancy of most third parties; if additionally, the Democrats and Republicans continue to polarize, this new centrist third party may expand its electoral base.

THE PRESIDENTIAL ELECTION

The question of interest to realignment analysis is not so much who will be elected President in 2000, as what will be the nature of the party coalitions in that election. In terms of change in electoral coalitions, the 1964–1972 realignment was easily the most compelling in American history, an observation demonstrated in Chapter 1. In that realignment, the white south left behind its historic roots in the Democratic Party and switched to the Republican Party in Presidential elections. No previous realignment saw such a radical shift in the coalitions of the two parties. Nor will the coming realignment.

Nevertheless, a realignment is coming. It represents the marriage of the critical realignment of 1964–1972 to the secular realignment of the next thirty years, in which historically conservative Democrats in general and the white south in particular shifted toward the Republicans in Congressional elections. The result is that Presidential and Congressional election coalitions resemble each other more now than they have at any time since the peak of the New Deal party system (see Chapters 1 and 7). The practical outcome will be that divided government will be much less frequent in the first half of the twenty-first century than it was in the last half of the twentieth.

Who will be elected President in 2000 cannot safely be predicted more than a year in advance of that election. But the coalitions revealed on the electoral map can be. Whether Albert Gore or Bill Bradley is the Democratic nominee for President, the Democrat will run strongest in the northeast quadrant and on the west coast. Whether the Republican is George W. Bush or someone else, the Republican will run strongest in the south and interior west (see Chapter 1).

Scientific public opinion polls with sound methodologies are almost always correct at the moment they are taken; they are not meant to be predictions, and are not "wrong" if the winner of the election in November is not the winner of the poll a year, or months, or weeks before the event. But if current polling were to prove to represent the election outcome, Bush would be elected by near landslide proportions. If that happens by the margins currently indicated, Gore or Bradley would carry very much the same states as Michael Dukakis in 1988, mostly in the northeast. Gore would be swept down south, and would not even carry his home state of Tennessee. In the less likely event of a Democratic landslide, we will see the Republicans carry some, but not all, of the states of the south and west (what is now the "Republican L" and was the "Democratic L" in the days of William Jennings Bryan). Finally, in a very close election, the Democrat would win in the northeast quadrant and the west coast; the Republican would win the south and interior west. These patterns are so consistent that Gore would have to battle for Tennessee and might even be elected without the support of his home state. Even Bill Clinton could carry only four southern states in his two elections, and he needed national margins of 5 to 9 percentage points to do it. Even with another realignment in the offing, these patterns of political geography are unlikely to change any time soon. Indeed, if Bill Bradley were to win a close election in 2000, he would probably become the first Democrat elected President without carrying a single southern state.

THE CONGRESSIONAL ELECTION

Six of the last eight Presidential elections have resulted in divided government, in the first five cases a Republican President and a Democratic or divided Congress. In 1994 the Republicans won control of both houses of Congress for the first time in fifty years, and they have retained Congress ever since. In 1996, while President Clinton was re-elected on the Democratic line, the Republicans retained Congress. In 1998 the Republicans again retained both houses; the Senate by 55 to 45, and the House of Representatives by 224 to 210.

The pattern of split tickets and divided government seems clear. The power of incumbency in elections for the House has been generally cited as a central explanation of divided government. But Chapter 7 presented an alternative explanation presenting evidence that ideological polarization between the parties in Presidential elections since the 1964–1972 realignment, unaccompanied by the same ideological polarization in Congressional elections, explains many of the divided outcomes between the two levels. This ideological model of split-ticket voting did not question the obvious power of incumbency in House elections. But it did demonstrate an ideological slant to split-ticket voting and divided outcomes in Presidential and Congressional elections. Since 1972, the largest incidence of divided outcomes has occurred in Congressional districts and states where incumbent conservative Democrats have been running for re-election to the House or Senate while a more liberal Democrat was losing the Presidential election to the Republican. This particular pattern was most evident in the south. Slowly however, through retirements and more occasional electoral defeats of incumbents, the south trended toward the Republicans in Congressional elections, a trend that reached decisive proportions in the Republican victory of 1994. After nearly three decades of voting Republican for President and Democratic for Congress, by 1994, the white south was voting Republican for Congress, too.

If this analysis is correct, Chapter 7 concluded, the increased occurrence of divided government was not a linear pattern but a dialectical one. That is, so long as large numbers of conservative Democrats split their tickets, divided government would be the outcome; but once historically conservative Democrats were voting Republican tickets, unified partisan control of the Presidency and Congress would be the

more frequent result of national elections. Given the smaller coun-
termovement of one-time liberal Republicans toward the Democrats,
this would not necessarily install the Republicans as the majority party.

This theory cannot be discounted by the reversal of the long pattern
of Republican Presidents and Democratic Congresses in 1996, when the
Democrats retained the Presidency and the Republicans retained Congress. Incumbency advantages are strong enough to explain the divided
outcome, even as the rate of split-ticket voting was declining for the
second consecutive Presidential election. And incumbency advantages
would explain why coattails have been permanently reduced in length
since about 1952. But while the dependability of unified party control
of the executive and legislative branches will not likely return to the
levels of the New Deal period, it is likely to occur more often than not
well into the twenty-first century.

CONCLUSION

The value of any science, social as well as natural and physical, is
found in the verifiability of its propositions. The 2000 election will
probably be a fair case with which to test the predictions of the ideological polarization model of realignment and party change presented in
this book. In the Presidential election, if Democrats do not run strongest
in the northeast quadrant and the west coast, and the Republicans do
not run strongest in the south and interior west, there will have been
an outcome nearly no one anticipated, which this model cannot explain.
That prediction on the electoral map is made with great confidence and
will surprise almost no one.

The predictions concerning the restoration of unified party control of
the Presidency and Congress are made with less confidence and will be
more controversial. In the 2000 election, the Democrats are unlikely to
make the gains they need to capture the Senate, whatever the outcome
of the Presidential election. But the Republicans enjoy only a narrow
margin in the House of Representatives, where a loss of seven seats
would hand control over to the Democrats. Therefore, it is quite likely
that the party that wins the Presidential election will win a majority of
seats in the House of Representatives, as well. If the results of both the
Presidential and Congressional elections are very close, the jury will
still be out on the ideological polarization model. If one party wins the
Presidency by a substantial margin and makes gains in the House to
win a majority, that will be evidence that the model is worthy of serious
attention. If, however, one party wins the Presidency by a considerable
margin and loses the House, this author will go back to the drawing
board, chastened, but ready to try again.

Figure E.1
Party Leaders and the Ideological Spectrum: Comparing 1964–1972 with 2000

		1964–1972		
		Democrats		
Kennedy	Humphrey	Johnson		Wallace
McCarthy				
McGovern				
	Rockefeller		Nixon	Goldwater
				Reagan
		Republicans		

		2000			
		Democrats			
Jackson	Kennedy	Bradley	Clinton		
	Wellstone		Gore		
		Bush*	McCain	Forbes	Buchanan
		Dole*			Quayle Bauer
					Hatch
		Republicans			

*either one

Selected Bibliography

Aldrich, John H. *Why Parties? The Origin and Transformation of Party Politics in America*. Chicago: University of Chicago Press, 1995.

Ambrose, Stephen E. *Eisenhower the President*. New York: Simon and Schuster, 1984.

American Political Science Association Committee on Political Parties. *Toward a More Responsible Two Party System*. New York: Rinehart, 1950.

Andersen, Kristi. "Generation, Partisan Shift, and Realignment: A Glance Back to the New Deal." In Norman H. Nie, Sidney Verba, and John R. Petrocik. *The Changing American Voter*. Cambridge: Harvard University Press, 1976.

————. *The Creation of a Democratic Majority: 1928–1936*. Chicago: University of Chicago Press, 1979.

Apter, David. "Ideology and Discontent." In David Apter, ed. *Ideology and Discontent*. London: The Free Press, 1964.

————. *Ideology and Discontent*. London: The Free Press, 1964.

Archer, J. Clark, Fred M. Shelly, Peter J. Taylor, and Ellen R. White. "The Geography of U.S. Presidential Elections." *Scientific American* 259 (1988): 44–51.

Aronowitz, Stanley. *False Promises: The Shaping of American Working Class Consciousness*. New York: McGraw-Hill, 1973.

Bain, Richard C., and Judith H. Parris. *Convention Decisions and Voting Records*. Washington, D.C.: Brookings Institution, 1973.

Baker, Ross K. "The Presidential Nominations." In Gerald M. Pomper, Walter Dean Burnham, Anthony Corrado, Marjorie Randon Hershey, Marion R. Just, Scott Keeter, Wilson Carey McWilliams, and William G. Mayer. *The Election of 1992: Reports and Interpretations*, pp. 33–71. Chatham, N.J.: Chatham House, 1993.

Barnard, Ellsworth. *Wendell Willkie: Fighter for Freedom*. Marquette, Mich.: Northern Michigan University Press, 1966.

Barone, Michael, Douglas Matthews, and Grant Ujifusa. *The Almanac of American Politics 1976*. New York: E. P. Dutton, 1975.

———. *The Almanac of American Politics 1978*. New York: E. P. Dutton, 1977.

———. *The Almanac of American Politics 1980*. New York: E. P. Dutton, 1979.

Barone, Michael, and Grant Ujifusa. *The Almanac of American Politics 1982*. Washington, D.C.: Barone and Co., 1981.

———. *The Almanac of American Politics 1984*. Washington, D.C.: National Journal, 1983.

———. *The Almanac of American Politics 1986*. Washington, D.C.: National Journal, 1985.

———. The *Almanac of American Politics 1988*. Washington, D.C.: National Journal, 1987.

———. *The Almanac of American Politics 1990*. Washington, D.C.: National Journal, 1989.

———. *The Almanac of American Politics 1992*. Washington, D.C.: National Journal, 1991.

———. *The Almanac of American Politics 1994*. Washington, D.C.: National Journal, 1993.

———. *The Almanac of American Politics 1996*. Washington, D.C.: National Journal, 1995.

———. *The Almanac of American Politics 1998*. Washington, D.C.: National Journal, 1997.

Barone, Michael, Grant Ujifusa, and Douglas Matthews. *The Almanac of American Politics 1974*. Boston: Gambit, 1973.

Bartels, Larry M. *Presidential Primaries and the Dynamics of Public Choice*. Princeton, N.J.: Princeton University Press, 1988.

Bean, Louis H. *How to Predict Elections*. New York: Knopf, 1948.

Beck, Paul Allen, and Frank Sorauf. *Party Politics in America*, 7th ed. New York: HarperCollins, 1992.

Bell, Daniel. *The End of Ideology: On the Exhaustion of Political Ideas in the Fifties*. New York: The Free Press, 1960.

———. *The Coming of Postindustrial Society: A Venture into Social Forecasting*. New York: Basic Books, 1973.

———. *The Cultural Contradictions of Capitalism*. New York: Basic Books, 1976.

———. *The Winding Passage*. New York: Basic Books, 1980.

Black, Earl, and Merle Black. *The Vital South: How Presidents Are Elected*. Cambridge: Harvard University Press, 1992.

Brands, H. W. *T.R.: The Last Romantic*. New York: Basic Books, 1997.

Broder, David. "Introduction." In Seymour Martin Lipset, ed. *Emerging Coalitions in American Politics*. San Francisco: Institute for Contemporary Studies, 1978.

———. "Democrats." In David Broder, Lou Cannon, Haynes Johnson, Martin Schram, and Richard Harwood. *The Pursuit of the Presidency 1980*. New York: G.P. Putnam's Sons, 1980.

Brown v. Board of Education of Topeka, Kansas 347 U.S. 483.

Buell, Emmett H., Jr. "The Invisible Primary." In William G. Mayer, ed. *In Pursuit of the White House: How We Choose Our Presidential Nominees*. Chatham, N.J.: Chatham House, 1996.

Burnham, Walter Dean. *Critical Elections and the Mainsprings of American Politics*. New York: Norton, 1970.

———. "Insulation and Responsiveness in Congressional Elections." *Political Science Quarterly* 90 (1975): 411–435.

———. "Party Systems and the Political Process." In William N. Chambers and Walter Dean Burnham, eds. *The American Party Systems: Stages of Development*. New York: Oxford University Press, 1975.

———. "American Politics in the 1970s: Beyond Party?" In Jeff Fishel, ed. *Parties and Elections in an Anti-Party Age*. Bloomington: Indiana University Press, 1978.

———. "American Politics in the 1980s." In Walter Burnham. *The Hidden Crisis in American Politics*. New York: Oxford University Press, 1982.

———. "Into the 1980s with Ronald Reagan." In Walter Burnham. *The Hidden Crisis in American Politics*. New York: Oxford University Press, 1982.

———. "The Reagan Heritage." In Gerald M. Pomper, Ross K. Baker, Walter Dean Burnham, Barbara G. Farah, Marjorie Random Hershey, Ethel Klein, and Wilson Carey McWilliams, *The Election of 1988: Reports and Interpretations*. Chatham, N.J.: Chatham House, 1989.

———. "Realignment Lives: The 1994 Earthquake and Its Implications." In Colin Campbell and Bert A. Rockman, eds. *The Clinton Presidency: First Appraisals*. Chatham, N.J.: Chatham House, 1996.

Burns, James MacGregor. *The Deadlock of Democracy: Four Party Politics in America*. Englewood Cliffs, N.J.: Prentice Hall, 1967.

Butterfield, Roger. *The American Past*. New York: Simon and Schuster, 1957.

Campbell, Angus. "Surge and Decline: A Study of Electoral Change." *Public Opinion Quarterly* 24 (1960): 397–418.

———. "A Classification of Presidential Elections." In Angus Campbell, Philip E. Converse, Warren E. Miller, and Donald E. Stokes. *Elections and the Political Order*. New York: Wiley and Sons, 1966.

Campbell, Angus, Philip E. Converse, Warren E. Miller, and Donald Stokes. *The American Voter*. New York: Wiley and Sons, 1960.

———. *Elections and the Political Order*. New York: Wiley and Sons, 1960.

Campbell, Colin, and Bert A. Rockman, eds. *The Clinton Presidency: First Appraisals*. Chatham, N.J.: Chatham House, 1996.

Campbell, James E. "Explaining Presidential Losses in Midterm Congressional Elections." *Journal of Politics* 47 (1985): 1140–1157.

———. "Predicting Seat Gains from Presidential Coattails." *American Journal of Political Science* 30 (1986): 165–183.

———. "The Revised Theory of Surge and Decline." *American Journal of Political Science* 31 (1987): 965–979.

———. *The Presidential Pulse of Congressional Elections.* Lexington, Ky.: The University Press of Kentucky, 1993.

Cannon, Lou, and William Peterson, "GOP." In David Broder, Lou Cannon, Haynes Johnson, Martin Schram, and Richard Harwood. *The Pursuit of the Presidency 1980.* New York: G.P. Putnam's Sons, 1980.

Carmines, Edward G., and James A. Stimson. *Issue Evolution: Race and the Transformation of American Politics.* Princeton: Princeton University Press, 1989.

Carter, Dan T. *The Politics of Rage: George Wallace, the Origins of the New Conservatism, and the Transformation of American Politics.* Baton Rouge: Louisiana State University Press, 1995.

Centers, Richard. *The Psychology of Social Classes.* Princeton, N.J.: Princeton University Press, 1949.

Chambers, William N. "Party Development and the American Mainstream." In William Chambers and Walter Dean Burnham, eds. *The American Party Systems: Stages of Development.* New York: Oxford University Press, 1975.

Chambers, William N., and Walter Dean Burnham, eds. *The American Party Systems: Stages of Development.* New York: Oxford University Press, 1975.

Cherry, Robert W. *A Righteous Cause: The Life of William Jennings Bryan.* Boston: Little, Brown, 1985.

Chester, Lewis, Godfrey Hodgson, and Bruce Page. *An American Melodrama: The Presidential Campaign of 1968.* New York: The Viking Press, 1969.

Clubb, Jerome M., William H. Flanigan, and Nancy H. Zingale. *Partisan Realignment: Voters, Parties and Government in American History.* Boulder, Colo.: Westview Press, 1990.

Coletta, Paolo E. *William Jennings Bryan.* 3 vols. Lincoln: University of Nebraska Press, 1964.

Congressional Districts in the 1970s. Washington, D.C.: Congressional Quarterly, 1973.

Congressional Districts in the 1980s. Washington, D.C.: Congressional Quarterly, 1983.

Congressional Districts in the 1990s. Washington, D.C.: Congressional Quarterly, 1993.

Congressional Quarterly Almanac 1964. Washington, D.C.: Congressional Quarterly, 1965.

Congressional Quarterly's Guide to U.S. Elections. Washington, D.C.: Congressional Quarterly, 1997.

Cook, Rhodes. "Dole's Job: To Convince His Own Party." *Congressional Quarterly Guide to the 1996 Republican National Convention.* August 3, 1996, pp. 7–11.

Cooper v. Aaron 357 U.S. 566.

Cornwall, John. Economic Breakdown and Recovery: Theory and Policy. Armonk, N.Y.: M.E. Sharpe, 1994.

Cotter, Cornelius P., and Bernard C. Hennessy. *Politics without Power.* New York: Atherton, 1964.

Crotty, William. *The Party Symbol: Readings on Political Parties.* San Francisco: W.H. Freeman, 1980.

———. *Party Reform.* New York: Longman, 1983.

———. *American Parties in Decline*, 2nd ed. Glenview, Ill.: Scott Foresman, 1984.

Davis, Kenneth S. *FDR: The New York Years, 1928–1933.* New York: Random House, 1994.

DeTocqueville, Alexis. *Democracy in America.* New York: Doubleday, 1969.

DeVries, Walter, and V. Lance Terrance. *The Ticket Splitter: A New Force in American Politics.* Grand Rapids, Mich.: William B. Eerdmans, 1972.

Dewey, Thomas E. *Thomas E. Dewey on the Two-Party System.* New York: Doubleday, 1966.

Donovan, Robert J. *Eisenhower: The Inside Story.* New York: Harper Brothers, 1956.

DuBoff, Richard B. *Accumulation and Power: An Economic History of the United States.* Armonk, N.Y.: M.E. Sharpe, 1989.

Edsall, Thomas Byrne, with Mary D. Edsall. *Chain Reaction: The Impact of Race, Rights, and Taxes on American Politics.* New York: Norton, 1992.

Edwards, Lee. *Goldwater: The Man Who Made a Revolution.* Washington, D.C.: Regnery Publishing, 1995.

Eisenhower, Dwight D. *Mandate for Change.* New York: Doubleday, 1965.

———. *Waging Peace.* New York: Doubleday, 1965.

Eisner, Marc Allan. *The State of the American Economy.* Englewood Cliffs: Prentice Hall, 1995.

Elazar, Daniel J. *American Federalism: A View from the States.* New York: Harper and Row, 1984.

Fairclough, Adam. "Was Martin Luther King a Marxist?" In E. Eric Lincoln. *Martin Luther King, Jr.: A Profile*, pp. 228–242. New York: Hill and Wang, 1984.

Fiorina, Morris P. *Retrospective Voting in American National Elections.* New Haven: Yale University Press, 1981.

———. *Divided Government*, 2nd ed. Boston: Allyn and Bacon, 1996.

Fishel, Jeff, ed. *Parties and Elections in an Anti-Party Age.* Bloomington: Indiana University Press, 1978.

Ford, Gerald R. *A Time to Heal: The Autobiography of Gerald R. Ford.* New York: Harper and Row, 1979.

Free, Lloyd A., and Hadley Cantril. *The Political Beliefs of Americans.* New Brunswick, N.J.: Rutgers University Press, 1967.

Gallup, George H. "The Gallup Poll," November 22, 1979. In George Gallup. *The Gallup Poll: The Gallup Poll 1979.* Wilmington, Del.: Scholarly Resources, 1980.

Germond, Jack W., and Jules Witcover. *Whose Broad Stripes and Bright Stars? The Trivial Pursuit of the Presidency 1988.* New York: Warner, 1989.

Gourevitch, Peter. *Politics in Hard Times: Comparative Responses to International Economic Crises.* Ithaca, N.Y.: Cornell University Press, 1986.

Greenstein, Fred I. *The Hidden Hand Presidency: Eisenhower as Leader.* New York: Basic Books, 1982.

Hadley, Arthur T. *The Invisible Primary.* Englewood Cliffs, N.J.: Prentice Hall, 1976.

Hadley, Charles D., and Harold W. Stanley. "The Southern Super Tuesday: Southern Democrats Seeking Relief from Rising Republicanism." In William G. Mayer, ed. *In Pursuit of the White House, 1996: How We Choose Our Presidential Nominees.* Chatham, N.J.: Chatham House, 1996.

Hartz, Louis. *The Liberal Tradition in America*. New York: Harcourt, Brace and World, 1955.

Hinckley, Barbara. *Congressional Elections*. Washington, D.C.: Congressional Quarterly, 1981.

Huckfeldt, Robert, and Carol Weitzel Kohfield. *Race and the Decline of Class in American Politics*. Urbana: University of Illinois Press, 1989.

Humphrey, Hubert H. *The Education of a Public Man*. New York: Doubleday, 1976.

Ifill, Gwen. "Pragmatism Is a Big Winner as Clinton Gains in New York." *New York Times*, January 21, 1992, p. A19.

Inglehart, Ronald. "The Silent Revolution in Europe: Intergenerational Change in Postindustrial Societies." *The American Political Science Review* 64 (1971): 991–1017.

———. *The Silent Revolution: Changing Values and Political Styles among Western Publics*. Princeton: Princeton University Press, 1977.

———. "Post-Materialism in an Environment of Insecurity." *The American Political Science Review* 75 (1981): 880–900.

Jacobson, Gary C. "Strategic Politicians and the Dynamics of U.S. House Elections." *The American Political Science Review* 83 (1989): 773–794.

———. "The Effects of Campaign Spending on U.S. House Elections: New Evidence for Old Arguments." *American Journal of Political Science* 34 (1990): 334–363.

———. *The Electoral Origins of Divided Government: Competition in U.S. House Elections, 1946–1988*. Boulder: Westview Press, 1990.

Jensen, Richard. "Party Coalitions and the Search for Modern Values." In Seymour Martin Lipset, ed. *Emerging Coalitions in American Politics*. San Francisco: Institute for Contemporary Studies, 1978.

Keech, William R., and Donald R. Matthews. *The Party's Choice*. Washington, D.C.: The Brookings Institution, 1977.

Kernell, Samuel. "Presidential Popularity and Negative Voting: An Alternative Explanation of the Mid-Term Congressional Decline of the President's Party." *The American Political Science Review* 71 (1977): 44–66.

Key, V. O. "A Theory of Critical Elections." *Journal of Politics* 17 (1955): 3–18.

———. "Secular Realignment and the Party System." *Journal of Politics* 23 (1959): 198–210.

———. *The Responsible Electorate*. Cambridge: Harvard University Press, 1966.

Kinder, Donald R., and D. Roderick Kiewiet. "Economic Discontent and Political Behavior: The Role of Personal Grievances and Collective Economic Judgments in Congressional Voting." *American Journal of Political Science* 23 (1979): pp. 495–527.

Kirkpatrick, Evron M. "Toward a More Responsible Two Party System: Political Science, Policy Science, or Pseudo Science?" *The American Political Science Review* 65 (1971): 965–990.

Koenig, Louis W. *Bryan: A Political Biography of William Jennings Bryan*. New York: G.P. Putnam's Sons, 1971.

Kramer, Gerald H. "Short-Term Fluctuations in U.S. Voting Behavior." *The American Political Science Review* 65 (1971): 131–143.

Krauss, Clifford. "Capitol Hill Starts Rounding Up the Usual Suspects." *New York Times*, February 14, 1996, p. A17.

———. "Democrat Sees Draft Scenario," *New York Times,* February 16, 1996, p. 26.

Kuhn, T. S. *The Structure of Scientific Revolutions.* Chicago: University of Chicago Press, 1962.

Ladd, Everett Carll. "The Shifting Party Coalitions—1932–1976." In Seymour Martin Lipset, ed. *Emerging Coalitions in American Politics.* San Francisco: Institute for Contemporary Studies, 1978.

———. "Pursuing the New Class: Social Theory and Survey Data." In B. Bruce Biggs, ed. *The New Class?* New Brunswick, N.J.: Transaction Books, 1979.

———. "Liberalism Upside Down: The Inversion of the New Deal Order." In William Crotty, ed. *The Party Symbol: Readings on Political Parties.* San Francisco: W. H. Freeman and Company, 1980.

———. "The Brittle Mandate: Electoral Dealignment and the 1980 Presidential Election." *Political Science Quarterly* 96 (1981): 1–25.

———. "Like Waiting for Godot: The Uselessness of 'Realignment' for Understanding Change in Contemporary American Politics." In Byron E. Shafer, ed. *The End of Realignment? Interpreting American Electoral Eras,* pp. 24–36. Madison: University of Wisconsin Press, 1991.

———. "Political Parties and Presidential Elections in the Postindustrial Era." In Harvey L. Schantz. *American Presidential Elections: Process, Policy, and Political Change.* Albany: State University of New York Press, 1996.

Ladd, Everett Carll, with Charles D. Hadley. *Transformations of the American Party System: Political Coalitions from the New Deal to the 1970s.* New York: Norton, 1975.

Lane, Robert E. "The Fear of Equality." *The American Political Science Review* 53 (1959): 35–51.

———. *Political Ideology: Why the American Common Man Believes What He Does.* New York: The Free Press, 1962.

———. "The Politics of Consensus in an Age of Affluence." *The American Political Science Review* 59 (1965): 874–895.

Lawrence, David G. *The Collapse of the Democratic Presidential Majority: Realignment, Dealignment and Electoral Change from Franklin Roosevelt to Bill Clinton.* Boulder: Westview Press, 1997.

Levine, Lawrence W. *Defender of the Faith, William Jennings Bryan: The Last Decade 1915–1925.* New York: Oxford University Press, 1965.

Levitin, Teresa E., and Warren E. Miller. "Ideological Interpretations of Presidential Elections." *The American Political Science Review* 73 (1979): 751–780.

Lewis, William Draper. *The Life of Theodore Roosevelt.* New York: United Publishers, 1919.

Lipset, Seymour Martin. *Political Man.* New York: Doubleday, 1960.

———, ed. *Emerging Coalitions in American Politics.* San Francisco: Institute for Contemporary Studies, 1978.

Lorant, Stefan. *The Glorious Burden: The History of the Presidency and Presidential Elections from George Washington to James Earl Carter, Jr.* Lenox, Mass.: Authors Edition, 1977.

Maisel, L. Sandy. *Parties and Elections in America: The Electoral Process,* pp. 55–73. New York: McGraw-Hill, 1993.

Mann, Thomas E., and Raymond E. Wolfinger. "Candidates and Parties in Congressional Elections." *The American Political Science Review* 74 (1980): 617–632.

Manuel, Paul Christopher, and Anne Marie Cammisa. *Checks and Balances? How a Parliamentary System Could Change American Politics.* Boulder, Colo.: Westview Press, 1999.

Mayer, William G. "The Presidential Nominations." In Gerald M. Pomper, Walter Dean Burnham, Anthony Corrado, Marjorie Randon Hershey, Marion R. Just, Scott Keeter, Wilson Carey McWilliams, and William G. Mayer. *The Election of 1996: Reports and Interpretations*, pp. 21–76. Chatham, N.J.: Chatham House, 1997.

———, ed. *In Pursuit of the White House: How We Choose Our Presidential Nominees.* Chatham, N.J.: Chatham House, 1996.

Mayhew, David R. "Congressional Elections: The Case of the Vanishing Marginals." *Polity* 6 (1974): 295–317.

———. *Placing Parties in American Politics.* Princeton, N.J.: Princeton University Press, 1986.

McClosky, Herbert. "Consensus and Ideology in American Politics." *The American Political Science Review* 58 (1964): 361–382.

McKnight, Gerald D. *The Last Crusade: Martin Luther King, Jr., the FBI, and the Poor People's Crusade.* Boulder, Colo.: Westview Press, 1998.

Murray, Robert K. *The 103rd Ballot.* New York: Harper and Row, 1976.

National Party Conventions, 1831–1996. Congressional Quarterly, 1997.

Neal, Steve. *Dark Horse: A Biography of Wendell Willkie.* Lawrence: University Press of Kansas, 1989.

Nie, Norman H., and Kristi Andersen. "Mass Belief Systems Revisited: Political Change and Attitude Structure." *Journal of Politics* 36 (1974): 541–591.

Nie, Norman H., Sidney Verba, and John R. Petrocik. *The Changing American Voter.* Cambridge: Harvard University Press, 1979.

Nixon, Richard M. *RN: The Memoirs of Richard Nixon.* New York: Grosset and Dunlap, 1978.

Nordloh, David J. *William Jennings Bryan.* Bloomington: Indiana University Press, 1981.

Novak, Robert. *The Agony of the G.O.P. 1964.* New York: Macmillan, 1965.

Parmet, Herbert S., and Marie B. Hecht. *Never Again: A President Runs for a Third Term.* New York: Macmillan, 1968.

Paulson, Arthur. *Political Attitudes of the Unemployed: Interviews with Fifteen Men.* Unpublished Ph.D. dissertation, University of Colorado, 1985.

Philips, Kevin. *The Emerging Republican Majority.* New Rochelle, N.Y.: Arlington House, 1969.

Polsby, Nelson W. *The Consequences of Party Reform.* Oxford: Oxford University Press, 1983.

Polsby, Nelson W., and Aaron Wildavsky. *Presidential Elections: Contemporary Strategies of American Electoral Politics.* New York: The Free Press, 1991.

Pomper, Gerald. "From Confusion to Clarity: Issues and American Voters, 1956–1968." *The American Political Science Review* 66 (1972): 415–428.

———. "The Presidential Nominations." In Gerald M. Pomper, Ross K. Baker, Walter Dean Burnham, Barbara G. Farah, Marjorie Randon Hershey,

Ethel Klein, and Wilson Carey McWilliams. *The Election of 1988: Reports and Interpretations*. Chatham, N.J.: Chatham House, 1989.

———. "Alive! The Political Parties after the 1980–1992 Presidential Elections." In Harvey L. Schantz. *American Presidential Elections: Process, Policy, and Political Change*. Albany: State University of New York Press, 1996.

Pomper, Gerald M., Ross K. Baker, Walter Dean Burnham, Barbara G. Farah, Marjorie Randon Hershey, Ethel Klein, and Wilson Carey McWilliams. *The Election of 1988: Reports and Interpretations*. Chatham, N.J.: Chatham House, 1989.

———. *The Election of 1992: Reports and Interpretations*. Chatham, N.J.: Chatham House, 1993.

———. *The Election of 1996: Reports and Interpretations*. Chatham, N.J.: Chatham House, 1997.

Pomper, Gerald, with Susan Lederman. *Elections in America: Control and Influence in Democratic Politics*. New York: Longman, 1980.

Presidential Elections, 1789–1996. Congressional Quarterly, 1997.

Rabinowitz, George, and Stuart Elaine MacDonald. "The Power of the States in U.S. Presidential Elections." *The American Political Science Review* 80 (1986): 65–87.

Ranney, Austin. *Curing the Mischiefs of Faction: Party Reform in America*. Los Angeles: University of California Press, 1975.

Rosenman, Samuel, and Dorothy Rosenman. *Presidential Style: Some Giants and a Pygmy in the White House*. New York: Harper and Row, 1976.

Scammon, Richard, and Ben Wattenburg. *The Real Majority*. New York: Coward-McCann, 1970.

Schantz, Harvey L. "Sectionalism in Presidential Elections." In Harvey Schantz, ed. *American Presidential Elections: Process, Policy, and Political Change*. Albany: State University of New York Press, 1996.

———. *American Presidential Elections: Process, Policy, and Political Change*. Albany: State University of New York Press, 1996.

Schattschneider, E. E. *Party Government*. New York: Rinehart, 1942.

Schlozman, Kay Lehman, and Sidney Verba. *Injury to Insult: Unemployment, Class, and Political Response*. Cambridge, Mass.: Harvard University Press, 1979.

Schneider, William. "Democrats and Republicans, Liberals and Conservatives." In Seymour Martin Lipset, ed. *Emerging Coalitions in American Politics*. San Francisco: Institute for Contemporary Studies, 1978.

Schwartz, Bernard. *A History of the Supreme Court*. New York: Oxford University Press, 1993.

Sexton, Patricia Cayo. *The War on Labor and the Left*. Boulder, Colo.: Westview, 1991.

Shafer, Byron E. *Bifurcated Politics: Evolution and Reform in the National Party Convention*. Cambridge: Harvard University Press, 1988.

———, ed. *The End of Realignment? Interpreting American Electoral Eras*. Madison: University of Wisconsin Press, 1991.

Silbey, Joel H. "Beyond Realignment and Realignment Theory: American Political Eras, 1789–1989." In Byron E. Shafer, ed. *The End of Realignment? Interpreting American Electoral Eras*. Madison: University of Wisconsin Press, 1991.

Skowronek, Stephen. *The Politics Presidents Make: Leadership from John Adams to Bill Clinton.* Cambridge: Harvard University Press, 1997.

Smith, Margaret Chase. *The Declaration of Conscience.* Edited by William C. Lewis. New York: Doubleday, 1972.

Springer, Donald K. *William Jennings Bryan: Orator of Small-Town America.* Westport, Conn.: Greenwood Press, 1991.

Stanley, Harold W., and Richard G. Niemi. *Vital Statistics on American Politics.* Washington, D.C.: Congressional Quarterly, 1994.

Stokes, Donald E. "Spatial Models of Party Competition." In Angus Campbell, Philip E. Converse, Warren E. Miller, and Donald E. Stokes. *Elections and Political Order,* pp. 161–179. New York: John Wiley and Sons, 1966.

Sundquist, James L. *The Dynamics of the American Party System: Alignment and Realignment of Political Parties in the United States.* Washington, D.C.: Brookings Institution, 1983.

———. *Constitutional Reform and Effective Government,* rev. ed. Washington, D.C.: Brookings Institution, 1992.

Tufte, Edward R. "Determinants of Outcomes in Mid-Term Congressional Elections." *The American Political Science Review* 69 (1975): 812–826.

Tugwell, Rexford G. *Grover Cleveland.* New York: Macmillan, 1968.

Turner, Frederick Jackson. *The Frontier in American History.* New York: Holt, 1947.

Verney, Douglas V. *British Government and Politics: Life without a Declaration of Independence.* New York: Harper and Row, 1976.

Wallace, Patricia Ward. *The Politics of Conscience.* Westport, Conn.: Praeger, 1995.

Wattenberg, Martin P. *The Decline of American Political Parties.* Cambridge: Harvard University Press, 1990.

Weed, Clyde P. *The Nemesis of Reform: The Republican Party during the New Deal.* New York: Columbia University Press, 1994.

White, Theodore H. *The Making of the President 1960.* New York: Atheneum, 1961.

———. *The Making of the President 1964.* New York: Atheneum, 1965.

———. *The Making of the President 1968.* New York: Atheneum, 1969.

———. *The Making of the President 1972.* New York: Atheneum, 1973.

———. *Breach of Faith.* New York: Atheneum, 1975.

White, William S. "Seven GOP Senators Decry 'Smear' Tactics of McCarthy." *New York Times,* June 2, 1950.

Wilcox, Clyde. *The Latest American Revolution? The 1994 Elections and Their Implications for Governance.* New York: St. Martin's Press, 1995.

Willkie, Wendell L. *One World.* New York: Simon and Schuster, 1943.

———. *An American Program.* New York: Simon and Schuster, 1944.

Wilson, James Q. "Realignment at the Top, Dealignment at the Bottom." In Austin Ranney, ed. *The American Elections of 1984.* Durham, N.C.: American Enterprise Institute/Duke University Press, 1985.

Witcover, Jules. *Marathon: The Pursuit of the Presidency 1972–1976.* New York: Viking Press, 1977.

Index

ABOUT THE AUTHOR

ARTHUR PAULSON is Associate Professor of Political Science and the University Pre-Law Advisor at Southern Connecticut State University. He is a life-long student of parties and elections who has written articles in this subject area.